he takes her from her childhood in China to her receipt of the Nobel Prize for Literature in 1938. That award created a dichotomy between her life as she would have liked to live it and what was expected of her by a world in which her fame had now reached a new pinnacle. The next critical point for her was the death of her husband, more than twenty years later in 1960. New relationships then entered her life, and she plunged even more deeply into the humanitarian causes to which she has somehow always managed to give of herself unstintingly in spite of her prolific writing. After thus completing her story chronologically, Mr. Harris devotes the last part of his book to what he considers the essence of his subject, namely the woman behind the writer.

Included in the book are the revealing parallels between many of Pearl Buck's fictional characters and the real people of her life; long quotations from her personal journal, never before published; letters from intimates casting additional light on her and her career; several of the many poems she has written for her private joy; and above all, the many revelatory passages from recorded conversations.

For the readers of her books and stories, for those who have listened to her speak, for the admirers of her work on behalf of the mentally retarded, of Amerasian children, and of other causes—for all the "several worlds" in which she has lived, this is a book to deepen one's knowledge and understanding of Pearl S. Buck.

PEARL S. BUCK

A Biography

Clara Sipprell

PEARL S. BUCK

A Biography

by Theodore F. Harris

IN CONSULTATION WITH

Pearl S. Buck

The John Day Company
New York

Acknowledgments and a Note
About Quoted Passages

Considerable portions of this book consist of direct quotations from Pearl S. Buck. In order to minimize interruption of the flow of the text, lengthy passages quoted from her are, with a few exceptions, printed in the same type as the body of the text and without quotation marks, but distinguished by a vertical line in the margin extending from the beginning to the end of each such quoted passage.

All quoted passages not otherwise attributed are from tape-recorded conversations between Miss Buck and the author. Sources of specific quotations other than those identified in the text and other than tape recordings are as follows below. (Numbers cited are page numbers of the present volume.) If any quoted passage is presented as unpublished which has appeared in print, this is only through the failure of diligent search to disclose the fact of publication, in which case apologies are hereby offered to the publisher thereof and to the reader of this book.

19–30: *My Mother's House*, by Pearl S. Buck. Richwood, West Virginia, Appalachian Press, 1965.

31–43: An article by P.S.B. in *Fortnightly Review* (June, 1932).

43–76: Unpublished manuscripts by P.S.B.

78–81: *My Mother's House, op. cit.*

123: *The Child Who Never Grew*, by P.S.B. New York, The John Day Company, 1950. Copyright, 1950, by the Training School at Vineland, New Jersey.

159–163: An article by P.S.B. in *Bucks County Realtor*, Doylestown, Pennsylvania.

175–177: Unpublished manuscript by P.S.B.

202–204: Reprinted by courtesy of the Chicago *Tribune*.

218–238: *The Chinese Novel,* by P.S.B. New York, John Day, 1939.

241–243: *Opportunity: Journal of Negro Life*. Reprinted with permission of the National Urban League, Inc.

259–263: "Equality," in *What America Means to Me,* by P.S.B. New York, John Day, 1943.

To P. S. B.:

Thank you for giving so much of yourself
to the world and to me.
—T. F. H.

Preface

I T IS impossible to judge a biography of one's self except in the area of accuracy. I told Mr. Harris before he began writing that I made only one stipulation, namely, that whatever was put between quotation marks, as having been said by me, had really been said by me. We provided for this by the use of tapes.

As to his qualifications for the task of writing the biography, I can only say that he knows me better than anyone else does. Ours is an unusual relationship, based upon mutual confidence and understanding. The result is that I have been able to talk with him freely and at length and to answer his questions with complete frankness. I cannot be responsible, of course, for his personal opinions about me and these we have not discussed. But he has presented the facts of my life accurately and, I feel, with perceptive comprehension. He has researched my books thoroughly and with intuitive insight that is satisfying, at least to a writer.

—Pearl S. Buck

Contents

Foreword

THE most pleasant part of the task of writing about Pearl S. Buck's life has been my association with the woman herself. She is delightful, an intellectual of the purest form, interested and inquisitive to the final "Why?", and above all, entirely human. I have been closely associated with her for five years now and one thing that stands above all else in my memory is her wit. When I reread what I have written of her, I wonder if I have put enough emphasis on this aspect of her personality. I think probably I have not, for it is difficult to deal lightly with subjects of such deep concern. A vital part of her unique greatness is that she merges good humor and wit with knowledge and understanding of the more tragic aspects of life in our world today. I can think of no one with whom I would rather have breakfast, luncheon, cocktails or dinner, or sight-see or drive or go on a picnic or to a coffeehouse or a concert; in short, I can think of no one with whom I would rather be at any time or any place. Words are her tool; and no matter how heartbreaking an incident, she can always manage a phrase that makes it easier to bear. She is loyal to her friends to a point beyond imagination, and equally as fierce to her enemies.

I should like to have had seventy-six years to write this book; perhaps then I would have been able to record each detail of a life which at this point has taken that long to live. This, of course, is not possible, and in the morning I must mail the manuscript to the publisher.

I shall miss it now that it is ended. It has been my constant companion for over three years. Its pages have traveled with me to more than two hundred and fifty American cities, and to other countries, too. Some of them have been written high above the Pacific during two trips to and from Asia. It is amusing that I, who habitually misplace items in the course of my regular work, have never lost the manuscript in these thousands of miles. It has traveled in a small black attaché case, and there has not been a time when I was not aware of its location. While on foot I have carried it, and in the car, office, dining room or bedroom it has been at my side. On those few occasions when it could not possibly accompany me, it waited patiently in my room, and I missed it desperately, often making excuses designed to get me back to it earlier than planned. But even when the black case is not with me, its contents are. In a meeting, or interview, or luncheon, or during a casual conversation, I hear her make a particular point and my brain takes leave of the present and makes note: "Now let's see, I shall write that into such and such, expressing it thus . . ."

Anyone who writes knows well the feeling for a manuscript. It is like the chef remarking to himself, "Hmm—not bad? I wonder if it needs a bit more salt?" or the artist who thinks, "Now let's see, possibly a little red in this corner. Not too much now! Just a touch!" A book is so final. Once the manuscript is gone, the word pictures can never be changed, the ingredients can never be increased or decreased. The broth is brewed, the die is cast. Alas, is there one of us who has not felt hopelessly inadequate and unsure when the pot is taken from our hands, the manuscript gone, the black case empty? When the book is in print I shall place the first copy in the black case, together with the manuscript, and give all three a resting place in the gallery of the Pearl S. Buck Foundation. They belong there with the mementos of the life they contain. I shall leave them there and go on with her, for we have a bigger work yet to do and we must go on our way with no backward glance.

T. F. H.

PART I

In the Beginning

I remember when I was born—
I do remember!
Through eternity I slept,
By its quiet waters swept,
In its silence safely kept.
All unknowing, night or day,
All unthinking, there I lay.
. . . Suddenly, by life compelled,
I was free, no longer held;
Free to hear and feel and cry;
Free to live—or free to die;
Free to be that which am I.
I remember when I was born—
I do remember!

—P. S. B.

How does a life begin? Pearl S. Buck has compared a book's beginning to the creation of a star in the heavens. A swirl of particles in the skies, a swirl of ideas in the vast space of one's mind, gather to form a substance. The process describes the creation of a life, as well. An idea is born in the mind of a man; a hope, developing into desire, grows into reality; love for a woman takes form in a child. A living creature thus begins its long trek through life.

For Pearl Buck the trek began with her birth in her mother's childhood home in the village of Hillsboro, West Virginia. It was the first coincidence in a series of coincidences that have formed her life and made her a living legend in her own time. For the marriage of her parents was in itself a coincidence. Had her mother married the man she loved as a girl, the child would have grown up in the beautiful surroundings of the wide valley and high mountains of Pocahontas County. The man Caroline Stulting loved was young and handsome, a neighbor's son, a suitable match except that he drank. Fearful of what her life with him might be, Carie refused him, denying her love. In his place she accepted Andrew Sydenstricker, the sixth and next-to-the-youngest son of a well-known family in Greenbrier County. It was a family of scholars, men noted for their linguistic skills. Of the seven sons, six of them ministers, Andrew was unique because he chose to be a missionary to China. Carie could scarcely have found a husband more unlike the gay and debonair youth whom she loved. And how could she have agreed to go to so distant a country as China, this young woman of twenty-three, except that she longed to go away as far as possible, once the decision was made?

In China, two years before the birth of the important child, destiny took a hand again. Carie and her four-year-old daughter fell ill on the same day with cholera, then usually fatal.

"Because of the seriousness of the illness I must work constantly to save one life, and I can save only one," the doctor told Andrew. "You must choose which."

How bitter a choice! He had just lost one child in death, and now he must decide between his wife and daughter. Yet for him there could be no hesitation.

"Save my wife," he said, "but with our Chinese amah's aid, I will try to save my daughter, too."

Try though they did, with the doctor's direction, Andrew and the amah could not save her and only Carie lived—yet in such sorrow she could not recover her health. The doctor ordered them to return to the United States, where they remained for two years. Thus it was that the child of Carie and Andrew whom the world was to know best was the only one conceived and born in the United States; thus did fate choose the obscure town of Hillsboro, West Virginia, as the birthplace of one of the world's great literary figures. The time was early in the morning of June 26, 1892.

Of her birth Pearl Buck says with characteristic insistence:

I remember when I was born. I am sure I remember. How else can I account for the intimate knowledge I have always had of my mother's house? I have never lived there for more than a few weeks at a time, and not many times. The first time I walked into it on my own feet I was already nine years old. Yet already I knew every room that I was to see. I knew how the grapevine grew over the portico. I knew when I entered the door that the parlor was to the left and the library to the right. True, a later generation had changed the library to another use, but for me it was the library and music room. It was still the music room where a musical family gathered to play organ and violin and to sing.

Up the stairs with the hand-carved balustrade is the room where I was born, my mother's room. Facing the house, it is the room at the front, on the left. When I entered, nine years old, I remembered being born there. Whenever I enter it now, I remember. I see the wide old-fashioned bedstead. I see the dressing table between the windows—there was a dressing table, although it has not been there in my lifetime after I was taken by my parents to China when I was three months old. But it was there, I maintain, when I was born, because I remember it. And I remember some sort of chest at the foot of the bed and two easy chairs. There were white ruffled curtains at the windows, and from those windows one sees the broad lawn and the big maple tree. When I was born, there were other trees, too, but they are gone. From the visit when I was nine years old, I remember the dew shining on the grass in the morning sun.

Do I remember the rest of the house? Yes, but from later years. My grandfather's room was behind the library. He had a table that fitted into a corner, above it a bookcase. The table is now in my own living room here in Pennsylvania. Other rooms? Yes, I remember them all, and especially the old dining room on the ground floor, next to the buttery where the milk was kept. There is a great old fireplace in that room, and I remember logs burning in it on cold and misty mornings. I love those morning mists. When I was nine I woke early and curled myself by the window to see the dawn, rising through the mist. The trees were shadows and the air was still. By ten o'clock the day was clear and mists were gone. The old dining room has not been used for a long time— not since the new dining room was built some fifty years ago.

I cannot account for the birth of memories, but they are in me and they center about the room where I was born. I distinctly see my mother as she looked when I first saw her. I feel myself in her arms, looking up into her dark eyes. She had a vivid, pretty face. Only last year, when I visited West Virginia again, an old lady patted my arm.

"I remember your mother because she was so pretty," she told me.

It is how I remember her, too. Her face changed, of course. It grew thin and pale with age and illness, although she was never old—not really. She came of long-lived ancestors, and she died in China, young at sixty-four, of a tropical disease, which no one knew then how to cure, but which we know now can be cured by massive doses of Vitamin B. But when I first saw her, newborn child that I was, I saw a warm, welcoming face, a gay face, a loving face, the dark eyes glowing and the soft chestnut brown hair falling about it. She had beautiful hair, dark but with gold in it, and she always wore it long and coiled on top of her head. I have a photograph of her when she was a bride at twenty-three. It is her wedding picture. My father, calm and handsome and self-assured, is seated but she is standing, her left hand on his shoulder, looking out at the world with those dauntless dark eyes of hers. Flesh of her flesh that I am, I know she was frightened, but dauntless, nevertheless.

That is the face I saw when I was born. I like to know, as I do know, that she rejoiced at my arrival. Three children she had lost before I was born, all small, the eldest four, the youngest six months. All are buried in the hot Chinese earth. It was because of their deaths that I was given the privilege of being born in my own country. It is a privilege I treasure, for I am the only one among my brothers and sisters who is so born. Yes, she was happy to see me. I know, for we exchanged looks, I remember her cheek against mine. She was a brown woman, her skin a soft brunette cream. I suppose this came from her Dutch ancestry and the French Huguenot strain through her mother, my grandmother. I did not inherit her brown looks. Instead I have the fair skin, light hair and blue eyes of my father's ancestry. What I inherited from my mother is inside me. I love people too easily, as she did. But then my first memory is of love. To be able to think back, as I can, to feel one's way back to the first moment of the new life outside the womb and to remember, as I do, nothing but love, overwhelming love, provides the atmosphere for one's whole life. So loved for one's self, one loves in return, easily and richly—and sometimes too often and too faithfully. For this gift of loving, I thank my beloved mother.

Do I remember nothing of my prenatal life? I have tried to remember. I can see the setting quite clearly, the lovely spring, the gentle summer of the West Virginia mountains. My mother's house is not in the mountains. It is set on a plain at the foot of the Alleghenies. There she was born and there she grew and she loved the mountains as long as she lived.

"I will lift my eyes unto the hills," she would murmur in times of sadness.

I heard those words how often, a refrain in my memory in the years when she was far from home! I never understood their full meaning until I returned to my mother's house and saw those mountains for myself. They are a part of me, although I have never lived among them. No, I cannot remember anything before I was born, in the days of prenatal sleep. I can see her in my imagination, moving about the house, among her brother's family. Her elder brother inherited the house after the fashion of the generations, and he reared his children there. I see her enjoying apples from the orchard, grapes from the vines that grew over the barn as well as over the portico. I see her engaged with flowers and vegetables in the garden behind the house. I see her before I was born but not with my own eyes. I slept those months away. I grew unawares. She was creating me day by day, my body shaping from the good food she ate, the milk she drank. I am made of American materials. My brothers and sisters were fed upon Chinese foods but I am American. I was conceived in my own land and there I was born. Does this matter? Somehow to me it does. Yes, I have tried very often to remember what it was like before I was born, but I see only my mother always busy, her old gaiety returning. I know that I had something to do with that return, for, as I said, she wanted me. She was happy that I was coming. But this is all after-seeing. I cannot see myself, small and curled inside my nest and sleeping.

My first vivid memory, therefore, is after I was born, when first I looked into her face and she looked into mine. That I do remember, and that exchanging look I have carried with me all my life. We recognized each other. I was her child and she was my mother. In later years, however much we disagreed, and we could disagree, we understood each other because we were so much alike, both quick in mind and strong of heart and not easily afraid. We could and did take opposite sides as I grew up. What trouble I might have caused her had I grown up willfully in my own country I do not know. But I grew in China, where one is taught to respect one's elders, and I respected her. My old Confucian tutor, with whom I spent my afternoons, saw to that. Under his tutelage I rose when my mother came into the room and remained standing until she bade me sit. I cannot say that I always behaved so decorously when he was gone, but his lessons took effect. Naughty as I could be in other ways, I was never saucy, nor did I answer back as I hear children do nowadays. And my Chinese training holds for another generation, for I do not allow impudence or even sauciness from my own children.

Let me not hasten. Let me savor every moment of my life in my mother's house. I was born in June, the most beautiful month of the year, in my opinion, especially in those West Virginia mountains. My mother nursed me at her breast. I know that, for she told me more than once, laughing, of my refusal to substitute a bottle for her breast. This took place when I was three months old and on the high seas on our way to China. She was always seasick and her milk dried. She had feared this would happen and was prepared with bottles. I refused the rubber nipple, I am told, with good nature but with stubbornness. Thereafter I was fed from cup and spoon by my father, a tedious task in a rolling ship, especially for a tall, somewhat lordly man, undomesticated from birth to death.

Let me not hasten! It is too soon to talk of the high seas. The first three months of my life in my mother's house were tranquil ones. I flourished, I am told, and was alarmingly precocious but I remember a sense of well-being which leads, perhaps, to precocity. The household revolved around the newborn child. A cousin helped to take care of me and washed my minute garments herself. My mother said that she brought them to her every afternoon, clean and fresh and smelling of pure water and sunshine. The matter of my name took some time. We have good names in our family and it was difficult to choose. My mother was Caroline and her mother was Johanna. Both names were denied me. Caroline was given to my younger sister, born seven years later in China, and I gave it again to my first daughter. Johanna I have given to my youngest daughter. My name, finally decided upon, was Comfort, another family name. My mother chose it with deep meaning, for at heart she never recovered from the loss of the three children who died before I was born. She gathered them together and had buried them in the cemetery for white foreigners in Shanghai. Three little mounds are still there, I suppose, unless that resting place has been dishonored in these strange new days —three little mounds under the shelter of a simple marble stone bearing the names and the dates of the beginning and end of these brief lives on the planet Earth. Whenever we went to Shanghai, in later years, my mother always led me to that place. We brought simple bouquets of daisies and lilies, or whatever flowers were to be had, and laid them on the green turf. There we stood, my mother and I, she remembering while the tears rolled down her cheeks, and I troubled but not remembering because I never knew the two sisters and the brother. Yet these three who came before I was born and went away again too soon somehow seemed alive to me. My mother had once bought a beautiful jewelry box in Italy, of carved sandalwood inlaid with ivory. In it were no jewels for herself but a few small possessions of the dead children. My sister Edith, I remember, four years old at her death, had a bracelet of delicate blue glass, the sort that Chinese little girls wear and which I suppose was given to her by a Chinese friend. With it was a tiny silver thimble for her middle finger. In the box was a silver chain belonging to my eldest sister, Maude, who died, aged six months, upon a ship in the Yellow Sea between China and Japan. It was the sort of chain that Chinese babies wear to keep them locked to life. There was a silver padlock, very small and finely worked, attached to that chain. Of my brother Arthur, who died in a few swift hours in one day, at the age of eighteen months, there was a lock of soft dark hair. The other locks, one pale gold, one dark, belonged to my two sisters.

I perceive that in spite of intention, I am wandering from my mother's house across the sea to my other country, that land I once knew so well, and to the people whom I have not ceased to love. Let me return again and yet again. My name was Comfort, and my mother took comfort in me, and that has made me happy. I wonder sometimes if she takes comfort in me still, wherever she is. So much has happened since she died. I had not begun to write books when she left me to join the ones who had left her before I was born. She named me Comfort. A wry wish that she had left it at that creeps into my thoughts. I have never liked my other name. It sounds well only in Swedish. Years later when I went to Stockholm for a special occasion, the newspaper carried the name as La Perla, and I liked it then.

"Why did you name me Pearl?" I asked my mother when I was old enough to ask questions—which I fear was far too early. Indeed, my unending questions sometimes drove my poor mother to distraction. "Why—why—why" was the ceaseless refrain of my childhood, and has continued thus all my life. So distracted did my mother become when I was a small child that sometimes she begged me not to ask a question for fifteen minutes. I always granted this request, but I remember, too, that I always drew my small chair near to the clock on the dining room wall and sat counting off the minutes, only to begin again when the second hand reached the exact point.

"Mother, why—"

She was a woman of infinite patience where a child was concerned. I never remember a cross word or her voice raised and never, never any physical force. But then she was a lady, well bred by birth and education.

"Why did I name you Pearl?" she repeated.

I remember the tenderness in her voice, in her eyes, so dark in the vivid face.

"Because," she went on, "you were fair when you were born. Your hair was gold, your skin was white—yes, actually you had pink cheeks and a rosy mouth and the bluest eyes. You looked like a little pearl."

I saw the small pearl of a child and felt shy that she was once myself. It is dangerous to name a child by what she appears at birth. She changes, she grows from unknown genes, and I have never felt that Pearl was my name. Yet in Chinese it is rather pleasing, "true gem," one that is natural and fundamental, growing about a wound in a living organism. I like to think that perhaps there is a significance here and that somehow I did provide, however inadequately, a comforting encasement for the wound my mother carried deep inside her being when her three children died.

For three months then, I lived in my mother's house, the center of my family life, an amiable child except for a five o'clock affliction, a colic, I am told, that sent the family into consternation, since I was a healthy infant and grew with normal speed. For two hours each day I was not good company, it seems, until at seven o'clock the colic disappeared and I smiled again, resuming my usual good nature. Whether the cause of this malaise each day was the result of my mother's overindulgence in apples, of which she was inordinately fond, or some other less obvious reason, will never be known. I have no memory of the affliction and for me it is only hearsay. But I have the habit of forgetting what I do not care to remember. Thus with my own children, all of whom I am sure were normally naughty, I can now remember only their charming traits of goodness and amiability. I cannot bring to mind any of the problems that we must have had. Ten children and no problems? Impossible, my reason tells me! Yet I remember only years of joy and laughter.

The day came, a day in late September, when my parents decided that we must leave my mother's house and set forth on the long journey to China. My eldest brother, a lad of twelve, was with us, and we made a little party of four. Knowing my father, I am sure that he rejoiced to be on his way back to his work. I have a secret conviction that my mother's family, too, were not sorrowful at his departure. He was not a person who accommodated himself. Wherever he was he remained the tall slim figure of a scholar, intent upon his own study and research. I know he absented himself often from my mother's house on errands connected with delving into ancient languages as well as preaching in neighboring churches. When he came back no one was quite as much at ease as we were in his absence. I think he felt this and was sometimes a little sad. Yet he must have known, too, how much he was respected in my mother's house, and with him his ancestral family.

For he came of a notable family, famous for their learning but also for their independence, not to say stubbornness. Last year, in the centenary year of my birth state, I was invited to return for celebrations. In the evening of the first day I did what I had not done before. Accompanied by an old cousin, I visited the cemetery where my ancestors are buried. It lies on a peaceful hilltop near the small beautiful town of Lewisburg. Standing on the hill, I was impressed by the row of white tombstones beneath which those lie from whom I am the descendant. All faced in one direction save one. This one was the tombstone of the father of my father. He is of course my grandfather, but I think of him primarily as my father's father. His tombstone, among all the others, faces the opposite direction. It is a gesture as lively as though he were not dead. I made inquiry of my cousin.

"How is it that this one tombstone faces the opposite way from all the others?"

"We've never known how that happened," my cousin replied.

A twinkle shone in his eyes. "He must have got up in the night and changed it when he saw how all the others were facing."

Something of that spirit was in my father, although whatever might have been perversity or perhaps only a humorous mischief was in his case tempered by reason. Yes, in my mother's house he was certainly treated with respect. There is a legend, true or false, that when he decided upon my mother as his wife, he then being a man of twenty-seven and my mother a girl of twenty-two, he advanced upon the house as upon a fortress, having previously made known his matrimonial intentions by letter, in order that no time be wasted. My mother's father, a man of short stature but indomitable spirit, marched out of the door, head erect, to meet my father and prevent him from carrying out his outrageous purpose of taking my mother to China. The family in my mother's house were also not of missionary stock. Their ways of living were comfortable and somewhat worldly, it must be said. It had never occurred to them that missionaries were anything but a set of unaccountable fanatics. As for China, was there any reason why a sensible man would leave his home and family, not to mention his own country, and set out to preach to Chinese, who already had several ancient religions of their own?

My grandfather met my father halfway down the walk. He carried his cane as usual and he brandished it in my father's face.

"You shall not have my daughter!" he shouted.

My father looked down from his tranquil height, his cerulean eyes amused.

"Oh yes, I shall," he retorted, and continued his way to the house.

The courtship was a formal one, I am told, but speedy, and my mother was married on the twenty-second day of July, the year of 1880. The bridal pair set out at once for China, my father forgetting, it has been said, to buy a second ticket until the last minute. It was a significant forgetting. I never heard my mother mention it, and a cousin told me the story. This is not to say that my father was derelict in his duty to his family, when that duty was pointed out to him. It was simply that he lived in the world of books and ideas and philosophy.

As for my mother, she continued, I think, to live in her own house. I think in spirit she never left that gracious white house at the foot of the Allegheny Mountains. Underneath the white painted wood the house, she told me, was of red brick. I imagine that my great-grandfather and my grandfather, being city men of Utrecht, Holland, did not like the idea of living in a wooden house. The inner structure, doubtless, they thought should be of stronger stuff. I know how they felt for when I returned to my own country to live I could not imagine myself living in a house made of wood. It is too frail, or so it seems to me, accustomed as I am to the houses of China, built of brick or stone or in peasant villages in the north of thick adobe walls. My own house is built of Pennsylvania field-stone, and it has stood for nearly a century and a half, for the walls are like the walls of a castle. A house of wood? Yes, it can be very beautiful, especially in New England, where the towns are made of white houses with green shutters, but a match put to wood makes a fire, does it not? Therefore my own house is of stone, and my mother's house was inwardly of brick. From Utrecht her grandfather and father came with three hundred other souls, a church full of good people and with them their pastor, all in search of religious freedom. For a brief period there was religious strife in Holland, but it lasted so short a time that had they been patient, in six months' time it would have been over and they could have stayed in their comfortable houses, enjoying their wealth and culture. Where I would have been had they done so, or would I have been at all is a puzzlement. Certainly I would not have had a Lincoln-like saint for a father, and I cannot imagine myself as I am without him.

The shipload of good people, bringing their wealth with them, was woefully and disgracefully cheated upon reaching the land of their choice. I do not know the full story of their arrival, for it remains a painful family memory. I do know that my ancestors bought woodlands in what was then Virginia and into the forest they went, city people who had never seen a mountain in their native land. They had no conception of what it meant to build even a simple log cabin and wily settlers robbed them without mercy. In the end they sold the woodlands and moved to the beautiful plain at the foot of the mountains, and there built the house like a city house. Vague discussions I never fully understood when I was a child and I have not heard since, conveyed to me nevertheless that the valuable early lands were sold at an absurdly low price, and had the family held them, they would have been immensely wealthy today. Be that as it may, they could not live in the forests. They were not forest people. They were city folk, accustomed to theater and music and books and all the rich culture of an ancient European nation, and they starved without it. My mother's house was enlivened with memories of European culture. It became a part of her education and nature and later of mine. To me, growing up in China, she imparted the best of the West, while I lived in the greatest and oldest culture of the East, and was thus doubly endowed. For this thanks be to life.

Throughout all my growing years, then, I was aware that my mother's real life remained in her own house across the sea. She made homes in China that were exquisite in taste. All my memories there are of quiet cool rooms, flowers everywhere, simple delicious meals, and pervading order. There was no disorder in any home that my mother created. Yes, she created every room except the room where my father lived, which was called his study. There he allowed no curtains and no flowers, and the floor was bare. Books covered the walls, and a vast desk stood in the middle of the room. His typewriter, which he took care of himself, though with difficulty, for he had no mechanical ability, was on a small separate table. Somehow that room had nothing to do with the rest of the house. It was always near the front door and accessible to Chinese guests, grave gentlemen in long gowns, men of erudition, who carried on endless scholarly discussions with my father in lofty Chinese language. Sometimes the guests were my father's helpers at various mission stations who came to collect their salaries or receive directions. Whatever and whoever they were, all seemed remote from our family life, which was in the rest of the house. There we found merriment, for my mother was of gay disposition, although she had certain moods which darkened the day for us and which we never understood. Only when I was much older and knew the private story of her life did I guess, and only guess, for she never confided her secret thoughts and feelings to any of us. But when she was what we called "quiet"—that is, when the laughter and the quick grace and the gay talk were settled—we were troubled.

"What is the matter?" we asked.

"Nothing," she would reply. "Nothing at all! Am I never to be allowed to be quiet?"

We could not answer this reasonable question, and were only quieted in turn. In quiet we played apart, subdued and puzzled until her gay self came back to us. Ah, there were depths in her that none of us ever knew! Whatever the personal shadows, basic to all was her unchanging longing for her home and her country. She was too young when she left that home of hers, and it remained forever in her memory as the home of her childhood, the place where her beloved mother lived and died, and where beauty was. She was friendly to the Chinese as she was friendly to all human beings, but she did not, I dare to say, love them as my father did or as I always have loved them and do love them now.

There were reasons for this. The Chinese are delightful but careless, whereas my mother was fastidiously neat and clean. I never saw her wearing a soiled or wrinkled garment, and all her personal belongings were dainty and fine and well kept. Our house was comfortable but immaculate, and her Chinese servants had first of all to be clean in every way. Raw foods and salads she made herself, because she did not trust their hands, and although she taught her cook to make the lightest cakes that tongue ever tasted, and his hot breads were delectable, she would not let him touch them with his hands. She had been beautifully trained by her French mother, her standards were impeccable, and less than the best she would not tolerate.

Speaking of cakes, my mother's fresh coconut cake I have never found elsewhere matched. The coconuts were local, and were bought in their original hairy state from the market by our Chinese cook. Every step was enchanting to me, as a child, in the making of this fabulous cake. The coconut was drained of its milk, nature having provided three tender spots in the hard shell. The drained shell was then cracked and the white meat separated. It came off with a dark skin that had to be sliced off. The pieces of fresh white meat were then washed and grated by hand on an old-fashioned grater, an agonizing task, for unless one were careful one scraped one's fingers, in which case my mother's sharp eyes always detected pink stains upon the snow-white coconut meat. No tinned coconut can possibly equal in flavor the taste of a fresh coconut, and not only a fresh one, but one plucked newly from the palm trees. I was reminded of that fact last year when in India I sat at breakfast on an outdoor terrace and watched bare-legged boys climbing the coconut palms, rope in hand, to cut the clusters of nuts and lower them gently to the ground. These were the day's supply for the guests. One bought a nut at the stand and had the milk drained into a glass to drink warm and sweet and then waited for the coconut to be cut into squares and peeled.

The years passed. My mother's house became more than the house in which I was born. It became the symbol of security and peace in a world where there was neither security nor peace.

How strange the chance, too, that she gave this child the name Comfort! Could she have sensed, even then, that the name of her child would one day be linked with comfort by people throughout the world? Or was she thinking only of her own life, and the tragedy therein, and realizing that this child would bring her comfort? Or was it simply that Comfort was a Stulting family name carried by other women before her? Questions whose answers have long lain buried with Carie in a grave in China!

Pearl Comfort Sydenstricker was taken to China with Carie and Andrew and her brother Edwin, then twelve, when she was three months old. Yet, though her early memories are of China, she was an alien in that land and a stranger to the land of her birth. I have thought many times that perhaps it is this beginning that partly explains the deep sadness that often comes over her face in repose. Can it be that the tragedy subtly evident in her whole being—and this in spite of her quick sense of humor and love of gaiety—could have begun with the feeling of being different, of not belonging? Could it stem from a Chinese heart and mind living in a body with Western appearance and American heritage? Could her basic loneliness originate from the fact that she is not at home with either side of herself? She has said: "I'm not quite at home anywhere and somewhat at home everywhere."

Americans do not think as Chinese do. They do not act or react in similar ways. Their values are different, their philosophy of life unlike ours. Pearl Buck was reared among the Chinese. Her first language was Chinese. She was tended by a Chinese nurse,

Wang Amah; she had Chinese playmates; she lived in a Chinese house near the Yangtze River in China. Of her nurse she says:

She is one of the two clear figures in the dimness of my early childhood. Foremost stands my mother, but close beside her, sometimes almost seeming a part of her, I see, when I look back, the blue-coated figure of my old Chinese nurse.

She was, even at this earliest memory of her, already old. There had been other babies before me and none of us ever had any other nurse. But death came to our house before I was born and took the two babies, very close together, and so when I arrived the old nurse received me with a tenderness which made me her own. True, doubtless she would rather have had me a boy. But even a girl was better than none. Doubtless, also, she would have preferred a child who had my mother's dark eyes instead of blue ones, and my mother's dark hair, too, instead of pale yellow floss.

But these defects could be remedied somewhat, at least to the extent of a Chinese cap with little Buddhas on it and fitting very closely so as to hide the unfortunate hair. My mother doubted the propriety of Buddhas upon the cap of a missionary child, but she was too softhearted to say anything when she saw how seriously the old nurse felt about it.

"We have lost those two," the old nurse said stoutly. "It is all very well to trust in a foreign god, but how can we be sure he has power over a country not his own? It is better to use all the gods there are, and surely the gods of the place where we live."

Nor would she be changed, and the little Buddhas remained in a stiff gold row upon the white baby's red cap.

There is a time when my mother's presence fades from my memory. Once I pondered on this deeply and I asked her: "Where were you, Mother, when I lived with Amah?"

"You were never alone with Amah," she replied, astonished. "You always lived with us."

But I seemed to remember a time when my world circled only about that small, blue-garbed figure. Then did I see no face but her brown wrinkled face bending over me, and I seemed to remember a fairly constant attachment to her hard brown hand, its forefinger very rough with needle pricks. At night when it was suddenly too dark to breathe I remembered being lifted out of my bed and cuddling down with greatest relief and comfort into a warm bosom. When I brought these memories into speech, my mother said gravely:

"She really should not have taken you into her bed—but I suppose it must have been that summer I had dysentery for three months and you were three years old. I was so weak I could not lift my hand from the sheet and I remember hearing the doctor say it was only a matter of days, and I resolved I would not die. But I had to let Amah take care of you all the time, and I used to be so afraid you would be ill! It was the hottest summer we ever had, and there was typhoid all during June and July and then cholera in the city. But you stayed fat and rosy—she used to put you into a little fresh white dress after your bath in the morning and bring you in to see me. I remember she even learned to curl your hair as I used to do and make it into a Thames tunnel on top. I know she would have liked better to brush it out as straight as she could, but she did it to please me, bless her old heart! You weren't ill a day all summer."

That was it, then! That was why I seemed to see my old nurse alone for a while with me. Then once more my mother came back, bringing a new baby with her, this time a brown-haired boy. He was too much for the old nurse and she was helpless in her adoration of him, a boy at last, and I was displaced in her arms.

For a time I do not see my old nurse so clearly. Evidently I was averting my eyes from the spectacle of her holding the new boy baby as she had once held only me. But all babies grow, and so did the boy, and he came to be rebellious and to want to use his own legs, and she found a strip of cloth to pass about him, and in the loop of the girdle he staggered about, as I had done, too, in my time, and as every Chinese baby does. The old nurse found time for the two of us again. By now I had reached the story age and I was insatiable.

"And what stories can I tell, who am only an ignorant old thing and I never learned the name of a letter in my life?" the old nurse would exclaim, squinting at the toe of the perpetual stocking she held over her hand to darn.

The remark we both knew to be merely polite, and I answered, in like terms:

"You do know more stories than any woman in the world!"

It was true that she had an inexhaustible supply of tales of magic, which she had heard chiefly from Buddhist and Taoist priests. The Buddhist stories were about wonderful daggers that a man could make small enough to hide in his ear or in the corner of his eye, but which when he fetched out again, were long and keen and swift to kill. Or they were tales of this god and that and what they did to men. Heaven and hell she told me about, too, the horrors of the Buddhist hell, and what heaven was and what the wheel of life that carries us along whether we will or not. I spent many an hour trying to think what I would like to be born into next time after I died.

I liked the Taoist tales better. They were tales of devils and fairies, and of the many spirits that live in tree and stone and cloud, and of the dragons in the sea and the dragons in the storm and wind. There was a pagoda toward the east of our house and I knew there was a dragon's head pinned under it. If ever he managed to wriggle loose the river would flood and swell until we were all drowned. But there was no danger, for it was a great, strong, beautiful pagoda, and there the dragon was, imprisoned and helpless.

Many and many a time when I was surfeited with magic I used to beg my old nurse:

"Now tell me about when you were little!"

This demand I made continually upon my father and my mother, too, and from them I heard the brave stories of early pioneer days in my own country, the country I had never seen; tales of fearless undertaking, of heroic religious independence, of a stern and God-fearing morality. Now I listened with equal interest and belief to the story my old Chinese nurse told me of her own childhood, and of how, in the very days when my parents were growing up in a little Christian village, going to church on Sundays learning their catechisms, she was living in a great old Chinese city upon the Yangtze River, going to the temple to worship, having her feet bound, thinking of marriage. She said:

"I cannot remember when my feet began to hurt me. I think they always hurt until I stopped growing. My mother was vain of her own feet and I was her only daughter and she said my feet must be as small as hers. She began to bind them when I was three.

The first thing I remember was my father leading me into the kitchen and making me sleep on the straw because I cried at night and kept them awake. But he did not beat me as some men do their daughters, and after a while I learned to moan inside myself. When I was married my feet were only three inches long and I wore tiny red satin shoes!"

I stared at my nurse's feet. "They are much longer now," I said skeptically.

"That is because your mother would have me let them free when I first came to live with you. One of my feet was sore when I came and she washed it and put medicine on it and it healed, and then to thank her I loosed my feet from their bandages to please her. Besides, it did not matter, because my husband was dead then and I did not want to marry another one."

"Let me see your feet!" I demanded.

Gravely she took off her cloth shoes, then her white cloth socks, and unwound the strips of white cloth she wore underneath, and so until her feet were bare. She lifted them for my inspection. The toes were still doubled under the soles of her feet, and the flesh was a strange color. I conceived a distaste for the sight.

"I am glad I don't have feet like that," I said.

"You should have seen them before," she replied and began to replace the bandages.

"Why do you wear those strips?" I asked.

"Because it would hurt me if I let my feet spread more," she said.

"Tell me about something else now!" I demanded, my curiosity satisfied.

Bit by bit, then, she told me the story of her life. On rainy afternoons when she sat in the nursery, or on sunny days when she sat in the servants' court, sewing, I put my little bamboo stool beside her and leaned an elbow on her blue-trousered leg and listened by the hour.

Her father had been a small tradesman. He sold candles made of cows' fat and painted red, and he sold incense and paper money to burn for the dead. His wife had been somewhat above him in station, but because she had been pitted by smallpox in childhood she could not marry her equal. Perhaps this mortification made her vain of her tiny feet, and made her so careful of her daughter's feet, too. I gathered from the story that my old nurse had been very pretty as a young girl. She said:

"You must know, child, that I had, when I was fifteen, a smooth pale skin, my hair was straight and very black and my braid swung to my knees, and in front I cut it to a long fringe over my eyes like a veil. My mouth was so red I needed not to paint it. My only fault was that my eyebrows were not even, and I had to brush them back with my brother's ink and writing brush. But my teeth were white and as even as the grains in a pomegranate."

I was too polite to express distrust of this, for my old nurse would not tolerate rudeness in us, and I merely stared very hard into that brown and wrinkled face. She had not more than six teeth, all told, at this time, and the mouth she said had been so rosy was sunken now into her toothless jaws, and the lower lip protruded. Her greatest comfort was that two of her teeth were opposite three others and so were still of use to her. One of the accidents she had that grieved her greatly was when she later fell down the cellar steps and knocked out two of these serviceable teeth. We children laughed, and she showed us one of her rare flashes of anger and called out a good hard name at us. But immediately she regretted it and she fumbled in her deep bosom and produced a handful of watermelon seeds, warm from her body, for us to crack. This was by way of apology, and we apologized, too, and all was well again.

As for her eyebrows, I could see they were too scattered. Her hair, as I sat staring at her, was still black, but very scanty, and patches of her bald head would have shone through except that on such places she had painted her scalp black. I knew this and took great interest in it. She used our black shoe polish and, after applying it, would ask us if any skin showed through, and we advised on further touches. At a little distance it was a very passable deceit.

"I was married young," she went on. "There were several matchmakers who wanted the business of betrothing me because it was so easy and they could make a good bargain for themselves. I was married young, too, because of the T'ai P'ing rebellion, and there were many soldiers about."

"What was the T'ai P'ing rebellion?" I asked.

"It was a lot of bandits," she said. "They came burning and killing into our city and it was said they did everywhere the same. They hated priests and gods, and they killed every priest they could and burned the temples. There was a temple near our house and it had seven stories to it, and was a very fine pagoda. The priests ran into it to hide. But the T'ai P'ings set fire to all the inner woodwork and burned up the priests and some say the smell of roasting men's meat is still there."

"How does roasted men's meat smell?" I asked with supreme interest.

"Very good," she replied calmly. "It is so good I have heard it said that when robbers take to eating it they crave it like opium and will eat no beast's meat afterward so long as they live."

"Does white man's meat roasted taste the same?" I asked.

This was an idea which had not occurred before to my old nurse. She held her needle still and looked at me thoughtfully for a while. But it would never do to pretend she could not answer, and at last she said with decision:

"The meat is more tasteless and it is full of water, because you wash yourselves so much. It is the difference between a water buffalo's meat, which is watery and coarse, and a cow's meat, which is closely shredded and dry and very fragrant to smell, when cooked with soy sauce and fresh ginger."

"Then what?" I demanded, this point being settled.

"Well, and then," she went on, running her hand skillfully into the recesses of the heel of the stocking, "you must know that I was so pretty they did not know what to do with me when all those hungry rebels came crowding into the city. I was married, and my husband loved me, and my mother-in-law did not know where to hide me. Yet if they were killed, as anyone might be in those times, there would I be alive because I was so pretty."

I saw no connection here, however, being very young, and I stared and said, "Did they not kill pretty ones, then? I should think your husband would have been glad, if he loved you!"

But the old nurse had a sense of the fitness of things. She perceived the story had come suddenly into a blind alley and the best way was to rise and go to her kitchen and lift up the wooden lid of the caldron and call back:

"I left a bowl of rice and salted cabbage for you today! It is as you like it best."

The T'ai P'ings vanished, and I rushed to hang over the great iron caldron from whence she dipped up rice. Then from a bowl set away into the niche of the chimney she brought out salted cabbage and she fetched her own chopsticks, wiping them first carefully upon her apron. I fell to the dish with delight. Every poor man in the land ate it every day, but to me it was perennially delicious. Many a time I went apathetically to my mother's carefully planned table, preferring this peasant's fare. But when a good half of the bowl was gone and the sharp edge taken off my hunger, I looked up from the bowl to ask, for I had been ruminating as I ate:

"What did they do with you then, if you were so pretty?"

My nurse answered carelessly, as though she had forgotten the whole matter:

"That? Oh, they put me down a dry well for a while and I sat on a little table they let down first, and every day they sent food down to me. . . . There, it is enough for today!" she ended suddenly. "Go and read your book."

This was the usual ending to any period of play or idleness, for my old nurse, although she could not read a word herself, was inordinately proud of the fact that, although a girl, I could read as well as my brother. True, she did not consider it important until I began to go to a Chinese school and learned to read Chinese. Then she used to boast proudly to her friends:

"This child of mine, although she is only a girl, has her stomach full of good Chinese characters!"

If I dallied and complained over my book, as often I did, being an extremely willful child, she would turn serious and admonish me:

"You shall learn to read! Here am I all my days like one blind, and if I want to write a letter even to my son I must go to the public letter writer and he puts in so many words I did not say that I can make nothing of it when it is written."

But I retorted stubbornly that I wished I were a little Chinese girl and need not learn, and well I knew I would like to be ignorant. At this she made her eyes so wide at me and thrust out her lower lip so far that I was awed and fell unwillingly to my book again.

In many other ways she spoiled us badly. My mother deemed it wise that I should learn to work, and she set for me the task every day of sweeping and straightening my own room and of making my bed. My nurse muttered:

"And why should this child work, seeing she is to be learned as a boy?"

Immediately I was comforted, knowing that the old nurse had her ways and means. So it came about that many a time when I went upstairs after breakfast I found my room spotless and my bed made and my old nurse whispered to me always:

"Child, put but a little more time on your books and I am paid!"

Where my mother first found our old nurse I did not know for a long time. I accepted her as having always been, as immemorial as my parents and as the very universe. So it was, until I was nearly grown, and then one day I asked my mother. She answered, hesitating somewhat in the reserve of her times.

"I am afraid, perhaps—when she was young, Amah was not such a very good woman. You see, the times were troubled and her husband died when she was young, and she was so pretty—"

"Then she was pretty!" I murmured out of my memory. My mother looked up in surprise.

"Yes, she was very pretty when I first found her, but not after you remember her, child! Her parents-in-law were killed in the T'ai P'ing rebellion—yes, most cruelly, I believe—and her husband died soon after. Her own parents had run away to escape the danger and she was quite alone. There was an evil landlord who pressed her very hard to—to—there were a great many evil stories told in the neighborhood—I heard she was quite without money. Some of the women said I took a grave risk when I brought her into our home to take care of my children. But I do not believe she ever said a wrong thing to you, did she?"

I thought of that brown mother of mine who was more than my nurse, and I said fervently:

"Never!"

As my Chinese nurse grew older we used to complain sometimes, because her temper tended to become somewhat short. She scolded me often, I know, because I was of a tomboyish turn and loved to climb trees, and this did not lessen darning. She would hold a ragged stocking knee over her hand and look at me reproachfully and thrust out her lip and say:

"Who would think this was a young maid's garment!"

Then she would admonish me in grave words as to how a young girl should sit and stand and walk, and how hold her head, and how speak if spoken to by elders. If this went on too long I usually grew oppressed by my shortcomings, being inclined to sensitivity, and when this stage was reached the old nurse invariably relented. Then she rose and went into her kitchen and appeared with, perhaps, a crust of hard-baked rice from the bottom of the cauldron. This she gave me, saying:

"I know you will do all good things, my child. Your heart is willing, that I know."

There is a power of comfort in a crust of hard-baked rice! And what pleasure she gave us in all the things she did for us! Chief of these was the hatching of chicks to be our pets. Every spring this was an event, and as soon as the edge was off the spring wind we went through the little farms in the valleys about us and with her we searched until we found a setting hen she liked. Then she bought here and there fresh eggs until we had twenty, and when we were home again she made a nest in an old box she kept from year to year for the purpose, and the nest was put into her own room where she could guard the whole process, and the hen established.

We were never allowed during these three weeks to touch either hen or egg, for the old nurse assured us that a Chinese hen would run right off the eggs and never come back if children with white skin and yellow hair showed themselves before her.

In spite of everything, however, the hen would occasionally abandon her task, and then if she was too flighty to be coaxed back to it, the old nurse would dispose the eggs carefully about in her own capacious garments and hatch them with the warmth of her own body.

At night she put the eggs under her quilt and slept half awake lest she lie on them. And what a moment it was when we caught

the half-absorbed look upon her face and saw her shrug herself gently and pull her hand up her wide sleeve and fumble in
her depths somewhere! She would whisper in a hushed voice:

"Wait—a chick!"

We waited breathless until she reached her hand out carefully
with the little damp, new fowl in it. How precious were such
chicks and what a tragedy if one died!

So she grew old in our house. She grew too old to do much, and
my mother contrived so that the finest sewing was not put into
her basket. But her age was really hastened because the good
daughter-in-law she had chosen for her son, who came to be our
cook, died. The young man was willful and insisted on marrying
a pretty, round-faced country girl he had seen at one of the farmhouses. He was an only son and could be denied nothing, and so
with a heavy heart the old nurse arranged the wedding. The
young wife was lazy and disobedient and spent her husband's
money on such foolishness as paper flowers for her hair and sweets
to eat. When the old nurse upbraided her she answered so inso-
lently the old woman could not bear it.

I remember one night as we sat at dinner the cook came running in, distracted and crying:

"My mother is killing herself!"

My mother jumped up and ran out, all of us at her heels. Then
in the gatehouse we found our dear old nurse, now white-haired,
beating her head violently against the wall in an attempt to knock
herself senseless. I saw my mother's eyes flash as she turned them
on the sullen young wife, who stood there half frightened, and
she cried:

"God will punish you for behaving in a way to make your good
old mother so sad!"

Then my mother took the weeping old nurse into her arms and
coaxed her and led her out into the quiet garden, and when the
old nurse wept on, heartbroken, and murmured that she must
die, my mother answered:

"You shall not die! Your life is mine. I have saved you twice;
once when I fetched you into my house, and once when you would
have died of cholera. You may not throw your life away."

It was true that one summer the old nurse had cholera and my
mother moved into that very gatehouse with her, away from us

all, and cared for her night and day alone and saved her at last from death. My mother was not one to mention such things, but in this extremity she did, and the old nurse responded and dried her eyes. But the young wife was sent away and we had a new cook.

Yes, once the old nurse saved my mother, too. At least my mother always said she did. It was after the birth of the last baby and my mother was very ill with a fever. The white doctor was there often—as often, that is, as my father could find him, for he was a man with a strange story, hidden away in this Chinese city, and he was drunk nearly all the time. At last everyone seemed to give up hope. Our nurse was very busy with the newborn one, for no other servant paid any attention to a girl child and one that had nearly killed its mother. But even so, she had time to comfort me; and when the new baby was washed and fed with milk from a tin can, then I crept into her old arms and asked, afraid:

"Will my mother die?"

She shook her head stoutly at this and replied:

"We will go tomorrow and pray at the temple—very early, before anyone is up."

The next morning she roused me and dressed me and we crept out of the house and went down the street to the temple, and we went in and the old nurse knelt before a little dark goddess in a corner and said her prayer and when it was said she thrust some incense she had brought into the urn there. There were gods everywhere, some urbane and smiling, some ferocious and terrible, but this little goddess was old and gentle-looking, and she stood with her hands folded quietly before her. Around her skirts were little baby gods made of gilded clay, as she was also. I asked:

"What goddess is it?"

The old nurse replied, "She is the one who helps all women in childbirth."

When we reached home again the old nurse took me into the nursery and said earnestly, "Now you must kneel, child, and pray to the white god, too, and so will every god be appeased."

I knelt then beside a little chair and put my hands together and prayed fervently. "O God, please let my mother get well!" And then after a moment's thought I prayed again, "And, goddess, you, too, please let my mother get well!"

And having thus prayed to all the gods I knew, I rose and we were both comforted, my old nurse and I.

But the old nurse was of a very practical turn, and while gods were all very well, there were also other ways. My mother told me the tale afterward:

"One night I was so weak I thought my life must slip away at any moment. Your father brought me the broth I had to swallow every two hours. As soon as he put the spoon between my lips I knew the taste was different. It tasted of fish, and I could scarcely bear it. But I knew I must take it, for there was no other ready and I felt too weak to delay. I thought perhaps the bowl had stood next to a dish of fish somewhere, and I forced myself to eat. Do you know, it is a strange thing, but I began to feel better, and the next day I was better!"

When my mother was well again the old nurse said with great triumph, "There is much these white doctors do not know. As for the gods, it is wise enough to pray to them, but who knows whether they are at home that day in the bodies of the images, and whether it is a day on which they will listen. No, in my home city when women have fever after childbirth there is a certain fish which, if brewed, will heal, and I brewed the broth secretly and put the bowl in place of that other bowl."

Who could say she was wrong—or right? There was my mother, well.

But the old nurse never gave up her own gods, nor would she ever become a Christian. My mother, feeling it her duty, explained, in the gentle way she had, the story of Christianity. The old nurse, listening politely, nevertheless would not go further than to acknowledge the possibility of a "white" god. If prayer were suggested, she said apologetically, "I cannot speak his talk! And how do I know if he understands Chinese?"

If told that God understood all languages, she would say, half coaxing:

"Then you pray for me, if you like! I do not mind if you pray! As for me, I have prayed so many years to my own gods now, they might be offended if I left off."

Some deep delicacy in my mother forbade any urging, and our old nurse lived on tranquilly to be very feeble. She died suddenly one night, when a pain laid hold on her old heart. She was quite fearless, confident that the round of life must begin for her again somewhere, and she rested in the commonplaces of life and was not afraid.

When her old body had been laid most tenderly into its coffin and the coffin sent away to be buried with her husband, the house was very sad for a while, and empty of a tender presence. Yet even though we grew used, and grown up, we know quite well and to this day that she left her share in us, her white children. Part of her went into us, as mothers are part of their children, so that now and forever her country is like our own to us, loved and understood, her people our own kin. And some essence from the gods in whom she believed lingers in our hearts still, and keeps us, when we think of our old nurse, too large for disbelief, too humble for any scorn.

So she speaks of her old Chinese nurse.

She loves her birth country of America, but her first knowledge of her own land is of ways strange and foreign to her. She loved her mother's stories about the stately old house in the hills of West Virginia, and of the people there, but these too were foreign to her. She did not understand how her own people lived, and why the differences between the two peoples. The eternal why! She said:

I can remember very clearly when it was that I first knew I was an American. I was perhaps four years old and Wang Amah was making me a cap to wear on the first day of the new Chinese year. Christmas she acknowledged grudgingly with small gifts as a foreign holiday not important. But she made tremendous preparations for the Big Day of Chinese New Year. My little brother and I had to be dressed in new garments from head to foot as all Chinese children were, and she herself made these garments until her eyes grew too dim to see.

A new cap was essential. Mine was always red, and it was bound with blue, and it had small gilt-washed Buddhas sewed on the very front. I knew that for some unknown reason these images distressed my father and mother and that they argued over their suitability for a Christian child. My father always ended the argument by commanding my mother to cut them off, and my mother always said she would as soon as she could manage it without hurting Wang Amah's feelings. The upshot of it was that, my mother being so softhearted, I wore Buddhas until I grew too old for them and then Wang Amah sewed little imitation green jade ornaments on my caps instead. I myself was fond of the Buddhas. By looking upward until my eyes crossed, I could see the tiny benign bold faces peering down at me.

"Buddha will keep evil and disease away," Wang Amah always said when I went outdoors.

"I thought God would do that?" I asked.

"Your God of course would do it in your own country," she said, "but he is not powerful here in China. Each country has its own God and here it is better to have Buddha on your cap. Besides, I have never been able to see even an image of your father's God, so how can I sew him on your cap?"

This was all reasonable, and so I played beyond the compound walls and walked the Chinese streets under the protection, I believed, of Buddha.

I knew vaguely, of course, that my family was different from those around us in more ways than the one of gods. We ate different food, for one thing, though I preferred Chinese food, and liked chopsticks better than a knife and fork. If I very often wore Chinese clothes, especially padded gowns in winter to keep me warm in unheated houses, still I knew my "real" clothes were not these gowns but my dresses and coat and hat and little aprons. And of course the English I spoke to my parents was my language, even though I spoke Chinese first and more easily.

But nobody put the matter into definite words for me until one day when, just before a Chinese New Year, Wang Amah was trying on my new cap. It fitted my head closely and covered my ears and curved into my neck, and a heavy silver chain, transferred from cap to cap as I wore them out, secured it under my chin. Wang Amah grumbled as she pushed my yellow curls into my cap.

"Ah, this strange hair! It is getting so long that a cap won't hide it anymore."

"Why must we hide it?" I asked.

"Because it doesn't look like proper hair, that's why," she complained. "It doesn't look human, this hair!"

I felt the burden of my misfortune. "Wang Amah, why do I have this hair instead of nice straight black hair?" I asked sadly.

"Because you come from an outer country, poor child," she said.

"Is America an outer country?" I inquired.

"Every country except China is an outer country," she said. Then she took pity on me and enfolded me in her arms and smelled my cheeks, which was the Chinese way of kissing. "Never mind," she said, "you cannot help it. I will hide it all under the cap and no one will see it. . . . Alas, there are your eyes! I cannot hide them."

"Why do you want to hide them, Wang Amah?" I asked in fresh dismay.

"They are so blue," she said, "and everyone should have black eyes."

"Why are my eyes blue?"

"Who knows?" she replied. "I only know that sometimes Americans have blue eyes." She thought of something else. "Ah, your poor mother!"

"Why is my mother poor?"

Wang Amah looked solemn and she pursed her full under-lip. "I have been with her for the births of all you six children, yet never once did she know what color your eyes would be when you were born, or what your hair. Four of you had blue eyes, poor souls, like your father's, and only two brown, like hers." She smelled my cheek again. "But you all have lovely white and red skin. When people talk to me about your eyes and hair I tell them to look at your skin, like white jade, and your lips and cheeks red as this satin."

Thus I knew that I was American, and I never forgot it. I had a country somewhere of my own, where children were like me. I am aghast when I think of how many little Chinese children must have had to struggle in later years with the lies I told them about that country of mine. I can only say I believed the lies as heartily as I told them. There were the long conversations I had with Precious. Precious was the first child of my Chinese sister, Golden Cloud. I had always thought of course that Golden Cloud was one of our family by birth. Two elder sisters of mine and a brother had died before I was born. Golden Cloud was enough older than

I was to have been married and to have a baby girl soon after I myself was born. I was fond of Golden Cloud, whom I called Chieh-chieh, which was the Chinese word for Elder Sister, because she was so pretty and gentle. She called me Mei-mei, or Younger Sister, and my parents she called Father and Mother. So it did not occur to me for a long time that her beginnings were different from my own. I did not even wonder about her Chinese looks. Everyone looked like her and most of the time I thought I did, too, or I didn't think at all.

But I said to Precious, soon after discovering that I had another country, "This isn't our country, you know. All of us in this house have another one, very far away."

Precious looked astonished. "Me, too?"

She had a little pigtail tied with red wool yarn and it was always braided so tightly that it drew up the skin of her brow and enhanced the already very Chinese cast of her features.

"Certainly," I said.

And then I began to tell her what America was like, America that I had never seen, but to which I belonged, and, I thought, Precious and her mother, Golden Cloud, and her father, Clear Decree, also. I told her, I remember, that in America there were no beggars, no poor, no thieves. This was important for there were many beggars in the city near which we lived. On Sundays when we went to church they snatched at us with hands like the skinny claws of fowls. If they had leprosy my mother said we must give them something quickly and run away. The sad leprosy-eaten faces made my dreams hideous, sometimes, at night. Even as a child the thought of the poor made me cry and spoiled the taste of food in my mouth. In my country there could be no poor.

As for thieves, we had them quite often. They slipped into the compound gate when it was open and the gateman not looking, and they hid in the bamboos and the shrubbery until night. Sometimes we only knew they had been there by finding a pair of dingy cloth shoes on the doorstep in the morning. When a thief left his shoes he meant that he had tried and failed and was coming back again. We dreaded that return. I didn't want any thieves in my country.

Precious looked pleased. "Shall I tell my mother?"

"Of course," I said complacently.

What she told Golden Cloud I don't know, but Golden Cloud must have said something to my mother. For that night before my prayers my mother told me how it was that Golden Cloud came into our family.

Years before I was born my mother had a friend. She was a Chinese lady about to die in late childbirth, and in desperation she had sent for the "foreign doctor." But the mission doctor was a man and she could not bear the strange touch. So my mother went along to act as a nurse, and with difficulty the lady and her child were both saved.

When the lady saw the child was a girl she turned her face to the wall. "All this—for nothing!" she whispered.

But my mother took the girl baby in her arms and said, "It is not right for man to despise woman, but for a woman to despise a woman is the utmost wrong."

After the lady got up from her bed she remembered those words and she and my mother talked a great deal about them and became warm friends. Then she told my mother why she had given birth to the child at all. She considered it shameful at her age, as all Chinese women consider it shameful to have a child if they are past the age of forty. Yet she was a beautiful woman and her husband had loved her for many years, and though he was rich he had never taken a second wife. Then she heard that he was giving his attention to a pretty singsong girl and she thought that if she could have a son, it would recall him to her. But a daughter, of course, was no use in this. So one day she gave Golden Cloud to my mother.

"Take her for your own," she said. "I feel I am going to die."

My mother refused to allow her to think of death. But one morning not long after, an old woman servant brought Golden Cloud, then a year old, to our house. The lady had swallowed opium the night before. It was the night when her husband had brought home the young girl to be his concubine.

This was the first time I knew that Golden Cloud was not born in our house and that my parents were not hers.

"So you see Golden Cloud is Chinese and not American, and we can never take her and her husband and children to America," my mother said.

"What is Chinese and what is American?" I asked.

"They are two different kinds of people," she said.

"But Golden Cloud is just like us," I said.

"So she is," my mother said, "and I can't explain Chinese and American. Nobody can. Go out and play with Precious and don't think about such things."

Yet I did think about it. I thought a great deal about it. I never felt quite so close to Precious again, though I loved her as much as ever.

Many years have passed since Precious and I played with my dolls under the bamboos in our compound and I forgot her for long times together. I have lost sight of her. She was always the worst of letter writers, and now who knows where she is, with half of China driven inland toward the west?

She must be middle-aged now, but if she is I feel sure she has the same round red-cheeked face that she used to have. Her cheeks were firm as apples and in winter scarlet with wind and soap washing. Her little plump hands were purple and chilblained and her round full mouth always smiling, and her eyes were as brown and bright as polished chestnuts. She bore up wonderfully under the weight of being a girl. It was more than one girl—many more. For the tragedy of Golden Cloud's life was her fertility in the matter of girls. She and Clear Decree lived in the small parsonage of one of the churches in my father's huge Chinese parish. Clear Decree's mother was dead, so that Golden Cloud had no mother-in-law to cope with, but Mr. Chang, Clear Decree's father and my father's assistant, said flatly that he would not consider that Golden Cloud had fulfilled her duties until she had a son, and for him a grandson. Mr. Chang was a bright-faced dapper old man with his scanty hair in a pigtail, and a small white goatee. He preached long sermons in a high voice, and in long prayers told God what he wanted. In church and at home he made it clear to Heaven that no benefits were any good unless he had a grandson.

When Golden Cloud gave birth to Precious, my parents felt anxiously responsible. It would have been so much easier for Mr. Chang's faith if Precious could have been a boy. However, after talk, Mr. Chang bore up and said he would forgive God this girl if there were a boy next time. It is incredible and horrible, but the truth is that within the year Golden Cloud had another girl. Christian courage demanded that Clear Decree and Golden Cloud pre-

tend that it was all right. They gravely named the second girl
Added Preciousness. She looked exactly like Precious and in a few
months had the same hard red cheeks and bright chestnut brown
eyes. Mr. Chang preached less and in his prayers there was now a
tone of definite threat.

"A boy next time, O Christian God," he prayed aloud where
anybody could hear him, "or else I had better have stayed by
my old gods."

Within a year Golden Cloud gave birth to a third girl, another red-cheeked, brown-eyed creature. There was now no pretense at courage. They named her Plenteous Preciousness, and all
the little girls knew what a mistake it was that they were not boys.
They were kindly and affectionately treated, and even Mr. Chang
was fond of them, but when he saw them together he would pull
his scanty whiskers and cry out, "If God can do all things, why did
he do this?"

I wish I could say that the next child was a boy, but it was not.
One after the other in the next three years Golden Cloud had
three more little girls. She and Clear Decree gave up any pretense
of their being precious and gave them the conventional names of
Beautiful Virtue, Beautiful Mercy and Beautiful Pity. To see
them in their fearful number on a Sunday morning, all red-
cheeked and dark-eyed, all six little black pigtails braided with
red wool, all six plump little bodies encased in clean blue cotton
robes, was to understand the tired, somewhat bewildered look on
Golden Cloud's face, the quiet resignation of Clear Decree's manner in the pulpit, and the belligerence of old Mr. Chang's upthrust
beard. By this time he had given up all preaching and
prayer, and spent his time on a bench in the sunshine smoking his
long bamboo pipes. He kept the six little girls in constant attend-
ance, and was sometimes melancholy and sometimes even bad-
tempered. But there were other times when he felt in the depths
of his padded robes and found cash for them to put on the candy
vendor's roulette wheel, and he was shamefully fond of the youngest and fattest girl, declaring that she would have made a fine boy.

The six little girls bore their condition without seeming to feel
inferior from it, and were too healthy and hearty and happy
to worry about anything. My mother worried a good deal because
Golden Cloud had lost so much face as the minister's wife in

Clear Decree's congregation and even my father admitted that
Providence had been inscrutable again.

Once more Golden Cloud was to give birth, but no one was
excited. A boy, we all felt, was beyond the range of possibility.
Old Mr. Chang, who heretofore had always taken an interest in
her condition and had bought special boy-guaranteeing medicines
and foods for her, this time pretended to know nothing about it.

And yet on a lucky autumn day Golden Cloud gave easy birth
to a beautiful boy. It was altogether unexpected. By this time no
one believed that Golden Cloud could have a boy, nor did she.
My mother was with her and she said that Golden Cloud, so calm
and seemingly unmoved as one little girl after another was laid
into her arms, when she saw the little boy cried until my mother
was frightened. She said Golden Cloud kept crying and murmur-
ing, "Now lettest Thou Thy servant depart in peace—"

"Stop!" my mother commanded her. "You aren't departing,
Golden Cloud. You have to bring up this boy."

They called the baby Grace of God. In a year or so he looked
exactly like the girls, red-cheeked and dark-eyed. But we all knew
he wasn't the same. He was a boy.

After all this was over I asked my mother, "Did you mind that
I was a girl?"

"No, indeed," she said indignantly. "I would have been
ashamed to mind."

"Why?" I asked.

"Because we are American," she said.

I talked less of America after that to the six little Chinese girls.
It would be cruel, like talking of heaven to people you knew
could never enter the pearly gates. And being too softhearted, as
was my mother, I endeavored to mitigate the sadness of the little
girls' lot. Did they feel badly about being girls? It was difficult to
look behind their round healthy faces. I said delicately, "You
know you really are just as good as boys."

Precious shook her head. She always spoke for the others.

"Oh no, we're not," she said cheerfully and laughed. They all
laughed.

"Don't you care?" I asked.

They cried in varying, cheerful voices, "Why should we care?"

"We can eat just the same," Precious said.

"And we play just the same," Added Preciousness said.

"And since we are Christians, we needn't bind our feet," Plenteous Preciousness said. They laughed heartily, and with them laughed the three little Beautifuls.

They never did care, I think. They grew up with me and we told each other everything. They did not change in their looks, they simply grew bigger. Mr. Chang died one year, holding his grandson's little hand in his as he went over, and Golden Cloud never had any more children. All six girls waited on their brother happily and brought him up through babyhood and boyhood. He never did anything for himself and by any law of psychology he should have been spoiled and pampered into imbecility. But he was not. He turned out to be a nice boy, with a calm and pleasant disposition. He loved his sisters equally and divided his favors between them. If one smelled his cheeks, he let them all smell him. He was not even very lazy. When he went to a boys' school whither his sisters could not follow him, he worked quite hard and proved himself a faithful though mediocre student. One of the Beautifuls developed unexpected brilliancy and when he began to earn money of his own, he helped her to go on to college.

And he was an exemplary son. When Clear Decree died too early of tumor in the brain, Golden Cloud and all the six girls looked to Grace of God. Though he was only about sixteen then he became the head of the family and with dignity and good sense he helped his mother to arrange marriages for the girls not yet married, for Plenteous Preciousness and all the Beautifuls, before he consented to be married himself.

But that was years later, when we were all growing up. When I knew him best, Grace of God was a fat placid baby, and we passed him from one of us to the other as we would a doll. Golden Cloud kept him in little red satin padded garments in winter and in summer his smooth brown skin was his only garment, except for a belly band against the summer complaint. We played house and he was the baby and we all took turns being the mother. He joined in very well and as he grew old enough would call any one of us mother in the game. I smelled his little dark cheeks as everybody did, for he was in reality a community baby, a miracle, an answer to years of prayer, a vindication of belief in God. Everybody in the little Christian church felt a share in him. After he was born Golden Cloud took on a look she never lost again, the look of a Chinese Madonna. . . . Dear Grace of God, it was a waste of life that one day years later, a Japanese bomb destroyed you and made you into dust!

These six little Chinese girls were the nucleus of my childhood. Six there were, but they were not a unit. The circle broke in the middle as they grew up. Three of them, the three Precious ones, were fat, red-cheeked and placid from birth until the last I saw of them before I returned for good and all to America. They were then married and surrounded by more fat and red-cheeked little creatures.

But the three Beautifuls grew up dark and pale and slender and they made endless trouble about getting married. They wanted to marry men of their own choice, or they did not want to marry at all, and which was more embarrassing to a respectable woman like Golden Cloud it would be hard to say. The explanation of it was, of course, that the three Precious ones grew up before there were too many new ideas yet from the First Revolution, but the younger ones, the three Beautifuls, were growing up when out of new Soviet Russia was pouring that strange flood of independence and freedom, revolt and tyranny. All of young China felt it, and so did the three Beautifuls.

I remember Golden Cloud, by then a mild-eyed widow, came to talk it all over with my mother. What, she inquired, would she do with her eldest Beautiful, who would not marry at all, in spite of four offers from local matchmakers for eligible young men? The eldest Beautiful merely said that she wanted never to marry. But who ever heard of a Chinese woman not married unless she were a Buddhist nun? And even nuns had usually been married once before they were nuns. And anyway, the Beautifuls were not Buddhists, and the way they looked made it impossible to think of them as nuns.

The second Beautiful said she might marry but only if she knew the young man first and decided she could love him. This was disgusting. Even Golden Cloud, the adopted daughter of an American mother, had not thought of asking such a thing. When Golden Cloud was twenty, old Mr. Chang had come to see my mother and had proposed marriage for his son, Clear Decree. Mr. Chang had seen Golden Cloud often enough on his way in

and out of my father's study when he came every month to collect
his little salary. He liked her soft voice and gentle ways. He feared
only that she might be indolent, but Wang Amah said no, Golden
Cloud was quite industrious about the house and a fair cook.

So he had proposed for Clear Decree and my mother, after
thinking it over, said she would let him know later. That night
she went into the room where Golden Cloud slept. It was a little
Chinese room in the midst of our American house. My mother
had furnished it with Chinese things just as she had kept all of
Golden Cloud's clothes Chinese. She said that she would have
been betraying Golden Cloud's dead mother if she had tried to
make Golden Cloud American.

So she went to Golden Cloud's bed and sat down and in the
darkness told her that Mr. Chang had come to ask her for Clear
Decree, and how did she wish to decide?

At first Golden Cloud said to my mother, "You decide for me."

To this my mother said, "No, I cannot. I am an American
woman. Not even my father decided for me who was to be my
husband. You must say for yourself whether or not you are willing
to be Clear Decree's wife."

After a long silence, Golden Cloud's voice came out very small,
"I am willing."

"Have you seen him?" my mother asked.

"Yes," Golden Cloud said, and added quickly, "only when going to church."

Men and women sat separately in the little Chinese Presbyterian mission church. But they came and went by the same big
door.

"Would you like to talk with him before you make up your
mind?" my mother asked.

"Oh, no!" Golden Cloud cried in horror.

She did not talk with Clear Decree until after the simple Christian ceremony in our parlor, and after the Chinese feast in the
dining room afterwards. My mother, telling us, always said that
of course she would never have allowed the marriage if she had
not watched Clear Decree grow up from a nice little boy into a
nice young man. And Golden Cloud and Clear Decree fell honestly and deeply in love after their marriage, which the old Chinese believed is the way a man and woman should fall in love.

There is an age for falling in love, and if suitable persons are not provided they will fall in love with unsuitable ones. And so it is the duty of parents and elders to observe the times of the young and to make sure that when the hour comes for falling in love, other young persons suitable and pleasant to the family are near at hand. And who is so fitted, they argue, to choose a wife for a son or a husband for a daughter as the parents who know the child from birth and better than he can know himself, and who so ill-fitted to make a lifetime choice for himself as one at the age of falling in love? So Golden Cloud believed, and was aghast now at the Beautifuls for ideas that had never crept into her gentle mind.

But gentle minds are the most stubborn. While Golden Cloud talked to my mother, the Beautifuls talked to me.

"If only our mother wouldn't make us feel we were martyring *her!*" the eldest Beautiful said.

"It would be so much easier for us if she were mean and cruel and beat us! Then we could run away with easy consciences. But how can we when she is so good?" inquired the second Beautiful.

"It is this turning of the cheek which is so hard to bear," said the third Beautiful. "It makes it impossible to go on saying what we think!"

The Beautifuls were handsome dapper young women with extremely slender bodies and short hair. They wore robes which Golden Cloud thought too tight and too short, and my mother thought so, too. And the long heavy black braids, tied with crimson yarn, that had swung down their backs all through their childhood were cut off to make smart sleek bobs. Golden Cloud had cried over this and into her pigskin trunk where she kept old baby shoes and the silver lock Grace of God had cut his teeth on and Clear Decree's water pipe, she put the three braids which somehow managed to look like little corpses when she held them in her arms and cried.

Of course it all turned out somehow. The elder Beautiful did marry because in her independent coming and going as a young woman teacher in the provincial school for girls she fell in love with the young professor of Chinese classics. And the second Beautiful married a doctor in the hospital where she was training to be a nurse, and the third Beautiful, to her own disgust, honestly preferred the man Golden Cloud wanted her to marry, and so what had been cause for noble independence and arguments about women's rights and a new day subsided into three happy marriages and a large number of fat babies.

When I last saw the Precious ones and the Beautifuls, they all looked placid and plump and comfortable. Marriage and babies had molded them into the same fundamental pattern. It is true that the Beautifuls had not let their hair grow, but the Precious ones had theirs cut off by then, because everybody was doing it. Quite elderly Chinese ladies found it convenient to have short hair, and comfort and convenience decide everything in China.

That storm in which I took such passionate part in my youth nevertheless laid seeds of cynicism in me for life. To struggle and declaim and take passionate part are all very fine in their time, but how quietly absurd they seem when the ordinary passing of time turns young rebels into middle-aged conservatives and marriage and children tame the wildest lovers and mold them into sedate partners and cautious parents! Now years later in my own country when I feel that quiver in my feet which is a sign of their urge to be off upon a quest of some sort, I think of the Beautifuls, those three placid matrons, who were once flying flags of youth and rebellion and revolution and I keep my feet steady on the ground.

"Wait," I say to my restless feet. "Wait!"

Ah, well! When I return to the earliest world I can remember it is of a window opening upon the Yangtze River in the river port of Chinkiang, that old city of the Chinese province of Kiangsu. It lies facing another old city on the opposite bank of the river, Yangchow, a city made famous by Marco Polo. They have not yet altogether forgotten Marco Polo in Yangchow, for he was governor there for three years. Five hundred and more years after that and about twenty years ago, wandering among little curio shops in the crooked streets, I found a small alabaster figure of a man dressed in Venetian garb. Cut into the base of the figure were four Chinese characters which said, "An honorable foreign heart."

But I knew nothing of Marco Polo in the days when I spent hours at that window upon the Yangtze. Behind me was the only home I knew—three rooms in which my mother, my little brother and I lived. My father was away most of the time on preaching tours, but he came home sometimes and then there were four of us. At night Wang Amah slept on the hatch that lifted in the narrow hallway upon a steep flight of steps. Down these steps we must go whenever we left home. We lived there because it was literally the only space my father could find to rent. The rooms I cannot remember. I must have eaten and slept and played in them. But I lived at the window when I was at home, and when we went out we walked to the hills outside the city.

Below the window lay the street called the Bund, because it ran along the river. The strip upon which we looked down was in the British concession, that piece of land like many others which England wrested from China after the Opium Wars to form bases for shipping and trade centers. Hour after hour during the day and the night steamers crept and sidled up to the squat hulks that lay offshore and discharged their cargo. Causeways connected the hulks to the shore and down these causeways all day and sometimes all night endless lines of coolies trotted with bags upon their bare backs, bags of sugar from Java, and rice from Kwangtung and jute and rape seed and tea and spices.

Every coolie had his queue wrapped around his head and his blue trousers knotted about his hard waist and in his hand a strip of blue cotton or a gray towel with which to wipe away his sweat. They were always sweating, these coolies, summer and winter, and their thighs and knees quivered under their heavy loads. Their eyes bulged, their faces wore horrible grimaces of strain, and their breath came out of them in singsong grunts and they kept step with each other and swung into rhythm to lighten their intolerable loads. Stuck into every queue was the bamboo tally stick that each man was given with the sign of his load. This he must hand to the tally man in the godown as he threw down his load.

Sometimes when we went out to walk we stopped and looked in the shadowy caverns of the vast godowns which held stored the wealth that poured into the port from all over the world, to be sent out again into inland China upon the backs of donkeys and mules and camels and men. There was always the same smell in the godowns, a mixture of hemp and peanut oil and the acrid sweetness of crude red-brown sugar. No one was allowed to go in, but once, happening to meet at a godown the English superintendent of customs, he led my little brother and me in with him, and showed us the long board of incline which took bags from one floor to another.

"A fine slide, what?" he said.

"Shall we slide?" I asked.

In great gravity he piled several jute bags together, for the boards were splintery, and then, he in front and we behind, we slid down. There happened at the moment to be no loading going on, and the upper floor of the godown had been quite empty. But as we came to the bottom a group of amazed coolies stood to receive us. They shouted laughter as we came to a stop, but the Englishman did not lose a flicker of his dignity. He rose, dusted himself off.

"Thank you for the ride," I said.

"Not at all," he replied. He nodded and marched off to his office, his head up and his eyes twinkling.

But I never even saw him again.

I suppose if I had at that time of my life, when I was about six, been given my choice of all the places in the world, I would have put aside Buckingham Palace and the White House and chosen a hulk on the bank of the Yangtze River. The gala days of my years then were when my mother went to call upon Cap'n and Mrs. Swan. The Swans were a stout Scotch couple who lived on the Jardine Matheson Hulk. They had comfortable rooms which had been the saloon and captain's quarters of the coast-going vessel which once the hulk had been. Cap'n Swan himself had been a captain on this very ship, but now he was a river master, and managed the comings and goings of the English company's steamers at the port.

We always chose a day and an afternoon when no steamer was tied to the hulk. Steamer days were impossible for visiting. In the first place Cap'n Swan was always in a swearing bad temper on those days and Mrs. Swan, who was a staunch Scotch Presbyterian, preferred not to have visitors, since it left Cap'n Swan more at liberty. The coolies did not understand Scotch swearing, but to have to check himself in the presence of visitors put a fearful strain upon the Cap'n. Besides, on steamer days the hulk was a hurly-burly of grunting coolies and dust and hustle and yelling. The coolies were implacable in their march. They swept over anyone in their way. I can remember being whirled aside by their sinewy brown legs as coldly as if I had been whirled away by wheels of machinery.

So we waited for calm afternoons and then at the decent calling hour of four we put on our best clothes and with Wang Amah along in a clean blue cotton coat to keep my little brother and me from climbing ropes and railings, we crossed the causeway to the hulk. The causeway was a terror in itself. The heavy boards were laid three or four inches apart, far too close, my reason told me, for children of four and six to fall through. But those spaces seemed to grow wider as we stepped over them and opened to show the swift wicked brown river beneath. My head swam as I stared down at that current. I was transfixed by the smooth evil movement of implacable water, so that to this day I cannot see the gathering of an ocean wave without knowing it cruel and having to fight against yielding to its power. And once in my own country when I stood at the head of Niagara Falls and watched the turn of the river over the great ledge beneath it, awful in its smooth power, I was caught back into the supreme terror of my childhood, the terror of the Yangtze River, so smooth, so swift, so dimpled with whirlpools and eddies that it was taken as fate that any who fell into those waters never came up again, even for rescue.

But the hulk, once reached, felt sturdy and strong beneath the feet, and the Swans, plump and hospitable, stood waiting to take us down the decks and over the door thresholds as high as my knees—"so that when the deck was awash it couldn't leak into the saloon," Cap'n Swan said. And then we went into Mrs. Swan's cozy cabin, where we laid off coats and hats on a real bunk, and where everything was still exactly like a ship's cabin. After this we went into the saloon that Mrs. Swan had made over to look as much as possible like the parlor in a Scotch Presbyterian manse and before a grinning little Franklin stove we sat down at a round table and had an enormous Scotch tea, with scones and jam and strong English tea and sweet biscuits and shortcakes and fine pound cake and fresh raisin cake and "sweeties" for the children. My brother and I had large cups of cambric tea and watched Cap'n Swan drink out of an enormous moustache cup that said on one side "A Present From Glasgow" in gold letters mixed with pink roses. Even so his moustache was too long and he had to suck it dry.

The talk during tea was exactly as though we were not on a hulk in the Yangtze River, but in a respectable small home somewhere in Scotland. No mention was made of China or the Chinese, but my mother and Mrs. Swan talked about children and clothes and the few white people in the city. We children ate steadily and when nothing more was possible, slipped down from our seats and each with one of Cap'n Swan's rough forefingers clutched in our hands we went out for a walk on the deck. He took us to what had once been the bridge and showed us his simple weather instruments and his telegraph apparatus and we peered into his telescope. Sometimes a ship came unexpectedly. We listened, not daring to breathe while he found out where the incoming ship was. "Noo, then, she's joost aboot cleer of Ching Shan." We, bilingual little beasts that we were, knew that he pronounced the Chinese name with completely the wrong intonation but we would not for worlds have corrected him.

Sometimes when luck helped us, he would lift us to a chair and let us peer through the telescope and then the smoking speck on the river's horizon would be a steamer complete from bow to stern, so magnified that we could see the English flag at her stern, and the people on her decks.

"Noo then," he would cry, "I must joost be about mah business."

He hustled us off to the saloon and always whatever my mother and Mrs. Swan were talking about would be hushed. It was women's talk, I suppose, women exiled and trying to make homes in an alien land. Three of my mother's babies lay buried in Chinese soil, and Mrs. Swan's twin boys were there, too. Their pictures were on the improvised mantel behind the stove. Upon the silk that draped it they stared out at everybody over their large embroidered collars.

But whenever we came in Mrs. Swan cried out, hearty and cheerful always, "Noo, mah dearies, here you are again! Wull you no have a bit more of the cake or a sweetie? No? Then some sweeties to take home."

And she packed two small bags of hard Scotch candies and shortcake and pressed them into our willing hands.

"Mother, a steamer's coming," we said. And that meant we must go home.

But sometimes there was no steamer coming, and then Cap'n Swan told us stories of the days when he went up and down the China coast and skirmished with the pirates at Bias Bay and ran down their junks. It made grand exciting stuff to hear, but Mrs. Swan sighed and shook her head and begged him to stop.

"Give over, do," she said. "Those days! I never saw your ship sail off without my heart droppin' to my boots. And never a way to get a word from you 'til you come sailin' in again!"

"Ah, them was the days," Cap'n Swan said.

"Not for me," Mrs. Swan declared.

Cap'n Swan knocked the ash from his short pipe. "If women was give their way, they'd keep men nussin' babes all their life long."

"If men had their way, there'd be none left, man, woman nor child. Wars and racketin' would end the race," Mrs. Swan said, looking as grim as a round and rosy face would permit.

"Hark to the woman," Cap'n Swan said good-naturedly.

"Aye, do," Mrs. Swan said smartly. " 'Twould do you good to hark to me once in a way."

He did not hark to her, of course, in any important way, else she would not have been doing Scotch homekeeping on a Chinese river hulk. He smoked his black pipe and raged at the Chinese on weekdays, kicking their bottoms if he grew too angry, and then went to the little English church on Sundays where he worshipped God devoutly and believed that the yellow men were the white man's burden. Through those two I learned to know Scotland and its people, and years later when I went to that rugged thorny land, it was no strange place, but the home, familiar to me, of Cap'n and Mrs. Swan.

For sometimes there on the hulk when they talked of Scotland I felt it around us and that if I looked out of the portholes that Mrs. Swan curtained to seem like windows, I would see not the dark and savage river, nor the scattering evening light of the Chinese skies, the myriad lights of red candles made of cow's fat and holding reeds for wicks, nor the little tin lamps that burned bean oil and peanut oil and the new American coal oil, but I would see the rough dark hills of Scotland. They carried Scotland with them, those two, in the burr upon their tongues, in all they said and wore and thought and did. Why did they live their lives in China and die at last to lie in Chinese soil forever? Who knows or can ever tell?

I asked their daughter that question once, but she did not know any more than she knew why she herself had come back to China. But she came, leaving Scotland. We knew of her existence, of course. Mrs. Swan spoke sometimes of Lisbeth, her daughter at school in Scotland, and for years Cap'n Swan carried a picture of her in his pocketbook, renewed from time to time.

"Aye, that's my girl," he would say whenever she sent him a new one. Thus over the tea table while I was growing up myself I watched Lisbeth growing up in Scotland, enough ahead of me to be a young woman with a pleasant open face when I was still a twelve-year-old.

When Lisbeth came back Mrs. Swan gave a tea party for her, and the handful of white people in the port—Mrs. Swan would not have thought of inviting any Chinese—came aboard the hulk to greet the plump, healthy, rosy girl in a ruffled pink dress, a little too pink for her own pink face and bright blue eyes. There was a flutter among the three or four English bachelors of the port of varying ages. A young unmarried white girl was rare enough to cause an agitation. But Lisbeth was a good girl and Cap'n Swan knew all the port scandal. Just before Lisbeth came, the youngest bachelor had succumbed to loneliness and example and had taken a pretty Chinese girl into his home. True, when he fell in love with Lisbeth he put her out again, but she had a baby afterwards, a strange little mongrel child. Cap'n Swan told Mrs. Swan and Mrs. Swan told Lisbeth and Lisbeth cried a great deal. But she was a good girl and steadfastly refused to go to the young Englishman's home, and after a year or two the wife of one of the missionaries died and after another decent year, Lisbeth married him and took beautiful care of his two motherless children and made him a faithful wife for twenty-five years of her own. And the young Englishman took another Chinese girl into his house and drank too much and grew sore and cynical about women. "Any woman is as good as another," he was fond of saying and kept on saying years later when his head shook with palsy and he was as yellow as a lemon with Yangtze Valley malaria.

But by that time the Swans were in their graves and the hulk was gone and the English ships plied up and down the river no more, and the clean parklike bit of land that had belonged to the English had been returned to China. Then Chinese swarmed in and out and the macadam streets were as filthy as the cobbled streets of the old city and the park benches along the Bund, once kept freshly painted and only for white folk, were peeling and decaying and cracking under the load of any Chinese loafer, beggar, student or coolie who chose to sit upon them. . . . The Swans belonged to the times they made and the England that was, lord of the East as well as the West.

But that river keeps rolling along. It has not changed a whit. I learned to know its every mood during the hours I spent at the window. On a crisp spring morning it looked as innocent as beauty itself, the sun caught in all its pointed yellow wavelets and shining upon brown and white sails and painted junks and bobbing sampans. Ferries plied safely back and forth, laden with people, and gunboats from America and France lay quiet with only their flags astir. Along the shores farmers, while they plowed or manured their green cabbages with the watered night soil they saved in great vatlike jars, kept their fishnets deep in the water. Whenever they stopped to rest they sauntered over to the riverbank and pulled a rope and the nets came swinging up out of the water. There was nearly always a fish in those nets. Then the farmer took a long-handled wooden dipper and dipped up the shining twisting silver shapes and had fish to eat with his cabbages or to sell at the market.

But there were other days when the river boiled like a muddy cauldron. Storms could beat upon it as fiercely as though it were a sea, and in the rough waters I have seen a ferry ease over upon its side and slide hundreds of people off as though they were insects, and turn still farther until it floated bottom up. Those black bobbing heads were visible only for a moment and then the river sucked them down. Nobody went to their rescue. A strange superstition locked men's hearts so that seldom was a hand put out to pull up even a child who fell into the river. It was believed that the gods decreed who was to drown, and if any human being defied the gods and saved a drowning man that man would live only to do evil. He would kill someone or commit a crime and the one who saved him would be responsible, and few dared to take the responsibility. Even the boat folk who lived in the mat sheds upon their flat-bottomed wooden boats let the river keep what went into it.

And fair weather or foul, the restless river kept gnawing at its farther banks. On that side the land was good farmland and the river bit it off, foot by foot, so that in a few generations a family could lose its entire farm. And then on the other side, where the city was, the river threw up a wide flat of mud that was a nuisance because the hulks had to be continually moved farther and farther away and the overloaded coolies had that much farther to walk.

That was the way the river was, and is, forever. The Yangtze River is the wildest, wickedest water upon the globe, and the most beautiful. It was as wide as an inland sea where our window looked across it. The farther shore was a gray-green line. For a thousand miles the river is wide and deep and full of fierce and changing currents. Then it grows narrow and runs between rocky cliffs and is fiercer than ever. It is an open, frank sort of fierceness, though, in the gorges. The fierceness that is horrible is the smooth dimpling golden spread of the lower Yangtze, which looks so amiable and still when one stands upon the shore and sees the waves lapping innocently at one's feet. But from an airplane you can see the real beast, for the river is never still. It moves with a long slow rush to the sea, a torrent as implacable as Niagara and more awful because it is so long, so slow.

And the terror to a child of climbing off and on the river steamers that anchored in mid-river when the river ran low and too shallow at the hulks! More often than not we had to get on or off at midnight, and by the light of swaying oil lanterns the yellow water rushing silently past the ship seemed to reach toward me to pull me under. The gangways were narrow rickety stairs of rope and boards and the only handrail was a soft waterlogged rope that gave at the touch. And the gangway never reached down to the bobbing sampans at its foot. The boatmen held up their dark bare arms and I had to jump into them, never sure of their grasp. But they did not fail. They plucked me out of the air and clutched me and lowered me to the flickering shore lights, while the muddy water sped past, a few inches below the edge of the boat.

I had good reason to fear that transfer from ship to sampan.

I had seen more than one Chinese slip into the widening moving strip of water between the two. When that happened, the body disappeared instantly. Not even white men thought of rescue, for rescue was impossible. The river was always first. Bodies were not washed up, or only miles below upon a muddy beach so far away that no one knew or could recognize the dead.

Such is the Yangtze, and there is no other river to equal it for beauty and for cruelty. The loveliest scenery in the world is to be found along its curving shores. Islands feathery with bamboos and studded with exquisite temple roofs tiled with porcelain, farmlands rich with alluvial deposits, little villages with cobbled streets running straight down to the river, cities whose walls guard them on three sides, and the Yangtze is the fourth, cliffs and mountains, the Yangtze has them all. It has spoiled me for any other river in the world. Even my own Father of Waters seems mild and small to me in comparison. I have seen Mississippi floods, and they are terrible and death-dealing, but I am grateful that they are nothing like the gargantuan Yangtze floods that swallow up valleys for miles inland and make islands of distant mountains. I stood once on Purple Mountain in Nanking, many miles distant from the river, and it was a great island, and lapping at its base, fifty feet deep over farmhouses and fields, were yellow Yangtze waves.

And yet two Americans once fell into the Yangtze and were not drowned. It was the very year of that flood, too. Charles and Anne Lindbergh had flown across the Pacific, north to the Orient, and their plane had come to rest on the quiet, lotus-studded waters of Lotus Lake, outside the walls of Nanking. I was among the crowd of Chinese that day who gathered to watch the plane glide down and come to rest, and with them I watched the Lindberghs come ashore in one of the small pleasure boats that plied upon the lake. The crowd parted and fell back before the tall young American and his little brown-eyed wife. They looked grave and tired and Lindbergh was worried about his plane, as he had reason to be. A flock of boats full of laughing excited people was gathered about it, and one young Chinese leaped upon the plane to pose for a snapshot his friends were taking. A guard had to be put about the plane.

I remember only one other thing. In that Chinese crowd a little

American boy, seemingly quite alone, pushed his way through to see his hero. He used his elbows and got to the front in time to see Lindbergh pass. I saw his face light up with worship.

"Hello, Lindy!" he cried.

Lindbergh, who had heard that call so many million times, did not answer or turn his head, but walked gravely on. He did not hear it and the light died out of the little American boy's face as he burrowed his way back into the Chinese crowd.

Yet it was only a few days after that that the Lindberghs took to their plane again and flew over the floods and did the splendid reconnoitering of destitute, water-surrounded towns and villages that formed the basis for relieving and saving thousands of lives. And just as they were leaving, their plane taking off from the Yangtze, a wing tipped and they were thrown into the river. The Chinese said the river reached up and pulled at the plane in revenge. By all Chinese experience and belief they should have drowned, but they kept up until they were rescued, to the awe and astonishment of everyone, and most of all the Chinese. A touch of magic went into all Chinese reminiscence about the Lindberghs thereafter.

"The old demon couldn't pull them under," the people said. "That's because they were American."

We left the river when I was eight because my father found a home for us. Our new house stood upon a low round hill, one of the many that are outside the walls of Chinkiang. There are a whole flock of these gamboling hills around that city, separated by tilled and fertile valleys that are green even in winter, where Chinese cabbage flourishes through the soft quickly melting snows of the Yangtze Valley. Small houses of earth and thatched with rice straw clustered among the rich fields are the farmhouses, and the ones nearest our house were as familiar to me in their interiors and in all the life that went on in them as a square brick bungalow on the hill that was my own home.

In those years I slipped instantaneously out of one life into another, depending upon the geography of the moment. Thus a fairly decorous American child rose in the morning from her bed and washed herself and put on her clothes and tied on the apron that all little American girls wore in those days and brushed her hair and went downstairs to breakfast of porridge and toast and eggs with her American family. Almost the only Chinese note at that meal was Liu Er, the manservant who brought the food in and put it on the table. He did not stay to serve it, because my parents wanted to be alone with us, to instruct us in table manners and to direct us for the day.

After breakfast we had prayers, and our contribution to that, as children, was a verse to be recited. The verse was chosen always for shortness, but it was a stern rule that there was to be no obvious repetition. Thus, "Jesus wept" could not be used more than twice a year by the same child without the piercing blue beams from my father's eyes being turned upon the offender and chilling her to stone with terror. My father's memory for Bible verses was prodigious. The result was that though we children became masters of short verses, we were hard put to it sometimes. There are fewer short verses in the Bible than one thinks. I remember my five-year-old sister one day piping out, "I am a companion to dragons and a brother to owls." This verse, while certainly in the Bible, my father received with awful gravity, relieved only by a twinkle in my mother's bright brown eyes. My father spoke.

"I do not consider your choice a suitable one," he said to my small sister. Her blue eyes filled with tears and he softened. "Do not use it again," he commanded, and went on.

And after the hymn and scripture reading and my father's prayer, always too long for my bare knees upon the rough Chinese matting on the floor, the business of being American went on. American lesson books were piled neatly on a desk in the sunny dining room, and there I must go and one by one attack the lessons my mother had assigned the day before. I do not remember any particular interest in them except to get them done, for the sooner I finished, the sooner I was free. So unless it were one of those soft spring mornings when work was literally impossible and I drove my mother frantic by darting in and out of the garden, I tried to hurry through my lessons and get to the real stuff of life.

In this fashion I galloped through American history and geography, for though we lived in China, I was taught no more of the history and geography of that land than if I had lived in Peoria, Illinois. I am glad this was so. Years after when I was sauntering about my own country, discovering one place after another, all the scraps of information which geographies gave me in those days fitted together, still fast in my flypaper subconscious memory. Out of it came long-forgotten things I knew and doubtless would not have known had they not been compulsorily stuffed into my brain as I sat by the window looking out over the lovely Chinese country about which I learned but not in books.

Whether my mother could "hear" my lessons or not depended on whether a Chinese visitor were there. Nothing else was allowed to interfere with lessons. My mother timed all her household tasks to leave flexible an hour to hear my lessons anywhere in the morning. But if a Chinese came to see her, then even lessons must wait, for Chinese came first, not only because they were Chinese, but because there might be an opportunity to bring to someone, directly or indirectly, the Christian message which was the reason my parents were in China.

How glad I was when I peeped into the little reception room that was furnished in Chinese tables and chairs and saw a visitor there! For then the tedious hour of recitation was postponed indefinitely, and I could skip out of the house and into another life.

I must have had a happy childhood, for it seems to me that the weather was always good. I remember always the full bright sunshine, semitropical as it was, pouring over the bamboo-covered hills and into the deep green valleys. This is ridiculous, for everybody knows that there is an exasperating amount of rain in the Yangtze Valley, and in summer a rainy season when for weeks it rains steadily. Yet the prevailing atmosphere of my memory is sunshine. When I compel myself to think of rain and what I did when it rained, I remember walking barelegged, with straw sandals on my feet, along the narrow raised paths between the rice paddy fields, and sheltered as I went by a hat as big as an umbrella on my head. It was made of a double layer of woven bamboo, and between the layers were laid flat bamboo leaves, and not a drop of rain came through. I remember slushing through delightful yellow mud on the road toward an old fort and searching for spent bullets that the rains washed down from the target practice fields. I have no dull memories of rain. But then I have no memories of a moment of boredom or tedium of any kind in my childhood. Why limit it to my childhood? I have not had such a moment in my life. Maybe it did rain a good deal, after all.

I do not remember having any toys except a doll, a box of blocks made of unpainted wood, and a paint box. But I had plenty of things to play with of one kind or another. I made kites by the hundreds, after the pattern Liu Er taught me, out of split reeds tied to the shape of stars or birds or butterflies and pasted over with opaque Chinese paper. To fly these I had to go out of the compound so as to escape the big trees, and to get as high as possible I climbed always on top of the highest grave. The graves did not show in the summer under the long grass, but after the grass was cut for winter fuel, they showed very clearly. Americans newly arrived were always depressed by these graves, for the Chinese have no cemeteries. I heard a young American girl cry once:

"Why, you live in a graveyard!"

"Where?" I asked, staring out of the window. And for the first time I saw that our hills were covered with graves. But they could hold no gloom for me by that time. I had spent too many happy years at kite-flying upon them, and running through their waving grass.

I am afraid, moreover, that I used to enjoy Chinese funerals. Whenever I saw a long line of white-clad mourners winding up our hill I managed if I possibly could to slip through the gate and hover on their outskirts and watch. It was seldom a wholly sad occasion. Usually the dead one had died months or even years before and the coffin had lain in some home or temple waiting for a lucky day. The mourners climbed the hill cheerfully, on foot if they were poor, or they were carried in sedan chairs if they were rich, and the whole affair was something of an outing. There was incense to be lighted, a white cock to be killed and the blood spilled, and brightly colored paper images of men and women and houses and furniture and money to be burned. The members of the family passed the coffin in turn, each to bow, and at the proper time the nearest relative cried loudly for the allotted time while the rest of the funeral party waited, squatting on their heels or lounging about the grass in the summer sunshine. Funerals were seldom held in winter.

This was all interesting and I edged nearer and nearer and had my part in supplying material for observation and remarks. They took it for granted that I could not speak their language, and I let them think so as long as nothing too untrue was said. But sooner or later it was said. Sooner or later someone said:

"The foreigners take the eyes out of babies to make pills to cure malaria."

Or they said, "Foreigners are opposite to us in all ways. They are born with white hair and die with black."

Even to the millionth time I heard them, these absurdities were too much for me. I felt upon me the necessity to defend my own people.

"Everything you say is lies," I remarked pleasantly.

The effect of this was instant. There was always a moment of stunned silence. Did they or did they not understand what I had said? they asked each other. They understood, but could not believe that they had. A rapid question or two, tossed among themselves, a quick comparison, and it was irrefutable that they had understood this strange foreign child. But this only alarmed them. Why had they understood? They could not speak the foreigners' language. Was there some foreign magic I had that made it possible for them to know what I had said? Once an old grandmother shrieked aloud when she perceived her own understanding.

"Ai-ya, I am going to die!" she cried. "I can understand the talk of foreign devils!"

But sometimes they merely came to the conclusion that all languages were the same. Even after protracted conversations they were often unconvinced that what I spoke was not my own tongue, though admitting it sounded exactly like theirs.

For of course once my silence was broken conversation was inevitable. Questions had to be asked on both sides. They had to ask what I ate and drank in my country. Did everybody in my country look like me? In my ignorance I always said they did, to be as soundly astonished as any Chinese years later to discover that my countrymen were yellow and red and black, composed of all races upon Earth.

Then their questions inevitably took a personal turn. How many were in my family and what did I wear under my dress and were leather shoes not hot and heavy on the feet? When I was small I lifted my short skirts and explained my petticoats and drawers, until my mother taught me better. The inevitable question asked, though never in the presence of adults, was whether or not foreign babies were reproduced in the same way Chinese

babies were. Rumor had it that they were not. I could not answer this question because I did not know myself how Americans
had babies, though I cannot remember when I did not know about
Chinese babies. Many of my days were spent with playmates in
courtyards where the women discussed freely and in detail this
chief occupation of their lives. So I had long ceased to have any
curiosity or interest in the matter except delight in the idea of
any new baby. I loved babies always and one of the happiest things
about China was the prevalence of babies. When I asked
my mother concerning the Americans, however, in order that I
might pass on the information, she looked strange, and the answer she gave me was the only one I had for years. She said
as severely as she ever said anything:

"When Chinese ask you that question, tell them that God made
us all alike, and in His image."

I am afraid many a funeral I thus attended was broken up by
conversations. The Chinese are an eager, friendly, curious, informal race, fond of children anywhere, and they often neglected
the corpse and turned to the small white child who had appeared
so strangely out of the long green grass. Sooner or later a woman
would call out:

"How is it you are here alone?"

"I ran away," I always said. This absolved my mother from
blame. Nice little girls did not wander about without their amahs
—and it always provoked loud appreciative laughter. Funerals
on those hills usually ended in cheerful good humor on all sides
and in much coaxing on the part of the mourning family for
me to go along home with them. I yielded to this only once, however, for a bamboo switch was waiting for me in my father's right
hand when I reached home after an entire day when nobody knew
where I was. It was a beautiful day and I was fed and amused and
admired by various members of a large well-to-do family, all complete strangers to me, and I was returned safely home at nightfall. Home seemed a sad contrast for a few minutes—an agitated welcome, tempered with indignation and a scolding, and
vehement commands for the future.

But there were some funerals at which I said nothing. They
were what I called "real funerals"! The dead was the well-beloved,
whose face would be seen no more, and the women wept and could

see nothing else for their weeping. I usually waited until out of their wailing I learned who had died, husband, father or son, and then I fled, in tears myself, to throw myself upon some other grave to cry for what reason I did not know, except that Death, usually a cheerful part of life, could be a sad and awful thing.

I used, at such times, to ponder a great deal about death. What was it? My little brother died of diphtheria when I was seven, and I was very ill of it, too, but not too ill to know that he was put into a box and taken to the Christian cemetery. "A Brave Little Christian Soldier"—my mother had a Chinese stonecutter carve the letters into our local Chinese marble. He was a gallant boy, wonderfully courageous even at five when he died in terrible suffering. That was Death. Sometimes it was like that, in spite of the heaven my parents said was waiting. But if my mother thought our four dead children were in heaven why did she weep as long as she lived when she thought of them? I used to ask her that and she shook her head until her tears dropped on her breast. "When you are older, you will understand," she always said. And that day did come, as it comes to us all.

But there was another kind of death, the sort the Chinese more usually died, a happy sort of party they planned for the end of their lives. As age came on, old men and women I knew ordered their coffins early and had them made exactly as they wanted them. Nearly all the homes where I came and went at will had a coffin or two ready for the oldest members. They were made of a very heavy special wood, perhaps cypress, and varnished a bright black. The enormous lid fitted tightly down, the whole thing made a handsome piece of furniture, and everybody grew used to it and it became as familiar as a bed to the old one who was to sleep in it at last. Indeed, he grew attached to it and fond of its presence and shouted against a careless child who scratched it in play. It gave him a feeling of security and continuity with the family. When he died one day, any day, he would simply lie quietly there, the lid sealed, and for days, perhaps even months, the family life would go on about him as it did now. There would be no sudden burial. On some chosen lucky day he would be taken to the family plot and buried in his proper place among the ancestors, and his name kept among the clan tablets and worshipped at the several times in the year set for such a purpose.

Yet the Chinese, sentimental as they are, do not carry even sentimentality beyond the possibilities of what is convenient. The dead are kept alive in the family circle for a hundred years, then they belong to the ancestors and are given no more attention, and a cycle of new dead begins. But a hundred years is a long time. It is three generations and that is long enough to live after one is dead.

It was a good way for a child to learn about death, to see it accepted as a part of life, to know it held no terrors for the old waiting one who smiled with comfort to think of his last bed provided for him and always in his sight. There was even a deal of humor about it. Mild jokes were made with the old one and sometimes if he grew angry over a trifle he threatened to get into his coffin prematurely. Sometimes he actually did it. I remember such a predicament in the home of one of my best friends. The head of that family was the great-grandmother, a wonderful old thing of ninety with a temper as high and hot as at nineteen, and being peevish at having lost one of her last two teeth so that she could no longer chew meat, she grew angry one day because her granddaughter-in-law did not cut the pork small enough, and after cursing her she climbed into her coffin.

What, then, to do? The whole family gathered to coax and cajole and her sons and daughters-in-law and their sons and daughters-in-law all knocked their heads before the coffin, but she would not budge. Fortunately the newest baby boy, just then learning to walk and neglected in the family crisis, fell down and bumped his head on the cobbles in the courtyard and then the old lady bounced out of her coffin to superintend his restoration and to bawl at them for not being careful about her great-great-grandson.

Even shrouds were robbed of all horror. In certain regions it is customary to make shrouds of bright red cloth, at least for women, and in families not too rich to be prudent, it is the common habit to make a shroud for anyone who is old enough to begin to expect death as a natural event, and then let the old one wear it for a while as a garment. The purpose of this is purely practical, but the results are sometimes extremely trying.

Thus in another family I once knew an old lady who wore out five shrouds before she finally was buried in her sixth, and that was a new one, after all. The first one was made when she was sixty-five, during an attack of dysentery. The family were all grateful that she lived to wear the shroud, and it was padded with cotton for winter and old Mrs. Ling wore it under a decorous black sateen coat. She wore it out and a second one was made, and some jokes cracked which Mrs. Ling could join in and be rather proud of herself for her vitality. But when her busy daughter-in-law had to make a third shroud, there were no jokes, and old Mrs. Ling was slightly ashamed of herself. At every illness that winter she announced that she was going to die. Three different times I went in to say good-bye to her, and to promise to continue my friendship with her granddaughter. But, alas, for her shroud, each winter for years we went through the same performance.

Poor old soul, one winter I came upon her sitting in a warm corner of the courtyard alone, recuperating in her fourth shroud, and she wailed into my sympathetic ears, "I just don't die! I can't help if I don't die, can I?"

"Nobody wants you to die, foster mother," I said, trying to comfort her.

It was true, none of them wanted her to die. There was even a good deal of admiration in the village for this doughty old body that would not give up. People outside the family took the whole matter as a joke, though the family were embarrassed by it.

Mrs. Ling herself grew angry about it at last and blamed it on some wicked mischievous spirit who was simply teasing the family by keeping her alive, and she went to special temples and burned extra incense—and went on living and wearing out shrouds. At last, when she was well over ninety, she did succeed in dying one day, in great triumph and peace of mind, in her sixth shroud, and was given an enormous funeral and the whole village turned out to it.

So how could death ever be a terror to me after that? When my turn comes to be laid into the soil of my country, in the little American village near my own home, I shall approach the hour with the tranquillity I learned in another land. When I was a child in China I saw death too often face to face, and too easily as a friend, to be afraid of it if it comes as a natural part of life. Under pagan skies I learned the truest meaning of brave Christian words, "O Death, where is thy sting? And, Grave, thy victory?"

. . . But I should not be telling the truth of what I learned about death in my childhood, if I did not tell more. Sometimes, as I wandered alone over the Chinese hills, I came upon strange and tragic fragments of human bodies. They were always the fragments of little bodies—most often of little girls, but sometimes of very small boys who had died of some illness in families too poor for funerals, or of babies who had been born dead. It was not customary to give babies funerals or even to bury them.

These little bodies, wrapped in matting and laid on a hillside, were always found by the half-savage village dogs and worried and mangled and partly eaten. I was perhaps eight when I first came upon the almost perfect head and left shoulder and handless arm of a tiny baby. We had just left the Bund then and the river and were living in the hills outside the city, and nobody had prepared me for this sort of death. I remember my first awful repulsion and horror. I was about to run away with all my might, when something pathetic and lost in the tiny face struck me to my heart and I went to look at it and then to cry. A baby, to be so left! I hunted for a stick and found a hole into an old collapsed grave, and put the poor little remains into it, first lining the hole with soft green grass. Then I dug and patted the earth about and made a tiny mound and put wild flowers on it, and went away still crying. With the curious reticence of childhood I told no one of the incident. I believe I never told anyone of it, and these words I now write are its first recounting.

Yet it had its importance, because that was the beginning of a fierce crusade I carried on all during my childhood, in the cause of the childish dead, against the dogs. I devised weapons of pointed bamboo sticks, or a long bamboo split to hold a stone I bound into it with wire, and thus armed if I saw a dog or sometimes several with their heads dropped and their shoulders hunched over something I flew at them with my weapon. It was a dangerous thing to do, I know now, for the yellow curs were vicious and snarled horribly. But they were curs and receded before my fury. If I had shown fear they might have flown at me. But passionate for the cause, I had no fear, for the moment however, and with the poor salvage in a grass-woven bag I always brought along, I had another of those lonely little funerals of my own, never telling anybody. Sometimes I buried only a bit of a hand or a skull or even only a bone, but sometimes it was more. They were always children and always very little ones, and I always buried them with flowers, or if it were winter with a twig of evergreen or a bit of bright tile or a pretty pebble.

I never learned to love dogs after that. Even today, in my own country where dogs are made much of and cared for better than children are sometimes, I cannot love them. I see their beautiful coats, their strong healthy bodies, their friendly playfulness and I can admire their animal beauty. But their jaws are the jaws of dogs, and when I look into the dog eyes, I see the eyes of other dogs, the enemies I fought against in a child's crusade for children helpless and distressed and dead before their time.

. . . And out of all this, what was I taught about death when I was a child in China? That death is beautiful and good when it comes without violence and as a natural culmination of a life lived to its proper climax, but that death by violence is evil and hideous because it is unnatural and contradicts life.

My father, who was a fisher of men, fished some strange ones. We were one winter harassed by a small band of robbers who hid in the distant hills and descended upon the farmhouses around and robbed and pillaged. We expected this sort of thing in famines but it was not a famine year, and everybody was indignant. The leader of the band was an old soldier, a man famous for his military deeds in the past, but he had lost his place because he had killed his superior officer and fled to the hills.

My father determined to make an opportunity to see this man and did, by simply going to the mountain temple where the robbers lived. He found this chieftain a rather well-educated man, and his manners gentle and seemingly without violence. He allowed my father to speak to him of religion, and they went from religion to talk of robbing and warfare. Then the man told my father frankly that he engaged in this not for what he would gain by it, but because he had become so used to the excitement of killing people that if he should give it up he would find life dull and stupid. He had left his wife and children, because the ordinary things of home were intolerable to him. My father, telling us of it, made us feel the ominousness of that man, sitting so quietly and telling of the pleasure he found in killing. The man called it "war" and "battle" and "a soldier's life," but my father said his real joy was in seeing people die, and in the wild sense of power he had when he could kill.

The man was not a maniac. He was simply an ordinary man who had become used to extraordinary stimulation. For death can have a strange pull and power of its own, so that men become like animals who have tasted blood and then thirst after it unquenchably. The pursuits of peace and of ordinary life seem flat and tasteless to them.

I remember that night we sat about the little iron grate full of coals in our sitting room, my father, my mother and I. I think they forgot I was there, because I had been listening, fascinated by the dark tale. My mother said, her mobile face full of repulsion, "More than we know, that is the explanation of war." Then she caught sight of me. "Go to bed," she commanded me, "this hasn't anything to do with you."

But it had. My young girlhood was to be spent under the shadow of the Great Wars, and today, when my life is not yet near its end, the shadow is over me again, and over millions like me, the shadow made of those who love to kill, who choose death and not life.

All of the people and incidents in the foregoing quotations were part of her childhood. They are real to her, and I feel they show truly the surroundings in which she grew up.

The childhood characteristic that remains strongest in her today is her curiosity. Carie often declared, laughing, that she was plagued by the forever flowing questions of this daughter, whose inquisitive mind could not comprehend how the people her parents talked about far away in America could do what they did, in the ways they did, when the Chinese knew the proper way to do everything! And why, the child must have thought, did the mother speak so longingly of the distant home? Yet the child was never to forget for a moment, either, that she herself was different, a white child in a brown country.

This insistent memory is, I believe, the reason she understands so well now the plight of a displaced child. Even today she is still displaced. In discussions by critics and journalists of what they call the leading American writers, she frequently is not mentioned, perhaps because she is not thought of as American by many American critics. Yet she is fiercely loyal to her own country. When she was driven out of China by the Communists and returned to America at forty years of age, she bought a house and land of her own, so eager she was to have roots and to belong in her own country. She loved China and her home and friends, yet there, too, she was an alien. She tells me that she has always loved the Chinese, a people happy and gay, yet she has feared them, for she has long known that some day they would take revenge for the cruelties of white people in their country. Yes, she has seen unbelievable cruelty committed by white people in Asia and she has told me often that her greatest dread is of the day when the dark races rise up and rebel against the minority of the world's population that is white. She has told me that all through her years in China she was conscious of this possibility. Her fear began perhaps in 1900, the year the Empress Dowager, about whom she wrote in her novel *Imperial Woman,* was enraged by the encroachments of white men on China's soil, and sent forth a royal edict:

"All white people are to be killed!"

So might the child and her family have been killed, as others were killed, except that the wise viceroy in Kiangsu province, where they lived, inserted the negative "not" after the word "are," thereby saving their lives at the risk of his own.

In the hallway of the third floor of the Pearl S. Buck Foundation's house on Delancey Place, in Philadelphia, between her library and her bedroom, where she often spends quiet hours working or resting, stands a Chinese chest made for this Chinese gentleman. Its clasp is the symbol for the male and female elements in the universe, the Yang and the Ying, and its interior holds many small drawers and secret compartments. It was made for that viceroy after his own design, a unique piece of furniture, and his daughter presented it to Pearl Buck when she left China years later. It is handsome here in its final home, its polished wood and gleaming brass a constant link between her ever-present past and this moment.

It is another page in her story—a small but necessary part, for without the man who owned that chest, there would be no story. She says:

I know, from the vantage of these years, that the change did not come suddenly, but it seemed sudden to me, a small child living within the shelter of our Chinese home, with parents and kindly Chinese friends and devoted Chinese servants. Suddenly, then, it seemed that I was no longer the happy child of favored people. Instead I became a member of something called the White Race, and without knowing it I was one of a group of persons who were attacking China, dividing the country and exploiting the people. All unknown to me, much too small to understand such matters, this sort of thing had been going on for a long time. It was true that England and European nations were constantly demanding pieces of Chinese territory and concessions in trade. France had taken an enormous slice of China and called it Indo-China. It is the same territory where now American men are fighting in Vietnam. Germany had taken land and cities, and I could see with my own eyes in the city near which we lived that England had taken land along the Yangtze River, had walled it off, and within the walled area Englishmen and their families lived as though they were in England. On the river itself English ships carried passengers and goods, and there were French, German and Japanese ships as well. But the Western nations were the worst, for they were the most predatory and they had the weapons.

China was near the end of a dynasty, too, and following the traditional Chinese pattern when a dynasty neared its close, young men of strength and influence were eyeing each other as rivals for the throne. In Peking, the old Empress Dowager, Tzu Hsi, was clinging desperately to the last stronghold of her power. Revolutionists had crept even into the palace and she was too old and tired to try new ways herself. Her only solution for Western encroachments was to get rid of Westerners. The great T'ai P'ing rebellion she had put down some twenty years before, at the cost of twenty million Chinese lives, and she was right, perhaps, in thinking that the men of the West were now her chief enemies.

She searched desperately for help and found none. Within the palace she trusted no one, for she had found rebels even among the tutors of the young Emperor. They had corrupted him, she believed, persuading him that China must modernize and learn from the West. To her this was unthinkable and she determined to rid the nation of Westerners. To this end she summoned a fanatical Chinese secret society, called the Boxers, who boasted that they had magic powers which made them immune to foreign bullets. In her desperation she believed them, and thus in the year 1900 my world changed as a result of an imperial edict sent forth by the Empress, in which she ordered the death of every white man, woman and child.

Our Chinese home was no longer a shelter and place of safety. Anxiety pervaded the atmosphere and my parents tried to decide whether we should leave for Shanghai and the protection of our own government officials there or stay with our Chinese friends. For our friends, too, were in peril. The imperial edict included all Chinese Christians as traitors and persons worthy of death.

The long story of those perilous days I have told in my book, *My Several Worlds,* and I need not tell it again. The importance of it here is that in my childish mind my mother's house in faraway America became for me the symbol of safety in a dangerous world. It was a confusing time for a small child. My whole life was changed. I was no longer allowed to wander beyond the compound walls. My favorite place in the long pampas grass outside the gate was forbidden. Snakes I had been warned against, yet the danger now was not from snakes but from angry people. For suddenly we were all changed, it seemed. We were not the friendly American family we thought we had been, living in a friendly Chinese community. Even my father's friends no longer came to the house. No one came to the house. Our servants remained faithful but they were afraid, too, of what might happen to them and to their families. We were responsible for "slicing China up like a melon," as the old Empress put it, and for the exploitation of the Chinese people. When I had this long word, "exploitation," explained to me I could only see the Chinese coolies unloading the foreign ships down on the English Bund, at the river's edge. It had always troubled me to see those men, their slender half-naked bodies sweating and trembling under heavy loads, each man carrying a tally stick in his free hand which he must present to the Englishman sitting in a comfortable chair under the shade of an umbrella.

The stick must tally with his record, or the coolie would not be paid for his labor. I had seen many a quarrel in which the Chinese always lost, and it always made me sad. I understood the Chinese language as my own tongue and I sympathized with a coolie's agonized explanations, which never saved him from punishment, for the Englishman could not speak Chinese and depended on an interpreter who said what he thought his master wanted said. How often did I long to break in with my own childish explanations, and had indeed tried to do so more than once, to no avail, for the lofty white man only stared me down or told me to mind my own business. So how could we, my family and I, be responsible for injustice and exploitation?

Nevertheless, it seemed we were.

"Let us go home to your house in America," I begged my mother.

She shook her head. "Not yet."

We did go to Shanghai, however, and stayed there, my mother and baby sister and our Chinese nurse and I, while my father remained alone in our Chinese home. There in that city we lived for nearly a year and there my mother had time to tell me stories of her home and her people, who were also mine, it seemed, although I did not know them.

During that year the siege of Peking took place. The old Empress Dowager fled with her court, and did not come back again until the imperial forces had been defeated and the Boxers proved charlatans. New treaties were made, the Chinese subdued but resentful, and after the next summer we went back to our Chinese home. But it was never the same again, never secure, never safe. One never knew when the resentment would break forth in some new explosion.

Meantime, a harsh peace was made between Western nations and the old Empress. She yielded with grace but she knew her end. The change had come and though we white people seemed safe, I knew we were not. Our friends were our friends again and the warm personal relationships continued, but we felt ourselves islands in the great sea of change about us. There was no real heir to the Dragon Throne, no one strong enough to breast the storm of revolution that had its heart and impetus from young men and women who had learned of the West through missionary

schools. As for me, I knew that my real home was in another country, with my own people—this, though I was a stranger there. By
the accident of history I was now compelled to take my place with
those whom I did not know and who did not know me but to
whom I belonged by ancestry and birth.

There is searching in Pearl Buck, a searching so deeply em-
bedded that it is difficult for one to fathom, but I am convinced
that it stems from a basic need to belong somewhere. She has
said to me:

"Somehow I have always been an object, rather than a person.
As a child, I was white with yellow hair and blue eyes in a country where everyone knew the proper color of eyes and hair was
black, and skin was brown. I can remember my Chinese friends
bringing their friends to look at me because I was different. By
the time I came to this country I was different again. I was already
what people call famous. People came to see me as they would
an object, not a person."

She spent her early life in the dim world of in-between. Hence
this small child retreated into her own world and began to watch
the passing parade of people as though from afar. She is very
much involved with life and world affairs, but not with people.
She still has that detached air as though she were watching the
feet of people passing the garden gate of her house in China. When
she was three years old and forced at times to stay within the compound, the gate was so near the ground that, try though she did,
she could see no more of people than from the knees down. She
was deeply interested, but detached behind the safety of the garden gate. Now she closes the "garden gate" of her private life, her
inner being, and sits in safety watching, interested and involved,
but, in a way, still detached. Yet she enjoys her life thoroughly
in spite of the loneliness one knows is there. Especially, I sometimes think, she enjoys undertaking the impossible. But many
times when I am with her I perceive the feeling she describes in
the last line of *A Bridge for Passing*. She is still that woman waiting at a window open to the sky.

Perhaps part of this detachment was due to her father's detachment from other missionaries in China. She often explains with
obvious pride that her father was no ordinary missionary. He be-

came a distinguished Chinese scholar, learned in Confucian philosophy and Buddhist theology. His greatest work of scholarship was to translate the New Testament from Greek into the Chinese vernacular, in order that it might be more easily read by the Chinese. Among his other literary works were a brilliant comparison between Buddhism and Catholicism and a reference book of Chinese idioms. True to his faith, he met even sorrow with a calm spirit. Whatever the misfortune he accepted it as God's will. Carie, however, could be rebellious, and as I have said, could even declare that God might be wrong. Thus, from her father the child inherited the basic belief that all men should be free to have their own faith, and from her mother she had the determination that she would be responsible for her own life.

"I make up my mind what it is that I want to do and then I go straight to it. I never worry about how I'm going to do it for if I did I am sure I would never get it done," she said one day. Nevertheless she has not always made wise choice of what she wanted to do. For example, one important decision that was obviously a mistake was her first marriage.

"I married a handsome face," she told me, reluctantly but truthfully, "and did you ever try to live just with a handsome face?"

Of the marriage there was born only one child, and this one with the metabolic inability to assimilate proteins, which is called phenylketonuria. In those years the difficulty was not preventable, as it is today, and mental retardation resulted. At an early age it was apparent that Carol was not normal. This, too, became part of her life.

Her first marriage was dissolved many years later. Of that, more when the time comes. But somewhere in those years there was an experience outside marriage that moved her deeply. It ended in the accidental death of a brilliant man to whom for many years she was deeply and privately devoted. She has transmuted that experience into a novel, *Letter From Peking.* The complete woman, she wrote thus of love in that book:

"For it was in this house that we first consummated our eternal love. We were not married. I write it down. I have never told our heavenly secret to anyone, nor has he. I am sure he has not. He says he loves only me, whatever happens, and so he has not told.

Say it may have been wrong, but I am glad now for what I chose to do."

Later, in the same book, she wrote:

"I read novels sometimes in the winter evenings while Rennie studies his books for school. The novels describe again and again the act of physical love between man and woman. I read these descriptions, wondering at their monotony and their dullness. The act of love can, then, be meaningless! I wonder at such degradation, and then I realize that it is degraded because the two who perform it are degraded. I thank the beloved who saved me from such desecration. I understand now the desolate look in women's eyes that I often see. For it is the man, not the woman, who is responsible for the beauty or the horror of the moment when the two meet. When a woman receives in exaltation and is given in haste, she is desecrated. She has been used as a clay pot may be used, and she is more than clay. She is spirit."

It is unimportant whether the foregoing quotations are exactly autobiographical. It is the privilege of a writer to grasp a situation as it stands and complete it in her own mind. The world will never know how much actually happened and how much took place merely in the vast areas of a great creative imagination.

Of him, whoever he was, she has spoken to me thus:

"He was half Chinese, and I noticed in him a tendency to lean to his Chinese side, a sympathy with his Chinese mother, which made me know that he needed a Chinese wife. I could never fill his needs. I could never be his wife, and so, we parted. He has a Chinese wife, and I believe he was happy."

Who is to say that Rennie, in *Letter From Peking*, is not the son she never bore, with all of the qualities she would have wanted in such a son? It is the privilege of a writer to take a situation from his own life and develop it to its fullest. But the hurt is there, the people are there, the situation is there. It could have happened. How much actually did is not for us to know.

It is of little wonder to me that she has never been inclined to write the autobiography so many people have hoped for, for it has all been written in her many books. Therefore, it is in her books, in their rich variety, that we must find her. In *East Wind : West Wind* she tells the story of a young Chinese maid, disappointed in love and marriage, finding it not what she had been led to believe it to be. Thus a woman has told her disappointment in her own marriage and has given hope to other women that this is something with which one can live if one makes the adjustments necessary in order to lead a healthy, reasonably happy life. The adjustments? They led her to transfer her interest to her work as a writer and as a lover of human life.

She expresses in the character of Madame Wu in *Pavilion of Women* her feelings concerning the life of a woman after forty. She believes that a woman's life is not finished simply because she ceases to be the bearer of children. She has treated the "change of life" with the same wisdom prevailing in all of her works—in fact, in her life itself. Incidentally, perhaps the reason she minimizes the importance of her first famous book, *The Good Earth,* is that, as a portrayal of Chinese peasant life, it necessarily contains less of herself. I have asked her about O-lan.

"Where did you find her?" I asked.

"Out of all the women I knew she emerged," she told me.

There are characteristics of O-lan that I recognize, nevertheless, but she is a glimpse of the Chinese Pearl Buck of many years ago. She is no longer part of Pearl Buck today, forty years later. But then how could she be? That earlier woman is changed indeed.

The two books in which she has the least interest are *China Flight* and *The Young Revolutionist,* perhaps because they are simple storytelling. Could it be that there is no Pearl S. Buck breathing in those pages? She has said:

"I wrote those books for money and I cannot do that and do well. I must write with no thought of whether the book will 'sell.' I write because I have something to say and I say it!

"When I contracted for *The Young Revolutionist* it so happened that I was in the United States with my retarded child, for whose care and future I was solely responsible. For her sake I needed money, for I knew all too well the cost of lifelong care for such a child. I have always earned my own living and I was not a missionary. I was a teacher at Chinese universities. I was well paid as teachers go, but now I had to earn much more. A Christian organization said to me: 'If you will write a book for children with a Christian ending, we will give you five hundred dollars.'

"Thus I contracted for *The Young Revolutionist.* I returned to China then and first wrote *The Good Earth* because it was in my mind, waiting. Then, reluctantly, I fulfilled my contract for *The Young Revolutionist.*

"If I have ever had a guilty feeling it is for that act of writing for money. I have regretted other things I have done, certainly, but none so much as that. Yet I needed money for my child, and five hundred dollars was a lot of money to me then."

One of her dearest friends said of her works:

"She had something to say, and she said it in her first book. She has been saying it ever since."

How shallow the mind that takes that remark to be cruel, for it is not! The same conviction of hope expressed in the first book she ever wrote (though published later), *The Exile,* is contained in the book she has most recently published. It is tempered with age and the wisdom acquired through the years, but it is there and it rings loud and true! It has been said that "there is more fact in fiction than in history," and certainly this is true of the works of Pearl S. Buck.

Hers has been a rich career and it grows richer with the years. How did it begin? She was tutored at home by her mother and a Confucian scholar.

"My mother employed him to teach me Chinese, and I've always been grateful for that because he taught me so much. He taught me good manners, too. My mother was very punctilious about manners. She didn't stand any nonsense. Nor did my father! My tutor taught me respect for teacher and parent. Of course, the Chinese made a greater impression on me then than anyone else. They were the most real people in my life and there were so many of them. They were always kind, very kind. And they had such wonderful holidays. My mother was sensible and good about having us celebrate their holidays. At the Feast of Lanterns we were always allowed to buy lanterns—rabbits, birds, butterflies, flowers. I remember I had a horse lantern, too. One could put the horse's head in front and the tail behind and walk in the middle. I had a gay sort of childhood."

Throughout her education, learning was made a game for her, and it is the game she enjoys most today. She developed a thirst for knowledge of the world, begun, she says, by her discovery of

Charles Dickens, whose novels she began to read at the age of four. In the Foundation house we still have part of that original treasured and much worn set of Charles Dickens from her home in China—torn, because the books were thrown about when her house was looted by a Communist mob. Dickens had more influence on her writing than anyone else, she says, except her mother, who required her to write something each week. It was a wise demand, for thus she early put into words her thoughts and dreams, her impressions of the life about her. Her mother, she says, was never critical. Instead, she always encouraged her young daughter to express her true self in whatever way she chose. The first writing of Pearl S. Buck known to be published is on my desk as I write this. It is contained in the "Letters to the Editor" column of *The Christian Observer,* a newspaper published in Louisville, Kentucky. The date is April 5, 1899. The letter is signed Pearl Sydenstricker, Chinkiang, China. Obviously much influenced by the missionary environment against which she later rebelled, it is headlined "Our Real Home in Heaven," and reads:

DEAR MR. CONVERSE:

I am a little girl, six years old. I live in China. I have a big brother in college who is coming to China to help our father tell the Chinese about Jesus. I have two little brothers in heaven. Maudie went first, then Artie, then Edith, and on the tenth of last month my little brave brother, Clyde, left us to go to our real home in heaven. Clyde said he was a Christian Soldier, and that heaven was his bestest home. Clyde was four years old, and we both loved the little letters in the Observer. I wrote this all myself, and my hand is tired, so goodbye.

She says now:

I can still remember my sense of wonder when I saw that brief letter. I can even remember the way it looked upon the page. It was a short letter, conveying nothing of interest or worth, I am afraid, and carrying in it a hint of my mother's idealism, always expressed in religious terms and against which even then I felt rebellion, although I loved her too well ever to express it to her.

It is perhaps fortunate that she died before the open rebellion took place. Nevertheless, it was exciting, even at six, to realize that I could write something in distant China and see it not too much later in an American newspaper, among all the other American letters.

This early success, if it may be called such, made me willing, if not always eager, to follow my mother's suggestion again and begin writing regularly, a year or so later, for the old Shanghai *Mercury,* a newspaper published under British auspices in Shanghai. A kindly editor offered prizes each month for the best stories and articles by children, and this became a source of regular pocket money for me by the time I was ten years old. Not only that, it gave my always softhearted but stubborn mother an excuse for exacting from me weekly an essay or story. She had, I found out afterward, a secret conviction that I would some day be a writer, and while she never told me this, she did encourage and coax me to put into writing some of my experiences and ideas. Strangely, when I began to write poetry, she objected strongly and for this I have never known the reason.

My first poem was a long one, written on a Christmas, and again published in the *Mercury.* It attracted enough attention so that I had to recite it at the Christmas celebration in the boarding school in Shanghai where for a term or so I was an unhappy pupil. My pleasure in this poem was also somewhat weakened by certain didactic ideas which my mother wished me to insert into the last verse or two, and against which I felt revulsion. I had not the heart, again, to refuse her, and so again I yielded. These early experiences in editorial compulsion have made me an unruly writer ever since and to such an extent that I insisted, years later, that my publishers return to an influential book club the contract, already signed by the club, for a certain novel of mine because editorial changes were asked for lest I offend certain religious groups.

As soon as I escaped from my mother's benign but restrictive literary influence, I began to write furiously and recklessly the most remarkable trash, nearly all of which, I am glad to say, is now lost in the ashes of civil wars in China. The early efforts of writers are as touching and as ludicrous as the efforts of a baby learning to walk. The miracle is that after falling down innumerable times, he does learn to walk, and keeps on walking.

The big brother "away at college," mentioned in the letter to the *Observer,* died years later in the United States, a great and brilliant man, much admired and respected. True, this only living son distressed his mother sometimes by drinking. Carie was understandably sensitive on the subject, because of her own unhappy first love. Perhaps, too, this is the reason the daughter drinks only when sociability calls for it. She is by no means a prude, however, and I wonder sometimes if she enjoys the shock value of the distinguished, white-haired, much honored author, Pearl S. Buck, saying, "I'll have a Bloody Mary," as she lights up the small cigar she seldom finishes!

But of drinking she has said, "I don't enjoy feeling my brain is not at its best. As for inhibitions, I've spent a lifetime developing them, and I don't intend to lose them!"

She considers her brain a sacred trust and never does anything that might impair its full functioning. She refrains from any activity, however pleasant or convenient, that might endanger it. She hates flying, for example, and avoids thinking about it until the last possible moment. When she can no longer avoid it, she leans back and closes her eyes for the takeoff. Does she pray? I doubt it! She is convinced that there is a power somewhere, but she takes the stand that she "will be surprised at nothing." The only answered prayer is work "and who knows what comes after?"

Although she lived in a Christian atmosphere as a child, she does not remember her parents as sentimental Christians. Her father never preached to her, for example. He read a brief passage from the Bible to the family in the morning, in English, and reread the same one at night in Chinese for the servants. And they prayed.

"Not me!" she exclaims. "I never prayed aloud—I, a woman? *He* prayed! My father was a Southern Presbyterian, not as narrow as most, but no woman was allowed to lift her voice to God while *he* was there."

One of her earliest memories is her mother's passionate disagreement with St. Paul for saying that "The head of man is Christ, and the head of woman is man."

"Well, it's in the Bible," Andrew reasoned.

Carie, however, maintained her independent position by simply removing herself from the argument, by laughter, and her usual remoteness from the local scene. In a sense, she says, her mother always remained remote, gay but remote.

"She was, I think, not close to my father, not 'in love,' and she was not close to us in demonstrated love. For example, I don't remember her ever putting her arms about me. Yet my parents were always frank with us. We knew the problems. If we had financial difficulties, we knew it. They discussed their work in our presence and we knew that we came second to it."

If there is any single emotion or experience that she misses from an otherwise perfectly happy childhood, it is, I think, a sense of physical closeness with her parents. She has told me she feels that parents should embrace their children and that children need the security of knowing and feeling that they are loved. She remembers this close physical contact only with her Chinese nurse, Wang Amah, and not with her mother. Throughout her childhood, she took part in much that Wang Amah did. The old Chinese nurse was always doing something interesting.

"You know how a child is with a nurse. One depends on her and leans on her. If anything went wrong, I ran to Wang Amah. I have, in a sense, a closer physical 'mother' feeling with her than I had with my own mother. I don't remember my mother taking me on her lap or caressing me in any physical way whatsoever. But I used to climb into Wang Amah's lap and I remember going into her room, a neat little room with a Chinese bed, in the servants' quarters. As I told you, she was always hatching something —chickens or silkworms. If the weather grew too cold, she would put the silkworm eggs and even chicken eggs inside her padded garments so they wouldn't get chilled. It was so exciting because every year she raised these things, just for fun. I took a great interest. She sat on an egg once and broke it. I knew exactly what had happened. I remember the stricken expression on her face. It was so funny!"

She can remember listening for hours to the stories of Wang Amah's youth. She would sit on her lap and snuggle her head into her blue cotton Chinese robes. She remembers the clean, earthy smell she loved.

"The close feeling that you would normally get with your

mother, I got with my Chinese nurse. But Wang Amah was an illiterate woman, uneducated. I could not confide in her."

Nor could she confide in her sister, seven years younger than she.

"I played with the little sister as one would with a doll," she told me. "It was my duty, indeed my pleasure, to rock her to sleep each day. I remember the rocking chair. It was low, with a high back. My mother must have bought it somewhere in Shanghai, for the Chinese had no such chairs. I have seen many like it in old American houses. At the same hour each day I would take my little sister on my lap and rock her to sleep. But I could not talk to her. She was only five when I was twelve and we had nothing in common. It was strange, this relationship between an older sister and one younger. Whatever it was, I loved her dearly and always."

As a child therefore she was close to no one in her family. She confided in no one. None ever knew how close she was to the Chinese, and of her lone jaunts into the village to visit the homes of Chinese she knew. There were many things I am sure Carie never knew. For example, the three copper cash, given to her for Sunday School collection each week, that she always spent for peanuts!

"I ate them very fast, so as to finish them before I arrived at church in my sedan chair. We went to church twice each Sunday. In the morning we attended the Chinese service and in the evening there was an English service for the English and the few Americans in our city. And I remember being restless in church. I was so restless! I knew that underneath the pulpit there was a tank of water, for it was a Baptist Church, Southern Baptist, and I used to wish and hope sometimes that the pulpit would give away so that the minister would fall into the water. I remember being so small in that church that my head wouldn't reach the top of the seat. It had an open back, and there was just one board, a narrow board, at the top of the back, and my head didn't reach it. With all my wriggling, one day I fell through into the laps of the people behind me. I was deeply humiliated, I remember, and sat very still after that. I thought God was punishing me."

Her early years are shadowed with memories of her father's work and his constant disagreement with the other missionaries, and of her mother's recurrent moods of sadness, but these were on one side, her American side. On the other, there was the warm Chinese community around her. And there she lived. She watched the lives of her mother and father, but she participated in the lives of the Chinese. Even when she visited her own country the first time, when she was nine years old, she felt she was definitely only a visitor. Constantly with her there was the distinct feeling within that she would return home to China and her friends there.

She gained no general impression of America at that time other than one of size. She is unable, when questioned about that visit, to provide any sequence. Scenes come to her but not in order. The family crossed the Pacific by ship and sailed through the Golden Gate. She remembers that they stopped for a few days in San Francisco to sight-see. Not long ago we had luncheon, the two of us, in the main dining room of the historic Cliff House in San Francisco, and she said:

"Strange that I don't remember anything about the time we spent here in 1901 except this restaurant! We had luncheon here one day, my parents and I. I remember the sun was very bright, and those rocks"—she pointed out the window at the rugged shoreline and Seal Rocks below the cliff—"there were seals on them then. We left San Francisco soon after that and went to visit my grandfather. That was the only time I saw him, for he died between that visit and when I returned for college at sixteen."

On the way to her birthplace in West Virginia they made another stop in a small town in Missouri to visit one of her uncles.

I don't remember much about Marshall, Missouri, except that it was a very hot Sunday when we were there. Oh, it was hot! And we had to go to church, of course. I had always thought my father preached too long, but this uncle—oh dear, I thought he would never get through. He went on and on. And it was so hot! I remember how bored I was. Afterward we sat outside on the lawn under a tree. I lay on the grass on my stomach and listened to my elders reminisce. I always listened as a child and I learned a great deal that day. I don't remember of what they talked, but I know I listened for a long time. It was in Marshall that I tasted ice cream for the first time. It was homemade and I found it delicious. And it was there I saw a trundle bed for the first time. My parents' bed in the guest room was a big four-poster with a canopy. At night they pulled a smaller bed out from under it and my sister and I slept there. I remember what fun I thought that was. It was like sleeping in a drawer. We left there then and went to my grandfather's house.

I remember clearly the day of our arrival. The journey had taken a full month, first the travel down the Yangtze River to Shanghai by English steamboat, then the voyage across the Pacific Ocean and finally the train trip across the continent. My uncle met us at the station in a carriage drawn by two horses and we drove in state to the house. I saw it at the far end of the wide green lawn and under the maple trees, for the carriage paused while the gate in the white fence was opened. It was exactly as my mother had said, a white house with vine-covered pillars supporting a portico. It looked what it was, a comfortable, dignified family home, a home in which I had a part because it was my birthplace.

The carriage rolled to the front door, and there we were met by a white-haired gentleman whom I took to be my grandfather, and so hailed him, but he told me he was only my Uncle Cornelius, and in a moment there was a still older white-haired gentleman, very straight and stately, and he proved to be my grandfather. After we dismounted, I, separating myself, stopped again to look, to drink in the scene, to verify all that had been in my mind and then to realize that it was even more beautiful, more wonderful, than my mother had said. True, there were the inevitable changes inside the house, the different use of rooms that each generation must make in order to settle its claim upon a house, but my mother's room was the same. It is this room that I still remember best. There is something awesome about the return to the spot where one's life began. As I have said, it seemed to me that I had seen it all before, as indeed I had, and again I saw myself as a newborn child here, where I had first opened my eyes. Bit by bit I remembered it all, and I set down those memories as they came to me.

Later we went to Lexington, Virginia, because my brother was at Washington and Lee University. We only stayed in Lexington for a few months through the winter, and that was my first experience with wood fires, too. We had little coal fires in China, but in that house we had big stone fireplaces with huge logs. I remember sitting by the fire on long evenings with my mother. I was with my mother much of the time in that house. We had an old Negro servant, but my mother spent a lot of time in the kitchen. I remember her singing as she worked. I went to school while we lived in that house. It was just for a few months. I don't remember anything about that school except that I don't think I learned very much. It was my first experience in an American school. I was in the third grade, and I do not remember learning anything. As a matter of fact, my mother had carried me far enough in our Chinese home so that study was unnecessary. Nothing about that school seemed important to me then nor does it seem important now.

I do remember a boy, though. He had red hair and green eyes, and he followed me around all the time. He must have been a very stupid boy, for he was older than I and in the same grade. Oh, how I hated him! He was very naughty.

After I went to bed one night in that house, I heard my mother crying. I remember I came down to see what had happened, and I saw her sitting there. She just sat quietly and wept. I saw my brother then. I didn't understand that he had had too much to drink. Now I remember how he lay on his stomach with one arm hanging off the bed. His face was very red and the air all around him was vile with the smell of whiskey. I didn't speak to her. I didn't ask questions. I just sat on the floor beside her chair. I took her hand in mine and put it to my cheek and held it there. Soon she quieted her tears and we went to bed. I still remember my brother lying there face down and the sickly smell of the air all around him. I didn't understand then why she cried. I know now she must have been thinking of the tragedy in her own life. The man she really loved she did not marry because he drank. For her beloved son to succumb to the same evil must have been a great deal for her to bear.

In the spring they returned to her grandfather's house in West Virginia. She was happy in that house, but they stayed only a short time and returned to China.

"The only memorable event was that the following summer,

after a series of visits to aunts and uncles and cousins, we ended with the month of August at my mother's house, a time of pure delight in which I learned to ride horseback, ate quantities of grapes and other fruits, and took part in every activity about the place, from moving the dasher of the churn up and down in the buttery and watching great lumps of butter washed and shaped and put away, to riding in hay wagons. Life was one day of joy after the other, and those weeks did much to wipe away the memories of a changed China, the China to which we had always to return and did return in early September."

They sailed for China from Vancouver, for Andrew distrusted the discipline aboard American ships. He was convinced, for reasons unknown, that only aboard English ships was proper discipline maintained so that in case of storm or fire, captain and crew would assign lifeboats first to the passengers. She did not see the United States again until she returned for college at almost sixteen.

In all our talks about her youth, I can find only one close friend, Dolly, and she was Chinese. During a Christmas when I visited her in Vermont we talked about Dolly. There was little snow and the mountains were bare, to the dismay of the owners of the ski lodges in the area. We sat by the wide window in her enormous living room with its beamed ceiling. She designed that house herself after the Chinese fashion, and though the builder told her it could not be built, she persisted. Now it rises out of the mountainside and so fits the surroundings one scarcely knows it is there until suddenly one comes upon it. Even then it is deceiving, for on the side one first approaches it stands almost level with the hill. But then one enters a family room forty feet wide and sixty feet long with flagstone floors of natural Vermont slate, red in color. One entire end of the room is a fireplace, formed by huge gray stones, taken from the field fences. The hearth is two feet off the floor and the fireplace is so wide that one can walk inside it. Birds sometimes fly down the chimney, and have to be let out through the door. Along one side of the vast room are kitchen and dining area. A grand piano is on one side of the fireplace; a chess set stands ready. The only other rooms are her bedroom, the guest room and baths, although there are bunks in the attic for an occasional overflow of visiting children.

Her own room is a long rectangle, at one end a stone fireplace, at the other her work area. In a corner is a rock garden. A spine of rock runs down the mountain and into the room, and she plants it with small ferns and dwarf pine. Her writing desk is built into another corner where in both directions windows overlook the terrace and Stratton Mountain. There are windows everywhere.

How did we happen to be in Vermont in winter? Her four young Amerasian daughters like to ski and it has been her habit to go to Vermont with them each year after Christmas Day. For once she decided to try a Vermont Christmas instead of making the usual rush the day after the big holiday. I, as a bachelor with no remaining family, was invited with a friend to spend Christmas with them. Early on the day after Christmas we sat, just the two of us. The girls had determined to ski on the slight snowfall of the day before, and my friend had gone along to take pictures of the gaiety. A fire crackled in the fireplace, and the new snow glistened in the warm morning sun like jewels tightly packed. She sat in her favorite chair, comfortably dressed in what she calls her green country suit, of a tweed material. She gazed out of the window with a distant look as she spoke.

There was no one really close to me. You speak often of my loneliness and you are quite right, but I was not aware of it then. Now I realize that I was a solitary child. There was Wang Amah, but as I have said, she couldn't read or write. My mother was busy and my father was gone much of the time. Of course, there were books. I lived mostly in books. I did go to a Chinese girls' school for a couple of hours a day, just for a year or so, and I had one friend there to whom I was quite close in a schoolgirl fashion. I can't remember anyone else and that habit of not having anyone close clung to me, I suppose, for when I went to college it was much the same. Yet I enjoyed life immensely and was very interested in other people. They talked to me freely of their lives and their troubles, and I used to think about all this a great deal. It didn't occur to me, however, that I had anything to confide to anyone, even when I was growing up. I especially loved my mother in those years, but I was older before I really loved my father. Yet I didn't talk with them much, or with anyone. I remember the Chinese school, because there I made my first personal friend. I remember her very well. Her name was Dolly. Oh, yes, she was Chinese. She was, I think, an orphan. The missionary women who ran the school had given her the name Dolly. She was a very pretty girl. Of course the years have separated us, and I had forgotten her, really, until that year when I met her son in this country, and he told me about her. He even brought me a gift from her, a beautiful magenta tea set. It is there on the shelves. [She motioned toward the bookshelves under the high windows along the opposite side of the room.] I'll always keep it, for I was fond of her. She was the first person with whom I exchanged my girlish confidences. My sister was much younger than I, remember? I never took her with me on my little forays into the villages and at the foot of the hill.

I doubt my mother knew how much time I spent with Chinese. I always did things by myself. I was very welcome in these Chinese peasant houses, and the people were sweet to me. The House of Earth* was just such a peasant's house. I have been in many houses like that, for all Chinese lived in the same kind of house basically. Rich man's house or poor man's house, it was the same. A rich man's house was more elaborate and beautiful, of course, but the plan was always the same and the furniture was arranged in the same way. But my friendship with Dolly was my greatest pleasure in those days. Like the girl in *East Wind : West Wind,* Dolly Wei was caught between past and present in changing times. No, she isn't actually that girl. I don't know of any character in my books of whom I can say, "It is she" or "It is he." I cannot explain the process of creation. Yet when I speak the names of my characters, they stand here before me as though they were in this room. You speak again and again of my loneliness and I realize there is truth in it. Perhaps, being surrounded by the people I have created, I don't need other people. They are all here, my friends, and they seem real to me. I don't live vicariously, however. I just don't distinguish between the people in my books and the people outside my books. One is as real as the other. Yes, my people are absolutely real to me. I think if I hadn't known somebody like that I wouldn't be able to make them. For

* The farmhouse setting of *The Good Earth,* and the phrase used as overall title for the trilogy of *The Good Earth, Sons* and *A House Divided.*

example, when I think of Jonathan, in *The Townsman,* I do think of a real person—now dead, alas! He was my husband's Uncle John. I went to visit him only three times, but he was just such a person as my Jonathan. He, too, was a schoolteacher. And Maggie in that book—of course her life went differently, but I think there was much of my husband's mother, my dear mother-in-law, in her. She was born in England and she came over here and I'm sure she was just such a child as Maggie. Of course, I embroider on them and there is much of me added, but they are real. I suppose that is why I have never been conscious of being lonely, even as a child!

Was she born the kind of person who lives in books and creates friends to avoid being lonely? Or did she, because of loneliness, turn to books for friends, eventually to create her own? Who knows the answer? And even if it were known, could it explain how such a talent was developed?

The years between that first visit to the United States and her college years went fast for her, for they were filled with learning. Yet, she says:

"Those were difficult years. My Chinese friends, the neighbor girls, that is, were already being groomed for marriage. Their feet were bound so they could not run and play. They sat and learned to embroider. My father had built a house up in the mountain where we spent the hot summers, and I found a few American girls there, but not many, and I was shy with them. I spent much time with my mother during those years. She taught me to cook and sew and to keep house. Not that she ever expected me to do these things myself any more than she did them—she did not! She fully expected me always to have servants, as I always have. But she said, 'How can you know if a servant is doing things properly unless you can do them yourself?' My mother was right, and though I have never had to keep my own house, it's been useful knowledge for me."

It was one wintry afternoon, when we were sitting in the library in the Foundation house, that she spoke those words. The conversation had drifted to some of the pieces of furniture there which she had brought from China and thence into her childhood. She had spent one of her usual days, crammed with appointments

—a dancing lesson, a French lesson, luncheon with someone, a visitor from out of town. It was over now. The housekeeper had served us sherry and had gone away to prepare dinner. We relaxed and talked. I asked questions and she answered in her easy fashion. The tape recorder ground away noiselessly in the corner.

"Does that thing make a noise when it's done?" she asked. She is always slightly distrustful of machinery.

I told her we would know when the tape ran out and remarked that we would have to get a less obtrusive recorder.

"Oh, I don't mind these sessions," she said. "If you are to tell an accurate story, it's something we must do."

She sat facing the fireplace over which hangs the portrait of her that was painted before she won the Nobel Prize. I remarked at the somewhat aloof expression on her face in that portrait, her Mona Lisa look, I call it.

"I was annoyed, I suppose," she laughed. "It took forever to paint, and I thought it a complete waste of time. I vowed never again to have my portrait painted. I never did, until just recently when we had the new one done for the drawing room. But I told the artist who did the recent one that I would only sit twice, and I only sat twice. He worked mostly from photographs he took on the first sitting."

While she talked, my eyes rested on the old Chinese desk that faces the fireplace from the opposite side of the room. It rules the room, and rightly so, for it is the most important piece in it. In fact, the room was designed around that desk, and there it stands in all its dignity, exactly as it did forty years ago when she used to sit before it to write her Chinese books, in an attic room in her Chinese home in Nanking. She writes at this desk today when she is in Philadelphia. It is a large desk, with latticework at the bottom so that the scholar can keep his feet off the cold floor. Behind it is a Chinese chair that looks uncomfortable but is surprisingly comfortable when one sits in it. Behind the chair is a wall of books, books on every subject, all read, all valuable. Between the windows opposite the door stands a grand piano, for she loves to play, and must have a piano wherever she spends time. There is a chess set here, too, for we both enjoy chess in the evenings after dinner.

I put my glass of sherry down on the ancient bronze Chinese drum that serves as a cocktail table between the lattice-backed couches facing each other from each side of the fireplace, and asked her when she first began to take an interest in boys. She remembers receiving her first "love letter" when she was but twelve. It was a summer evening when the Chinese postman delivered it and she was sitting on the veranda with her mother.

"I opened it, very proud to have a letter of my own," she said, laughing. "When I read it I felt myself blushing fiery red. I tore it to shreds and stuffed it through a crack in the floor with my toe. I was barefoot, I remember. And my mother laughed very much."

Her first real experience with American boys was after college however.

I think I was never interested in boys my own age. They were too young for me. The first man who interested me was on the ship with me going back to China. In fact, there were two men, one at least twenty years older than I and the other about ten years older. I liked the younger one.

I suppose the first time I thought I was in love was on that ship going back from college. Yet I knew I didn't want to marry the man. I can't remember his name, but I remember the name of the older man, the one I didn't like! He was rather short and had bad teeth and a little moustache. He afterwards wrote to me from the Philippines and I never answered. He said to me, on board ship, and I remember I was shocked:

"I'd like to know you better, but of course we all know you are engaged to this . . . ," whatever his name was—Philip something-or-other.

And I said, "That's not true. I'm not engaged to Philip."

And he said, "Well, you're not thinking about anybody else."

I couldn't deny it. It was true. I wasn't thinking about anyone else. I was then about twenty-one. Philip was about thirty-one, maybe thirty-five. It was a shipboard romance, and somehow I knew it. When I got home, he wrote to me but I didn't answer. I was already plunged into responsibility. I could see that my mother was very ill and that my sister needed my help, for she was at the adolescent age and had strong feelings of inferiority. It was my first sense of my responsibility for my family. I didn't want to marry anyone. Yet the shipboard experience was good for me. I suppose it was the first time I had ever kissed a man with all my heart and let him kiss me. Yet I knew perfectly well that I didn't really care for him. I suppose I knew he wasn't my equal, and that in the long run of life, he wouldn't be enough for me— and I would be too much for him! I suppose I was in need of some physical expression, but I was very grateful that I had not let it go too far. Nevertheless, I think that I was first conscious, then, really conscious, of my own looks. I suppose that's something love does for you, any kind of love, especially if one is a girl. I never had thought of my looks very much. In those days one couldn't use cosmetics, else people would think you evil. That was one thing that this man did for me. He made me value my looks. He made me see myself and that was good. I had a tendency to be withdrawn. Yet it seemed I was one of those girls who, without any effort, do attract—and I didn't try, I really didn't, because I was interested in too many people and things.

I had a hard time when I went home to China, however, for missionaries were very conservative. There was a group of young American men, I remember, three or four Standard Oil men, who lived on the Bund, in the British concession of our city. I remember one big fellow especially—I forget his name—with whom I went out once or twice, whereupon the missionaries sat in judgment on me and said I could not go out with a young man and continue to be a teacher in a missionary school. They said the Chinese would talk. It was true! I had a real struggle for I had perfectly natural impulses, and I wanted to go with young people and there were no American girls of my age. While I had my Chinese friends, they too were very restricted. Most of them were still having marriages arranged. Yes, it was a very difficult time. I was caught again between two peoples, two cultures. I was helpless.

The small old French clock on the mantel began to chime, and she stirred restlessly, as though a little weary. I knew the spell was broken and the session ended.

"What time is that?" she asked. "Eight o'clock? Do you think dinner is ready?"

I knew it was, but I telephoned the kitchen anyway. Dinner had been waiting for some time. We took our sherry with us and descended the curved staircase to the second floor landing between the drawing room and the dining room. We entered the dining room through the arched doorway. The round table is of highly polished natural wood, six feet in diameter. The beige carpet had just come in that day, for it had to be especially woven for the room, octagonal in shape. The chairs are empire, covered in avocado velvet, one of her favorite colors, and contrast with the muted gold tones of the drapery at the windows. Over the pink marble fireplace there is a large clear mirror. The opposite wall is covered with smoke-blue mirror, and the crystal chandelier over the table glistens in the light of its twenty-seven electric candles, reflected back and forth thousands of times, from mirror to mirror into infinity. We sat in the armchairs at each end of the room, the two of us, as we have many times since. Behind her, through double arches, are a twenty-five-foot hall, another arched doorway and the drawing room. Behind me she looks through an arch into the stained-glass solarium with its statue and fountain. There I know we shall have blossoms, in season, transferred from the two greenhouses in her country house. She loves her flowers, and I am glad there is a place for them here. Yes, this house on Delancey Place has lent itself graciously to her and I know she will be with us here always. We chatted lightly over dinner that evening about the house and the things we want to do and see. I wondered as I watched her there, so serene and self-contained, if we would ever recapture the mood of our previous conversation. Recapturing a mood is all but impossible for most people, and it is seldom that a conversation can be resumed after the mood is gone. Mood and conversation are communicable between us, I am happy to say, and so says she.

We returned to the library later for after-dinner coffee. There was still an hour remaining before her car came to take her back to the country house. I switched on the recorder and she took up where she left off.

"I remember the first years home again in China. I married, as you know, choosing an American. Why? I think I was simply ready to be married. It was difficult for us to meet while we were engaged, for Chinese tradition forbade it and my parents were very sensitive to Chinese opinion. We did write letters during the winter while we were apart, and I should have known. But I was very young—too young for my years emotionally, I think, as

I now remember myself. The next spring he asked me to be his wife. By that time I had made up my mind to marry him, though against the advice of my parents. They realized I was basically an intellectual and he was not. That's not to say I'm a cold person. No! The physical in life means a great deal to me, but mind and body must go together, no matter how much I may love a person."

As she talked on that evening, I could not avoid a nagging question that crept again and again into my consciousness. Even though I had been given license to pry, so to speak, into the personal life of this woman, still I felt a hesitation. Yet I could resist no longer. She has written profoundly of love between man and woman. I put my question:

"What about Gerald, in *Letter From Peking?* Where did he come into your life?"

She hesitated, too. I could see that she was revealing her strange life as she had never done before. But she went on bravely:

"Gerald? He was the half Chinese I told you of before. I had first known him when I was in the Shanghai boarding school. His father was American and his mother was Chinese. I met all of his family when I used occasionally to go to their home. Of course his name was not Gerald. We became friends, we fell in love in our young fashion and I could see already that he was very torn between his American and Chinese sides. He was five years older than I and he went to college in Shanghai. We drifted apart when I went away to college in America."

A clear gong sounded twice. This time it was the doorbell breaking the spell. I knew her car had arrived and she would be leaving, but I wished our talk did not have to end.

"How is it that your husband didn't realize your unhappiness sooner?" I asked.

"We will talk more about him the next time," she said.

There was a knock at the door and the housekeeper told us that the car was waiting. Again we walked down the stairs, for an elevator is a dull way to travel through a beautiful house. We walked past the drawing room, the dining room and down into the foyer, where hangs Chen Chi's painting of "The Good Earth." This distinguished Chinese artist had presented his pictorial idea of her book to her some years earlier. It was on loan to a museum for many months, then it hung over a couch in her country house until it found its permanent home here, rightfully taking its place among her most treasured belongings.

The evening was pleasant outside on the street, and I lingered a moment before I reentered the house. Just inside the door there stands a gilded Kwan Yin. We had waited so long for her to arrive that we almost gave up hope of her ever being there. We had even considered something else to go in her place. Now that she is there, however, we agree she is right for the house. I smile at her as I pass, remembering that the other day when we were discussing this book, she objected strenuously to a title I had suggested—"Let's call it *And Her Name Shall Be Comfort.*"

She turned on me, laughing. "I don't think I've ever been a comfort to anyone! I think in my own quiet way I've upset many lives and made many people very uncomfortable."

My title died an instant death. Yet was it not ironic that the woman who did not want her book called "Comfort" nevertheless wanted the Goddess of Mercy in our entrance way? Upon whom does the goddess bestow her graces, those who enter or those who leave this house?

I turned out the lights, preparing the house for the night, and I thought over our talk as I went upstairs. For a vital young American woman, wanting a normal happy life, to be compelled to live in the restricted atmosphere of a group of missionaries had been difficult. Her childhood memories are of their quarrels among themselves and their disapproval of her liberal-minded father. Writing of her father in *Fighting Angel*, she says:

"Then there was that question of religious denominations. One of the astounding imperialisms of the West has been the domination over the Chinese of Methodists, Presbyterians, Baptists, and what-not to the number of well over a hundred different sects of the Protestant Christian religion alone. This has been in China more than a spiritual imperialism—it has been physical as well. There has been much talk of political spheres of influence, of Japan and Germany and England and France dividing China into areas for trade and power. But the missionaries divided China, too. Certain provinces, certain areas, were allotted to certain denominations for religious propaganda and there was supposed to be no overstepping.

"Andrew, of course, was a born overstepper. . . ."

This was all very fine for Andrew, but what of Carie and her daughter? Andrew was accustomed to turbulence in his childhood home. His father and brothers argued constantly over religion. But Carie was a gentle soul, unaccustomed to such an atmosphere. She retreated more and more into herself, for she found little real companionship among the Chinese. How could she, educated as she was? Her daughter's biography of her was properly named *The Exile,* although the working title of that book was *His American Wife* or *The American Woman,* and the publishers renamed it years afterward when it was published. The child, seeing her mother withdrawn from the missionary group, withdrew also. Where and how and to what would she withdraw? I have asked her, for example, about the years between her return to China, after that childhood trip, and her college years. She has not much to tell. That period of her life means little to her now—a vacuum except for a few bright memories. She remembers, for example, a young American couple who spent a year in her home. Strangely enough we met the woman of that couple only recently in Sacramento, California, and she told me she remembers the lonely young girl in China. It was customary in China that when new Americans came they lived in someone's house until they could find their own. The American couple were in love with each other and the young girl saw for the first time in her life the relationship between a man and his wife in a happy marriage. The adolescent struggle is difficult for any girl, and very difficult for one caught between cultures, as this one was.

This warm American life was going on inside her house, but outside there was great turmoil. Those were the last years of the old Empress' life, described so clearly in *Imperial Woman.* Yet even after her death in 1909 the Chinese family traditions held, and they lived in peace for a few more years. The young American girl began her writing during those years—poems and stories —and all the time, too, she was diligently studying Chinese with her mandarin teacher, who came in every day. She read Chinese and English books, and she poured out thoughts and feelings in her writing. Nevertheless, those were years of uncertainty, I think, for I have heard her repeat herself over and over again:

"I wondered if I would ever be a good writer."

"I knew I had to be a writer, or I would die!"

"Would I ever be able to write?"

Meanwhile, her Chinese friends were swept into their own culture of early marriages and family obligations, from which she was naturally excluded, and there were no Americans her age. And so, in loneliness, a writer was born. She observed the world about her and wrote down her observations.

I lay awake that night thinking of a lonely child, in the middle of a vast continent, writing out of her imagination all of the things she wanted to do and see and experience herself, blending dreams with what she saw going on around her. And this is the technique she uses today, which is probably why her characters and stories ring so true. Does anything remain of that early writing? I remembered, as I lay there, that she told me she had destroyed everything she had ever written when they left China to make the long trip through Russia, all the way across Europe and the Atlantic to America for her to start college. Russia made a lasting impression on her in all its vastness. She had actually been ready for college for two years before this journey, but Carie did not feel it right for her to leave home and go far away so young. She describes that long journey in detail in *My Several Worlds,* so I will not recount it now, except to add these words of her own:

"Once we began traveling and left China, I left behind me my mood of self-absorption. When I think back I realize in those years I thought of nothing but myself, really. That ended when we moved into the world."

They stopped for about six months in Switzerland, and she went to school in Neuchâtel, to learn French, although she longed to reach America and be with girls her own age. I ask her again about boys. She laughs.

"I didn't think about boys much. I was still in the Chinese tradition! What was the use of thinking about boys when everything would be arranged for one somehow anyway? I was much more absorbed in everyday experiences and the excitement of getting to know girls my own age, in my own country."

In her college years, she left China behind and plunged into the American world. Yet, 1911, when she was eighteen and entering her sophomore year, was a year of climactic revolutions, for the Chinese government was overthrown. There was no longer an empire and the Dragon Throne was gone. Her mother wrote to her of Manchu ladies in their silk robes hiding in the hills about her house, trying to escape with their lives. But they were killed, all of them. In those four years she worried constantly about her parents, remembering the Boxer years of her early childhood, yet her new life made its own demands on her. Her brother, now married, lived in Lynchburg, Virginia, where she attended Randolph-Macon Woman's College. He was editor of the local evening newspaper, and she spent holidays in his home. Her first year in college was one of drastic adjustment, but she determined to become as American as possible. Self-contained and detached, even there, she nevertheless took part in all the life about her, and by her junior year was elected president of her class.

Her senior year passed quickly. Commencement was over, leaving her with prizes in both fiction and poetry. I have asked her many times what sort of writing she did at such a young age, and she is really unable to remember much about it. In her files, however, I found an article dated 1911, and on questioning her learned that she had written it for the Randolph-Macon college magazine. One finds the same fresh approach in a Pearl Buck story written in her sophomore year that one finds in a Pearl Buck book written today:

A quaint little Chinese village it was, reaching down to the sea waves as they rolled gently over the sand up to the foreshore. A strange little village, too, with a certain air of drowsy mystery and Oriental languor. Perhaps it was the sunshine through the misty violet light on the circling hills, or the changing, wonderful blue of the sea, or the wind, laden with that delicate, subtle fragrance of mimosas, which rustled the slender, swaying bamboos and graceful willows. Perhaps all these had some share in it; yet there was something else, too, a dreamy sense of quiet and peace, of utter difference from the other places I had visited.

Into the blue of the sky merged the violet peaks of the Liang Mountains. Most beautiful of all was one peak white with snow, and to this the villagers pointed with superstitious awe, for underneath it lay chained a great Dragon which Whang-lu, the sea god, had caught out of the sea, and imprisoned beneath the White Mountain. No one might ascend the mountain, for upon the cloud, where no mortal had set foot, one might look down a deep crater and there see the dragon's head all flaming with fire, and some-times the smoke would pour forth from the dragon's mouth, and then dire misfortune would befall the little village. All this the children told me with wide eyes and bated breath as they gath-ered about me.

The village itself was built entirely of old boats, turned over bottom side up, with a tiny opening for a door. It was a pictur-esque enough idea, but the villagers had done it for the simple reason that for the last hundred generations all their forefathers had done the same thing, and for a son to have any other kind of house than the shell of his father's old boat would have been an unheard-of act of insubordination and of dissatisfaction with the village customs.

The years had passed lightly over the village by the sea, and had brought little sorrow beyond that which must come in some manner to all. The old men looked at me in my foreign dress from as curiously simple and child-like eyes, as they sat on the door-steps of their little boat houses, as did the round-eyed, fat and sol-emn little boys playing about in the sand.

The simplicity of the villagers appealed to me greatly. Their slow movements, placid expressions, and low, musical language seemed born of the quietness of the hills, the calmness of the wide sky and the unchanging sound of the sea. Had I seen the little vil-lage a thousand years before, probably there would have been the same languor and stillness and dreamy peace, and the villagers would have stared at me with the same frank look of childish cu-riosity that they bestowed upon me now as I passed.

The cobbled road was not easy to walk upon, especially when one was so foot-weary as I was that summer's day, and so when an old woman, placidly smoking a five-foot pipe and gazing reflec-tively into space, let her eyes wander to me, and a wide smile wrinkled her face, I accepted her tacit invitation and dropped upon the narrow wooden bench beside her.

"Good day to you, my daughter," she greeted me politely. "Have you had sufficient to eat this morning?"

"I have had the greatest sufficiency, I thank you, honorable mother," I replied as politely.

Nevertheless, she arose, saying "You will drink tea, though, doubtless," and went inside to prepare it. I waited patiently enough, and enjoyed to the full the scene about me. At my feet rolled two dusty babies, utterly guiltless of clothing and heartily enjoying the sunshine and dirt, and the gymnastics of their little mongrel puppy, with which they were playing. Nearby a most exciting fight was taking place between two youths of tender years, and about this duel was gathered an intensely interested crowd, their pigtails fairly quivering with excitement and anxiety as to the outcome of the fight.

Just then the old woman returned with two tiny bowls of tea, and I sipped mine loudly, as the fashion is over the sea, to express my enjoyment of it. Then, having declined a smoke of the five-foot pipe, I sat watching the quaint, wrinkled face of my old hostess, and she in turn looked at me, and then asked politely:

"Your honorable age, what is it, my daughter?"

I replied, and returned the courtesy, whereupon she said in her slow, old way:

"I, my daughter, am ninety and nine. This"—sweeping her hand through the air—"is my native village."

Then I saw my opportunity and asked, "Most revered and ancient of women, tell me, whence came this village, and what was its beginning? I see that it is old, and you, who are so much richer in years, can doubtless tell me of its origin."

She puffed meditatively at the long pipe, gazing over to White Mountain, and then answered slowly:

"Yes, child, I am very old. I can tell you what my grandfather told me, and his fathers told before him, but listen, child. You must believe all that I tell, lest these waves that roll so near us hear and see your unbelief of a sacred tale, and tell of it to Whang-lu, the great Sea God, whose place is in the bottom of the sea, and he will bear wrath against you, and when next you cross the sea, he will raise mighty storms against you. So listen, child, and I will tell you the Sacred Tale of the Village by the Sea."

Then she assumed the high, chanting voice of the professional Chinese story-teller, and began thus:

"Long years ago, when there was no Village by the Sea, and at night the roar of the waves against the rocks would echo from the lonely hills, and the Trees grew thick and dark even to the beach, when no human creation of the great Whang-lu lived in the shelter of the White Mountain, Whang-lu, the Mighty One, would rise from the waves, and shaking his wave-drenched locks, would walk upon the sands at eventide to enjoy the World of Air.

"One day, as he paced the beach with mighty strides, a roaring came over the sea, and he stopped to listen. Slowly the waves grew larger, and fell more heavily at his feet, the sky darkened, and the North Wind lashed the water to white foam. Then was Whang-lu exceedingly angry, for he had commanded no storm, and who was there who might interfere with his domain—he, the Mighty One of the ocean? So thinking, he was about to hurl himself into the depths of the sea, when suddenly he saw a strange sight. Over the waves came a mighty beast, like a dragon, a terrible dragon, and with one foot uplifted, it glided over the sea, its silvery scales shrinking and widening as its great body coiled on the face of the waters. The foam was white for leagues about it, and behind it was a shining wake three hundred miles long. Most dreadful of all, was a man held between the teeth of the monstrous beast, and the man was writhing in the pangs of death.

"When Whang-lu saw this sight, his heart went out in fierce wrath against the dragon, yet he feared, for the dragon's uplifted foot bore but four claws instead of five, and by this he knew that the beast was sacred and mighty in strength, passing the strength of human comprehension. Then was Whang-lu afraid, but when he saw the man in the dragon's mouth, his strength returned, for, my child, this man was wondrous to look upon, of divine beauty. His hair and eyes were of onyx darkness, his skin like gold, and the nails upon his fingers were six inches long!

"Nearer the beast came, foaming and lashing with its mighty tail, but Whang-lu was strong again in heart, and in a loud voice he cried:

" 'I, who am Lord of the Sea, do bid you to cease your way upon my waters, and to give me that man whom you have seized!'

"Then the dragon cast forth fire and smoke from between its scales, and answered:

" 'I am Lord of Fire and Smoke—dare you stop me? I obey none!'

"When it answered thus, Whang-lu was glad, for is not water stronger than fire and smoke? So he cried louder than before:

" 'I, Whang-lu, Lord of the Waters of the Earth, of Rains and Rivers, Lakes and Mighty Oceans, I bid all the waters of my possessions to come hither and overcome the flame and smoke in this beast!'

"No sooner had he spoken than a mighty rushing was heard, and rain fell from the sky in streams, and rivers and lakes and seas rushed together, and there was quenched the fire and smoke within the dragon, and it lay as dead upon the sands at Whang-lu's feet.

"But the man leaped up, strong and beautiful, and worshipped the great sea god for his power and mercy. Then Whang-lu bade the waters cease, and lifting the White Mountain by the strength of his hands, he placed the dragon beneath it, and there it lies to this day.

"The man, when Whang-lu asked him from whence he came, said that from the Emperor of Heaven's home in the Land of the Morning Calm he had come, and that as he was bathing in the Sea of Sunlight nearby the dragon had approached him and seized him, and whither it would have taken him, none knew.

"When the man spoke thus, Whang-lu was pleased with him yet more, and bade him stay on the seashore forever, and raise up to him a race of golden-skinned, black-eyed mortals. So saying, Whang-lu gave him a great shell to live in; a shell such as one does not see in these days, round and high, and all rosy within, like the sky at evening. More than that, Whang-lu gave to the man his own beautiful daughter as wife. Thus they founded the village and we, who are their descendants, are eternally thankful to Whang-lu, the Supreme Ruler of the Sea, who preserved our ancestor from death. Moreover, we are a divine race, for we spring from the Emperor of the Land of the Morning Calm.

"Look!—" Here the old woman broke off and pointed to the water at her feet. "See how close the waves have crept to listen! Beware how you speak now, for they hear."

We were silent for a little while after the story. The grimy babies sat bolt upright, with solemn eyes and awestruck faces; the boys had stopped fighting and were listening and even the rollicking puppy was quiet.

Finally, I saw that night was not far away, and already the sun had gone behind the hills, and so I arose, and bidding my old friend farewell, thanked her and started on my way. Scarcely had

I passed a few paces, when the old woman hobbled after me, and whispered these words in my ear:

"One word more, my child. You are young and strong and ambitious for many things, but never climb to where the white snows lie on yonder mountain, for the spell that lies on the dragon, the spell of the lakes and seas, will be broken when mortal footprint is left on the whiteness of the snow. It is the seal of the Sea God."

After graduation she was ready to go home, and home was still China. But now World War I began, and this brought delay. Of course, no one knew what this war meant. No one knew what nations would become involved, or on which side; and with so much unrest in the world, it was decided that she would not return immediately to China.

She accepted a summer position in her own college as assistant professor in psychology—her major—and it was not until November, 1914, that she was allowed to go home. There she found her mother very ill with the tropical disease sprue.

"I devoted myself to bringing my mother back to life," she has told me. "All my energy I poured into the task. I remember one dreadful night when it seemed she must die. I was alone with her and in her utter weakness her eyes closed, and she whispered to me:

" 'Child, is this d-e-a-t-h?'

"She spelled the awful word. I remember how my whole being rose to deny it.

" 'I will not let you die!' I cried out.

" 'You are very comforting,' she said, and fell into a peaceful sleep.

"She did not die—not then. She grew well enough to live a few more years, and I began teaching in a boys' school."

It was a boys' day school in Chinkiang, on a hill opposite the one on which she lived. There was a valley between, the same valley in which she had played as a child. Now she walked in it daily as a young schoolteacher, with what hopes and dreams I do not know. I drifted into sleep at long last with vague visions of a young girl wandering through beautiful valleys in China, while

all of the revolutionary turmoil of a warlord era went on around
her.

One afternoon not long ago we were scheduled to go to a neighboring city, about four hours away, to attend a benefit for the
Foundation. She arrived promptly, as is her habit, and we were
off. We sat in the back of her big car, and talked. I always enjoy
these trips for they give us a chance to discuss the many things
that come up in our work, and I am able to learn more about her
past life. The chauffeur guided the car to the expressway, and I
reminded her that she had promised to tell me more about her
first husband. She continues to say that there really is not very
much to tell. This is typical of the woman I know. Her personal
philosophy keeps her living in the present and planning for the
future. She learns from each experience in her life, retains what
she has learned, and casts out what is left as useless. She does this
as coolly as one operates a machine. With the finality of one who
pushes a button, she says, "Now that is past. It is over. There is
no use dwelling on that. We must think of what is yet to come."

Pieced together from bits I have gathered, mostly on that trip,
here is the story:

She met John Lossing Buck that summer of 1917 in the mountains in China. She saw him only four times alone before they
were engaged, and even those meetings were considered improper.
A young lady in China in those days simply did not meet
with her husband-to-be before they were married. Her parents
made these exceptions only because he was considered a guest in
their home. They tried to tell her that he was not the right
husband for her, to point out that she was an intellectual by heritage and education, and that he was not. But she felt that he
would change, that association would make a difference. They reminded her of the fact that he never read and that she was constantly with a book. Her stand was that he would read when he
had the proper chance and atmosphere. Even if he was not an
intellectual, she felt that they would have other things to share.
Her parents asked frankly how she would endure the close companionship of marriage with a man so different from herself.

The truth is, I think, that there is a biological age for marriage,
and she had reached it. Perhaps she felt the need for independ-

ence from her parents. She had been away at college and come home, had nursed her mother until she was as well as she ever would be, and now it was time for her own life. The circumstances of her life had simply been too constricted for her, and she felt that she had to escape. Even before she decided on marriage she determined on another step that would also have been an escape. She had written to an American woman who lived in Yunnan, that beautiful province in South China. This woman was an independent teacher, a missionary, yes, but the attractive quality was that she was independent. She had built her own school and now she needed an assistant. Pearl Comfort wrote to her and said she would like to come. This decision distressed her mother, and she put it aside. But her mind was made up that she wanted to begin a life of her own. Rather suddenly she decided to get married instead. And she did.

They moved then, newly wed, into northern China and the little old-fashioned town of Nanhsüchou, in the province of Anhwei. She became the head of a girls' school and settled down to making her own life.

Her creative instincts went to work now in the making of this first home of her own.

"It was a lovely little Chinese house," she told me. "We had a lawn and a flower garden, enclosed in a compound wall. Beyond our wall was the city wall, and we lived in its shelter. There were only four rooms, but what pleasure it was to arrange the furniture, hang the curtains, paint a few pictures for the walls, to hang the Chinese scrolls! I was happy and busy. When all was finished— well, what next? I took over the girls' school, I invited a girlhood friend, a young Chinese woman, to be my assistant—alas, she wouldn't stay because she missed the rice she had always eaten in the South and she did not like the wheaten bread of the North. Well, I found someone else, and I made new friends."

It was not long before she found herself confronted with periods of great personal loneliness. She began to realize that her parents had been right, and that she would never find companionship in this man she had married. She resorted then to her love of order and beauty and found comfort, as she says, by throwing herself wholeheartedly into making the house a home and a place of simple beauty. It was a work of pleasure. They did not have much money and she enjoyed seeing how much she could do with little. She bought Chinese silks and had curtains made. There was such personal pride and joy in making her first home that in the beginning it scarcely mattered with whom it was shared. But, the house furnished, she became depressed again, this time by the surrounding landscape. She had been accustomed to the lush, mountainous land of her childhood, and North China is flat and almost a desert. She loves to walk, but then it seemed scarcely worthwhile to go beyond the city walls.

"If I walk ten miles outside the city the landscape is the same," she complained.

Of course she never thought of divorce. It was unheard of in old China and there had never been a divorce in her family. But she did run away into her own thoughts and interests. She read books in the evenings, for example, for conversation grew increasingly difficult. Books were in her tradition and a part of her life, but her husband failed to develop an interest in reading. She readily admits that she was undoubtedly as difficult for him as he was for her.

Without defining her determination she began to live her life as she wanted it. One advantage of marriage, she discovered, was the greater freedom it gave her to accept invitations to Chinese homes. She learned to know the Chinese people of this northern region and became deeply interested in them, an interest that continues to this day. Out of such experience, Wang Lung and O-lan appeared and *The Good Earth* began to take form in her mind. She was not conscious of gathering material, but the story grew. This is still the way she works. She travels and lives in the world, never conscious of creating a story. When she sits down to write, however, she draws on the vast wealth of knowledge and personal experience she has stored up through life itself.

She tells me, for example, of a young American doctor who, with his wife, came to live and work as a missionary in Nanhsu-chou. The wife could never adjust to China and refused to leave the compound. The doctor needed help, however, and Pearl Buck supplied it.

"It was an exciting, absorbing experience," she says. "Our work took us into many places. I remember a peasant's hut and a child born dead, but we saved the mother. I remember a dark and rainy night and a concubine's room in a rich man's house. The concubine had hung herself. We came too late, the doctor and I. I remember the lovely dead face. And how many were the wounded soldiers that we tended! We had them brought into the little brick church, men from the armies of warlords contending for power in those troubled times."

Out of such wars came her novel *Sons,* which I consider to be one of her finest books. The Tiger is a character never to be forgotten. I feel as though I myself have known a warlord. I can understand all the little wars in China and the importance of them to the people involved. Her powers of explanation are so great and her command of English so deft, that one lives and breathes with her characters. To read her books is to live in the times of which she writes.

A few nights ago we sat in the Foundation drawing room to have coffee after dinner. The housekeeper had created a masterful dinner. "When dealing with a lady of the stature of the mistress of our house," she said, "one tries to please." And please she did. She had spent all afternoon finding just the proper filet of lemon sole and had prepared it the way her "Mistress of the House" likes best. She had sliced fresh eggplant and browned it lightly in butter. A loaf of hot bread and a tossed salad completed the menu. She had had to prepare additional eggplant for Pearl Buck, she so enjoyed it. This is extremely rare, as she usually eats very little of anything. She makes it her habit to eat only when hungry, drink only when thirsty, and sleep only when sleepy.

As a matter of fact, she does absolutely nothing she doesn't have to do except work. She eats only because if she doesn't she will become ill. She sleeps only because she knows that one must rest in order to live properly—but not rest too much—and she averages about five hours sleep per night. I know, for I have tried to keep up with her. It is a task I find impossible, though I am nearly forty years her junior. The only thing she does of which she doesn't enjoy the actual mechanics is writing. She has said it is the most tiresome work one can choose, and her mind invents various excuses each day to prevent her from beginning to write. Begin she always does, successfully resisting the urge to play the piano, stroll in the sun, work with her flowers, read a book, or do any one of a hundred or more things she enjoys. She takes a firm stand with herself: writing is what she chooses to do with her life and she writes. She wants to produce books, she likes to tell stories. She takes great pleasure in accomplishment and has often told me that true joy, real happiness, lies in the completion of a project.

I had watched her across the table during dinner. She is a magnificent woman—beautiful, feminine, soft, but not in the least degree dainty. I have tried often to picture her as she must have been in those days before she returned to this country. I have seen portraits and photographs, of course, but it is always difficult to breathe life into such artifices. Flat and colorless she was not, but, as nearly as I can ascertain, time has been her dearest friend, for age has certainly graced her with a beauty beyond what I see in her early likenesses. Brilliant blue eyes, wide-set in a face lined with character, a strong nose and full sensitive mouth, delicate coloring of cream complexion and striking white hair that is always simply but neatly arranged—this is she. It is our habit when we travel together, as we frequently do on business, to take a two-bedroom suite in the hotel, with a shared sitting room between. We try always to have breakfast in the suite, as this enables her to enjoy her favorite meal without the risk of intruding autograph seekers and fans. We meet often as early as six-thirty or seven o'clock in the morning, and while she usually wears one of her many Chinese robes, I have never seen her without her makeup complete to the most minute detail, including mascara. Her straight hair, almost waist-length, is always gathered into a soft, neat, shell-like bun on the crown of her head. The whole effect is one of complete poise and beauty. Faced with this present woman, I find it difficult to picture in my own mind the unhappily married young woman of those early years in China.

As we sat in the drawing room, we discussed its decor, for it had just been completed by the decorator and was of prime interest to us. It was during this conversation that she made a remark which I found very revealing. The room had been appointed in a French period with which Chinese furniture or accessories do not combine. Elegant gold and black candelabra, reflected in mirrors, hung on each side of the fireplace. The mirrors hung over olivewood commodes that we agreed looked like cancerous growths on the base of the wall.

"Those things must go," she said firmly. "They look as if they have mumps! How could anyone decorate a room like this and expect me to be comfortable in it when the only things I am really ever at home with are Asian?" She paused to reflect. "Do you know," she went on, "whenever I go to Asia, I fall back into the old patterns of my life there. One never recovers from Asia! It makes no difference where in Asia I go—Korea, Japan, India, it doesn't matter—suddenly I'm at home again. I love the people and they know it. They, in turn, accept me as theirs. It's not that I don't love my country—I do. But perhaps I'm never as comfortable with any Westerner as I am with an Asian."

And therein lies my key to her books. In China, a young American woman with such feelings would be equally as torn between two cultures as was the young Chinese girl in *East Wind : West Wind;* Pearl Buck must have experienced the same frustration and dismay at facing a lifetime within the context of her marriage. She turned to other interests, since divorce, as I have said, was as impossible in her circle as it was in Chinese society. Yet it was during this period in northern China that she became pregnant. She wanted a child, for she had always loved children. In this same year her husband was invited to Nanking to teach agriculture and they decided to move out of the new house they had built outside the city of Nanhsüchou and go south again to Nanking. She missed her Chinese friends a great deal, particularly at first, for she had no Chinese friends in Nanking as yet, but she was happy preparing for the expected child. Politically it was a restless, disturbed year. Ten years had passed since the overthrow of the Imperial Throne and ardent young revolutionists had not been able to build a new government. Soviet Russia moved into the vacuum. Her own revolution had been successfully accomplished in 1917 and she offered to help the young Chinese to organize their struggling revolution. The invitation was accepted and in 1921 the Communist Party was formally recognized in China.

In the midst of such turmoil she lived, centered in her personal joy. Her child was born in 1921. She remembers the first time she saw Carol, born an apparently normal child, beautiful and intelligent. That was the year's joy, but there was sorrow, too. When the baby was only six months old, Carie died. She was buried on a rainy October day in the Chinkiang foreign cemetery, where a little son had been buried years before. After her mother's death, she went to work immediately to paint the word portrait later to be known as *The Exile*. She has said that she found great comfort in writing that book, for she was putting into permanent form her memories and her impressions of her mother. Years later, she did the same for her father, creating portraits that are true to two who were indeed *The Spirit and the Flesh*—the combined title used for the two biographies together. Andrew and Carie live and breathe in these books, and the Nobel Prize Committee in 1938, in the citation for the Nobel Prize, described them as "masterpieces of biography."

The Bucks were given a house for their use that year in Nanking. She had wanted that house, for it had a big garden and a view overlooking the mountains, and she enjoyed furnishing it to her taste, and there they lived for ten years. Meantime, it became evident that something must be done for her father and her sister, who since Carie's death had lived together in the house in Chinkiang. Her father was absorbed in his work and her sister was lonely. She saw that her sister was unhappy, that her life was being crushed by the responsibility of caring for Andrew, so she proceeded to relieve the situation in the fashion natural to her. She went to the seminary in Nanking that her father had originally founded years before, and with some personal pressure obtained a professorship for him. She then encouraged her sister to enter the Chinese language school in Nanking. Father and sister came to live with her. Her sister later married and moved to another city, but her father stayed in her house until his death at eighty. She says:

"I learned at last to know him and to value him as man, as scholar, as saint. He lived in my house all those years, a gentleman distinguished and learned. We came into a new relationship, a friendship, with mutual respect and affection."

When Carol was four years old they spent the summer at a seashore in North China. She has always loved the sea, and this was a happy holiday. Playing on the beach with Carol, riding horseback through the bare mountains, she tried to ignore her fears. The child, though healthy and active, had still not developed speech or comprehension. What could be the matter? She heard one day that an American psychologist, a woman, was lecturing on child development. She went to the lecture and, listening, realized how far behind her own child was.

"Tell me what is wrong," she begged the woman.

The woman told her that something was very wrong, but she could not tell what. After a consultation of doctors it was decided that the child must be taken at once to the United States for diagnosis and treatment. The happy summer ended abruptly. In a few weeks they were on the ship.

In late summer of 1925 began the rounds of visits to specialists that she describes in *The Child Who Never Grew*. No one was really able to tell what was wrong. There was no record of such a case in the history of her family. Finally, a doctor at the Mayo Clinic told her that, whatever the cause, the child was hopelessly retarded.

"I don't know of any blow in all my life that was as rending. It was as if my very flesh were torn," she says of that scene. "It was beyond belief, and yet I knew I had to believe it, and shape my life around the fact."

I look at her now. Many years have passed since that blow, and I am reminded that time, so falsely named the master healer, is a veil through which we cannot see. She did not recover from that blow. Until this day she has not recovered and, what is more, she never will. I am reminded of a definition of "A Mother's Heart," which I read recently. It described how a young man, trying to marry an unscrupulous maid, years ago, reduced himself to pleading. "Please! Anything you wish I will get for you! Just tell me what it is!" The maid, thinking to be rid of him, said, "Go forth then, and cut out your mother's heart and bring it to me. Only then will I know your love is true!" And the young man did go forth, and he did cut out his mother's heart. He held it in his hands and he ran with it, eager to please his love. In his haste, he stumbled and fell. His mother's heart rolled from his hands and through the sand, and a voice came from it saying, "Did you hurt yourself, my son?" Such is pain. Such is heartbreak of a kind that can be known only by one who has borne a child in her womb and watched it blossom forth into life, a creature of beauty, and then must sit and watch it suffer, unable to relieve.

And there is an unusual plant of which I am reminded. It is a beautiful bright green fern, but if one touches it, it withers. There in the bright sunlight it cringes like a thing struck. It closes it leaves and withdraws its beauty and appears to die, but it does not. If one waits many long minutes, it ventures forth one leaf, and then another, until finally it appears to be the same as before the touch—yet is it?

In *The Child Who Never Grew* she describes the scene in detail and I shall tell it only briefly here. She has often described to me those moments in one's life that crystallize into permanence, a phase of time often short, sometimes long. The length of time becomes unimportant when one is overwhelmed by a tragic occurrence. Each minute detail of such an experience is remembered as though it had taken days, weeks or even months to come about, when actually the events took place in only a matter of minutes. She describes such a moment when a doctor first spoke frankly of her child's illness, a crystallized event for which she claims she will be grateful as long as she lives. She says frankly that to have been told the child could be well would have meant a gratitude still higher, but as long as that was impossible she feels deep gratitude to a doctor at the Mayo Clinic who came quietly out of a small room opening off the corridor as she was leaving with the child. She describes him as a small, inconspicuous person, wearing glasses, and definitely German by looks and accent. She had seen him only once or twice in the head doctor's office when he had brought in a sheaf of reports and then had gone away without speaking. She recognized him now, although in her sorrow she had seen him previously without attention. He beckoned for her to follow him into the empty room and she went in, still half-bewildered, her child clinging to her hand. His voice was almost harsh, his eyes were stern, but he spoke clearly, though in broken English. He demanded to know if she had been told the child might be cured. She stammered that she had not been told she could not be cured.

He told her then the bitter truth, that the child could never be normal. He went on to say that she should not deceive herself for in doing so she would wear out her life. She must give up hope and face the truth, for he knew from experience that the child could never be well. He told her almost brutally, but with kind intent, that the child would be a burden on her all her life and she must get ready to bear that burden. He forced her, for the first time, to face the fact that the child would never be able to speak properly or to read or write and would never be more than about four years old. He cautioned her against letting the child consume her and told her that she must find a place where Carol could be happy and leave her there and live her life for her own sake as well as for the sake of the child. She remembers the words exactly as he spoke them and knows now years later that he really suffered while he spoke. The child laughed and danced when she saw her mother's face distorted with weeping and she remembers continuing down the empty hall feeling as though she were bleeding inwardly and desperately. She has said, "It was a long time ago and yet it will never be over as long as I live. That hour is with me still."

And so it is. Those of us who know her well can see the pain that is there behind the bright blue eyes. It is there always—at chess, at dinner, when she laughs, when she dances—it is still there. But the laws of compensation have blessed her. In her I have found a compassion for and understanding of her fellowman unequaled by any I have seen or heard of before.

And yet, there is a discipline that can also be traced back to that blow. For sorrow disciplines or destroys, and she has chosen discipline. She will not, indeed cannot, endure any form of disorder in her life. When a person tells her that something, for example, however small or seemingly unimportant, will be done at a certain time, she expects, in fact demands, that it be done as promised. Her father was strict, yes, and she was brought up in a disciplined Chinese life, but that would not in itself account for her response whenever a slight transgression against time has been committed. An individual can be late for a luncheon appointment, or a member of her staff forget to repair a small household article as she requested, or her secretary leave undone a minor detail of her daily work. Then her blue eyes sparkle with inner fire as she exclaims, "One's word should count for something, surely!"

Is her inner desire to do everything well an effort to prove to herself that she is capable of perfection and, therefore, will tolerate nothing less? She cares little for what people think of her. If she writes a book and many people read it, she is glad. She wrote it to be read. But that they agree with her is not important.

She seldom reads the reviews of her books. Nor does she reread her books. She writes them, and is then finished.

"They are past, and I have new ones to write," she told me once. "I must think of these if I am to finish my work."

She is fiercely proud of her work. Only the other day she came into the office at the Foundation to keep an appointment. She entered through the big double doors that separate the conference room from the entrance hall and waiting room. She looked especially beautiful, wearing a simple tailored suit in that shade of blue she loves so well. It is a rich blue, about the same as her eyes. Her step was strong, deliberate, and from the light in those eyes, I knew something was wrong.

"Look at this!" she said. She threw an envelope on the table and sat down. I ignored the papers and asked her to tell me what was wrong.

"Some editor tells me how I must write!"

The envelope held a children's story she had written for a magazine. It was a charming story about three foxes, and she had referred to the main character as the "little" fox throughout the story. Wherever the word "little" appeared it had been carefully crossed out and the word "littlest" written above it in a neat handwriting.

"I never use the word 'littlest'! It's a silly word. How stupid! They want something written by me, and then they let someone edit the very essence of me out of it. Why didn't they tell the editor to write it in the first place?"

She is exacting on herself, and she will not allow others to lower her standards. As I have said, she is intensely proud. It is not false pride. There is not an ounce of falseness in her being. She takes great personal satisfaction in accomplishment, but praise means nothing to her professionally. To know within herself that she has come as near perfection as possible in a task she has set for herself brings her great joy.

Imagine this love of perfection, of excellence, and imagine then the tragedy of discovering that the child one bore would forever be far less than perfect!

To a parent of a retarded child who said to her that it would be better if the child were dead, she replied, she told me, as follows:

"One must not start killing people, not even by wishing them dead. One simply must not—or where will it end? Hitler did just that. He first killed the mentally ill, declaring them useless. Then of what use were cripples or retarded children, or the aged? He killed them, and after them it was Jews, and then anyone who did not agree with him. Where does one draw the line? At the beginning! One must not take a human life, for any reason."

She was alone in her care for the child. It became entirely her responsibility to provide for the child's future. She put her feelings into words as follows:

"People were kind enough, but no help came from anyone. Perhaps that was my own fault. Perhaps I made my surface too smooth and natural so that no one could see beneath it. Partly that, perhaps, and partly it was, too, because people shrink from penetrating beneath surfaces. Only those who know inescapable sorrow know what I mean.

"It was in those days that I learned to distinguish between the two kinds of people in the world, those who have known inescapable sorrow and those who have not. For there are basically two kinds of sorrows, those which can be assuaged and those which cannot. The death of parents is sad, for they cannot be replaced, but it is not inescapable sorrow. It is natural sorrow, that which one must expect in the normal course of life. The crippling of one's body, irremediably, is an inescapable sorrow. It has to be lived with and, more than that, it has to be used for some other sort of life than that planned in health. The sorrows which can be assuaged are those which life can cover and heal. Those which cannot be assuaged are those which change life itself and in a way themselves make life. Sorrows that pass may be assuaged, but living sorrow is never assuaged. It is a stone thrown into the stream, as Browning put it, and the water must divide itself and accommodate itself, for it can never remove the stone."

I have tried to get from her the story of the years between that sad discovery in 1925 and her divorce and second marriage in 1935, and she has tried to tell me the story, I know, for there are no secrets between us. Our understanding of each other, and our mutual respect, have resulted in a friendship too deep to be cluttered or marred by such things as secrets or forbidden topics of conversation. But she can tell me very little.

"Those were difficult years. I have tried so long to forget them, and the unhappiness and confusion they held. Even if I could remember, must we bring them all back again?"

And I have told her indeed we must, for those are important years.

I awoke this morning, scarcely two hours ago, and I was vaguely conscious of being somewhat weary. I was aware then that I had dreamed in the night, and in my dreams I had spanned years of living in moments, perhaps. There were past scenes re-enacted in the present, and scenes unfamiliar to me that I take to be my subconscious effort to view the future. Caught as I was in that drowsy world of half-sleep, suddenly it was all clear to me and I reviewed each event in my mind in my efforts to doze off and once again enjoy the drama being presented for me alone. Then the buzzer of my interphone sounded and I was told that breakfast was being prepared. Instantly that dream world was gone and as I dressed I could not recall the events so clear to me only a few minutes before. I understood then her difficulty with those years. I know perfectly the happenings of my dream, and yet I cannot sort them out and put them into any semblance of order. She knows what happened in those years, yet it is all but impossible for her now to put people, places and events into order. Hence, I can give the story only as I have gathered it from her. Her exact words in describing those years? "They were just a hodge-podge!" she exclaims. I present them thus, therefore.

In 1924, on her way to the United States with her husband and Carol, she began to write again. On board ship she wrote "A Chinese Woman Speaks," a story later to become known as "East Wind." She had had mild success with two essays, one published in *The Atlantic Monthly*, entitled "In China, Too." The second, "Beauty in China," was published in *The Forum*. There were no more until "A Chinese Woman Speaks."

This story came out of the turmoil of China at that time, the struggle of East and West. She was very conscious of revolution in

China and of the great impact of the West. She had found her own circle of friends in Nanking, the intellectuals, and there is one she remembers in particular. He was a young man named Hsu Tse-mo, a Chinese poet, a handsome man with a face she describes as "like a Buddha, not a fat Buddha, but a slender, handsome Buddha. That man had the most beautiful hands I have ever seen. They were graceful and strong with long and slender fingers. He called himself 'the Chinese Byron.' "

She was aware of the conflict in this young man, indeed in all her young Chinese friends, caught between the old and the new. She was intensely interested in this important change and read everything written about it. Out of this interest, and out of these friends, grew "East Wind." In the story she imagined herself as a young Chinese girl, an easy feat for her, marrying a young man such as Hsu Tse-mo. The story was submitted to *Asia* magazine and then was promptly forgotten in the turmoil of her own life in those stormy years of civil wars. It was published in the April, 1926, issue.

Her first adopted child was born on April 6, 1925. I say "first" for she now has a grand total of nine. This baby, a girl, was three months old when the adoption became final. She had tried to adopt a baby before but agencies disapproved of her taking a child to China. She continued her efforts because of the ever deepening loneliness in her life. She felt she must have someone to whom she could turn for comfort, and there was no one, nothing. If she could have hated her first husband, perhaps that very hatred might have been a comfort. Yet for her the opposite of love is not hate but indifference. There was, of course, no comfort in the retarded child, for she did not respond in any way to efforts to train and teach her except to become tired and nervous. At last, however, she found another child.

She described the scene to me thus:

"I was sure that there must be a baby somewhere who needed me. I found her in a small orphanage in upstate New York. A friendly Presbyterian minister took me there and the director led me into the nursery. There were twenty babies in their cribs.

" 'Take your choice,' the director said.

"Was there ever such a choice presented to a young mother? I went from crib to crib. At last I came to one where a very small, very pale little girl lay, her eyes closed. She seemed scarcely to breathe.

" 'How old is she?' I asked.

" 'Three months,' the director said, 'and she has never gained since birth. She weighs only seven pounds. She will not eat.'

" 'I want her,' I said.

"He argued against it immediately. Why should I take a child doomed to death? But I insisted. I felt a strange instant love for the exquisite dying child. I took her in my arms and carried her away. The very next day she began to eat. In a fortnight one wouldn't have known her. She was actually plump. My husband and I finished our work for our masters' degrees and took our two daughters back to China with us."

Today I look at this tall, handsome young woman and find it hard to believe she could ever have been other than healthy.

In coming to the United States in 1925, she had arranged to study at Cornell for her master's degree. That year at Ithaca, New York, was the only year of her life she can remember when she had no servants and had to do her own housework. Not that she has ever really minded household tasks, but her life has always been so full of her work that she has never had the freedom to indulge in housework. There are certain duties, however, that she reserves for herself, even today. For example, she always arranges the flowers for her home. She loves their beauty and creates artistic, colorful arrangements, always fresh, for she does not tolerate one blossom that is even slightly wilted.

The highlight of the year at Cornell was the writing of her prize-winning essay entitled "China and the West." It won first honors in the Laura Messenger Prize competition and a purse of two hundred dollars. Little as this may seem now for a Pearl Buck essay, it was more money than she could imagine at that time.

She smiles, remembering the important event as she describes it to me:

"It was foolhardy of me to enter that contest, for it was in the history department and I was majoring in my own field of English literature. I had a few free weeks between classes, however, and I decided to write on the history of the relationship between

China and the West. I needed money and that was the largest prize the college offered. I spent many hours in the library, and finished my essay—a long one—and handed it in. Our names were not attached to the essays, for the judges were not allowed to know who wrote them.

"Then I told my English professor what I had done.

" 'You're mad,' he said cheerfully. 'The prize always goes to a history major.'

"I tried to remain hopeful, nevertheless. In a few weeks I heard a rumor that a Chinese student had won the prize. I began to be more hopeful. Another week and my name was announced as the winner. The importance to me of this prize was more than money. It gave me confidence as a writer."

She used that essay for a lecture she gave years later at the Academy of Music in Philadelphia. It is not surprising that an essay written by her could be a lecture nearly twenty years after it was written and still be considered timely. In reading *What America Means to Me,* a collection of her essays and speeches published in 1942, one realizes that she speaks essential truths about people, and these do not change with time. She makes her points with never-failing accuracy, and there is musical flow in her use of English.

"Are you conscious of style?" I asked her.

To which she replied, "I hear words clearly, as though they were spoken to me, and I write down what I hear. People who knew me in college never thought I would write prose, they thought I would write poetry. I very nearly didn't write prose, but, thank God for my pocketbook's sake, I did."

These words tell the story better than I shall ever be able to do, of exactly how she feels about this gift of hers. Writing is her work and she writes.

Before leaving America, she sent "A Chinese Woman Speaks" to Brentano, at that time a publisher as well as a bookseller. They told her that it was too short for a novel and asked her to expand it. She refused to do so; for it is her habit, when she has said what she has to say on a subject, to consider it finished. She does not pad. Instead, in this case, she conceived the idea of a second story, to be entitled "West Wind," and wrote it on shipboard returning to China. *East Wind : West Wind* was then sent to Bren-

tano, but they did not like the two-story idea and returned it
to her. Of course that was a blow, but she went to work immediately
on a novel, which she completed in the early spring of 1927. Before she could send it to a publisher, the second revolution was
in progress in China. The victorious revolutionary army entered
Nanking and attacked the foreigners. Houses were burned
and looted and in the fury the manuscript was lost.

"Probably it was no good," she comments.

Between 1927 and 1930, there was little time for writing—not
that she had given up, but there was simply no time. Caught between wars and revolutions, her own life was too difficult for her
to think about anything else. She has told of those years of Chinese history in *My Several Worlds,* and I will not repeat the story
here except to recall that in 1927, when the Communists seized
Nanking, she fled with her husband and two daughters to the
mountains in Japan, where they spent a summer. She has pleasant memories of that summer and of their little Japanese house in
the forest by a brook. In sorting some papers not long ago I found
a copy of a letter from her to Miss Marietta Neff, then an editor of
Asia magazine. I cannot imagine why she would have saved this
one of many letters, but it does give definite insight into her feelings at that time, and I include it here with appreciation. It is
dated April 15, 1927, at Unzen, Japan:

> My dear Miss Neff:
> Thank you for your letter of March the 4th. I am glad you can
> use one of the manuscripts. I meant the two to be more or less
> samples of a series. I'll try another on the Chinese student as a
> student, having known him as such in both mission and govern-
> ment universities.
> You will note my change of address. The papers have told you
> how all foreigners were forcibly ejected from Nanking by the
> Nationalist troops when they came in. We were among the for-
> eigners and like the others, we lost everything we had in the way
> of home, clothes, and so forth. It was the most sudden event
> imaginable. We heard at the breakfast table that the revolutionists
> were marching into the city, and we were glad, because the days
> of fighting had been tense ones, and also because we, as a group
> of foreign university teachers, were heartily in sympathy with the
> national aims.

Then in fifteen minutes we were fleeing for our lives. Our faithful servants came running to tell us that the Nationalists were killing foreigners, and they helped us to hide. It was true, for our vice-president, Dr. Williams, had already been killed—shot instantly when he did not give up his watch to a band of soldiers. We hid all day—thirteen hours to be exact—in a tiny hovel where a poor woman, whom I had helped, lived. We could not make a sound, since the soldiers were all around us—and "we" includes two babies under two and my seven-year-old. But they were very good. All day we listened to the most hideous shouting and crashing in of gates and doors. Our servants crept in to tell us that the soldiers were urging the common people in to take out things, since now everything was to be in common, and there was to be no more private property.

Others were less fortunate than we, and had to face the mobs and were beaten and shot at and robbed of their clothing and rings and even spectacles, and some were killed. At four o'clock in the afternoon the English and American men-of-war in the harbor seven miles away began to fire shells and instantly the mobs quieted, a bugle blew, and the soldiers were called off. But several houses had been burned, and we heard the crashing walls for a long time. We were finally rescued by our faithful Chinese friends who did all they could to help us—our students and our Chinese faculty who were as much astonished and horrified by what had taken place as we were. We white people remained huddled together in one building, over a hundred of us, not knowing until the very end whether they planned to kill us or not.

The Chinese press has tried to avoid responsibility for the Nationalists, and Nationalists have tried to put the blame on retreating Northern soldiers, but those of us who passed through the experience know better. The Nanking Chinese recognized the dialect of the soldiers. It was Southern. Besides, we had seen the Northern soldiers retreating in good order all the previous day. The consensus of intelligent opinion among the foreigners and of *honest* opinion among the Chinese is that it was an attack planned and premeditated by the Nationalists of the Communist group, who are bitterly against any foreigner who is not a red Russian. Of course the great question in China now is, who is going to win—the Communists or Conservative Nationalists. That is the real fight. After all, we foreigners as such are only pawns in the game. It may be that the Nanking affair was simply a plot to make trouble for Chiang Kai-shek, the Conservative leader—no one knows.

Forgive my writing at such length! I thought you might be interested, perhaps. Meanwhile, we are very glad to be here, perched in a tiny Japanese house among pines on a mountainside, perched indefinitely, I suppose. Most of our group are through with China, and have sailed for America and their respective countries, but I have an insatiable curiosity and want to hang about a bit to see what else is going to happen.

Yours sincerely,
Pearl S. Buck

Incidentally, my manuscript for a novel, which I had just finished, was scattered to the four winds with everything else in the house. I console myself by thinking it probably was not any good. At any rate, it was a lot of work—gone for naught. But perhaps I may consider it a work of genius, since no one can ever tell me differently, now!

She was in Japan a few years ago and she returned to see the house of that summer, and there it still stood—much the same as it had been before, but closed and silent in the pine forest. It was good for her to see it, I think, and to know that at least something in her life was unchanged by time.

She tells me of that return in these words:

"Ah, yes—that return after half a lifetime away! I was in Japan working on a film—you may read about that in *A Bridge For Passing*. I had a longing to see Unzen again and the little Japanese house in which we had taken refuge. So one afternoon a Japanese friend motored me up the hairpin curves of the mountain and there Unzen lay, much enlarged and commercialized. I could no longer recognize the way in the maze of new buildings. We stopped a young woman and asked her if she knew anything about some houses where Americans had fled from a Chinese war. Her face lighted.

" 'My grandfather knows.'

"She ran to fetch him and he did indeed lead us through the town and across a narrow gorge, which I remembered. Yes, there the house stood, empty. I lingered a while and then went away. Leaving the city, I pressed a gift of money upon the old man.

He fended off the gift but I insisted and he accepted unwillingly. A few minutes later we heard someone calling. It was the young woman. She handed me a package.

" 'Grandfather says you used to buy these rice cakes for your children.'

"It was quite true. I had forgotten but the old man had not."

So much had changed for her, and so rapidly, that I marvel at her seeming inner peace and tranquillity. I say "seeming," for I know that there is no real peace in her entire being. How could there be peace, when she is driven from within by the realization that there is not enough time left in life for her to do and say and see all of the things she wishes? How can one be plucked from country to country, culture to culture, people to people, and retain any sense of belonging to any race or place? To me there can be only one real answer. That day in Nanking when the Communists were killing all Westerners and she was faced with death, I know that she took stock of her life as it was and decided upon what she would like to be able to do and what she would have done otherwise—and vowed that if she managed to leave that place alive, life would be different.

"In those hours in that little hut," she says, "I realized that I had not been living in the world. I had lived in a Chinese community, deeply involved with the life there, my house, a beautiful garden, my neighbors, the community events. I'm convinced that had it not been for that day I would never have left China, because my whole life was there. On that day my cord to China was broken. It was all destroyed—my house, the garden, and I listened to the crackling of the flames and I knew that it was all no more. Life, as I had known it, was ended. In a way it was like a birth. I was thrust out of my familiar surroundings and into a new world. I realized that if I lived beyond that day it would have to be in the entire world and not just in my secure part of it."

She owes her life from then on to a Chinese peasant serving woman, and the world of literature owes that simple woman so deep a debt of gratitude that here I must tell all that I know about her, for without her we would have no Pearl Buck as we know her. Yes, that peasant woman, to me, is the most important person in her entire life, and I shall forever be personally grateful to her. Briefly, the story is this:

One winter morning in those years of unrest after the death of Sun Yat-sen, her breakfast was interrupted by a knock at the door. She opened it and a woman stood there, a ragged dusty woman from the North, as could be discerned from her bound feet and baggy trousers. The woman came in and told her that she was Mrs. Lu, the wife of a gardener employed by the family in northern China. Her husband had run away and left her when the famine came. The people of the south were expecting many refugees from the famine but this woman had come early for she was pregnant. She had previously lost five children from what she referred to as the ten-day madness, which is simply a type of tetanus resulting from an infection in birth.

"I came to you," the woman said, "because I have no one else. I have nothing but this child still to be born."

"I didn't welcome her in my heart," Pearl Buck says, "but I was sorry for her and let her come in."

The woman moved into a little house behind the garden near the gate and there she lived until the child was born. She wanted that little house, though it was formerly a henhouse and really not fit for a human being, nor would she under any circumstances go to a foreign hospital. She had given birth to so many children she knew exactly what to do, she insisted, and she wanted no one with her when the baby was born. She gave birth this time to a tiny, fat boy one December morning. All went well for a few days; then the mother reported that the baby was ill. It seemed she had poured iodine on the baby's navel as a disinfectant, and the child almost died from the burn.

"I took the baby into my own room," Pearl Buck has told me, "and he decided to live." Before he was a month old his father, the runaway husband, appeared and the family was reunited. They rented a small room in an earthen house just over the compound wall and life went on.

It was a strange, uneasy winter. The revolutionary forces had dug in around the city and everyone waited for the spring when they would march again. White people were hopeful but distrustful, depending upon their feeling for the Chinese people. No-

body knew exactly what Communists were, for bandits and brigands had joined their ranks and what they heard about Communists was what they had always heard about bandits and brigands. No one knew which was which. She has described the
Nanking incident fully in *My Several Worlds,* from which I quote
a few paragraphs that capture the horror of the moment:

When I remember the fateful morning of March 27, 1927, I
see it in a scene, as though I had nothing to do with it. A little
group of white people stands, uncertain and alone, on the early
green lawn of a gray brick house, three men, two women, three
small children. The wind blows damp and chill over the compound wall. The sky is dark with clouds. They hold their coats
about them, shivering, and they stare at each other.

"Where can we hide?" This is what they are whispering.

One of those women is me, two of the children are mine. The
other woman is my sister. The two younger men are our husbands,
and the tall dignified old gentleman is our father. The nightmare
of my life has come true. We are in danger of our lives because
we are white people in a Chinese city. Though all our lives have
been spent in friendly ways, it counts for nothing today. Today
we suffer for those we have never known, the aggressors, the im-
perialists, the white men of Europe and England who fought the
war and seized the booty and claimed the territory, the men who
made the Unequal Treaties, the men who insisted upon extra-
territorial rights, the empire builders. Oh, I was always afraid of
those white men because they were the ones who made us all
hated in Asia! The weight of history falls heavy upon us now,
upon my kind old father, who has been only good to every Chinese he has ever met, upon our little children, who have known
no country except this one where now they stand in danger of
death.

"Where shall we hide?" we keep asking, and we cannot answer.

The pleasant house which until now has been our home can
shelter us no more. The rooms stand as we left them a few minutes ago, the big stove still burning in the hall and spreading its
heartening warmth, the breakfast table set, the food half eaten. I
was just pouring the coffee when our neighbor, the faithful tailor,
came running in to tell us that the revolutionists, who in the night

had captured the city, were now killing the white people. He stood there at the table where we were all sitting, happy that the battle was over, and he wrung his hands and the tears ran down his cheeks while he talked.

"Do not delay, there is no time—Teacher Williams lies dead already in the street outside the gate!"

Dr. Williams? He was the vice-president of the Christian university!

My father had breakfasted early and was gone to his classes at the seminary, but only just gone, so immediately the houseboy runs to bring him back. My sister and I know only too well now that death is possible, and we get up quickly and find the children's coats and caps and our own coats and we all hasten outside the house that is no longer a shelter, and here we stand in the chill wet winds.

Where can we hide?

The servants gather around us, half fearful for their own sakes. They know that if they are found with us they too may be killed. Nobody knows the ferocity of the revolutionists. We have heard such stories.

"There is no use in hiding in our quarters," the amah says. "They will find you there." She falls to her knees and puts her arms around my older child and sobs aloud.

Oh, where can we go? There is nowhere. We hear the sound of howling voices in the distant streets and we look at each other and clasp the children's hands. My old father's lips move and I know he is praying. But there is nowhere to go.

Suddenly the back gate squeaks on its hinges, the little back gate in the corner of the compound wall, and we all turn our heads. It is Mrs. Lu, who lives in a cluster of little mud houses just over the wall in a pocket of an alley off the street that runs in front of the house. She comes hobbling toward us on her badly bound feet, her loose trousers hanging over her ankles. Her hair is uncombed as usual, rusty brown locks hanging down her cheeks, and her kind stupid face is all concern and alarm and love.

"Wise Mother," she gasps, "you and your family, come and hide in my little room! Nobody will look for you there. Who would harm a woman like me? My good-for-nothing has left me again and I and my son are alone. Come—come—there is no time!"

She pulls at me, she embraces all the children at once, and we follow her blindly, half running, leaving the gate open behind us. There are no houses very near, we have lived in one of the open spaces of the city, and we run across two or three acres of grass-land and old graves and between some neat vegetable gardens until on the far side of our wall we reach the handful of mud houses, in one of which Mrs. Lu lives. The people are waiting for us there, the kind poor people, and they receive us, her friends and neighbors, and they hurry us into the dark little half-room which is her home. It is indeed only half a room, barely big enough for the board bed, a small square table and two benches. There is no window, only a hole under the thatched roof. It is almost entirely dark. Into this narrow place we all crowd ourselves and Mrs. Lu closes the door.

"I will come back," she whispers. "And if the children cry, do not be afraid. We have so many children here, those wild soldiers will not know if it is your child or ours that cries."

The Communists had reorganized forces and they were the leaders. Even Chiang Kai-shek was with the Communists, the foreigners were told, and the Communists were building upon hate, the hate for the foreigner, the injustices of the past. For many long hours she huddled in that small room and the Chinese woman brought them the only food they had, risking her own life of course, but steadfastly trying to save them. Then suddenly in the last hours no one came. The sound of the cannon from American warships, on the river, miles away, lasted a long time and they wished someone would come but no one came. Then there was silence for two hours or more before friendly Chinese came to take them to the university buildings, where they awaited transfer to an American warship and freedom. She recalls this incident vividly but shudders today when she thinks about it, and she acknowledges quite freely that except for the loyalty of that peasant serving woman she would undoubtedly have died at the hands of the Communists.

Such is her amazing story. It is difficult for me to understand now how one could endure such terror as she must have known and emerge from it with any remaining sanity. But I am sure that after living through such experiences one would be in either of two extreme states: completely broken in spirit or infused with renewed faith in one's right to live in a way that results in happiness. I do not know how those who were with her on that day came away, but I know how she came out of that hut and how she felt as she sailed down the Yangtze River to freedom. I know also that she has not forgotten. There is in her today so tranquil and yet so firm a determination to do as she wishes that I shrink from considering what would happen if for any reason she could not accomplish that upon which her mind is set.

In the autumn after the summer of 1927, in Japan, she and her children took a train trip throughout that country and thus came to know and love the Japanese and they remain a favorite people with her today. She stayed at country inns, she tells me, and everyone was so kind to her and to her retarded child that they quickly won her heart. On her Green Hills Farm in Pennsylvania there is a place here and a spot there where the delicate Japanese influence expresses itself in decor and even in her gardening. Yesterday we were discussing that trip in Japan, long ago, and I asked where her husband was and why she made the journey alone with the children. She looked puzzled.

"You know, I really don't know! I can't imagine why I was alone, but that shows how unimportant my marriage had already become to me. He had his own life and he was living it. I was preparing for mine."

And prepare she did. After the stay in Japan they returned to the house in Nanking to try to rebuild what was left. It was during this period of reorganization that she bought the Chinese desk that now stands in the library of the Foundation house. I have wondered often if when she bought that desk she understood that it was the key which would open the long-closed door of her true being and release her from the bonds of "what is expected." She places upon herself always the determination to succeed, and she has displayed that in each phase of her life. She is a woman different from the world around her and no matter how she resents these differences, they exist, nonetheless, and she has had to learn how to live with herself. Being different from others is not easy, for then one is never completely close to other human beings. No matter how intimate may be some of her external relationships, she still has that inner place where she lives alone with her people—the people she has created. She experiences their likes and dislikes, their loves and hates, their lives, and while this creation is going on she must not have a life of her own, for if she does, it influences her writing. I know how the men in her life must have felt when she retreated thus, for I have felt a pang of resentment myself when I have found that there is no place for me in that part of her being. She cannot share the creative process with anyone. I suppose one could say that she experiences much vicariously—if one can create and then experience vicariously from the creation!

Her people! She knew them all. They were there in her inner being, ready for her to bring them to life. Were they to live? She saw the possibility of her life's ending in Nanking with her people never having lived. She knew she must write. She bought that desk and put it in an attic room of the house where she could go and be alone with her people.

It was a handicap, she found, to be so far from her market and the readers she hoped to have, for she received at first the inevitable rejections, and realized that she must have a literary agent in the United States to handle these details for her. In an English bookshop in Shanghai she found a worn, secondhand copy of *The Writer's Guide*. In it were listed the names of two American literary agencies. She wrote to both, asking if they would handle her work. One declined on the ground that "no one wanted to read stories about China." The second replied cautiously, asking to see a sample of her work. When she sent him *East Wind : West Wind* in the spring of 1928 he agreed to try to sell it. This was David Lloyd.

Meanwhile, she turned again to the problems of life. She had still to make permanent arrangements for her retarded child. In 1929 she took Carol to the United States again, this time to look for an institution where the child could be cared for and happy. The story of this search is told in her short book *The Child Who Never Grew*. Suffice it here to say that she found the place she sought at The Training School, in Vineland, New Jersey. She had heard of this school even when she was in China, a place, she was told, "where happiness comes first." Here, then, her child must live, but how would she find the money? A thousand dollars a year at that time was a large sum and she wanted two years free of teaching so that she could write the novel that was ready in her mind.

Happily there was a doctor then in New York who had become her friend and advisor. He told the wife of a friend of his about the child and, moved by the story of a brave young mother trying to care for a retarded child alone, the woman gave the doctor two thousand dollars as a loan to help Pearl Buck with her problem. She left Carol in the training school with her care paid for two years and she prepared to return to China.

On the way she stopped to visit a friend in a university in Buffalo, New York. While there, the news came to her that *East Wind : West Wind* had been accepted by a publisher. So absorbed had she been with the problem of her child that she had neglected to tell her agent that she was not in China, and cablegrams had followed her around the world only to find her not far from New York. Next a congratulatory letter came from her publisher with a luncheon invitation for them to meet. She replied and then let weeks pass, much to his surprise, he told her later, before she accepted his invitation. They met at last, neither dreaming at that time that one day they were to be husband and wife. The next day she left for China with her adopted daughter, then almost four years old.

When they were home again, as soon as her husband left for work each morning, and she had made the house beautiful with flowers, she would climb to the attic room and spend hour upon hour with Wang Lung and O-lan. She lived their lives with them. She took Wang Lung from a peasant's country house to a great house of wealth in the city and returned him to the House of Earth to end his life where it began. In two months the story was finished. She typed it twice herself, boxed the manuscript and mailed it to her agent. It was immediately accepted by her publisher, who suggested that it be entitled *The Good Earth;* her own working title had been simply *Wang Lung.*

Next she fulfilled her contract for *The Young Revolutionist* and began to write *The Mother.* This was a short book, the story strong and dramatic. It was so different from *The Good Earth* that she decided it was "no good," as she says, and threw it into the wastebasket. I think she knew the book was good—too good, and I think she did not want the world to know that she herself was capable of the emotion and passion felt by this woman. She wanted to destroy the evidence. At any rate, the houseman was ill on the day she threw the manuscript away, and absent from his duties. Consequently, the wastebasket was not emptied as usual. Before he returned the next day, she retrieved the manuscript, but she put it away. It was not published for several years.

Meanwhile the sons of Wang Lung haunted her attic, and she began to know them as well as she had known their parents. They too became a story. The following is a letter written to her publisher after *Sons* was finished:

3 Ping Ts'ang Hsiang, Nanking, China
October 14, 1931

Mr. Richard J. Walsh
The John Day Company
New York
My dear Mr. Walsh:

Thank you very much for your letters of September the seventeenth and twenty-first. I am very glad *The Good Earth* is still managing to hold its end up.

A day or two ago I sent the manuscript of my next novel to Mr. Lloyd. As always, I am completely unable to know whether it is worth anything or not. But at any rate it is gone. It portrays a somewhat different side of Chinese life, and again my main purpose has not been to portray conditions but people. I have called it *Sons,* and if you find the book worth having, I hope that title can stand, because *Sons* is what I mean. I shall not be unreasonable, however, if you feel it impossible, for I am very distrustful of my own judgment in all such matters. As to the time of publication, it must, of course, be as you think best. I am glad to have the manuscript out of China, however, in these extremely distressing times, with the possibility of war and sudden exits daily before us.

You may be interested to know that I have had several applications from Chinese to translate *The Good Earth*. A rising young novelist, a cousin of Dr. Lin Yutang, by the way, who is in New York now, writes me:

"One week ago I received a copy of *The Good Earth* from my uncle, Dr. Lin Yutang, who lives in New York now, with a letter urging me to translate it into Chinese.

"After I read it all over, I was largely astonished by your splendid achievement. As a little Chinese writer myself, I have devoted my attention to our peasants, and I found your novel tells more truth than many famous foreign professors, who have written several volumes of books dealing with Chinese peasant life.

"Your novel, I am sure, will be largely appreciated by Chinese readers. Would you be so kind as to give me the honor to translate it? During the last two years I have translated some foreign novels, including Remarque's *All Quiet* and its sequel, Henry James' *Daisy Miller,* M. Gorky's *The Bystander,* and Renn's *War.*"

I have been pleased that even the most chauvinistic—and how chauvinistic we have them—have granted my sympathy with my Chinese characters. It has been a relief to me, for so many of our ardent young patriots feel that to show China as less than a heaven upon earth and a perfect state is to show dislike and unfriendliness. Well, I have been very lucky.

I told Mr. Lloyd to tell you, but since I am writing I might say myself, that Mr. Cyrus Leroy Baldridge, whose drawings you may know, passed through here not long ago, and would have me sit for my portrait. I do not know how to judge the result. I mention this in case he sends the drawing to you. But more important is the fact that I thought his Chinese drawings and sketches the very best I had ever seen and the most true; this in case you ever need an artist on Chinese subjects.

You may be sure I was pleased to sign the contracts for the next novels, although I cannot guarantee their worth in any sense. But I have two more now quite clearly ahead of me, and shall work away on them at my pleasure. I have never told you, perhaps—nor is this for publication—but there has been a family circumstance which has kept me bound for more than ten years. I have always known that I would write—must write—but with this responsibility of care for someone quite helpless, I had never any time of my own, unless I sacrificed the one dependent, and only last year was the bondage removed, and I received my honorable discharge. But all these years while my hands were busy, these novels have been making themselves in my head, and therefore are they ready now to be put down. If the books come fairly rapidly, therefore, it is not necessarily hasty writing, but simply the putting into writing of material long pondered and mentally revised many times. The actual writing of *The Good Earth* was less than two months, in addition to other duties I could not wholly put away as the wife of a very busy husband, and the mother of a big busy house. I explain this so that you will not feel me too quick in my books.

Sincerely yours,
Pearl S. Buck

Her stories came from her now in a great rush, like the waters of the mighty Yangtze in a flood. The people she had created, the tales she knew, came from her fast, anxious to live, to be written down before they were lost forever. The hours she wrote increased each day until often she was exhausted. Money poured in from *The Good Earth* as it continued on the best-seller list for twenty-two months. With this money she set up two lifetime trust funds for her retarded child so that she would always be taken care of. She repaid the original two thousand dollars and discovered then that the loan had been made by the wife of an executive of the New York *Times,* Mrs. John H. Finley, her devoted friend thereafter. She even built a bathhouse for the Chinese women in her neighborhood as she had determined to do years earlier.

"I laugh when I think of that bathhouse! The reason for it was that women in our city had no warm bathhouse for winter use, their homes being unheated, whereas men did. So, wanting to share my good fortune in earning some money, I built the bathhouse. It was a good one with plenty of tubs, soap and hot water. Not everyone appreciated it, however. I remember one day when I was inspecting it I heard an old woman grumbling. 'All this bathing,' she complained. 'I'm not sure it is a good thing. Before we had this fine bathhouse I could be comfortable all winter with no baths, whereas now, I begin to itch at the end of three weeks if I don't come here for a bath!' Most of the women enjoyed the bathhouse, however, and brought their smaller children with them."

Then she made improvements in her own home. In short, she did everything she had wanted to do.

What was happening to the woman herself? I surmise that she never thought of herself. She was too occupied in being herself, her own self, the creative writer. Was she changed? I think she was changed without knowing it. Her Chinese friends knew no difference, but her American friends were awed and perhaps somewhat uncomfortable to realize that the quiet detached young woman, dreaming and aloof, had suddenly become famous.

"I think they didn't like me," she says now, remembering.

Perhaps it was only human for them to fear that person in their midst who was better at everything, it seemed, than they were. At any rate, more and more it came about that her only companionship was in the attic with her people.

At this time she was still unaware of the tremendous impact *The Good Earth* was having on the people of the United States. She remembers showing her father a bound copy of *The Good Earth* and laughs today when she remembers his question.

"How much money do you think you will make from this book?"

"Oh, about twenty thousand dollars," she answered.

"That's a lot of money for a novel," he said of the book that was to earn her more than a million dollars. "That's very nice, I'm sure, but I'm afraid I can't undertake it."

And he never did read her works. As a matter of fact, she can never remember his reading any novel. He was a scholar and had no taste for fiction. Her father died in 1932, at the age of eighty, without ever knowing of the fame that was to come to his child. It was the year of the big flood in China and she remembers that even though the Yangtze was seven miles away there was water all around them. The water never rose to their house, for it was on a low hill, but the city streets were all under water. Her father was spending some time with her sister up in the mountains, as was his custom each year, when her sister wrote to her that he was desperately ill with a tropical dysentery, and then for days no news came. The telegraph wires were swept away in the flood. Of course her desire was to go to him, but the river boats were not running so she could not go, and by the time she had news it was of his death.

"I could not get to the funeral," she says, "but later I did visit his grave. It was high on a hilltop and I stayed for hours, remembering his long and brilliant life, so little appreciated or even understood by his fellow missionaries. There was something symbolic in this lofty resting place, the noble mountains encircling, and the wind blowing the clouds down from the sky."

It was in this year of the great flood that Charles Lindbergh flew to China to survey the damage. She recalls that she was chosen to be among the reception committee to meet him at the airport and then was invited to dine with him and his wife at the American Embassy.

"He was a quiet man," she reflects. "He said very little during dinner. Afterward he took out big maps and spread them on the table and we all discussed the flood damage. The real danger was from typhoid and tropical diseases. There were so many dead things in the water—people and animals and such. He was a pleasant man and I enjoyed meeting him, even under those circumstances, and his wife was gentle and lovely."

Tragedy was enacted all about her in China, but in America, where people were quite unaware of the flood, *The Good Earth* was chosen by the Book-of-the-Month Club, and sales soared. Will Rogers, at that time at the peak of his career, commented on it and was quoted thus in the New York *Times*:

"It's not only the greatest book about a people ever written, but the best book of our generation. So get this and read it."

Millions of people everywhere in the world who believed every word that Will Rogers spoke went out and bought the book and read it. It was translated into many languages and her publishers and agents reported record grosses. She feels that the greatest single contribution to the success of *The Good Earth* was the comment made by Will Rogers. He tried to visit her in China that year and she was eager for the meeting, for she wanted to thank him in person. The floodwaters from the Yangtze prevented him from coming to the part of China where she was, however, and so she was compelled to wait for another day.

Late in 1932 *The Good Earth* was awarded the Pulitzer Prize for the best novel of the year, and again sales soared. It is typical of her to pay no heed to awards and prizes. We were arranging a display for the Pearl S. Buck Foundation recently and I asked her what physical form the Pulitzer Prize took.

"You know, I can't imagine what that was. I don't think it was anything. I know I was in China and I heard about it by cable."

"But there must have been a plaque or a certificate or a medal or something," I insisted.

"No, I don't think so," she said in a timid little voice, like a child who has committed some wrong. "I know there was some money, and I spent that, but I don't remember anything else. I suppose there must have been more, but I don't know about it. I'm afraid I've forgotten."

Meanwhile, she had been doing research on translating the great, classic novel of ancient China, *Shui Hu Chuan*. She had already learned to divide her workday into periods of creative work and noncreative work, a formula she still adheres to rigidly today. In the mornings she wrote—stories, novellas, novels, about life around her and her created people. In the afternoons she worked on the translation. She shut herself in the attic each day and her life withdrew more and more from those around her into the ever-expanding recesses of her inner creative self.

With *Sons* finished and sent to her agent, and her translation of *Shui Hu Chuan* now also finished, her foremost thoughts were of her retarded child, alone in the United States. A few days ago we were discussing this period of her life:

"I left her all alone for three years and that, I know now, was wrong for me to have done. It was wrong for her and for me. After all, she had never been separated from me before and for it to be so sudden and so complete was hard on us both. True, I paid a woman friend to go and see her, and she reported to me each month, but it was not the same as visiting her myself. I vowed I would go back to see her at least once a year."

Fortunately, it was time for her husband's sabbatical year. They made their plans to return to America, and left China in July, 1932. On shipboard with her she carried the manuscript of her translation, now entitled *All Men Are Brothers*.

"I didn't let it out of my sight! It was so much work—four years long—to complete, and I didn't want anything to happen to it."

Her publisher met them at the train in Montreal and he told her afterwards that he knew at once that he was going to marry her. Of that she had no inkling at the time, of course. They went to New York to attend an important welcome dinner planned by her publisher at the Waldorf Astoria. It was August, a month when literary critics and all so-called important folk were out of the city. Nevertheless, they returned for the brilliant occasion. She had been asked to speak, but, overcome by shyness, she could not make a speech of her own. Instead, she read Shih Nai-an's preface to *Shui Hu Chuan*, written five hundred years ago:

A man who lives until he is thirty years of age without marrying should not then marry. A man who has not been governor before the age of forty should not then seek for a governorship. At fifty years he should not found a home, nor at sixty set out upon travels. Why is this said? Because the time for such things is past and he will, if he undertake them, have little space left to him in which to enjoy them.

When the morning sun has just risen, palely bright, we wash head and face, wrap the kerchief about our head, take food, chew a bit of this or that, and when the work of this is done we stand and ask, "Is it yet noon?" Noon has already long come. This is as it is in the hours before noon. From it may be known how pass the hours after noon. So one day is over. How do a hundred years differ from it? There is only sadness when we think of it. Where can joy be found? I ever marvel that people say, "How old is that one this year? How many are his heaped years?" —What is this "How many"? They are the heaped years. Can anyone bring them back and count them? Can anyone see that which is past and gone? It is gone. Even as I finish this very sentence the time which has passed before it is gone. Sorrow is this to the heart!

Of all joys nothing brings more joy than friendship and the most joyful part of friendship is quiet talk together among friends. Who can deny this? Yet it has not always been easy for me to gain this companionship. Sometimes the wind blows and it is cold; sometimes rain falls and the road is muddy; sometimes I am ill; sometimes when I go to seek my friends they are away and I miss them. At such times I feel I am in prison.

I have only a little poor land. I plant for the most part grain for wine. I cannot drink much wine myself, but when my friends come they like to drink it. My door is near a river and on its banks lie the deep shadows of beautiful trees. There my friends gather and stand about and sit down and walk as they please. I have only four old women servants to cook rice and vegetables and such dishes. The others are but children; large and small, there are ten odd of us, although the young ones can at their best but run about for us and greet guests and escort them when they go or bring in the cards of those who come. When they are idle, men- and maid-servants, I teach them to make brooms and to weave mats—brooms to sweep the floors and mats for my friends to sit upon.

When my friends are all come there should be sixteen of us but there are not many days when all can come. Yet except on days of great winds or of mighty rains, there are few days when none come. Usually six or seven gather together each day. When my friends are come they do not necessarily drink wine; if they like to do so, they may, but they need not if it is not their wish— each man to his own heart. We do not depend on wine for our happiness. Conversation is our delight. What we talk of is not the affairs of the nation. This is because not only do I feel it right to keep to my humble position, but also because our place is far distant from affairs of state, and political news is only hear-say and hearsay is never true and it is a waste of saliva to talk of it. Neither do we talk of people's sins. Men under Heaven have no sins originally and we ought not to malign them. What we speak of ought not to be such as to frighten persons. What I speak of I want people to understand easily; although after all they cannot understand, because I speak of that of which they have never heard and moreover every man is intent on his own affairs.

My friends are all contemptuous of high place. They are wide of heart and they understand everything and so what they discourse upon has its influence on all, and therefore when our day's talk is over, a matter is ended. Yet there is no one to write out our words, although sometimes I think I will put down what we have said in a book to leave to those who come after us. But until now I have not put it down thus. Why? When the desire for fame is over, the heart grows languid. We discourse for pleasure and the making of books is tiresome. Moreover, when we are gone no one will read what we have said. Or if perhaps this year we make the book the next year we will surely regret it.

In this book there are seventy chapters. When my friends were gone and I sat alone under the lamp, I wrote in idleness. At times when the wind blew and the rains fell and no one came then also did I write. Turning the book over and over in my mind it became at last such a habit to me that it was not necessary even to open my book and take up my brush and prepare something to write and read for my own diversion. For when at times I walked along my garden wall or at night covered by my quilt I lay awake, or when I picked up the end of my girdle and twisted it in my fingers, or when I stared unseeing at some object, at such times the stuff of which my book is made came crowding into my mind.

Some may ask thus: "You have said already that you did not make a book from your discourse with friends; why then have you now made this book alone?" But if this book is made it is without fame, and if it be not made no harm is done. When the heart is idle and there is nothing to force its will, whether the reader is good and learned or evil and unlearned, anyone can read this book. Whether the book is well done or not it is not important enough to worry over.

Alas, I was born to die! How can I know what those who come after me and read my book will think of it? I cannot even know what I myself, born into another incarnation, will think of it. I do not even know if I myself afterwards can even read this book. Why therefore should I care?

—Shih Nai-an of Tung-Tu

She remembers little else about that summer in America, except that they spent time with her husband's family and that she visited Carol often, always going alone, for no one else was interested enough in the child to visit her.

When autumn came she went often to New York, too, for she was news and everyone wanted to meet her. It was a different home in Ithaca now from the one she had endured on a previous trip, although once more in Ithaca, where her husband was to continue his studies. They settled into a comfortable house and while her husband went off to school, she was swept into the whirl of cocktail parties, luncheons, dinners, press conferences, speaking engagements, shows and concerts—much like the one in which she lives today. These, too, became a part of her life. One would think it might have been simple for her to move into New York City and live her own life. For anyone else it would have been simple, but not so for her, for she still had to have a home and children, however incomplete the relationship may have been. She helped her husband with his studies, especially languages, and took deep interest in her younger daughter's first experience in an American school.

In 1931 the Theater Guild had purchased the dramatic rights to *The Good Earth*. The dramatization was written by Owen Davis and his son.

When I returned to America I saw that play in rehearsal, and I knew it would fail. I remember that so well because it was a rehearsal quite near the opening day. I was discouraged because the American actors were so un-Chinese, even in the abrupt, ungraceful fashion in which they walked. I was used to the graceful movements of the Chinese. It was a shock to see these awkward Americans, dressed in Chinese clothes. Nazimova took the part of O-lan and she was very good.

The play failed on Broadway as I had known it would. But the real disaster was that the Theater Guild had acquired the motion picture rights with the play. They sold them for $100,000, which was a considerable sum in those days. Owen Davis received $25,-000, and I $25,000. It is all I have ever had from the motion picture *The Good Earth*.

About three or four months after the Foundation was established, I saw the film announced for the thousandth time or so that it has been shown on television. I wrote to Metro-Goldwyn-Mayer and said, "Your company has made millions of dollars on this picture. I have made $25,000. I am not asking anything for myself now, but perhaps your company would give some money to the Amerasian children." To this letter I never have had a reply. And every time that picture is shown on television I think of that unanswered letter with a deep bitterness.

To return to the days long ago, before the film was made, I remember having luncheon at Sardi's with a member of the firm of Metro-Goldwyn-Mayer. He asked me if I had any particular wishes about the motion picture, and I said I hoped they would use Chinese actors in the leading parts, to which he replied that this was impossible because of the American star system.

Then I returned to China, and the next I knew about the picture was when in the same year I met a representative of Metro-Goldwyn-Mayer, who came to see me and told me the picture could never be made in China since the Nationalist government was opposed to it because it portrayed the Chinese peasant instead of the Chinese intellectual.

He told me that his studio had been burned down in Shanghai, an act of sabotage, and that he was returning to the United States, which he did. He was on his way when, for some personal reason, which I think was not connected with the picture, he committed suicide. The next year Metro-Goldwyn-Mayer sent a large group of people—actors, producer, director and camera people—to China to choose a village and take local color scenes, the main part of the picture to be filmed there. I heard of all this through two sources, for I had nothing to do with it. I heard through the American Consul, John Davis, who was a friend of mine, and I read about it in the Chinese newspapers. It made a great deal of commotion.

The newspaper editorials said that they feared, in spite of every effort on the part of the Nationalist government to prevent it, that there would be dirty children, or an unfortunately sloppy woman in the picture and so give a bad impression of China. They finally allotted one village to the motion picture company, and they insisted that the women all wear clean jackets and flowers in their hair. They also objected to the water buffalo, which they thought would make China appear medieval, and they wanted to substitute a tractor, although at this time there were only two tractors in the whole of China and even so it would have been impossible to use a tractor in the small fields. I did not concern myself with the picture, however, since I had not been asked to do so. I heard no more of it for several years and I did not know whether Metro-Goldwyn-Mayer was proceeding with it. I knew there were some other unfortunate circumstances, for example, when their people got back to the United States and to Hollywood, they found the containers of the film were full of acid. Somebody had again sabotaged the picture. Of the total film as later shown, only twelve minutes was salvaged of the film taken in China, and the rest of it had all to be done over again in the United States—even the famous locust scene, filmed, I think, in Kentucky. The picture was dogged by bad luck and I think a good many people in Hollywood thought that there was a sort of Chinese witchcraft in action. Thalberg, who was a very good director, died during the producing, and the man who took his place was glad to have finished the picture and said so one night in his home after dinner, or so it was told to me, and he was standing by the chimneypiece where there was a heavy oil painting hanging on the wall. When he had spoken these words the picture fell down and almost crushed him.

I can't remember the exact year the film was completed. I do know that I was living in America. I refused to go to the premiere, because I was afraid I might not like the picture and would be in an embarrassing position if I were at the opening and had to say on the air what I thought of it. So I waited, and two days after it opened I went quite by myself to see the picture. I don't remember what the reviewers said about it. I doubt I read those reviews, because I didn't want to be influenced by them. But, as I said, I went alone to the theater and sat in the gallery and watched the picture. When it was over, I heard the comment of two men behind me as I got up to go. One of them asked the other how he liked the picture, and that one replied, "It's all right, but I'd rather see Mae West."

I never saw the picture again until decades later, and then I saw it once on television and found it too painful, so that I have never looked at it again.

Years later, when Katharine Hepburn was starring in *Dragon Seed,* I went to Hollywood with my family, not to see the new picture, but to make speeches for war relief. We were invited to spend one day on the set in the Metro-Goldwyn-Mayer studio. There I met again the original water buffalo, which had been brought from the Philippine Islands to play the part of the buffalo in the story. I was compelled to have my picture taken with the beast, and everyone thought I was very strange because I was afraid of it. But what they did not know was that all water buffaloes hate white people and go after them immediately, and since these animals are very big and very determined, it is something like being pursued by a rhinoceros, except it has two horns instead of one. A white person with any brains at all would certainly not enjoy standing near enough to one of these creatures to have a picture taken. I did pose for the photograph, but at a sensible distance.

And that is the end of *The Good Earth* film, so far as I am concerned. It was a tremendous success in Asia. I think the Chinese were somewhat stunned that Westerners could have produced such a picture. I might add that even today this picture is drawing record crowds in Japan. A famous Japanese director very much wished to make a Japanese version of *The Good Earth* a few years ago but Metro-Goldwyn-Mayer, continuing its greedy ways, refused to allow this. I am sorry, because I am sure the Japanese would have made a new and beautiful version of my book, and a new filming is needed.

Speaking of *Dragon Seed,* I remember two things with amusement during the day I spent on the set. While I admire Katharine Hepburn greatly as an actress, she is not Oriental and she insisted upon wearing a man's costume in this film, because she found the Chinese man's costume more becoming to her than the woman's costume. Also, I noticed that the hills in this film were terraced, in spite of the fact that there is no terracing in the area of Nanking, the locale of the story. This was amusing enough, but I noticed further that some of the terraces ran perpendicularly up and down the hill, instead of horizontally. This amazed me so much that I asked the reason why, and was told that the horizontal terracing was monotonous and that the perpendicular lines relieved the monotony. This and a number of other mistakes compelled me to ask why there was not a Chinese advisor to correct such things. The reply was that there was indeed a Chinese advisor. I sought him out immediately and asked him why he did not give better advice. To this he replied mournfully, "I do try to correct the mistakes, but they say, 'Oh, never mind—the Americans won't know the difference.' "

So much for these films! Other films were made of *China Sky,* a magazine story of which I thought very little, and later a very bad film, though replete with stars, entitled *Satan Never Sleeps.* This picture was in gorgeous color, which only emphasized its unfortunate aspects.

No, I remember one more film experience, which was memorable because it was no experience at all. Warner Brothers, with great enthusiasm, bought the film rights to my short novel *Letter From Peking,* but never made the film. I suppose the script lies dusty and forgotten in their files. I inquired about it a few years ago and was told that Vermont, its locale, seemed too remote and they were toying with the idea of making it in Santa Barbara. This idea sent me into fits of laughter, and I still laugh when I think of it.

On her frequent trips to New York from Ithaca in 1932 and 1933 she had luncheon often with her publisher, Richard J. Walsh, Sr. It did not take long for them to become friends. He was a charming and handsome man, well versed on many subjects, and she found him attractive.

The first sign of a personal relationship between them is found in a letter from her to him which he had kept among his belongings.

November 4, 1932.

Dear Mr. Walsh:

I did not think until after I had left you yesterday afternoon, how very selfish it was of me to leave the editing of that long speech upon you, who are already so busy. I cannot excuse myself —it seemed suddenly at that moment a relief to me not to see the thing again. But please don't hesitate to send it to me, if it will relieve you, if it is not too late.

At no time while I was with you either could I put into spoken words what it meant to me to have you come straight to me after the speech as you did and let me see your understanding. While I was talking I had the strangest and most horrible feeling of loneliness sweep over me, so that twice I could scarcely go on. Afterwards I felt quite cut off from everyone and utterly spent. So perhaps you can see it meant how very much to me to have you understand what it meant for me to have opened a door I had never opened before, and that in the presence of so many. I hated it very much, and yet I had to do it for the once. I am greatly glad it is over.

But your quick appreciation there is only part of your whole attitude to me which I should like you to know I value more than I shall ever tell you. I am coming to see that the ideal relation between a publisher and the writer whose life-stuff he considers worth presenting to the world is a very delicate and important one. It is of the utmost importance to me that I happened upon a man like you rather than upon another sort. I can see perfectly that had you not been what you are, I might have been dwarfed in my work in all sorts of imperceptible ways. As it is, I feel stimulated to do my very best. Sympathy and understanding appreciation are so delightful—I am not used to them—and it is for me wonderful—I mean, so far as my work is concerned, I have not since my mother died years ago lived among people who value such things or consider them of importance or who understand my supreme interest in writing.

But you must not let me impose on your sympathy, which I value so much, and take on yourself tasks I ought to do myself.

Miss Bucher tells me there is some luncheon—is it?—of publishers in January at which you wish me to speak. Of course I will do so with pleasure. Have you any suggested topic? I could speak on the contrast between Chinese and Western novels or some such literary subject, or on a particular phase of modern fiction in China, or on a more personal—that is, literary personal —subject. I should like you to suggest what you wish, and I will do what I can. You know the group and you know me, and can tell me the better what our common meeting ground would be.

You have won my warm regard.

Sincerely yours,

He wanted another book but was dismayed by *All Men Are Brothers*. He frankly told her he did not know if anyone would ever read a long Chinese novel. It would be an expensive book to publish and he was not at all sure he wanted it. But she had not written another book, except for *The Mother,* which she had put on the shelf and did not want to submit. Nevertheless, he knew that the public could not be allowed to forget Pearl Buck. He put together a collection of her shorter works and brought it out in 1933, entitled *The First Wife and Other Stories.* In the meanwhile, he moved straight toward his personal purpose and asked her to be his wife.

She smiles now when she tells the story.

"It was madness. I told him, 'I have a husband and children; you have a wife and children. It's unthinkable! I won't even discuss it!'

" 'Do you think I like it?' he answered. 'Here I am, a publisher, and I've fallen in love with my best-selling author! Stupid of me—' "

Their conversations continued until her husband received his Ph.D. in 1933 and it was time to return to China. She did not know what to do. She was greatly attracted to her publisher, but their separate lives were involved, and there was her ever-present public and the press ready to pass judgment. She thought she knew where happiness lay, but she had been reared in two strong cultures, both of which were against divorce. On one side there was the Christian influence, and she retains today a strong sense of right and wrong. On the other hand, she has the Asian philosophy that states a premise in a question: "What makes you think, O Soul, you have a right to be happy? You have your life to live and there is no promise of happiness."

When she was vacillating over the possibility of her second marriage she very nearly did not go through with it because her prospective husband expressed pity for his first wife.

"She is so delicate," he said of her, "she has been protected so much that she will suffer to a greater degree than you could ever suffer, because you are strong. We must consider her."

"To the contrary," she told him with characteristic intolerance, "she can suffer only to her capacity. Her capacity is small and so she will suffer little, while I on the other hand, with my large capacity, can suffer enormously. If you are so worried about how she will suffer, you had better stay married to her! I shall go back to China!"

In this divided mind when she decided to return to China and leave her publisher in America, she went back through Europe with her husband and child. It was on board ship from Naples to Bombay that she told him of her dilemma. She has told me that she remembers it as yesterday.

" 'I don't want to hurt anyone,' I told him. 'But let me have a year in which to find out what I want to do with my life. Just one year with no promises, no ties, a year of complete freedom, will you?'

"He was taken by surprise. 'I thought I had made a success of our marriage,' he said. 'Have I ever stopped you from doing what you wanted to do?'

" 'No, never,' I said honestly."

When they arrived in Nanking she began to think at length about what she had done and what she would do in her year. If anyone had asked her then, I am sure she would have insisted that she intended to spend the rest of her life in China. When we were in Nevada together not long ago, she said:

"Divorce is such a horrible thing. It's so final and so rending. It destroys everything—it's like death. All those years a man and woman have spent together are lost. They can never be recovered.

It is all finished! I didn't know whether I could go through it. Besides, I wasn't sure I wanted to."

Such was the quandary she was in. She had not begun a new book, although she knew it would be about the grandson of Wang Lung. She knew the story but she could not work, for her life was too undecided and everything about her reflected this indecision. Upon this scene one day her publisher arrived. He had followed her to China. She has told me that their conversations were always along the same line.

" 'This is useless,' he said. 'You are not happy and I am not happy. You know you miss me and I miss you. This is absurd!'

" 'I don't know,' I insisted, 'I don't know what I'll do.' "

He stayed for a while in China and then he was gone.

While in China that last time, after her return in 1933, she thought at length about a side of American life she had not seen before. Crowds had greeted her everywhere she went and she was invited to speak many times to different groups on a variety of subjects. And while she was definitely impressed by this great country of hers, all of her impressions were not favorable. She became acutely aware, for example, of racial prejudice, a shock from which she has not fully recovered even today. As an illustration, I include a letter from her written at that time to an American newspaper:

Distance is an invaluable aid sometimes to clear vision and space is the great lens. So I found last year when I was away from China, the land where I had lived all my life. I had become so used to wars that they had come to seem almost a natural and necessary way of settling a dispute over a seat in government, or for the possession of a fertile stretch of country. I had grown accustomed to banditry so that I came to think it a natural result of poverty and social injustice. Flood and its consequence of famine I had come to accept as an act of fate, scarcely to be averted.

But when I went out of these conditions into a world where war is increasingly being thought of, at least, as anarchy, to be prevented by intelligent settlement of disputes, I began to see that war really is a stupid, endless quarrel and settles nothing.

When I found bandits treated as common criminals, arrested by police and put in jail, I realized that banditry is not a necessary result even of poverty, and is not to be accepted; when I saw floods anticipated and controlled, and famines averted, I realized that forethought and scientific knowledge, and not fate, are the means whereby even natural catastrophes may be averted or alleviated. I gained perspective, in other words, upon problems which had seemed too large to be solved so long as I was involved in them.

Now from the eastern half of the world where I live I look through this same clarifying lens of distance, back to my own country, America. I have always been proud to be an American. I would not, if I could, belong to another people. I am not an internationalist, if by being an internationalist one means doing away with the valuable individuality of nationalism. I believe in international cooperation for the solution of international life. But I want to see my country and all other countries retain always the valuable peculiar quality which makes each one what it is, which stamps it different from every other. I repeat, I have been glad to be American.

And yet, I would not be a true patriot, I think, if I were to excuse or condone in any slightest degree the incredible news which has come flashing across the cables even to this far China of the lynchings which have taken place in my country within very recent months and even weeks. Those who were lynched were my countrymen. That their race was not mine makes no difference—they were my countrymen. Because they were my countrymen, they had every right, no matter what their crime, to the privileges of the laws of our land. Their race, their crimes, have nothing to do with the question of their rights. When they were lynched they were treated with hideous and barbarous injustice. One receives with equanimity such news from savage islands or from the few remaining hinterlands of the world. To receive such news from my country, from America, my country which calls itself civilized, from which missionaries and philanthropists have been sent in such numbers to other countries and peoples, is inexplicable and to me heartbreaking.

I am quite aware that there are those among my countrymen who will say I do not understand the race problem. I reply, I do understand it. I have lived my life among colored races, a white child, a white girl, a white woman, with two daughters. There is no aspect of the race problem which I have not faced and completely understood. I have never seen any aspect, I cannot conceive of any aspect, which could extenuate the savage bestiality of lynching.

I understand, too, mobs and what mobs can do. Unceasingly I am grateful for the experience of having known personally what colored mobs can do when they are inflamed against white people. It makes me more sure that I can be nothing but the more bitterly ashamed where mobs of my own race behave in such a way, and this against one defenseless creature.

Do I know the crime, I am asked, of which those lynched have been guilty? Again I reply steadfastly, it makes no difference to me. If the assault had been against me, against my daughter, I would do my utmost to prevent the criminal from being lynched, not only to save him, for after all, he is only one, but to prevent that more serious, more terrifying, more dangerous crime, the spectacle of a civilized, even intelligent group of people returned suddenly to primitive savagery in their thoughts and actions, and by this return dragging us all back again, down, down the long uphill road we humans have come from the beasts we once were to the men and women we hope to be upon this earth. That poor one matters so little. It matters so much that all of us, even here in China, suffer shame, humiliation, depression at the knowledge that again the machinery of civilization has failed, and in a country, especially, to which China looks for guiding achievement.

For I as an American in China am now ashamed before the Chinese. I speak to them less hopefully of the inevitable passing of their barbarous civil wars, because in my own country is this subtle civil war, breaking out into such fearful open murder. I am less confident of their schemes of democracy, since I see that my own country, where the democratic theory has been most adequately put into practice, can yet allow, year after year, such recrudescence of the lowest, least democratic, least intelligent form of tyranny, the tyranny of the beast over the brain. I shall not be proud again until my countrymen make lynching a major crime. For to break the laws of justice, not only to a single human being, but to all human beings, by an act of such complete lawlessness as lynching, is infinitely worse than the killing of one man by another because it is the murder of one by many, and we are all implicated inextricably in such crime. I feel myself shamefully implicated. Sitting here at my desk in my quiet home, pausing to look over peaceful Chinese fields and hills, I am degraded.

So it seems to me today, watching my country across the clear distance of the ocean, remembering the surprise and cynicism I saw upon certain Oriental faces only yesterday when they read what my countrymen did to my fellow citizens.

I shall not walk proudly now for a while.

The attic room no longer held her. She wanted to get back to work, to write books she wanted to write, but she could not concentrate. Carol was too often in her thoughts then and she decided to go again to America for a visit. Preparations were made and she took her adopted daughter with her, said good-bye to her husband for the summer, and sailed for America. In Yokohama, to her surprise, her publisher appeared and boarded the same ship.

It was a new beginning, on her part, of many months of searching for decision; on his, of determined patience. She rented a house on Park Avenue in New York and spent the winter of 1934-1935 there, alone save for her daughter and the housekeeper. It was while living there that she took the first step toward decision. She would buy a house in the country and make an American home. She might live there alone—or she might not.

She was familiar with the countryside of Pennsylvania from going through it to see Carol, so she knew the type of house she wanted and the location. First, her house must be made of stone or brick, not wood. Houses made of wood were not considered permanent by the Chinese, for they were too vulnerable to fire. And she must have land, a lot of land, for she had been accustomed to space in China. With these points in mind, she went to a large national real estate concern with offices in New York and asked if they had such a farm in Pennsylvania. They had many and she spent some time going over photographs—then she saw a folder. On the front page was a photo about the size of a postage stamp, but she could see that the house was made of fieldstone, and stood on a slight rise. She did not want to be on a high hill, but the floods in China had taught her the value of being on high ground. It had a brook and a pond and it was very American, and the land upon which it stands once belonged to the brother of the Founder of Pennsylvania.

"I'll take that one," she said, like a child buying candy.

Some years later she wrote of that decision and of the house:

Bucks County had been here in Pennsylvania, U.S.A., for some two hundred years, but I did not know it when I was looking for a home in my own country, after half a lifetime in Asia. No, not the name but the houses were the charm. I chanced to drive one day through a lovely region of rolling hills, rich fields, woods and rippling streams, not unusual, yet the houses in this landscape were unusual. They were built of fieldstone, the color of the golden brown earth, shot through with shades of paler gold and touches of crimson. The roofs were slate and the walls were thick, and near the house there was always a great red barn upon which were designs in white. Where was I? I was reminded of vast old houses in Germany, of the south of France, and country houses in England.

I paused at a gas station. "Please tell me where I am," I said.

The attendant, a cheerful pink-faced boy, looked at me with suspicion. Was I all right?

"Bucks County, Pennsylvania," he said. "But I ain't never had nobody ast me that before. Mostly they knows."

The accent was unfamiliar, but I identified it later as Pennsylvania Dutch. I had heard of the region. I drove on, my eyes alert now, for I passed one beautiful house after another. I had seen no such houses elsewhere in the United States. They stood as solid as castles, facing south as the Chinese houses do, and surrounded by big trees and flowering shrubs.

I had been looking for a house to make into home—my first American home. I wanted not only a home but a hill, a brook, mountains not too far, and the sea within reach. New York had to be thought of, too, for that was my business center, and I had always loved Philadelphia, because it reminds me of London, so I wanted to be near Philadelphia, too. But the house was the thing. I did not want a new house. I had lived in old countries and in houses where generations had lived before me. I wanted again to live in such a house, my family fitting into the past as well as the present and future, part of the human stream, this time of my own people. An old house then, one at least a hundred years old, one that meant history, one where ancestors had lived and died. I had considered a house in New England, a lovely place, and since England is a beloved land in our family, some of us even born there, I wandered about in New England. Yes, its houses are old and beautiful, furnished with mahogany and antique objects from my other part of the world, curios brought back by early sea captains. New England houses are enchanting and often elegant but—well, I have never lived in a wooden house. Our houses in China were of solid brick with tiled roof, or they were of mountain adobe and deep thatch. I felt strangely unsafe in a wooden house where a misplaced match or a dropped cigarette could cause a holocaust. Perhaps memories of Japan crept in unawares. The fragile wooden houses there are built for earthquake, easy to escape from, but they burn in a few moments to small heaps of ash.

I spent hours that day wandering in Bucks County, stopping at one house after another, sometimes merely on the road, sometimes invited to come inside. I found hospitable folk, proud of their homes and farms. The houses were of two kinds, in general, the farmhouses, built by early settlers from South Germany, and manor houses built by the early English. William Penn was a large-hearted man and he made Pennsylvania a refuge for people from many countries, but Englishmen and Germans were the builders. Their houses still stand solidly upon the American earth, white marble date-stones set into the huge chimneys, announcing at least a century of life. All of the houses have fireplaces and big attics and good cellars, thick walls and many-paned windows and floors of wide pine or oak boards. Above all, they breathe the atmosphere of home. Not every house can be made into a home. Sometimes a house resists every such effort.

There was no time that day for further search, but I had my region. Somewhere here, two hours from the city, was the house that waited for me. I never thought, however, that I would find it so quickly, on a leaflet in a real estate office in New York, a stamp-sized picture of a house standing on a hill by a brook, against a background of trees. There my home was. I recognized it immediately, without ever having seen it, one hot July morning, when I chanced to stop at that particular office for no reason whatever, and I had never before stopped at any such office and never did again.

The next day I drove to the house and found it exactly as I knew it would be, a stone house, facing south, set on a hill at the foot of which a brook flowed. On one side of the house was a big black walnut tree, on the other a big maple, behind it the woods, and beyond it the hills.

"I want this house," I told the real estate agent.

"Better look a little more," he advised. "There's others nice, too."

I looked half-heartedly, knowing it was no use, a waste of time. I had found my house and I came back to it and paid my money down—a reasonable sum in those days, and the house had no telephone, running water or electricity. But these were incidentals, only necessary mechanics. The house was there, fireplaces big enough to stand in, wide oak floors, enormous chimneys, many windows, a farmhouse deep through the middle and easily added to, as the family grew. There was the look of home about it, too, although, the agent told me, no one had lived in it for seventeen years. It had been a home from its beginning. On the main chimney a white marble inset gave the date, 1835, and beneath it we found the names when we opened the panel of a door and found penciled upon its unpainted surface a legend:

"I, Joseph Housekeeper, made and worked this door. August 12, 1835, I married my true love, Magdalena."

Time passed and we made it into our home. I have read many books by disappointed city dwellers who moved to the country— books that tell of the difficulties and annoyances of country living, books that end by the people moving back to the conveniences of the city. I can only say that none of these difficulties has been mine. The house accepts everything we give it. It grew, it became warm and comfortable and colorful. The dark beams drink in the colors of curtains and carpets and bowls of flowers and fruit. The furniture is robust. We cannot use mahogany and lace. The house is too strong for delicate graces. We have lived here now for more than a quarter of a century, and my roots have grown deep.

The neighborhood suits the house. They are strong good people of kind heart.

Yet my house is only one of many, some of them much more handsome and more stately. My house looks well worn now. Dozens of children, my own and others, have raced through its halls and rooms on their way back and forth to the swimming pool and barn, not to mention the more mundane business of school and office. I cannot redecorate, even now when the children are grown, for they make great outcry that the house must remain exactly as it has always been for their children. I enjoy my friends' houses, therefore, those which are more carefully planned than mine, more beautiful in detail, although loyally I continue to like my own best. They all have the same atmosphere, the feeling of permanence which only age can give, the noble air of satisfaction in having lived largely, in space as well as grace.

We even have a ghost, as all solid old houses in our region have. They are seldom the ghosts of beautiful girls, I regret to say. Ours is the ghost of a stubborn Pennsylvania Dutchman, known as Devil Harry, and famous for his tricks and ways of getting ahead in the world. He walks, an old neighbor told me, every Christmas Eve, from our huge red barn down to the stone bridge over the brook. Is it true? I am not a seer of ghosts myself, though I wish I were, for it would add interest to life, but my neighbor is—or was, poor soul, for he has become a ghost himself at the age of seventy-seven, which I am told is the best age at which to become a ghost.

One can believe anything, as a matter of fact, about our old house. The walls are so thick, the cellars so vast and dim, the attics spacious, the beams of oak and well-nigh a foot in diameter—at least the heavy thunder beam that runs east and west through the whole house. Windows, as I said, are many-paned, and the glass is old and iridescent and the doors are the Dutch doors, the upper half swinging free from the lower half, a fine way to keep toddlers in the house and pigs and fowl out. The meadows spread gently down the slopes of the hills and fat Guernsey cows munch at the grass until the sun rises high and they lie in the shade of the sycamore.

A sycamore belongs with every Pennsylvania stone house, too, not the dapper white trees of the city, but great old gnarled crooked sycamores, tents of big green leaves in the summer and ghostly old shapes in the winter, their branches twisted and angular, the seedballs swinging at every tip of twig. They grow fast. The sycamore we planted at the edge of our terrace more than twenty years ago is a foot and a half in diameter. The bark peels off like a snake's skin every summer and reveals the satin-soft white new bark beneath.

The stately homes of Pennsylvania—yes, that is what they are. They are not elegant like the houses on plantations in the South, nor do they have the white beauty of the mansions in New England. But they endure. They were built for generations and for eternity, in the days when those two words seemed certainties. They have a noble history, whether they sheltered a farmer's family or the sons of William Penn and their progeny. They are solid and strong, and within their rooms, cool in summer and warm in winter with sunshine and fires, one finds shelter and peace for body and mind—even today, and perhaps tomorrow. As long as any house made with hands endures, these will endure, against time and against destruction.

The need for a home has always been and is today one of the strongest motivating forces of her life. And a home has a definite place in this busy life of hers, but, master of her being that she is, she keeps it in place. Her home, wherever or whatever it has been, is not the focal point of her existence, and yet it is that place to which she always returns. It is a center of life, many lives, and not only hers. It was important to her husband and is important to her children, but it has never absorbed her. She must know it is there, a haven, but her life itself centers about her, wherever she may be, and no single building, or for that matter no single country, is large enough to hold her whole interest alone or forever.

The foregoing quotation is from an article written for a real estate magazine in Bucks County, Pennsylvania, some years ago, and I find it necessary to correct a minor point here in a biography, where all things must be factual. She has a habit, when writing anything about her life, of eliminating all personal events that would require explanation. For example, she writes that it was the real estate agent who urged her to look at other houses.

This is not quite true. When she announced that she was going to look at a house, her publisher-suitor declared, "I must go with you. You are trying to set yourself up without me and I won't have that. If you must buy a home, then I must be a part of it. Besides, you don't know anything about houses, and you will get cheated."

It was he who made her look at other farms, though she had determined the first one was hers. It is a matter of history now that she bought it, and the work of modernizing—yet keeping the beauty and charm of the old—was begun. Electric lights had to be brought in and modern plumbing installed, for it was a simple old farm structure. Her publisher persisted with his talk of divorce and marriage and at last she agreed, early in 1935, to go to Reno. They knew well what they faced. Reporters would not be kind, publicity would be unfortunate. Elaborate plans were laid for her to disappear from the New York scene with one name and return to it some weeks later with another. Utmost secrecy was necessary. They planned to have no news break until all was done and thus all unpleasantness would be over with at one time, instead of prolonged through six weeks. This attitude is also typical of her now, thirty years later. Those of us who know her well know that she never under any circumstances procrastinates. If there is a task she must do which she finds particularly unpleasant, she tackles it first, deeming that the more quickly she gets it out of the way the less discomfort it will cause her. To her, thinking about an action is equally as exhausting as performing it, and therefore, energy being her most valuable asset, she always strives to use it wisely.

For these reasons I have found it somewhat difficult to understand her hesitation over a divorce and remarriage for such a long period of time. I expressed my puzzlement to her as we drove to Vermont one Christmas for our holiday. I remembered the time that we had had alone together the previous Christmas, when we had discussed Dolly Wei and some parts of her childhood, and hoped for the same opportunity this year in which we could discuss the years 1933, 1934 and 1935. We vowed that somehow we would find time during this week to get past my stumbling block of the marriage. I had spent much of the preceding year reading her personal correspondence files as well as all the cor-

respondence with her publishers during those years. Indeed, for
two years I had read nothing but Pearl Buck's books and was
beginning to feel saturated. There were still those areas in her
life, however, that remained a mystery and I knew of no better
way to get the story told than to have her tell it in her own words.
With this in mind I had carefully packed our tape recorder together with the gift packages and various other things necessary
for a week away from home.

We arrived at the mountain house and there was the usual
necessary hustle and bustle of settling in for a holiday, so that at
least four days went by before we managed to turn to our tape
recorder. We arose early on this morning, determined to set about
our work. With much excitement, her three daughters had bun-
dled themselves off for skiing, and we sat together in the privacy
of the big work area in a corner of her bedroom. The familiar
scene before me lent much to the mood. The window overlooks
the terrace and stretching below it is the valley, and above it Stratton Mountain rises on the horizon. It was unusually warm and
the snow was already beginning to thaw, much to the sorrow of
everyone concerned with skiing.

She settled herself comfortably on the rose-colored chaise
longue, and the sunshine streamed through the windows as she
began to speak:

It is very difficult for me to think in terms of time or the exact
calendar year. I suppose this is because my life has always been
divided between the Chinese calendar, which is in the four
thousand six hundreds, and the Christian, which is in the one
thousand nine hundreds. In the year 1933, when I returned to
China from India and the colonial countries, I still had no idea
of leaving China, except that I saw in the far distant future the
possibility of Communist rule, in which case all Americans would
have to leave. I didn't really face that then. I thought only in terms
of my personal life and whether I would make the tremendous
change in marriage and what I would do when I left China. I
don't make up my mind quickly. I think and think. And that
is what I did, weighing many events, one against the other. I was
not ready to make a final decision and I remember that [when she
went to America again in 1934] I left the house in Nanking

intact, just as it was. I thought only in terms of spending the summer in the United States in order to be near my retarded child. I had left her for three years before, and this proved to be very bad for her. She had developed symptoms of discontent which made her difficult to care for because she could not understand why I didn't come to see her. She did not realize that I was three thousand miles away across the sea. So I had decided that while I would spend every summer in the United States in order to be near her, I would spend my winters in China. That gave me a reason to postpone any decision, and so I didn't change the house but left everything exactly as it was. I remember leaving that day and thinking, "Well, I'll be back in three months, probably." The three of us, my younger daughter, my secretary and I, started across the sea and I really had every intention of returning. I doubted that I would make the radical change, perhaps because I had lived so long alone in my inner life that I didn't realize how much the companionship of a husband could mean. I have always had a warm place in my heart for that house because it was comfortable, and I had made it a home. It had a lovely garden and a beautiful view out toward the mountain. We sit here this morning in Vermont and look at a mountain, too, and it occurs to me now that perhaps this place satisfied an instinct of the past, which made it more comforting to me then to go up to my attic room and shut the door and look out on the double-crested mountain of Nanking.

Richard Walsh had been in Manchuria since we had decided to make no decision, and we met unexpectedly in Japan and traveled to the United States on the same steamer. I was still sufficiently undecided so that in the autumn I did not return to China. Instead, I took Malvina Hoffman's house in New York for the winter, a delightful place, which satisfied my interests in sculpture. She had many beautiful pieces which she kept there. She was away in Europe all year and my daughter and the housekeeper and I lived in New York through that winter. Those were the months of decision. The more I thought of going back to China and to my old life there, the more impossible I realized it was. Because of the sense of coming change in China, I knew it could never be the same China again. Moreover, the circumstances of my life and the success that had come to me separated me. It shouldn't have, but it had to, for the missionary group where the university was situated was rather narrow. I knew that I had to step out into the world even if I had to do it alone, and I still didn't know whether I was going to do it. I thought if I were to make the transition from Asia to the world I didn't know in the West, that I must have a house. I had never really owned a house, and I thought that if I had one of my own I could from that vantage point put down roots and make better decisions. Also, I wished to continue with my work and it seemed logical that I have a place where I could write well and feel at home. So that was how the house in Pennsylvania came to be bought.

I still think that I was so slow to make up my mind about marriage, if we are to talk about that, because the marriage I had had never meant enough to me to convince me that any marriage would mean much to me. Now that doesn't mean that I didn't have deep and long friendships with men, because I did, but I had found more outside of marriage than within it. Therefore I questioned very much whether marriage itself was valuable enough and would be the right step for me. I know I was dedicated to my work—not dedication so much as that I wasn't happy if I wasn't working. As I said, I had lived in a solitary sort of fashion all my life and I wasn't sure I needed marriage. All through that winter I was undecided.

A House Divided was published in 1935, so I must have written it in 1933 and 1934. Its title is very interesting because, if you remember, in that book the chief character leaves his country, China, and goes to Japan. When I went to America, that feeling of separation and division undoubtedly was the feeling out of which I wrote and though the story was entirely different from my story, some of the emotions perhaps were the same.

Then came the decision to go to Reno. It was a difficult decision because, as I said, I wasn't convinced—I never have been convinced—about marriage. I question very much whether marriage is a good relationship for me. I believe in relationships and I don't think people can do without them, but I don't know whether the demands of marriage are very wise for a person like myself to undertake. I enjoy housekeeping. I don't do any of the work myself, but I enjoy having a house—but then one can have that anyway, without marriage. I think perhaps the inconvenience of not being married in our society made me realize that I'd better get the legalities over with for, difficult as it was, it was the only practical way of living.

In short, after we had decided that we would be happier together, the only sensible thing to do was to get married. It was very difficult for him because while he was separated from his wife and he had grown children—yet I was his top author and traditionally a publisher doesn't marry his top author if he can avoid it. It has happened, but it is not considered a wise step. I certainly heeded the feelings I had and ignored the . . . what shall I say? . . . the nonsense of the interference in one's private life. I have the Chinese point of view—I remember one time, when Chiang Kai-shek was divorcing his several wives and marrying Madame Chiang Kai-shek, that I heard a conversation between a Westerner and a Chinese, a friend of mine. This Westerner said, "How will this affect Chiang Kai-shek's standing as a leader if he divorces his three legal wives to marry this one new wife?" With great dignity, my Chinese friend, who was a gentleman of the old school, said, "It will not affect him the slightest, because this is his personal matter. It is not the business of the public to inquire why he divorces three women in order to marry one. It is his inside-the-house business." I think I have that attitude. But I realize that in the United States one has no such privacy. At least, once one's name becomes known, there is no such thing as privacy, and, while I'd always done exactly what I pleased, made whatever friendships I liked, traveled with my friends as I wished, still it's a little different in the United States. This is a very curious-minded country. We like to know about our famous citizens and their private lives. It became a matter of convenience, therefore, that we had to take the final step. So we got it over with as fast as possible. Those weeks in Reno I remember with the utmost distaste, because Reno is a strange place in which to spend six weeks. The gambling and the nonsense that go on there, however, didn't really sink very deeply into me. What I learned to love was that Western country. I bought an automobile, for I had learned to drive before when I was in America, and I spent my time driving all over those deserts of Nevada. I had the mother of my husband-to-be with me. We were in the same hotel and we took as many trips as possible. I learned to love the desert. We went up to that strange city which was then deserted—Virginia City. It was a ghost of a town indeed. I learned about America through the history of our West. I don't recommend Reno nevertheless! I think divorce is an undignified proceeding, but I don't know how it can be avoided. I think a divorce should be easy and quick and I think marriage should be made difficult.

We were married that same afternoon the divorce was granted. I think I've given quite a detailed description of that occasion in *My Several Worlds*. I remember the morning of June 11, 1935, partly because I see the picture of it—I always see events in pictures. The one that catches my attention is the moment that I came out on the steps of the courthouse when it was all finished, out into the glittering sunshine. The desert sunshine is like no sunshine on earth, anyway. I remember I had on a white suit and hat, and Richard Walsh met me at the foot of the steps. He had come into the courthouse, of course, because he had been getting his divorce in a different room. I didn't know anything about that and I tried not to think about it. I ought to say that I knew his first wife. I visited in their home and in a curious way we were friendly. We were not exactly friends, because we were totally different people. She was not an unkind person, but rather sweet, and I think she understood that the separation between her and Richard Walsh had come long before. The truth of the matter is that there had been another woman between her and me in Richard Walsh's life. She knew about that situation, too, and so whatever break there had been was made long before I appeared on the scene. I don't think she knew the extent to which the relationship between Richard Walsh and this other woman had gone. Indeed, in a sense that relationship was a stumbling block to me, too. He was handsome and attractive to women, and when he recognized that this early marriage had not been a satisfactory one to him, it was inevitable that there be other matters, other people. That didn't trouble me, except that it was an added complication. But he told me that he'd never really been in love before, and once the final love strikes it does change many things in life. I don't think we ever discussed our past lives. I never talked about mine to him nor asked him about his. Frankly, I didn't care. I thought we were two people who were just as new in our approach to each other as Adam and Eve in the garden, let's say, and what had gone before really didn't matter. And then I had been reared in an entirely different culture from his, so I accepted naturally the facts of life much more simply and easily than they are accepted here. The definition of sin in different countries is interesting, because sin in China is not the same as sin in this country. I've grown up rather ambivalent, perhaps, in these matters.

Anyway, Richard was there waiting, that day in Reno. We were married and went by car to Lake Tahoe, which chiefly I remember as being bitterly cold. When we got there I immediately wanted to go swimming, which we did in the coldest water I ever felt in my life, though it was sunset. There was a porch on our cottage, and I remember the gorgeous sunset and the stars. That was a very blissful and happy time. It was such a relief to have made up my mind and to have the future clear. But it hadn't been easy, because I had not been happy in my first marriage. It was not an active unhappiness—let's say that I understood very well my first husband's good qualities. I don't think we ever quarreled. I don't remember quarreling. It was just a basic difference. There was really nothing to quarrel about. I had early learned to adjust myself to life and to live my life no matter where I was, so that while there was a great lack, there was no animosity. I still remember the last moment I saw him. He came to see me and to discover what could be done to save the situation. I realized that it couldn't be saved and the strange thing is that that kind of finality can take place without any anger. There was no anger. We were sorry, but I knew that it had to be. I couldn't go on. I have never forgotten that day, and though I have never seen him since and don't really care to, there is no memory of anger, only great compassion on my part because I realized that if I couldn't give that man love he was being deprived of something, too. Naturally, I hoped he would find it in another marriage, which I think he has. He married a very attractive Chinese woman who was his private secretary, and I think it's been a good marriage.

I feel compelled at this point to elaborate somewhat on the difficulties of her first marriage before leaving them forever. I am told that if a biographer has been led to draw his own conclusions he must then report all of the facts that have led to these conclusions in order that the reader may be sufficiently well informed to be led to conclusions of his own. Because of the hurt that I know she has suffered over this divorce I have insisted that all of the facts be well reported in an effort to set the record straight, so to speak. The only thing in life of which she is really afraid is evil and anonymous gossip. It is without logic or reason and attacks when one is not aware of the attack. For example, a friend once told her that she was at a women's luncheon and a woman who had never seen Miss Buck and did not know her said, "I do not like Pearl Buck because she divorced her first husband when she found he was going blind." The enormity of this complete lie might simply amuse her if she had no children. Her children know nothing of that former life of hers, however, and if when she is gone they hear such a lie they can only say, "I know she could not do such a thing." But they will have no facts, because she has told them none, hating to burden their minds with shadows. I think the facts should be known, therefore, and here they are.

She married her first husband at an age when she was mentally and biologically ready for marriage: that is, romantic, idealistic, and twenty-four years old, or nearly. She was extremely lonely in a Chinese mission station without a companion of her own race or age and among a group of grim quarrelsome missionaries. She withdrew into her own dreams. Her mother was ill and she was with her a great deal, caring for her night and day. At this strategic point there came into her life an agricultural missionary, not a religious missionary, for he had no such tendency in his nature, but he was young, strong and good-looking. He asked her to marry almost at once, and she said she would, although, strangely, at the moment of his proposal she had the only super-natural experience of her life, she has told me. She heard, after he had finished speaking, and before she replied, a voice saying perfectly clearly to her, "This is wrong for you, you will be sorry if you do this." But not believing, she went on. She supposes it was her subconscious saying to her what she knew but did not realize.

She was married for seventeen lonely, unhappy years. She doesn't think the marriage itself was unsuccessful because she determined not to allow it to be so. She saw almost at once that she had made a mistake but set her mind to have as good a home life as she could in spite of it. She kept a pretty and comfortable home, within limitations. She tells me that it seemed the only thing he liked to do was to "collect data." He enjoyed finding out about Chinese farm implements and ways of farming. This seemed to her excellent, for no one really knew much about Chinese farming. Together they began collecting data.

Early in the years he began to complain of not being able to bear light. He wore dark glasses always, and she grew concerned. She made shades for the windows out of Chinese cotton cloth, for they could not buy shades in China. As time went on and he grew worse rather than better, she began reading the books he had to use for his work and telling him the contents. This was in addition to her own teaching.

She told me that he felt it was foolish to do what she wanted to do for their retarded child, so she met all expenses. Had it not been for her the child would have been put into a state institution and forgotten as soon as possible.

His eyes continued to bother him, and as soon as she could pay for it, she had him go to a great eye specialist at Johns Hopkins. He had been examined many times and the verdict always was that nothing wrong could be found. She felt this great oculist could discover the trouble. The oculist accepted no patients at this time because of his age, but he had an interest in her books and said he would make an examination. He kept the patient under close observation for a week, made every test, and at the end of the week called her in and said to her privately, "There is nothing wrong with his eyes. The trouble springs from the desire to monopolize your attention and to avoid the trouble of reading. He has never really mastered reading. Ignore him when he complains, gradually take away the shades at the windows, and be too busy to read. He monopolizes you." This she did and his eyes gradually grew better, and then she made up her mind she could no longer endure the marriage.

She has written:

"I have been able to make another home, to gather together my darling children, to provide all I dreamed of for the retarded child. It is better that I have been able to do it alone and I would continue to keep silent except that the malevolence of unknown persons cannot be foreseen. If at any time it slanders my former marriage I simply say that for eighteen years I gave all I could, spiritually, and materially, and for eighteen years received nothing in return. I say this without bitterness. I made the best of it until I could no more. When the time came I left him still young, strong, able to do what he would do, provided well with money and free of all obligation to me or my children. I have the satisfaction of knowing that I helped him all I could. It is over and on my part honorably."

And I repeat at the close of this section what I have heard her say many times, "Here endeth the first lesson." So let us get back to the second marriage.

After the trip to Lake Tahoe, we started home. We went by train, because Richard had left the car somewhere near New York, and then we drove to the house I had bought, and we made it into our home. I've been thinking all morning—oh, I've thought about this before—that while I keep talking about my living alone, and that I've done things by myself, which is true, on the other hand, I don't know what I would have done without the important men in my life. There have always been important men and there's always been one especially, and still is, for my real friendships are very lasting.

Most men will say that there has always been a woman behind them. I can say there has always been a man behind me. So I would like to say here that I don't think I would have written the books I have, or have grown into the person that I think I am, or reached the success in my life that I have reached, or have the sense of vitality and potential growth that I still have if it were not for the affection, love, or whatever one wants to call it, that has been given to me from men. I am grateful, for I think these friendships bring something new into my life and have contributed a great deal to my growth. And I hope I have contributed something, too, to them.

I didn't write any big books in 1935. I was involved in adjusting myself to the American scene, in making a home of the house and getting acquainted with my husband. There's quite a difference between seeing a person a few hours out of a day and being with him twenty-four hours a day. It takes a much greater adjustment, especially if one is used to hours alone as I was. In my first marriage I was still alone and I could spend hours by myself.

That was a practical association, but in the case of a man like Richard Walsh one had a man who made great demands in marriage and who expected his demands to be met. And I delighted to give more. Nevertheless I couldn't devote myself to writing a big book that year. I don't know when I began to write again, but certainly during that first year I devoted myself to my marriage and to my country and getting used to American ways. That takes time and it takes devotion. I daresay that any articles I wrote during that time were only my local points of interest. I was interested in one thing after another. I was interested in seeing as much as I could of the United States, but time didn't permit digging deep, as one must when writing a big book.

The first two years in my country house I really worked, too, at the landscape of my house, to try to tame it. There was a brook, for example, that I wanted to guide through a different way to the pond. In China it could have been done, but not this brook! I remember I spent hundreds of dollars trying to build embankments to shape it. It was a mild brook during fair weather, but in rain it grew very sudden and swift and tore everything away. Finally I yielded to it and gave up. And that's the way it is today. I have retained the wildness and beauty of the countryside in which I live mainly by planting trees and making forests and cultivating the meadows. But it was a real struggle. Yet I couldn't have done anything wiser than buying a piece of land and a house. And I'm glad I bought a house that other Americans had lived in—an old house. That house has meant a great deal to many people and still does.

During this period then, from 1935 straight through until 1938 and the awarding of the Nobel Prize, she concentrated on studying the community life around her and familiarizing herself with these United States into which she had come to live. It must have been a strange experience, after forty years of life in a country such as China, and after seventeen years of marriage to a man such as her first husband, to find oneself confronted by the necessity of fitting into an entirely different set of circumstances—a new country, a new husband, a new community. Certainly it explains why there was no writing of any major importance during that period. I have come to realize that few people in the world have experienced her success and yet been left with such feelings of inferiority as she has. Perhaps inferiority is not quite the word I mean. She is well aware that she has a superior intellect, and that she is a superior author. Yet she suffers periodically from a lack of confidence that, to me, is almost inexplicable. Perhaps the only way it can be explained is to consider certain facts: for example, that her first and only birth child was retarded, for which I am sure she takes some blame; that her first marriage was a failure, for which I know she takes all of the blame; that she was criticized severely for her divorce and second marriage.

"No, no," she says here. "What you take to be a feeling of inferiority is the result of my Asian training, which teaches a woman to be quiet, persuasive, gentle, especially before men. This training was reinforced by my lordly father, who was convinced by birth and inheritance and Christian teaching that woman is subject to man."

Be all this as it may, certainly such experiences could strongly and deeply affect the confidence of anyone, at least for a period of time. Also, sometimes I wonder if she is not in awe of herself and of her own abilities. She considers the talent she has for writing a sacred trust and she is not always sure of her own ability to use it wisely. Perhaps this explains, too, the discipline she applies to her work. Whatever she does, she does with her whole heart, as is obvious when one views the results of her efforts.

In the early months of 1935 she worked, without pay, as consulting editor for her husband's publishing company. The following article, dated May 16, 1935, will give some insight into her feelings about the task of being an editor:

One of the interests of my life these days is a job—the job of being advisory editor of a publishing house. It is not only a job, it is an avocation, and more, it is a search. I suppose the hunting instinct is in everyone, to be satisfied by hunting something from golf balls to lions in Africa. As for me, I hunt books, and I know I am but one of many. In other editorial offices there are hundreds of others who hope, as I do, for the moment when we may pick up from the pile of manuscripts one which is a *book*. In the hope of that moment we read through thousands of typed pages, pages neatly typed and bound in a literary agent's covers, and pages badly done by some overworked clerk in his scant evenings. Whatever they are, these pages are for me always an exciting possibility until I have scanned them and laid them regretfully on the heap of manuscripts to be rejected. Yet however high that heap becomes I am not discouraged. I turn indeed with the more eagerness to the next one not yet seen. For somewhere, sometime, I shall discover that one for which I search, the manuscript sent in by some young unknown person who, writing in obscurity and perhaps poverty, discovers himself to me as the possible genius.

Not that a writer always discovers himself in this one way! He may be a silent, seemingly ordinary young person to be met anywhere, whose book is still struggling unshaped in his mind. To see the book, perhaps, to help it to be expressed, is also to complete the search at one point.

And I do not believe there ever was a better time than now for young genius to emerge. It is not, it is true, so hopeful a time for mediocre talent. Because people have less money to spend than they used to have, when they buy a book they demand more than they used to demand. If it is a book that bears reading more than once, so much the better. But there is no editor, no publisher, who is not combing his manuscripts eagerly for the new and real writer, and any signs of ability are detected. There is no truth in the often expressed belief of the unsuccessful writer, that it is only those with established names who can hope for attention. Authors with established names, if they produce trash—as the best of them may do, sometimes—are rejected, too. Quality is more important today than name.

So the search goes on. With me it has gone on now for six months, since I began to read manuscripts and talk with aspiring authors. I know that I have seen only a part of what is being written, but just at present, anyway, I see every manuscript that comes into the office of an average publishing house, and there are hundreds, and I have not yet found the book. I know that I need not be discouraged, because only once in several years does a book appear by a talented new writer.

Yet why should this be true? Of these hundreds of manuscripts I read many are surprisingly well written, some are also well conceived and intelligently developed. But that is the best that can be said and it is not enough.

The chief fault in them is, I think, a lack of reality. Of talk there is plenty but it is so often meaningless talk. There is action but it is action without vitality because it is causeless activity. There are people who do not live in spite of noise and movement because they are sporadic and unrelated to humanity. There is liveliness, but it is not life.

Yet our country is one of the most various in the world, richest in every sort of humanity. There should be scores of young authors flowering out of this rich soil into vivid writing. Surely they must appear. But it may be that our country is too varied and therefore confusing to the young. There is no pattern visible, no unity to be grasped.

Whatever the cause for delay, I do not give up the search. Every day fresh manuscripts are piled upon my desk. Almost every week I meet somewhere someone who wants to write a book. Some day the door will open and it may be the genius. Or perhaps some day I shall take up a manuscript, perhaps badly typed or on cheap paper and perhaps full of scrawled corrections, but perhaps, too, the first page will begin like music, sure and clear and finished. There, there will be the *book*.

Meantime she took up life in the neighborhood around her, without becoming really part of it. Yet today when one visits the village of Dublin, Pennsylvania, one is likely to hear, "I wonder what 'she' thinks?" "I wonder how 'she' feels about thus-and-such?" She has become what she laughingly calls "a sign post" in the countryside. People will say, "Do you know where 'she' lives?" or "It's on the road where 'her' house is."

She has a philosophical attitude about all of this and maintains her Oriental calm and dignity through everything. She spoke about her neighborhood in 1955 and I include her words here, even though they were written for a newspaper in India some twenty years later than our chronological order:

I live in a country region in the state of Pennsylvania. This state is large yet my community is typical, in general, although some of the great industries of the United States are in Pennsylvania, and some of the largest cities. We have mining areas, mountains, lakes, and rivers, but many communities are rural, like ours.

Most of the citizens here are farmers. The farms are not large, as American farms go. They average about fifty acres and they are family farms. Parents and children work together to try to make the farm a success. Fifty acres is barely enough to support a family and in order to have cash for daily expenses, the farming must be diversified, except that cows are the mainstay. True, some farmers grow only chickens, and are known as chicken farmers. But the dairy business is still the chief business. Cows are useful in maintaining soil fertility with their manure, as well as useful for their milk and meat. Almost everybody drinks milk and eats butter and beef. We have many cattle shows and country fairs, at which farmers exhibit their best animals and win prizes, and farm wives exhibit their cakes and jams and jellies and pies and loaves of bread and also win prizes.

Farm prices are always lower than other prices, however, and so the children cannot all stay on the farm. They must seek work elsewhere as they grow up, and many of them, both boys and girls, go into small local factories. Sometimes even the wives and mothers feel they must work, at least part time, in these small factories in order to help with the family income. Every family wants to own their house, some household conveniences and at least one automobile.

The village near which I live is quite typical in my home area. It has only one main street, and about fifty houses. The population is some three hundred people. There are two small factories in the village, one to make men's clothing and the other to make nylon stockings for women. These goods are shipped to large centers to be distributed. The work is piece work, and people are paid for the amount that they do, and not by the hour, but their pay is good, if they work hard.

The houses here in our village are of red brick, for brick is cheap in our vicinity. They are comfortable houses, neither large nor small, and the women would think themselves ill treated if they could not have an electric or gas stove, a refrigerator, a vacuum cleaner, rugs on the floor, curtains at the windows and nice chairs and a table in at least one best room. Sometimes they cannot pay for these things quickly, but must pay a little each month.

We have two garages in our village, a small inn, a small bank, two grocery stores, of which one is also our post office. We have a florist shop, an undertaker whose business is to care for the dead and their funerals, a well digger, a plumber, a hairdresser for women and two barbers for men. These two barbers compete with each other somewhat. One of them charges sixty cents for a haircut, the other fifty cents. We do not know which makes the more money, but certainly the fifty-cent barber has the most customers. He works all day and until nine o'clock at night. On Mondays he takes a holiday and goes fishing.

We have a doctor in the village, too. He is a young man, just out of the army, and he is a good doctor. I do not know whether he will be content to stay in such a small place. Perhaps as he gets experience he will move to another bigger town. If so, another young doctor will take his place. Certainly I should mention the fire company in our village. This company is made up entirely of volunteers. They work at other jobs but when the fire whistle blows, every volunteer, wherever he is, leaves his job and rushes to the fire house where the fire-fighting engines are kept and the whole company hastens to the scene of fire. Many houses and people are saved by this prompt action. The money to buy the engines and house them is contributed by the people in the village. The women sell food they have cooked or the community gets together to have a supper for which they pay, and the money is given to the fire company. Also the householder where the fire breaks out contributes a fee for expenses.

We have one church, a modest brick building, behind which is the graveyard. The graves are tended by the citizens, the grass cut, the walks swept. On anniversaries each family brings flowers to lay upon the graves of their dead. The minister of the church is a young man, he has a wife and two small children. He does his best to help his people and to strengthen their spiritual life. He gets discouraged sometimes because not all the people go to church but he keeps trying.

Our community is quite self-sufficient. The citizens look after each other's needs and business. The street is clean and people like to have their houses nice and their yards bright with flowers. Each family has a garden in the spring in order to save money by growing their own vegetables. Some families have a few chickens for eggs and meat.

The village lives a quiet life. The villagers learn something about the rest of the world through their radio and television sets, and something too from the local newspaper. They are kind people, and they do not understand why we cannot live together peacefully, all peoples upon one earth. Their sons serve in the army when the time comes, but they hope for the day when this too will not be necessary. They think that other peoples also do not want war, but they are puzzled about how to stop war. They often feel unhappy because they cannot understand the large problems of war and peace, but they try at least to do their daily work as well as they can. The village has its own problems. A few citizens are lazy or bad-tempered or they drink too much and the other citizens are sorry for this. There is a family feeling in the village.

Is this village typical of small town life in the United States? I think so. We have some large cities, but most of our people live in small towns surrounded by farms. The life in one is very much the life in others. The effort of each family is to support itself, to send the children to school, to stay together. Our village itself does not have a school, but there are good schools nearby, maintained by the State and paid for by a school tax which everyone has to pay, whether they have children or not. There are no fees for the children. The school tax covers everything including books, but not including the hot meal which the children get at noon. The meal, however, is very cheap, though nourishing. Even the poorer children get this one hearty meal a day. In our village we have no very rich and no very poor.

What do the people do for amusement? At night they look at television in their homes, parents and children, and they seldom go out. But on Saturdays the men and boys play baseball or football in an open field, and in the evening perhaps the family goes to a motion picture theater. The young people, boys and girls, may go with the family, but if they are older they separate and go alone. Sometimes they go to dances. They marry young and only a few go beyond high school to college. Were it not for military service abroad, most of our citizens would not have the opportunity to see a foreign country and its people. They love home, however, and seem to have no great wish to travel, although they are glad to see visitors from other lands. We do not have many of these, either. Most Americans are like our villagers. They love their homes, they like their own kind of food, they want peace above all, they have no desire to be aggressive toward other peoples or countries. They want to live and let live.

These are my neighbors. They are not different from the neighbors I had in China, or India or Japan. They are not different from the neighbors I had in England or France or Italy. A difference in food and housing, a difference in language, but no more. With all the world peopled by such as these, surely we can live in peace together.

From the foregoing passage, one is able to judge how she feels about her neighbors and her community. Now there should be some mention of how her neighbors feel about her, and we are fortunate to have an eloquent testimonial to this. Although she has not kept a scrapbook or a diary, there is a volume, begun in 1939, in which she has made handwritten entries. There is no particular order to it, and there are many months during which no entries were made, but it does give insights into her personal feelings regarding her life during the years since 1939. She refers to this as her "Treasure Book," and she has placed in it some of the things she has received that meant the most to her. There are many quotations from that volume in this book.

While reading through it one day, I came across a letter to her from one of her neighbors, dated June 26, 1963. I include it because I feel it is typical of how her neighbors feel about her, and reveals the respect she has won in her community.

Dear Mrs. Walsh:
As one of your neighbors, I would like to be among the first this year to wish you health and happiness on this, your seventy-first birthday anniversary. May the coming years bring with them health and contentment for you.

I would like also to take this opportunity to express to you my gratitude for the many happy moments you have given me, not only through your written words, which I have enjoyed through the years, particularly your story, *Come My Beloved,* but for those times whenever I pass your home and enjoy the trees and shrubbery you had planted so many years ago in your fields. Whenever I see the fields of pines and hardwoods, memories come back to me of other years and other people. One of my first memories is the time, when a child, we heard of some woman who had written a book and been awarded a great prize and was going to buy a farm near to ours, "out on the back road," where one day my father loaded us all in our old Model T Ford truck and took us out past "the place." I can see it now, standing rather alone on the horizon, very plain in appearance except for a large piece of red tin on the roof, where I suppose it had been patched. That was just about the last time we were ever by the house and just about all I can remember of it before you moved in.

Those were the years when our well would go dry in the summer and we had to haul water from your creek (in the days before it was straightened out and still had a few deep holes), dipping water in buckets and into small kegs and hauling it home for our stock, in our old truck. How thankful we were for that water!

I remember also how you acquired more acreage, farm by farm, and how you had so many small trees planted. Of the men who planted them and mowed around them close up with their scythes, Tommy Haines, Tom Hamill, Paul Kadner, Ed Crouthamel and my father, Bill Miller. All of these men have passed on now, but your ideas and wherewithal and the results of their labors are now providing all of us remaining with happy memories, and in the years to come will give our children a bit of green in their asphalt and concrete world.

I can remember hearing the men tell one time of you and your husband to be, how you would walk about your grounds together and you would remark, "Aren't those flowers lovely?" and he'd reply, in a rather singsong, abstract way, "Uh huh." We thought his answer and the way he gave it rather amusing under the circumstances and not at all what we would have expected. I remember seeing him a number of times when I worked on your "Green Hills Farm," always quiet and dignified, with his tweed coat and curved pipe with a shiny band, and always a kind greeting, though it seemed his mind was working on something else.

It was while I was working for you (1944) that I married the loveliest girl in the world, an opinion I still hold. We have three boys now, the oldest being fourteen. Your five children were at that time scarcely that old. My, how time does fly.

I remember as a child seeing your Cadillac, with John Maurer at the wheel in his uniform, and the once in a while glimpse of you we had as you rode by on your way to or from New York. And a close up look at your car, if we were lucky enough to be around when it was serviced at the local garage, was a *real* treat!

So many memories, and time passes so quickly. A more recent memory is the one we have of the Pennsylvania premiere of "The Big Wave," which my wife and I attended and enjoyed. Your "Welcome House" idea is indeed commendable, and I am sure is a source of joy to you and the many once sad and neglected young people you and others are helping.

This has indeed been a strange way of saying "happy birthday" to you, but I've wanted to say some of these things to you for a long time and now seemed a good opportunity. I hope I've made it clear that we are glad to have you in our community, and thank you for all you have done and are doing for not only this little spot but for mankind as a whole. If these few words bring back even for a moment pleasant memories to you then they will not have been in vain.

Once again, may health and happiness be yours in the years to come.

Yours sincerely,
John M. Miller

As soon as I read the foregoing letter, I wrote to Mr. Miller asking his permission to use it in this book, and I include two paragraphs from his letter in reply, giving me permission:

You may be interested to know a bit about this above-mentioned letter. It was written in the wee small hours on her anniversary morning, on what might be termed an impulse, and was not intended to be a literary gem, but rather an outpouring of one human heart to another, of things remembered and hastily put to paper in the hope that their utterance would recall to mind a happier time and the knowledge that someone noticed and cared.

You have indeed chosen a monumental task, which when completed will, I am sure, help to tell the world's people now, and in time to come, of one who cared enough to put into action the commandment, "Love thy neighbor as thyself." And my hope is that not only will it stand as a monument to her, but will inspire more of us to be more conscious of *our* obligations in like manner.

It never ceases to amaze me that, with a beautiful home in Bucks County, there is still a restlessness in her. Now it scarcely resembles the house with the "large piece of red tin on the roof" of Mr. Miller's letter. I remember well the first time I was there. It was in July, 1963. The story of that meeting has been told in detail in our book, *For Spacious Skies,* so I will not repeat it here, except to describe the scene as it impressed me that evening.

As I entered the drive, I at once felt I must be in the wrong place. I had been told this was a farm, and it did not look like any farm I had ever seen. The man in the country tavern at the cross-roads in Dublin, Pennsylvania, had said, "Ye go down that road exactly one mile. Then cross a little stone bridge and turn right at the first road. That's 'her' place."

I had followed his directions carefully and driven between imposing stone columns and onto a narrow, winding black-top drive. The sharpness of the turn nearly brought the car to a stop, and I was aware at once of a stillness. It was early evening in early July, and in that stillness I could almost hear growing life around me. There was a small moon, quarter or half, as I remember, and the dim moonlight cast deep shadows through the trees, and as the car lights picked up the next turn in the road they brought small spots of beauty out of the recesses of the wooded area. There is a pool with a fountain on the right as one enters. The fountain is a figure of a young child appearing to contemplate the mysteries of the water, and I could hear the fountain's faint trickle as the car rounded the bend toward the tennis courts on the left. Ahead I saw the huge red barn, and beyond that sprawled the house. I say "sprawled," for that is the only way to describe it. It rules the crest of a slight rise and appears to have begun as a small unit of life that spread out until it firmly clutched the spot where it sits. In the moonlight I could see a dogwood tree, trimmed in the Japanese fashion, that stands beside another pool that is directly in front of the main entrance. As I approached the door, the brown fieldstone house seemed to ramble on into the night on both sides.

A lovely Amerasian girl of about sixteen, one of her last four adopted children, answered my ring and admitted me to the entrance hall. I saw that it was one leg of a large U-shaped room, with rough hand-hewn beams. A big stone fireplace is on one wall and comfortable furniture is arranged as best suited for the occasion, for I have seen it since in many different ways.

The overall effect on me that evening was one of strange beauty —strange because here in an early American farmhouse were rare Chinese art treasures, some centuries old, neatly arranged on the tables.

I can see it all clearly as I write here, early on Saturday morning, in the fourth-floor sitting room of the Foundation house. The familiar strains of a Beethoven sonata come from the library downstairs. She is playing the piano, as she frequently does before breakfast, and she has been working on that sonata for some time. I wonder if she will ever be satisfied with her ability to play it. She was out late last evening, for she went to New York to attend a cocktail party given in honor of Madame Gandhi, now Prime Minister of India, on a visit to this country.

That first time we met she had just returned from spending almost a year in India, and as she came down the stairs that evening I was surprised by the dark, deep tan face made startling by the white hair framing it. She wore a pale green cotton suit and white, loafer-type walking shoes, and I thought to myself, "So this is *the* Pearl Buck! This is the world's most translated author, the only American woman to have won the Nobel Prize for Literature!" I don't know what I expected that evening, but the simply clad, painfully shy, almost frightened woman who stood before me was not it.

I know now that she is not really frightened of people, of course, but she is shy and that shyness takes over any time she is faced with a person or situation with which she is unfamiliar.

Our friendship grew from that first meeting, and since then I have asked her many questions about that house, for it fascinates me. And, after all, her life in the United States has more or less centered there. She says of the house:

Of course it was not like this when we first moved here. It grew and expanded with the children.

I don't know exactly why my husband wanted more children. He had a son and two daughters by his former marriage, who were kind to me. They were grown children then and were devoted to both their mother and father, and I really don't think they knew of the growing difficulty between them. His divorce and our marriage were a surprise to them. I don't know whether I could have gone through that marriage if there had been small children. My own daughter, my adopted child, was nine then

and she had never been close to my first husband. She was close
to me but not to him, and her adjustment was more to a new
country than to a new set of parents. . . . I think she found American life difficult, she has told me so, though she has made an excellent and successful career for herself. It was quite a break for
her to leave China because the Chinese are extremely tender with
children, much more tender than Americans are. At least they
were—I don't know how Communism may have changed China.
We gave her a year to adjust to the new situation and then my
husband wanted us to adopt more children. I think I wanted children, too, and I could not have them myself at that time for various reasons. I really don't think I wanted to produce another child
because, well . . . I'm not a maternal woman, we have to face it.
I don't have a physical sense of my own flesh and blood. In the
first place, it's not my own blood anyway. Every baby makes its
own blood. In the second place, I don't know much about my own
ancestors and I knew even less of his. They are all strangers to me
and I had not the faintest idea of what I might produce. When
you have children, you never know what you are going to produce. They are strangers and they may look like some distant
grandfather or great-grandfather or some other person you don't
know. I don't think my adopted children are as strange as my
own would have been, because at least I saw them before they
were mine. That may sound absurd, but such is the case and I can
only explain it by the fact that I am not primarily a mother. I
love children as human beings and I respect them from the moment they are born. I am glad my children are adopted. I think
if I had given birth to another child I would have had such a
sense of responsibility for creating a new life that I would not
have enjoyed it as much as I have taking children who are here
anyway, and trying to make them happier, and in making them
happy making myself happy, too. I have great respect for a newborn creature, but I would have no more affection or respect *because* it would be something I produced. In my marriage I was
always a wife before I was a mother. I think I value the relationship between man and woman more than I do the relationship
between mother and child. I enjoyed my children, and still enjoy them as human beings and as individuals, but not because
I'm a "mother."

My husband said he had enough girls and only one son, so we took two boys first. They were both infants. Then we took two more and they would have been both boys, too, except that I made a big stand for one daughter. In those two years, 1936 and 1937, we adopted three boys and a girl. I'm so glad I did make the fight for my daughter. I love my sons, but this girl has been a particular and special comfort to me. She is a deep, understanding person and has developed into a strong, wise woman, though she is a tiny creature. I think she is five feet two, but her spiritual stature and her good, quick mind have been a delight always. She is one I rely on very much. So, we had four small children. It was a great undertaking for me, though I must say I had plenty of help. We lived in New York then and only went to the country weekends. Every Friday there was a great exodus with four babies and a nurse and a ten-year-old daughter. We spent Saturday and Sunday at the farm and came back on Monday. Each week we made a great entrance to New York with hustle and bustle at the apartment house and all that sort of thing.

We had an apartment at 480 Park Avenue and I always remember the kindness of the people in that building. I had been told that people in New York were kinder to dogs than to children, but that was not true in our case. We had the utmost kindness from the doorman and the elevator man and all of the people who worked there. Even the policeman on the corner was kind. In those days we drove ourselves. We liked to drive. My husband did most of the driving but each Monday I would let him off at the office and go driving up Park Avenue alone. One day the policeman stopped me. I know I'm not the best of drivers, in the sense that I don't always pay attention where I should. I get interested in something that I see and forget whether I am going too fast or running a light. When he stopped me I thought, "Oh, dear! Now I've done something *stupid*." I waited at one of those crossroads and soon there was a lull in traffic and he came over to the car. I was all ready to take my ticket, though I could not think what I had done. I thought he would know. He walked up, looked at all of the children and said, "Well, I just wanted to see how they are all getting along this week." Then he waved us on. Really, I met with great kindness everywhere.

As the children grew, it became apparent we should move

to the country, although we had a big apartment, eighteen floors up, with three terraces, and we kept the children on the terraces. We never did take them to the park because I hated the sight of all the children in Central Park with their nurses always restraining them from running here and there. Our children had plenty of play space at first, but when they were three and four they were just too big to be kept on the terraces. So we made an addition to the house and moved ourselves down to the country. Then we took a small apartment in New York, for we no longer needed so many rooms. My husband and I spent two nights and three days in the city each week at first, and the rest of the time in the country. Later he liked the country so much that we moved all of his editorial work there, and only went to his offices when we were in the city one day a week. That was about the time he brought his son into the business, at my suggestion really—I suppose because in China the son always went into the father's business, and this publishing company is very much a family firm.

Those were busy years. Of course, I had many outside interests —I always have had. I write out of my own experience and I can't live in only one set of circumstances, one surrounding. I must have variety. My husband and I had the understanding before we were married that I must have the freedom I needed to live and create. He asked only one thing of me. He said, "I ask only that we stay together. Don't go away with the children in the summertime and leave me alone in the city. Whatever we do, let's stay together." It has been told me, and I don't care if it is true, that he particularly wanted children because he thought it would divert me from my many interests and give me a center. Perhaps so, but it worked out well enough. I still had my freedom. The only thing is, I must confess, I hated leaving the children even for a day. I say I'm not a maternal person, but I have a sense of responsibility for the small young creatures and I did hate to leave them.

Today all of the children she has just talked about are grown men and women, of course, and all of them have busy lives of their own. Jean, the daughter she fought for, lives across the brook from the house I have just described, in a second house on the same farm. I asked her to write a letter to me and tell me something of what it is like to be the daughter of Pearl S. Buck. Though she is a busy housewife, with five small children of her own, she promised to do so, and I respectfully and gratefully include her comments here:

Being the child of a famous person has been a wonderful experience for me, as it would be for anyone, because I have been able to learn and do things that, perhaps, if I had been in another family, would never have happened.

I am an adopted child; therefore, I came into a family who really wanted me as I was. I had an older sister and three older brothers, all of whom I might never have had, and most important a mother and father whom I could love in return.

My childhood was filled with happy times. We always did everything as a family. Mother and Dad both worked but, unlike most parents, their kind of jobs permitted them to stay at home except for two days a week, or less, when they went to New York. Before we were old enough to go to school we went along. For years we went to the Christmas program at Rockefeller Center, to Macy's parade, to the children's theater and all the museums and other interesting things that children can see in Philadelphia, New York, and Washington, D.C. We went on all the important trips, such as Hollywood, where Mother was working for war relief, and were always included in every part of every day.

I have always known the farm in Pennsylvania as my home and will remember forever how wonderful it was to have a garden, fresh milk, eggs, fruit, meat and everything. During World War II we were completely self-sufficient except for coffee, tea, sugar and a few other things. We had a big freezer and cold room in the barn and it was always full.

Mother thought it important that we learn to do things, often unpleasant things, like weeding, cleaning the swimming pool, keeping our rooms neat, etc. We thought these things to be horrible at the time, but I think all children think certain parts of living are awful.

One of the nicest parts about being Mother's daughter or son is that we can always be ourselves. She is famous, but she never encouraged us to do anything but what we would be happiest doing. I wanted always to be a teacher of young children.

I always remember Mother with her long beautiful hair and perfect complexion, taking time always to make a happy home for me and my brothers and sisters. I have always wanted to be just like her, as I feel so much a part of her. I feel loved and wanted and am so grateful that I was a chosen child, chosen by Mother, who is the most remarkable of women.

She is Pearl S. Buck, author, humanitarian when it is expected of her, but to me she is my mother, with understanding, love, gentleness, and all things that make her a perfect example of a complete woman.

This letter is typical of how her first adopted children feel about her.

Here it is time to resume the account of her career, for it is for her writings that she is most famous. This perhaps is unfortunate, for to me, great though they are, her literary works are merely her artistic expression and are not of primary importance compared to her other accomplishments. Her work for peace through world understanding, for example, overshadows *The Good Earth* one hundred times, not to mention her work for children, beginning with retarded children and expanding to her present program for the education and general welfare of the displaced children of the world, although her immediate project for the Foundation is the Amerasian children. I am fortunate, I think, in that when I met her I had not read a single Pearl Buck book, and therefore knew first the woman; then I knew the artist. I do not mean to convey the impression that I feel her literary works are of *no* importance, for that is the farthest thought from my mind. On the contrary, I feel that all of the prizes she has won are small recognition indeed for such a stupendous contribution to the world of literature as we have had from this one person. She considers herself a writer, and only a writer. How many times I have heard her exclaim:

"Indeed I am not a humanitarian! It's just that a writer must be involved in the mainstream of life in order to write, and I cannot endure disorder in any form. When I become involved and find a situation that is not right, then I must do something to try to change it. But it is the artist's sense of order that leads me to undertake such a cause as displaced children, not any humanitarian feelings. I always try to get someone else to do a job before I undertake it, and it's only when I fail to get anyone to do it that I do it myself. I am a writer, and my work is to write books."

And this is true—she is a writer. She is without reservation one of the greatest literary figures in the world today. But to me, personally, it is not nearly so important what she has made of her career as what she has done with what she has made from it. The head of an English Department of a high school was recently asked what he thought of Pearl Buck, and he said that she was unquestionably one of our most outstanding literary contributors because of her rare talent for relating to people of every level of intelligence. And I agree, but being a great author is only part of being the woman that she is, just as being a wife and mother is only a part of this woman, and to recognize only a part of her is to miss the essence of her that *is* the woman. If it were not for her basic human essence, there would be no great books. By the same token, there would be no other great works. It would not then disturb her to see disorder in the world and she would not care if there is no understanding between nations and races and therefore no peace. Personally, I feel it is the woman who is great and not just the various by-products. Of course her books are good. She wrote them, and she is a master of her art.

On the other hand, she could easily become a master pianist. She plays beautifully and has to restrain herself from spending valuable hours practicing each day when, as she says, "I should be writing."

She could have been a sculptor. The heads she did of her children are excellent and she has told me she had to give up sculpture for it was taking too much time.

Whatever she undertakes will be done well and the results will be great, because the woman is great. Writing is her chosen field and she has worked hard at it. She was not born just to turn out literary gems as from a factory.

She began, as I have said, with *East Wind : West Wind,* and while that book was a success, it was not until the impact of *The Good Earth* that Pearl Buck was in the news on a daily basis. In 1931 *The Good Earth* sold 1,811,500 copies, according to Alice Payne Hackett, in *Sixty Years of Best Sellers.** She goes on to say:

> *The Good Earth,* by Pearl S. Buck, topped all novels of the year, making a permanent place in our literature for itself and for her other novels of China. Mrs. Buck was awarded the Nobel

* New York: R. R. Bowker Company.

Prize for Literature in 1938. Her book marked the first appearance on these lists of a publication of The John Day Company. There were five novelists new among the best sellers in 1931, all of them women, all American but one.

Over in China, Japan seized Shanghai in her undeclared war on that country. *The Good Earth* headed fiction for a second year, with Pearl Buck's second novel [*Sons*], continuing the story of the same Chinese family, taking third place.

From *Twentieth Century Authors*, by Stanley J. Kunitz and Howard Haycraft,* I quote:

Her first book, *East Wind : West Wind,* though it received critical recognition, did not make much of a stir. But publication of *The Good Earth* in 1931 made literary history. It won the Pulitzer Prize, it became a successful motion picture, it gave its author the Howells Medal of the American Academy of Arts and Letters in 1935, and with her subsequent work it led to her becoming the Nobel Prize winner in 1938.

Meanwhile, in 1932, a speech and a magazine article in which Mrs. Buck, who had been a missionary since girlhood, criticized the personnel of foreign missions led to a heated controversy with the Presbyterian Board of Foreign Missions. Eventually, she resigned as a missionary, and one of her supporters on the Board resigned with her, in protest. The next year the Bucks returned to China. But in 1934 Mrs. Buck came back to New York alone, joined the editorial staff of The John Day Company, her publishers, and secured a divorce. In 1935 she married Richard J. Walsh, president of the publishing company and editor of *Asia*. They live on a farm at Perkasie, Pa., with her two daughters and four adopted children—three boys and a girl.

In 1925, Mrs. Buck (under which name she still writes) had come to America on furlough and secured her M.A. at Cornell. She is also an honorary M.A. of Yale. In 1936 she was made a member of the National Institute of Arts and Letters.

After eight Chinese novels, besides a translation of the classic *Shui Hu Chuan* (*All Men Are Brothers*), and two remarkable biographies of her father and mother, Mrs. Buck has turned to writing of the contemporary American scene. But she cannot escape the public identification of her with the Chinese background which she is so peculiarly fitted to depict: to the world she will

* New York: H. W. Wilson Company.

always be the author of *The Good Earth,* which still remains the best of her novels.

"The truth is," she told the Columbia School of Journalism, "I cannot be happy without writing novels, quite irrespective of whether they are read or not. I am one of those unfortunate creatures who cannot function completely unless he is writing, has written, or is about to write a novel."

Mrs. Buck is a tall, rather severely handsome "demi-blonde." She is liberal both in religion and in politics, and has emerged during the Second World War as a passionate spokesman for economic and political freedom of the "colored" peoples of the world.

When I read her the foregoing quotes, her single comment was, "But I'm not tall. I wish I were. I wonder why people always say I'm tall?"

And she is not tall, but there is a stateliness about her, and a bearing, that do make her appear to be tall. She is what I would call a striking woman, and it would be impossible to lose her in a crowd.

Literary critics have been, on the whole, very good to her. I include some examples of the reviews of the books for which the Nobel Prize was awarded:

East Wind : West Wind

A novel off the beaten path and a very good novel, too. Mrs. Buck has written with a fine simplicity and delicacy and charm. One would say *East Wind : West Wind* was an exquisite book, did not the word, in this connection, so often connote preciosity.
—Edwin Seaver, New York *Evening Post*

Only one who, like the author, has lived all her life in China, yet being American still holds to Western concepts of romantic love, marriage and the scope of filial duty—only a lover of China, but no convert to her code of family and clan supremacy over the individual, could have written this beautiful novel. . . . This is Mrs. Buck's first novel, a striking piece of work; indeed it does not suffer in comparison with the best of Lafcadio Hearn.
—New York *Times*

The Good Earth

A work of genius. . . . I have read *The Good Earth,* every word of it . . . slowly because I did not want it to end, and fast because I could not get enough of it. After the first few pages I forgot that I was reading about Chinese men and women. . . . It was as though I was living with these men and women, different from us only in the clothes they wear and the land they live in. It is a book I shall never forget and shall read again. It is a beautiful, poignant and tragic book. It is perfectly written. . . . I predict for *The Good Earth* a popular and distinguished success.

—Mitchell Kennerly

A rare, fine sterling piece of work. To find such a book gave me a thrill of delight. . . . I hope that as many Americans as possible will read it. . . . One of the few stories of oriental life I ever read in which all the characters seem human and understandable and possible to me, in which my sympathies were deeply engaged as in the life of the living people around me. *The Good Earth* makes us belong to that Chinese family as if they were cousins and neighbors.

—Dorothy Canfield

The Good Earth is a superb example of intuition . . . a unique book. *The Good Earth* is China. The people in this rather thrilling story are not "queer" or "exotic," they are natural as their soil. They are so intensely human that after the first chapter we are more interested in their humanity than in the novelties of belief and habit. Those who supposed that the life story of a Chinese peasant will be monotonous will have a surprise when they read this book. . . . Mrs. Buck has the story teller's gift. She sees life like a reel unrolling, scene after scene, each exhibiting character.

—*Book-of-the-Month Club News*

You will remember that *The Young Revolutionist* is the book that she really does not like. However, in order that this report be complete, I feel I must include this review:

The Young Revolutionist

This little novel from the pen of Pearl S. Buck can scarcely be regarded as a successor to *The Good Earth,* nor does it tempt comparison with that beautifully written and strangely moving chronicle of the Chinese peasant. *The Young Revolutionist* is altogether a slighter story, and a story written with a purpose. Mrs. Buck has set out to portray the conflict with which the youth of present-day China is faced, torn as it is in one direction by its old accustomed ways and its traditional religion, in another by new leaders and the growing sentiments of nationalism and patriotism, and in yet another by the teachings of the foreigners and missionaries who have the welfare of China at heart. It is a large and very real conflict, and in the person of 17-year-old Ko-sen, the idealistic son of a comfortable small land-holder, Mrs. Buck has found an excellent protagonist. If it had been written without bias, *The Young Revolutionist* might have been a very fine and moving novel. As it is, the reader is constantly oppressed by the feeling that Mrs. Buck is trying to make out a case, to construct the argument, that she is defending the role that the foreigners have played in the development of the new China, that she is justifying to herself and her readers the efforts of the missionaries to substitute new gods for old, because "men will have gods of some kind, and when old ones are gone they will build themselves new ones." Regardless of the merits of this case, its mere existence tends to destroy the dramatic force of the story. The appealing figure of Ko-sen, who emerges in the first chapters as vividly as Wang Lung in *The Good Earth,* becomes by the end of the book little more than a logical convenience for the advancement of symbolism.

In spite of this *The Young Revolutionist* is not without something of both power and beauty. Mrs. Buck writes superbly; she understands her characters, and she portrays them without a hint of that febrile exoticism which marks other interpreters of the Orient, from Lafcadio Hearn to Hollywood. The initial chapters of the present book are as fine as anything Mrs. Buck has done. In them she describes Ko-sen's illness and his awakening in the temple of the Ten Heavens to find his entire future dedicated to the service of the gods. The doctors had despaired for his life, and his parents, as a last resort, had taken him to the temple, promising him to the gods in exchange for his life. Since Ko-sen is an only son, his sister's betrothed will take his place in the household, inheriting his father's lands, and he, Ko-sen, will be regarded as officially dead.

Ko-sen's anguish at finding himself cut off from life, his rebellion against the unending routine of service in the temple, his final determination to risk the wrath of the gods by running away, and his enlistment, for lack of any other expedient, in the army of the revolution, are graphically and appealingly told. Except for the flavor of propaganda, and an occasional tendency to over-obvious symbolism, *The Young Revolutionist* is a very appealing narrative.

—New York *Times Book Review*

Sons

The characters are much more sharply individualized in *Sons* than in *The Good Earth* or perhaps they are merely rounded out. . . . There is more power in the new book, and a wider scope.

The power is diffused: the structure less compact. Yet it is captious to pick flaws in a book which has so much that is extraordinarily fine in it. The prose is superb, full of music and simple dignity.

Pearl Buck knows people, and she writes with an appreciation of the dramatic possibilities in even the humblest and simplest lives. She realizes how drab and wearisome the routine of a farmer may be, and yet how poetical and vital it can be. She knows the weakening effect of idleness and luxury and the brutalizing influence of too much power. Suffering appalls her, but she does not turn away from it. She sees happiness as fleeting, and loneliness as inescapable. In short, she has great wisdom and a bigness of soul which is the measure of her book's worth.

—Dorothy Canfield, *Book-of-the-Month Club News*

The First Wife and Other Stories

If any further proof were needed that Mrs. Buck writes with a realist's eye of the China which she loves, this collection of her short stories and sketches supplies it. She is vibrantly alive to the beauty which belongs to China's ancient way of life. . . . She will not let the poetry, the graciousness and charm which sprang from the old feudal order blind her to harshness and cruelty, both personal and impersonal, which existed side by side with those aspects which delight the Westerner; she never forgets how heavily these dark elements have bulked in the lives of China's millions; and she is to a high degree conscious of the tragedy inherent in the conflict which grows out of the impact of Western ideas upon the old civilization.

That awareness is the unifying thread which runs through this first collection of her shorter pieces. . . .

These are unforgettable little pictures of human desperation and of the unconquerable will to live. As her publisher, Richard J. Walsh, justly remarks in his introduction: "Few modern writers have done so much to further the common understanding of the human heart."

—J. Donald Adams

Never has Mrs. Buck attained greater heights.

—Philadelphia *Public Ledger*

Where could there be found prose more suited to the short-story form!

—New York *Herald Tribune*

The Mother

Amazing, I can find no more fitting word. In many ways *The Mother* is finer than *The Good Earth*. . . . I do not think there is anything you could say in regard to it which would be an exaggeration.

—Florence Ayscough

A true epitome of motherhood. There is no mother of whatever race who will not recognize some measure of herself in the Chinese peasant woman whose story this is. It is a unity and a driving simplicity and strength to a degree more marked than in any of Mrs. Buck's previous work. A story of the widest possible appeal to all who wish their fiction to be at once a rendering and an illumination of life.

—New York *Times*

A House Divided

The best book Pearl Buck has done since *The Good Earth*.

—Virginia Kirkus

With her inimitable sure unexcited touch, Mrs. Buck carries forward the story of the Chinese family with whom we all lived for a time in *The Good Earth* and *Sons*. . . . It is a rich, full-bodied, living novel, the absorbingly interesting story of the growth and development of one individual human soul. . . . An engrossing narrative of what happens to a number of singularly real human beings. . . . The reader lays down the book with a long breath of satisfaction.

—Dorothy Canfield

While sorting through an old suitcase full of her husband's papers, I found two more treasures and I include them here. They are the presentation speech for the Howells Medal and her acceptance. In 1935, Robert Grant stood before the audience at the Academy of Arts and Letters in New York and made the following speech. I feel that it more clearly describes the honor bestowed upon her that evening than I could in my own words:

Fifteen years have elapsed since the funds to provide a prize "to commemorate the name of our great American novelist" William Dean Howells, also the first President of the American Academy of Arts and Letters, were accepted. The donor of this gold medal provided that it should be given every fifth year in recognition of the most distinguished work of American fiction published during that period. The medal was designed and modeled by Ann Hyatt Huntington, now a member of this Academy.

Today is the occasion of the third award. The first recipient of one of these gold medals was Mary E. Wilkins Freeman in November 1925. The second was Willa Cather, to whom I had the honor, as Chairman, of presenting the medal in November 1930 for her book *Death Comes to the Archbishop*. It should be borne in mind that by the terms of the donation it appears clearly that the award is to be made for a definite work of American fiction published within the five years since the last presentation and not for the entire work of the recipient. A work of American fiction means a book written by an American author, but its scene need not be laid in the United States, or its theme have to do with our national life. It is to be borne in mind also that a five-year period necessarily eliminates from consideration favorite fiction which enthusiasts heedless of the passage of time might have chosen.

For the third time the medal is to be awarded to a woman, a choice acquiesced in by the four Academicians serving as the Committee, three of whom are men, and approved by a majority of the members of the American Academy of Arts and Letters. I have the honor to report that our choice for this distinction is Pearl S. Buck, now Mrs. Richard John Walsh, for her novel *The Good Earth*.

This story made public in 1931 and awarded the Pulitzer Prize for that year was recognized at once as a veracious picture of agricultural life in China worked out with distinguished skill and fidelity. In terms of human drama it gave the intelligent world a far better understanding of the common man in China than it ever had before. After reading of Wang Lung, the farmer's inveterate devotion to the fruitful soil, of his homely wife O-lan's pathetic selflessness and of their social evolution, one closes the patient chronicle with the admiring thought: "This is life to the core, it must be true." Except that I abhor the term as used by some in these United States to distort art, it is a proletarian novel in the best sense. The author of *The Good Earth* takes life as it is instead of standing civilization upon its head and asking us to glorify its dregs or the emotions of those who have just begun to think.

Pearl S. Buck is the daughter of American missionaries of Virginian extraction. Most of her childhood was spent at Chinkiang on the Yangtse River in a small bungalow built on the top of a hill which overlooked the great river and "the crowded city whose tiled roofs overlooked each other as closely as scales upon a fish." At seventeen she was taken to Europe and England and thence home to complete her education at Randolph-Macon College in Virginia. On graduation she returned to North China, where the next five years were passed. To quote her own words: "Part of the time we were the only white people there in that town and countryside and at no time were there more than six of us." Later she taught in the University of Nanking. Again she writes: "My chief pleasure and interest has always been people and since I live among Chinese, then Chinese people. When I am asked what they are like I do not know. They are not this and that, but people. I cannot describe them any more than I can my own blood kin. I am too near them and have shared too closely their lives."

Years ago I attended a so-called banquet given by the [New York] City Government in honor of emissaries from the Celestial Kingdom. The visitors were courtly men, evidently with refined sensibilities. Speech followed speech and the kernel of the eloquence was the superiority of American manners and customs and modes of thought and the desirability of their adoption by China. Not a single word was uttered the entire evening in praise of what China had produced or what was to be learned from China. I have often wondered what were the emotions of these Oriental visitors from one of the politest nations on the globe as they listened to this rodomontade. They gave no sign in their own gracious responses.

But this is only an aside. As has been already quoted, "They are not this and that, but people." It is to honor those who can write so convincingly of people, whether in the tragedy or comedy of human life, that the puppets cease to be puppets, and live and move and have their being, that this memorial to William Dean Howells was endowed. Because she has done this so unerringly and with such an artistic sense of values, I am commissioned to bestow upon the author of *The Good Earth* this medal of gold for the five-year period just ended.

She rose then, and to the audience said:

This occasion is especially welcome to me because it gives me a time and place in which to express not only my deep appreciation to the American Academy of Arts and Letters, but also my appreciation to the larger audience of my country. I feel grateful to my country because I find here, surely more than in any other country in the world, opportunity for a writer, unknown and obscure, with no influence of any kind, without money or particular friends, to come into recognition, to find generous praise and welcome and many friends. Surely no first manuscript ever written was sent forth in such doubt and uncertainty as was my own small *East Wind : West Wind*. It wandered, it is true, a long time. But there was someone to direct its wanderings, someone who saw a faint merit there—someone wholly a stranger to me—and at last it met another stranger, who, again only upon its faint merit and the remote hope of larger things to come he thought he saw in those pages, accepted it and published it. No one could have had more unpromising beginnings than I—to write of subjects so foreign, to live so far. And yet, at every step I have found open to the writer one opportunity after another. I am constrained by my own experience to believe that only complete lack of any merit prevents a writer from generous, often too generous, recognition here. And I am further persuaded to this belief because I now see for myself the eagerness with which all young talent is searched for, encouraged, and developed. I have as part of my own work these days the reading of many manuscripts which I do, partly to discover more of people's minds, but also and more for the delight of finding unknown gifted persons, who need the help that I did, and I am not in the least unusual. In many a publishing house, I do not doubt perhaps in all, there are those who, apart from any commercial interest—indeed, usually in the case of unknown authors, against all commercial interest—search for talent in the piles of manuscript before them. Mine is indeed a country of matchless opportunity for the artist. I cannot ask for more. When I remember the little distant poor room in which I began to write, and when I look about me today in your presence, I cannot but feel a great humility and gratitude for opportunity, so freely given, and so richly awarded, in America.

She put into words in that acceptance speech much of what is felt by many writers, I am sure. One works for many months on a book, and then sends it forth like a small child being sent to school for the first time, and must then wait and worry. Will it stand on its own merit? Will it find an understanding editor? Or will it meet with impatience and be pulled apart with no sympathy?

I am surprised that so many authors succeed as do, among the many writing today, for that wait is the most awful ordeal. Pearl Buck's advice to me has been: "Finish it—wrap it—and mail it to the publisher—and then forget it and at once begin another book, for if you wait to hear about the one you sent, you may never begin another."

And she did not wait. After *A House Divided,* she began another novel, got about three-quarters of the way through, then decided she did not really like it and put it to one side. She was still not firmly enough established in her own country to have new material. Needing money, therefore, she brought out *The Exile,* the biography of her mother she had written years earlier, and wrote a companion biography of her father, *Fighting Angel.* Again I quote from reviews:

The Exile

To the American reader of every type and class, it seems that no book could be more poignantly and vitally interesting than this. Merely as a story this book is as absorbing as any novel: it has suspense and excitement in its happenings, development and conflict in its characters, beauty and horror and strangeness in its changing background. . . . Though it tears the heart with pity again and again, it is no tragedy. And it is in deepest truth American. Clear, incandescent, gripping in its interest, written in a style of beauty and unerring rightness, this "Portrait of an American Mother" is an epic of our country. It is one of the noblest epics of our day.

—New York *Times*

The Exile is tender and moving, impassioned and intelligent, and as readable as any novel. I am sure Mrs. Buck has never done anything finer.

—Herschel Brickell, New York *Post*

The book of a novelist who not only loves life but looks at it clear-eyed. *The Exile* is a story of fact as exciting and as moving as any of her fiction. The events of the story are stirring, but they pale beside the story of the woman and her mastery of circumstances."

—Mary Ross, New York *Herald Tribune*

A moving picture of one woman's heart and home and life. It is a real book of fine literary quality interpreting one great human character.

—Sherwood Eddy, *Saturday Review of Literature*

Pearl Buck's most profoundly felt book, more moving, I think, than any of her books, with the possible exception of *The Good Earth*.

—Lewis Gannett, New York *Herald Tribune*

Swift torrents of emotion flow beneath its surface. . . . There are many who will feel that no matter how good *The Good Earth* was, *The Exile* is an even better book.

—Fanny Butcher, Chicago *Tribune*

Fighting Angel

Fighting Angel is a human document of tremendous meaning. It is a rich book, rich and varied, and packed with dynamite as few books are. It cannot but explode loudly on the reading public to whom it will tell several usually untold truths. . . . This powerful, moving, searching invitation to meditate deeply on human life.

—Dorothy Canfield, *Book-of-the-Month Club News*

To give an example of her own thoughts and feelings regarding *The Exile* and *Fighting Angel* I include here an article written by her in 1937 and published in the Chicago *Tribune*.

I am by nature a writer of fiction and not a biographer, and now, after having written two biographies, I have come to the conclusion that a writer is either novelist or biographer and seldom both, with equal pleasure to himself, at least. As a matter of fact, *The Exile* was never meant to be a biography—that is, not exactly. It was written many years ago, not for publication, but because there were children in my family who had never seen my mother and would never feel, as I had, the strength and color of her glorious personality. One hot summer I determined to occupy myself in putting down all I could remember about her, as honestly as I could, so that she would continue to live in our family as the generations grew. The memory of her burned as vividly in my mind as her reality. I wrote it all down with scarcely any change to be made. Years later, for a reason which I knew she would consider enough, the book was published.

Then it became evident that another story must be told—the story of my father. It was not possible to put them in the same book. They were not, in fact, the same story. So *Fighting Angel* was written, not so much as a memory this time as a real biography. And, having in one way or another, almost without knowing it, written two biographies, I put down for myself certain differences in the two kinds of writing.

The difference between the writing of fiction and biography is the difference between being free to roam in the hills and having to walk within a walled garden. In fiction the writer may choose whatever characters he wills out of the world and his imagination, and he may make them what he likes in appearance, behavior and character. All that is asked of him is that the various attributes and actions he chooses for a single character shall, taken together, present a unified whole so that, as the reader sees him, he will be alive and believable. In other words, the creator is limited only by his own creation. Having chosen a certain creature, he must not allow him to go beyond the bounds of his own possible nature.

But in writing biography there are innumerable limitations. The writer is given his materials. He has to portray a creature of a known nature, who has lived in certain known ways in a known time. The writer, thus limited, has only the freedom of how he shall use and arrange these facts. Yet even here the honest biographer has no real freedom. He has no right, for instance, to suppress any facts whatever about the life he has chosen to portray, because all of those facts have significance. It is, of course, obviously impossible for him to record every fact for the sake of space alone. He must eliminate, but when he does, it must be only duplication which he avoids. He must choose every salient incident and speech, everything which reveals a new aspect of his subject's nature. Sometimes these facts seem contradictory but he cannot suppress any of them, for in that very contradictoriness may lie still further truth.

Fiction is a painting, biography is a photograph. Fiction is creation, biography is arrangement. For the creative writer, biography is far more difficult than fiction, because he feels the limitations of a character already definitely created. The task in biography is the task of discerning the shape of the character in all the known facts concerning him.

There is one similarity between the writing of fiction and biography. Character must emerge clearly in each. The process is exactly opposite. In fiction the writer sees and feels his character first and then chooses the incidents and action to portray him; in biography he must study the incidents and actions and from them find his character. He cannot honestly introduce anything new in action or speech. In my own two biographies, for instance, every incident is authentic, every speech what I have heard said, or was told on reliable evidence was said. But nearly all I saw and heard myself, and remembered, having the curse and the blessing of a photographic memory.

I do not think I shall ever write other biographies. I like the freedom of creative writing. I like choosing and making my own characters. But I am glad to have put into some sort of permanence, nevertheless, these two beloved characters of my life.

She speaks often of liking the freedom of creative writing and yet she has told me frequently of the severe discipline needed in order to employ this freedom. As a matter of fact, the self-discipline needed to use any form of creative talent properly is one of her favorite subjects.

She has many creative interests—gardening, piano, sculpture, poetry, painting, flower arranging—and she manages to enjoy them all to some degree. The difficult thing, of course, is to keep all of these things in their proper place. I am reminded of her thoughts on the subject. We attended a banquet recently at which she spoke to a group of college students and their parents and teachers about music. The students were young scientists-to-be, who were being honored for their participation in the various musical groups in their college—glee club, band, etc. She was asked to speak informally about what music has meant in her life. She was magnificent! She wore a two-piece gown, a gold satin skirt with a top of black French brocade, the gold satin carried through to a cowl collar, and she was stunning to see. She leaned forward, her elbows on the podium, and spoke in a soft, quiet, intimate voice. Her wit brought intervals of laughter throughout the forty-five-minute talk. We who know her know that she hates each moment she is before an audience, but none of those listening would have dreamed that this is so. She told them of her childhood and her mother and father, and of her Chinese nurse and her Confucian tutor. She held them in a trance as she told of her first musical instrument, a Chinese one, somewhat like a harp. They laughed at her dislike of a guitar that her mother urged upon her, and they nodded knowingly at her love of Beethoven sonatas. And through all of this she wove her point —that the self-discipline necessary for making beautiful music is the same discipline an author needs to write great books, an artist to paint great pictures, a surgeon to perform an operation, a scientist to make a discovery. For that matter, the same discipline is essential for any great accomplishment in life.

"You have to work at life," she told them, "in order to find peace and contentment in that wonderful sense of beautiful accomplishment. Perhaps this is especially true of music. Music demands honesty. One cannot play music without honest work at practicing. No one is deceived, neither performer nor listener. Showiness does not deceive."

Young and old alike rose to their feet in overwhelming ovation when she closed, saying:

"And the greatest satisfaction comes not from without, but from within. The greatest rewards come not from the discipline applied by others, your teachers or parents, but from the most beautiful and severe of all disciplines, that which you exert on yourself."

Above all, this is what emerges from a close association with her. I can hear her saying, "Until you write that last page—indeed, the last word—you haven't a book."

True, she takes a series of small diverting breaks during a day, but her unrelenting love of perfection sends her back to her desk. Knowing this energy in her being, one finds it difficult to understand her periods of silence. The longest pause in her writing career came in the years just before the Nobel Prize. I questioned her about those years of noncreativity, and she replied thus:

I was in that ebb which comes after a first success and was beginning to have some self-distrust. I have two sides, among other sides, but one is a sense of . . . I suppose I might call it humility about myself. I don't think I tend to overestimate myself. Why? A residue from childhood, perhaps! My father felt that women were naturally inferior to men—not true, of course, for we complement each other in a most remarkable way. Moreover, I am always comforted by the number of stupid men that I discover. I am sure that there are just as many stupid men as women. But my father was really quite arrogant about it without meaning to be, in his ancestral German fashion, two hundred years though it was since his family came to America. I saw, in my mother's case, a brilliant woman who suffered from this false conception. My father had a fine mind, but he didn't give my mother full credit for hers, and this hurt her. As a consequence, I grew up with the feeling that girls were not as good as boys, not only because of my father and our rather formal household, but because the Chinese definitely considered woman below man. Of course I found this same feeling in my own country when at last I returned to it. There was no woman writer in the United States who was really ranked with men by the male critics—not while she was alive: The exception was Willa Cather. Even after she was dead I always have thought the acceptance was more or less a token, as a business firm or college takes in one or two Negroes just to show that they aren't prejudiced, when they really are prejudiced because they don't take in others. Even Willa Cather was too often mentioned as "a woman writer."

All this created a creeping doubt in myself about my own talents. Also, at the time you mention, although it was true that I had spiritually and mentally left China, I still did not really live in America. I was in a sort of no-man's-land. It was too soon for me to write about my own people, for I didn't know them well enough. Then, too, in this country of ours, after any first success, such as I had with *The Good Earth,* everyone is watching for the next book—"Is it as good as *The Good Earth?*" That was discouraging. People didn't say, "Well now, let's see what the next book will be. It should be something different from *The Good Earth.*" No, they want the same book over and over, and I knew I could never—and would never—write any book twice. I finish a book and I am ready for something new, in writing as in experience. Yes, it was a dark period, but I never told anyone. I did not discuss it even with my husband. My writing and my work as a writer I have always kept apart from personal relationships. I am talking more now to you than I have in my whole life to anyone on the subject of my work.

And from these intimate talks I have learned the story of those years as follows. The year was 1937; a new phase began—a beginning that brought her previous way of life to a complete end. The change was like a death, or a birth, or even a combination of both, for indeed these great and most important changes constitute efforts which any individual must undergo entirely alone. It is one's own separate will to live that takes control at crucial moments. I have been told by her that there is an extremely dangerous moment at the birth of life when the fateful decision must be made by each human being alone—to draw breath and live, or not to make the effort and die. Through long months of prenatal care the new being has slept without worry with all necessities provided. Suddenly without any warning this creature is thrust forth into an entirely new atmosphere. Its skin has never felt a touch and now it feels rough hands and fabrics. Its lungs are filled with liquid, which it must expel with that first great cry of a heretofore unused voice. I say *must* expel for indeed the liquid *must* be expelled before the lungs can be filled with the first breath beginning that entirely independent action which takes place an average of twenty times a minute for all the days of the creature's life. I am told that the strength of the individual decision to live must be stronger at that moment than is ever again required or the first breath will not be drawn and the creature will die. She has told me herself that many times in life when great change must be endured if one is to continue to live, one must remember that no change is so complete, no shock so great as that one at the beginning. She has said that often in her life she has had to stand alone and make up her mind that she would, indeed could, take a deep breath and go on.

The year of 1937 held just such a moment for her, for it was in that year, she has told me, that her decision was made to dedicate her life to her books with complete effort, and from that point on all else became secondary in importance. As I write these words my telephone rings:

"I have found a beautiful thought," she says, "a gem that I want to share with you." She read aloud: "The uncommitted life is not worth living. . . . We either believe in something or we don't. . . . Commitment is willingness to stand up and be counted. It is a human must for young and old, for black and white, for Christian, Moslem and Buddhist. It is skill plus goodwill. It is a thoughtful decision on the part of an individual to participate passionately in the events of his time. It is the dogged staying power coupled with the sensible idealism that makes the world go around. It has nothing to do with middle of the road. . . . Commitment will bring sadness as well as joy, loneliness as well as friendship, but whichever it is, it brings excitement and demands the use of all of a person's resources. Even beyond this, it increases our capacity for the generous enjoyment of life and colors all that we do with a concern for other people. . . . With Commitment we can move mountains. Without it we cannot move a molehill." *

This passage is pertinent to the very words I am writing, for in 1937 her commitment was made finally and surely. That commitment holds today and will hold for all the rest of her life, I am sure, for writing is her major work and will so remain long after all else is gone. To proceed: early on a summer evening, in June, 1937, she sat on the grass of a gently sloping hillside in Bethlehem, Pennsylvania, and listened to the performance of a Bach oratorio at the Bach Festival. With her was her second husband. She has told me that as she sat there, listening, her mind drifted over the years of her life, her early childhood in China, her first marriage, and the beginning years of her career as a writer.

* From an article by Dr. William G. Saltonstall, in *Odyssey*, journal of the U.S. Experiment in International Living (Spring, 1966).

She thought of the departure from China and of the final change to this country only three years before.

Three years? So short a time for so much to have happened! She had not planned to remain in this country when she left China in 1934. She had intended to spend only the summer and to visit her retarded daughter. The years since the trip had been stormy and difficult. The whirl of press luncheons, cocktail and dinner parties coupled with her publisher's persistent pleas for marriage had kept her in a state of constant indecision during the first years. The flow of her books was now stemmed by the adjustment to her new life. Her creativity in this period had to be devoted to home, family, husband, and country—each of these must find its place in her life, in order for her career to go on. Furthermore, a novelist writes out of experience and she had not yet gathered enough experience in her own country. She was away from her old material and there was not sufficient new material.

A novelist who does not create is the proverbial fish out of water. It is an unnatural state for the fish, and noncreativity is unnatural for the true novelist. The fish will die, as will the novelist, unless the unnatural state is made natural again. She knew she would write, indeed had to write, but what would she write? Besides, she was enduring new criticism. Even *The Good Earth* had just been severely criticized. One self-righteous woman in Kansas City declared she saw no reason for her fifteen-year-old son to "wade through filth" to get some supposed message at the end of the book. She went on to say, "I venture to predict that in twenty-five years or less, such authors as Theodore Dreiser, Eugene O'Neill and Mrs. Buck will be only bad memories." I wonder if that woman, were she here today, would be willing to eat those words? Nevertheless, *The Good Earth* was removed from the recommended lists of some high schools and junior colleges. While this sort of criticism helped the sales of Pearl Buck books to soar, it surely affected her confidence in her own ability as a writer.

She was not prepared either, she has told me, for the criticism of men against women which she found in America. She had heard it said of herself many times that "she is just a woman. She will never do anything really great."

Another factor, of course, was commercial. I heard her say,

not long ago, "I married two men in my lifetime who were unable to support me. Not that I would have wanted them to do so, but they would not have been able to, anyway. I have always supported myself and my family, and it's been a large family." She needed money in 1937, as she does today, as she always has and always will. She lives on a cash-and-credit basis, spending capital at least as fast as she gets it, and sometimes borrowing on royalties before they are due. She has made millions in her lifetime and she has spent it all. Not on herself! The fact is that very little of it has ever been spent on herself. She has only the barest wardrobe for a woman of her station. She has almost no jewelry, and most if not all of that was given to her. She has a few furs. She has always maintained a large house, for the sake of her family. There are people who will say, "But she has enjoyed her life and her family, and they were her happiness," and this is true. But even today she lives and works for others.

As she sat that evening listening to the music of Bach she thought of the past years and of her plans. Suddenly a voice broke in on her thoughts to announce the next portion of the oratorio to be sung: "This Proud Heart." She chose this to be the name of her next story—the story of a talented and creative woman and of the struggle such a woman makes for a normal life. She began at once and remembers it as a long and difficult book. It could not really have taken long to write, since it was published in February, 1938. However, I am sure that the soul-searching necessary to write this novel made the writing itself difficult. It is her most autobiographical novel and it presents a true picture of her own life at that point.

Susan Gaylord, the central figure of *This Proud Heart,* had to be based firmly in reality in order to serve the author's need for self-expression. She had to be talented and creative. But she could not be a writer; that would be *too* close to reality. A different form of talent was the solution. In 1934 Pearl Buck had lived for a short time in the house of Malvina Hoffman in New York. Miss Hoffman, already a renowned sculptor, was away and had leased the house to her complete with contents. It was during this period that she developed a deep interest in sculpting, for there were many of Miss Hoffman's works in her studio, as well as her tools. Drawing on this experience, the author made Susan a sculptor. Through her, the book told of the difficulty of being a superior person—of doing everything a little better than one's contemporaries.

She exercised the novelist's prerogative and let Susan's first husband die, for divorce, at that time, would have been no more true to character for Susan than it had been for her. The death of Mark is symbolic of the novelist's own decision to live her own life—no, not so much to live her own life as to *be* everything she knew she had to be. The sorrow she felt at her decision was like that felt at the death of someone close. Her sorrow was for him. Marriage was not, indeed could never be, everything in her life.

Yes, *This Proud Heart* is a very revealing book—so much so perhaps because its author is one who never feels finished with anything until all emotion has been written out and put down on paper in order that it may be viewed coldly, as a sculptor may view a figure, soul of his own soul, objectively. Only then can a writer feel himself cleansed of the energy-robbing emotions that prevent work even while driving one to it. A great writer, such as Pearl Buck, may take liberties in fictionalizing places, times and events, or even people—but the heart of the matter, the core, the emotions must be true.

The ending of that book is completely effective and is a typical expression of her philosophy at times when she learns that any sorrow or disappointment is in fact inescapable:

"Yes, she would grieve sometimes, at night perhaps, but in the morning she would get up and go to work, and then she would not grieve. She would forget to grieve."

The essence is there, the essence of truth so apparent in each word that has been written by Pearl S. Buck.

Now she was finished with all of that at last. It was all behind her now because it was written and she could close the book and look forward into the years ahead with no nagging tugs from the years past. She had expressed herself, she had had the proverbial last word, and no matter how bitter life may be, this is the sweet privilege reserved for the writer alone. For he can always write that last word, and it is final: "The End."

From the writing of that book one interest remained with her—Susan Gaylord's art. The book was published in 1938 and on New Year's Eve of 1939 she wrote in her "Treasure Book": "On this day I began a thing which I have long wanted to do. That is, I began to model in clay. I began with the head of my son John, and after three hours' work had caught a fair resemblance. I shall do a head of each child. What I remember most clearly now at the end of the day, is that I know John's face as I have never known it. I had really to see it before I could model it. I had thought I knew its every line since I love him dearly and watch him often, but actually to make this beloved little face required a new sort of sight. I shall never forget it now. This is the last day of the year. I feel no especial emotion either in looking back or forward. But this is because I have been absorbed and cannot think of time and its divisions—let life go on as it is—is all I ask."

At that time she was evidently more content than I have ever known her to be, if, as she wrote, she was content to "let life go on as it is"; now she does not accept life as it is and I cannot believe she ever really has. I think, rather, that she had committed herself for the next several years. She had contracted, so to speak, when she adopted the children in 1936 and 1937, for the years of their lives through to educated adulthood, and she must fulfill that commitment. The present is made up of the past and future, as far as one can see of each, and her own life lay before and behind her as clearly as a map. And now she could look only forward, with Susan Gaylord she had written "The End" on the past.

Then suddenly there came the most unexpected event of my life. How well I remember that day! It was in the autumn of 1938. I was sitting in my study in the big apartment in New York before we had moved to the country. I remember the very morning—indeed, the hour. It was ten o'clock, the children were out on the terrace with the nurse, and I was at work. Suddenly the telephone rang. I took up the receiver and heard my secretary's excited voice.

"You've been awarded the Nobel Prize!"

I didn't believe her, of course, but before I could say, "I don't believe you," another telephone rang, and I heard my husband saying, "You've won the Nobel Prize, it's in the papers today!"

Of course I still didn't believe it. "I think it's reporters' talk,"

I said, "and I shan't believe it until you have called Sweden by long distance and inquired."

Well, it was true. The award came to me at exactly the right moment, and exactly as Alfred Nobel had planned. For he had directed that the prize for literature was not to be given to long-established, old and successful writers. Instead, it was to be used to encourage young writers, and I was still young, as writers go. In fact, I was the next-to-the-youngest person ever to get the Nobel Prize for Literature. I believe Rudyard Kipling was a little younger than I. At any rate, to receive it at that moment gave me back the confidence I was beginning to lose. I was swept up into all the old publicity again. Incidentally, the prize was given for my work as a whole, which up to that time had been Chinese, and special mention was made of the two biographies.

The Exile I didn't write for publication, as I have often told you, but because I wanted to keep a portrait of my mother for my children. I did publish it eventually, because the young man whom my husband had left in charge of his business—while he was in pursuit of me!—had not done well, with the result that when he got back he found that he was near bankruptcy. I decided that if my mother had lived to understand everything, she would have wanted me to use her story to help us in our lives together. So I brought that manuscript out from its closet. It was published in *The Ladies' Home Journal* as a serial, and then it came out as a book. It sold very well and I invested my share of it in the company, and put the firm on its feet again. I did that twice— once with *The Mother* and again with *The Exile*. Both books I had never intended to publish.

Well, to proceed—of course everything was bustle for us to get ready to go abroad. The prize was to be given in the early part of December, and we both left the children, except that we took with us my young stepdaughter, my husband's daughter. She was rather at loose ends, for she stopped college and while she was still living with her mother, she obviously missed the background of the family home. Janice, my oldest adopted daughter, was in boarding school, not far from home.

I have made a very detailed account of that trip to Stockholm in *My Several Worlds*. You always complain that I don't reveal anything personal! Well, here is an item. I think the occasion of the awarding of the Nobel Prize was quite a test of my husband. He was an important man in his own field, which was publishing, but it must have taken considerable grace for him to have to be there in, so to speak, a sort of secondary position. Yet that was one of the moments of my life when I was compelled to act as a solitary person. There were certain responsibilities and obligations placed on me as the prizewinning figure, and I could not share them. I had to walk alone, and I understood that this was hard for him. It seemed like a separation. I am glad that his daughter was there, for she was with him at such times, as for example, when I had to walk alone up the aisle, when I had to cross that big platform by myself. He sat in the audience, while I was on the stage. He was much too big a man not to understand this, and yet I am sure the experience was trying. I know it was, for afterward he told me so. It was a part of my life, nevertheless, into which he could not enter. The days were busy and crowded. I had to be on public show the whole time, and when I reached my rooms at night I could scarcely talk, I was so exhausted. I felt I simply had to go to bed and sleep, but I wouldn't let myself. I made myself give the evening to him. It was often long past midnight, but I wanted to live over the day with him and let him talk about it so that he would have a sense of sharing it with me. It was the only way he could share it, for much of the time he had to stand aside.

It was all harder for me than it was for Dr. Fermi. Enrico Fermi was the other person to get the Nobel Prize, of course in his case for physics. There was only one science man and one literary person that year. Of course, when a prize is given, there is always only one literary person, but that year there happened also to be only one scientific person. His wife was with him, but it was easier to be known as the wife of Enrico Fermi than it was to be known as the husband of Pearl Buck. I really needed those four days entirely to myself, but I had always to think of the other person, too, and for the first and only time I found it difficult. In a way, I rather wished that I had been able to come by myself, but I know that would have been even worse for him. I don't think he could have borne it. Well, we understood each other.

My acceptance speech was quite short, but for the Nobel Prize lecture I was asked to speak on a literary subject. I had always, for years, kept notes on the development of the Chinese novel, thinking that some day I might write a book about it. I am a trained scholar, and whether I am writing or not I am always pursuing something else—as I am pursuing nuclear physics and related subjects now, when I am really not a scientist. I am a literary person, but I cannot restrain my interest in these other fields. I had been working on a study of the Chinese novel for ten years, because in China there was no real history of the novel. Chinese scholars always considered the novel outside the realm of good literature. Philosophy and history, poetry, were literature, but fiction was not. The Chinese word for it is "yea-shih," or wild literature. Wild stuff, meant to satisfy ignorant people! A novelist had no position. There were some famous novels, but they were still considered to be of no value. I gathered my notes and used them as a basis for my lecture. Later the lecture was published under the title *The Chinese Novel*.

That whole trip was the most brilliant occurrence of my life. The first night there was a big dance and a ball for the people. We went out on the great balcony of the Town Hall and the students from all the universities came. The Crown Prince danced with my little stepdaughter, and it was lovely to watch. The next evening was the occasion of the giving of the prizes. I only remember sitting on the platform beside Enrico Fermi and distinguished Swedish Academicians. Of course the speeches were in Swedish and I didn't understand any of it. We were told when to get up—each one of us in proper turn. I was given the prize first. I remember that I didn't want to turn my back on the King, but I did for an instant when I had to mount the stairs. Then I had to negotiate, backwards, the carpeted platform.

The next day the newspapers all came out with appreciative reports of my efforts. What did I think about when I stood before the King of Sweden? I remembered above all that literary agents and publishers once told me that I could never make a success writing about the Chinese people, because no one wanted to read about them.

For other reasons, too, it was difficult to be a woman receiving the prize.

I was not the first woman to receive the Nobel Prize for Literature. There had been three before me. I was, however, the first and only American woman ever to receive it. I think I was a little hurt that so many men writers wrote against my receiving this prize, not only because I was a woman, but because they considered that I was not really American since I had been reared abroad and wrote about Asian people. That was hard for me to bear. I think it was what I expected, but I was sorry to have it so.

The experience of receiving the Nobel Prize focused and put into sharp, clear example the difficulty of a woman's sharing her total life, even with the man she loved. I couldn't do it. It was physically impossible to share all aspects of my life with him, however much I wished to do so. Many times since then there have been occasions to which I was invited and he was not invited. To be sure, I usually turned them down, but there were times when I could not. There were invitations involving my giving important lectures when he had to be in the audience. I can only say that he bore this with the utmost grace, yet I was aware of it. I saw quite clearly that it doesn't matter how much a woman loves a man and responds to and respects him, and no matter how indispensable he is, there are parts of life that cannot be shared. Men have been an indispensable part of my life, and are today, but there are areas into which I must go alone. I think this sharp realization has made me a bit sad. Perhaps it is the isolation of the artist, and I am sure that in a man's life it would have to be exactly the same. A man who is successful does go it alone. He cannot take his wife with him in all areas either, and so it was with my husband.

The award was simply worded, and it was a gratification to her that it did not cite merely *The Good Earth* to the exclusion of her other work. To the contrary, in fact, it was given for the body of her work and it did not mention that novel or any other single book by name. It read: *For rich and genuine epic portrayals of Chinese peasant life, and for masterpieces of biography.*

Standing before the King, she accepted with the following words:

It is not possible for me to express all that I feel of appreciation for what has been said and given to me. I accept, for myself, with the conviction of having received far beyond what I have been able to give in my books. I can only hope that the many books which I have yet to write will be in some measure a worthier acknowledgment than I can make tonight. And indeed, I can accept only in the same spirit in which I think this gift was originally given—that it is a prize not so much for what has been done as for the future. Whatever I write in the future must, I think, be always benefited and strengthened when I remember this day.

I accept, too, for my country, the United States of America. We are a people still young and we know that we have not yet come to the fullest of our powers. This award, given to an American, strengthens not only one, but the whole body of American writers, who are encouraged and heartened by such generous recognition. And I should like to say, too, that in my country it is important that this award has been given to a woman. You who have already so recognized your own Selma Lagerlöf, and have long recognized women in other fields, cannot perhaps wholly understand what it means in many countries that it is a woman who stands here at this moment. But I speak not only for writers and for women, but for all Americans, for we all share in this.

I should not be truly myself if I did not, in my own wholly unofficial way, speak also of the people of China, whose life has for so many years been my life also, whose life, indeed, must always be a part of my life. The minds of my own country and of China, my foster country, are alike in many ways, but above all, alike in our common love of freedom. And today more than ever, this is true, now when China's whole being is engaged in the greatest of all struggles, the struggle for freedom. I have never admired China more than I do now, when I see her uniting as she has never before, against the enemy who threatens her freedom. With this determination for freedom, which is in so profound a sense the essential quality in her nature, I know that she is *unconquerable*. Freedom—it is today more than ever the most precious human possession. We—Sweden and the United States—we have it still. My country is young—but it greets you with a peculiar fellowship, you whose earth is ancient and free.

The next night, before the Swedish Academy, she delivered the following lecture, and I include it here. I feel it belongs in

this study of her life, for it gives the reader such a clear understanding of what elements have made her the great writer
that she is.

When I came to consider what I should say today it seemed that
it would be wrong not to speak of China. And this is none the less
true because I am an American by birth and by ancestry and
though I live now in my own country and shall live there, since
there I belong. But it is the Chinese and not the American
novel which has shaped my own efforts in writing. My earliest
knowledge of story, of how to tell and write stories, came to me in
China. It would be ingratitude on my part not to recognize
this today. And yet it would be presumptuous to speak before you
on the subject of the Chinese novel for a reason wholly personal.
There is another reason why I feel that I may properly do so. It is
that I believe the Chinese novel has an illumination for the Western novel and for the Western novelist.

When I say Chinese novel, I mean the indigenous Chinese
novel, and not that hybrid product, the novels of modern Chinese
writers who have been too strongly under foreign influence while
they were yet ignorant of the riches of their own country.

The novel in China was never an art and was never so considered, nor did any Chinese novelist think of himself as an artist.
The Chinese novel, its history, its scope, its place in the life of the
people, so vital a place, must be viewed in the strong light of this
one fact. It is a fact no doubt strange to you, a company of modern
Western scholars who today so generously recognize the novel.

But in China, art and the novel have always been widely separated. There, literature as an art was the exclusive property of
the scholars, an art they made, and made for each other, according
to their own rules, and they found no place in it for the novel.
And they held a powerful place, those Chinese scholars. Philosophy and religion and letters and literature, by arbitrary classical rules, they possessed them all, for they alone possessed the
means of learning, since they alone knew how to read and write.
They were powerful enough to be feared even by emperors, so
that emperors devised a way of keeping them enslaved by their
own learning, and made the official examinations the only means
to political advancement, those incredibly difficult examinations

which ate up a man's whole life and thought in preparing for them, and kept him too busy with memorizing and copying the dead and classical past to see the present and its wrongs. In that past the scholars found their rules of art. But the novel was not there, and they did not see it being created before their eyes, for the people created the novel and what living people were doing did not interest the scholars, who thought of literature as an art.

If scholars ignored the people, however, the people in turn laughed at the scholars. They made innumerable jokes about them, of which this is a fair sample: One day a company of wild beasts met on a hillside for a hunt. They bargained with each other to go out and hunt all day and meet again at the end of the day to share what they had killed. At the end of the day, only the tiger returned with nothing. When he was asked how this happened he replied very disconsolately, "At dawn I met a schoolboy, but he was, I feared, too callow for your tastes. I met no more until noon, when I found a priest. But I let him go, knowing him to be full of nothing but wind. The day went on and I grew desperate, for I passed no one. Then as dark came on I found a scholar. But I knew there was no use in bringing him back since he would be so dry and hard that he would break our teeth if we tried them on him."

The scholar, as a class, has long been a figure of fun for the Chinese people. He is frequently to be found in their novels, and always he is the same, as indeed he is in life, for a long study of the same dead classics and their formal composition has really made all Chinese scholars look alike, as well as think alike. We have no class to parallel him in the West—individuals, perhaps, only. But in China he was a class. Here he is, composite, as the people see him: a small shrunken figure with a bulging forehead, a pursed mouth, a nose at once snub and pointed, small inconspicuous eyes behind spectacles, a high pedantic voice, always announcing rules that do not matter to anyone but himself, a boundless self-conceit, a complete scorn not only of the common people but of all other scholars, a figure in long shabby robes, moving with a swaying haughty walk, when he moved at all. He was not to be seen except at literary gatherings, for most of the time he spent reading dead literature and trying to write more

like it. He hated anything fresh or original, for he could not catalogue it into any of the styles he knew. If he could not catalogue
it, he was sure it was not great, and he was confident that he only
was right. If he said, "Here is art," he was convinced it was not to
be found anywhere else, for what he did not recognize did not
exist. And as he could never catalogue the novel into what he
called literature, so for him it did not exist as literature.

Yao Hai, one of the greatest of Chinese literary critics, in 1776
enumerated the kinds of writing which comprise the whole of
literature. They are essays, government commentaries, biographies, epitaphs, epigrams, poetry, funeral eulogies, and histories.
No novels, you perceive, although by that date the Chinese novel
had already reached its glorious height, after centuries of development among the common Chinese people. Nor does that vast
compilation of Chinese literature, *Ssu Ku Chuen Shu,* made in
1772 by the order of the great emperor Ch'ien Lung, contain
the novel in the encyclopedia of its literature proper.

No, happily for the Chinese novel, it was not considered by
the scholars as literature. Happily, too, for the novelist! Man
and book, they were free from the criticisms of those scholars and
their requirements of art, their techniques of expression and
their talk of literary significances and all that discussion of what
is and is not art, as if art were an absolute and not the changing
thing it is, fluctuating even within decades! The Chinese novel
was free. It grew as it liked out of its own soil, the common people,
nurtured by that heartiest of sunshine, popular approval,
and untouched by the cold and frosty winds of the scholar's art.
Emily Dickinson, the American poet, once wrote, "Nature is a
haunted house, but art is a house that tries to be haunted." "Nature," she said,

> is what we see,
> Nature is what we know
> But have no art to say—
> So impatient our wisdom is,
> To her simplicity.

No, if the Chinese scholars ever knew of the growth of the
novel, it was only to ignore it the more ostentatiously. Sometimes,

unfortunately, they found themselves driven to take notice because youthful emperors found novels pleasant to read. Then these poor scholars were hard put to it. But they discovered the phrase "social significance," and they wrote long literary treatises to prove that a novel was not a novel but a document of social significance. Social significance is a term recently discovered by the most modern of literary young men and women in the United States, but the old scholars of China knew it a thousand years ago, when they, too, demanded that the novel should have social significance, if it were to be recongized as an art.

But for the most part the old Chinese scholar reasoned thus about the novel:

> Literature is art.
> All art has social significance.
> This book has no social significance.
> Therefore it is not literature.

And so the novel in China was not literature.

In such a school was I trained. I grew up believing that the novel has nothing to do with pure literature. So I was taught by scholars. The art of literature, so I was taught, is something devised by men of learning. Out of the brains of scholars came rules to control the rush of genius, that wild fountain which has its source in deepest life. Genius, great or less, is the spring, and art is the sculptured shape, classical or modern, into which the waters must be forced, if scholars and critics were to be served. But the people of China did not so serve. The waters of the genius of story gushed out as they would, however the natural rocks allowed and the trees persuaded, and only common people came and drank and found rest and pleasure.

For the novel in China was the peculiar product of the common people. And it was solely their property. The very language of the novel was their own language, and not the classical Wen-li, which was the language of literature and the scholars. Wen-li bore somewhat the same resemblance to the language of the people as the ancient English of Chaucer does to the English of today, although, ironically enough, at one time Wen-li too was a vernacular. But the scholars never kept pace with the living, changing speech of the people. They clung to an old vernacular until they had made it classic, while the running language of the people went on and left them far behind. Chinese novels, then, are in the "Pei Hua," or simple talk, of the people, and this in itself was offensive to the old scholars, because it resulted in a style so full of easy flow and readability that it had no technique of expression in it, the scholars said.

I should pause to make an exception of certain scholars who came to China from India, bearing as their gift a new religion, Buddhism. In the West, Puritanism was for a long time the enemy of the novel. But in the Orient the Buddhists were wiser. When they came into China, they found literature already remote from the people and dying under the formalism of that period known in history as the Six Dynasties. The professional men of literature were even then absorbed not so much in what they had to say as in pairing into couplets the characters of their essays and their poems, and already they scorned all writing which did not conform to their own rules. Into this confined literary atmosphere came the Buddhist translators with their great treasures of the freed spirit. Some of them were Indian, but some were Chinese. They said frankly that their aim was not to conform to the ideas of style of the literary men, but to make clear and simple to common people what they had to teach. They put their religious teachings into the common language, the language which the novel used, and because the people loved story, they took story and made it a means of teaching. The preface of *Fah Shu Ching,* one of the most famous of Buddhist books, says, "When giving the words of gods, these words should be given forth simply." This might be taken as the sole literary creed of the Chinese novelist, to whom, indeed, gods were men and men were gods.

For the Chinese novel was written primarily to amuse the common people. And when I say amuse I do not mean only to make them laugh, though laughter is also one of the aims of the Chinese novel. I mean amusement in the sense of absorbing and occupying the whole attention of the mind. I mean enlightening the mind by pictures of life and what that life means. I mean encouraging the spirit not by rule-of-thumb talk about art, but by stories about the people in every age, and thus presenting to people simply themselves. Even the Buddhists who came to tell about gods found that people understood gods better if they saw them working through ordinary folk like themselves.

But the real reason why the Chinese novel was written in the vernacular was because the common people could not read and write and the novel had to be written so that when it was read aloud it could be understood by persons who could communicate only through spoken words. In a village of two hundred souls perhaps only one man could read. And on holidays or in the evening when the work was done he read aloud to the people from some story. The rise of the Chinese novel began in just this simple fashion. After a while people took up a collection of pennies in somebody's cap or in a farm wife's bowl because the reader needed tea to wet his throat, or perhaps to pay him for the time he would otherwise have spent at his silk loom or his rush weaving. If the collections grew big enough, he gave up some of his regular work and became a professional storyteller. And the stories he read were the beginnings of novels. There were not many such stories written down, not nearly enough to last year in and year out for people who had by nature, as the Chinese have, a strong love for dramatic story. So the storyteller began to increase his stock. He searched the dry annals of the history which the scholars had written, and with his fertile imagination, enriched by long acquaintance with common people, he clothed long-dead figures with new flesh and made them live again; he found stories of court life and intrigue and names of imperial favorites who had brought dynasties to ruin; he found, as he traveled from village to village, strange tales from his own times which he wrote down when he heard them. People told him of experiences they had had and he wrote these down too, for other people. And he embellished them, but not with literary turns and phrases, for the people cared nothing for these. No, he kept his audiences always in mind and he found that the style which they loved best was one which flowed easily along, clearly and simply, in the short words which they themselves used every day, with no other technique than occasional bits of description, only enough to give vividness to a place or a person, and never enough to delay the story. Nothing must delay the story. Story was what they wanted.

And when I say story, I do not mean mere pointless activity, not crude action alone. The Chinese are too mature for that. They have always demanded of their novels character above all else. *Shui Hu Chuan* they have considered one of their three greatest novels, not primarily because it is full of the flash and fire of action, but because it portrays so distinctly one hundred and eight characters that each is to be seen separate from the others. Often I have heard it said of that novel in tones of delight, "When any one of the hundred and eight begins to speak, we do not need to be told his name. By the way the words come from his mouth we know who he is." Vividness of character portrayal, then, is the first quality which the Chinese people have demanded of their novels, and after it, that such portrayal shall be by the character's own action and words rather than by the author's explanation.

Curiously enough, while the novel was beginning thus humbly in tea houses, in villages and lowly city streets out of stories told to the common people by a common and unlearned man among them, in imperial palaces it was beginning, too, and in much the same unlearned fashion. It was an old custom of emperors, particularly if the dynasty were a foreign one, to employ persons called "imperial ears," whose only duty was to come and go among the people in the streets of cities and villages and to sit among them in tea houses, disguised in common clothes, and listen to what was talked about there. The original purpose of this was, of course, to hear of any discontent among the emperor's subjects, and more especially to find out if discontents were rising to the shape of those rebellions which preceded the fall of every dynasty.

But emperors were very human and they were not often learned scholars. More often, indeed, they were only spoiled and willful men. And the "imperial ears" had opportunity to hear all sorts of strange and interesting stories, and they found that their royal masters were more frequently interested in these stories than they were in politics. So when they came back to make their reports, they flattered the emperor and sought to gain favor by telling him what he liked to hear, shut up as he was in the Forbidden City, away from life. They told him the strange and interesting things which common people did, who were free, and after a while they took to writing down what they heard in order to save memory. And I do not doubt that if messengers between the emperor and the people carried stories in one direction, they carried them in the other, too, and to the people they told stories about the emperor and what he said and did, and how he quarreled with the empress who bore him no sons, and how she intrigued with the chief eunuch to poison the favorite concubine, all of which delighted the Chinese, because it proved to them, the most democratic of peoples, that their emperor was after all only a common fellow like themselves and that he, too, had his troubles, though he was the Son of Heaven. Thus there began another important source for the novel that was to develop with such form and force, though still always denied its right to exist by the professional men of letters.

From such humble and scattered beginnings, then, came the Chinese novel, written always in the vernacular, and dealing with all which interested the people, with legend and with myth, with love and intrigue, with brigands and wars, with everything, indeed, which went to make up the life of the people, high and low.

Nor was the novel in China shaped, as it was in the West, by a few great persons. In China the novel has always been more important than the novelist. There has been no Chinese Defoe, no Chinese Fielding or Smollett, no Austen or Brontë or Dickens or Thackeray, or Meredith or Hardy, any more than Balzac or Flaubert. But there were and are novels as great as the novels in any country in the world, as great as any could have written, had he been born in China. Who then wrote these novels of China?

That is what the modern literary men of China now, centuries too late, are trying to discover. Within the last twenty-five years literary critics, trained in the universities of the West, have begun to discover their own neglected novels. But the novelists who wrote them they cannot discover. Did one man write *Shui Hu Chuan,* or did it grow to its present shape, added to, rearranged, deepened and developed by many minds and many a hand, in different centuries? Who can now tell? They are dead. They lived in their day and wrote what in their day they saw and heard, but of themselves they have told nothing. The author of *Hung Lou Meng,* or *Dream of the Red Chamber,* in a far later century says in the preface to his book, "It is not necessary to know the times of Han and T'ang—it is necessary to tell only of my own times."

They told of their own times and they lived in a blessed obscurity. They read no reviews of their novels, no treatises as to

whether or not what they did was well done according to the rules
of scholarship. It did not occur to them that they must reach the
high thin air which scholars breathed nor did they consider the
stuff of which greatness is made, according to the scholars. They
wrote as it pleased them to write and as they were able. Sometimes they wrote unwittingly well and sometimes unwittingly
they wrote not so well. They died in the same happy obscurity
and now they are lost in it and not all the scholars of China, gathered too late to do them honor, can raise them up again. They
are long past the possibility of literary postmortems. But what
they did remains after them because it is the common people of
China who keep alive the great novels, illiterate people, who have
passed the novel not so often from hand to hand as from mouth
to mouth.

In the preface to one of the later editions of *Shui Hu Chuan*,
Shih Nai-an, who had much to do with the making of that novel,
writes, "What I speak of I wish people to understand easily.
Whether the reader is good or evil, learned or unlearned, anyone
can read this book. Whether or not the book is well done is not
important enough to cause anyone to worry. —Alas, I am born to
die. How can I know what those who come after me who read my
book will think of it? I cannot even know what I myself, born into
another incarnation, will think of it. I do not know if I myself
then can even read. Why therefore should I care?"

Strangely enough, there were certain scholars who envied the
freedom of obscurity, and who, burdened with certain private
sorrows which they dared not tell anyone, or who perhaps wanting
only a holiday from the weariness of the sort of art they had themselves created, wrote novels too, under assumed and humble
names. And when they did so they put aside pedantry and wrote
as simply and naturally as any common novelist. For the novelist
believed that he should not be conscious of techniques. He should
write as his material demanded. If a novelist became known for a
particular style or technique, to that extent he ceased to be a good
novelist, and became a literary technician.

A good novelist, or so I have been taught in China, should be
above all else *"tse ran,"* that is, natural, unaffected, and so flexible
and variable as to be wholly at the command of the material that
flows through him. His whole duty is only to sort life as it flows

through him, and in the vast fragmentariness of time and space and event to discover essential and inherent order and rhythm and shape. We should never be able, merely by reading pages, to know who wrote them, for when the style of a novelist becomes fixed, that style becomes his prison. The Chinese novelists varied their writing to accompany like music their chosen themes.

These Chinese novels are not perfect according to Western standards. They are often too long, too full of incident, too crowded with character, a medley of fact and fiction as to material, and a medley of romance and realism as to method, so that an impossible event of magic or dream may be described with such exact semblance of detail that one is compelled to belief against all reason. The earliest novels are full of folklore, for the people of those times thought and dreamed in the ways of folklore. But no one can understand the mind of China today who has not read these novels, for the novels have shaped the present mind, too, and the folklore persists in spite of all that Chinese diplomats and Western trained scholars would have us believe to the contrary. The essential mind of China is still that mind of which George Russell wrote when he said of the Irish mind, so strangely akin to the Chinese, "that mind which in its folk imagination believes anything. It creates ships of gold with masts of silver and white cities by the sea and rewards and faeries, and when that vast folk mind turns to politics it is ready to believe anything."

Out of this folk mind, turned into stories and crowded with thousands of years of life, grew, literally, the Chinese novel. For these novels changed as they grew. If, as I have said, there are no single names attached beyond question to the great novels of China, it is because no one hand wrote them. Beginning as a mere tale, a story grew through succeeding versions into a structure built by many hands. I might mention as an example the well-known story *The White Snake,* or *Pei She Chuan,* first written in the T'ang dynasty by an unknown author. It was then a tale of the simple supernatural whose hero was a great white snake. In the next version in the following century, the snake has become a vampire woman who is an evil force. But the third version contains a more gentle and human touch. The vampire becomes a faithful wife who aids her husband and gives him a son. The story thus adds not only new character but new quality, and ends

not as the supernatural tale it began but as a novel of human beings.

So in early periods of Chinese history, many books must be
called not so much novels as source books for novels, the sort of
books into which Shakespeare, had they been open to him, might
have dipped with both hands to bring up pebbles to make into
jewels. Many of these books have been lost, since they were not
considered valuable. But not all—early stories of Han, written so
vigorously that to this day it is said they run like galloping horses,
and tales of the troubled dynasties followed—not all were lost.
Some have persisted. In the Ming dynasty, in one way or another,
many of them were represented in the great collection known as
T'ai P'ing Kuan Shi, wherein are tales of superstition and religion,
of mercy and goodness and rewards for evil and well doing, tales
of dreams and miracles, of dragons and gods and goddesses and
priests, of tigers and foxes and transmigration and resurrection
from the dead. Most of these early stories had to do with supernatural events, of gods born of virgins, of men walking as gods,
as the Buddhist influence grew strong. There are miracles and
allegories, such as the pens of poor scholars bursting into flower,
dreams leading men and women into strange and fantastic lands
of Gulliver, or the magic wand that floated an altar made of iron.
But stories mirrored each age. The stories of Han were vigorous
and dealt often with the affairs of the nation, and centered about
some great man or hero. Humor was strong in this golden age, a
racy, earthy, lusty humor, such as was to be found, for instance,
in many of the books of tales, some presumed to have been col-
lected, some to have been written during the period. And then the
scenes changed, as that golden age faded, though it was never to
be forgotten, so that to this day the Chinese like to call themselves
sons of Han. With the succeeding weak and corrupt centuries,
the very way the stories were written became honeyed and weak,
and their subjects slight, or as the Chinese say, "In the days of the
Six Dynasties, they wrote of small things, of a woman, a water-
fall, or a bird."

If the Han dynasty was golden, then the T'ang dynasty was
silver, and silver were the love stories for which it was famous.
It was an age of love, when a thousand stories clustered about the
beautiful Yang Kuei Fei and her scarcely less beautiful predeces-

sor in the emperor's favor, Mei Fei. These love stories of T'ang come very near sometimes to fulfilling in their unity and complexity the standards of the Western novel. There are rising action and crisis and denouement, implicit if not expressed. The Chinese say, "We must read the stories of T'ang, because though they deal with small matters, yet they are written in so moving a manner that the tears come."

It is not surprising that most of these love stories deal not with love that ends in marriage or is contained in marriage, but with love outside the marriage relationship. Indeed, it is significant that when marriage is the theme the story nearly always ends in tragedy. Two famous stories, *Pei Li Shi* and *Chiao Fang Chi,* deal entirely with extramarital love, and are written apparently to show the superiority of the courtesans, who could read and write and sing and were clever and beautiful besides, beyond the ordinary wife who was, as the Chinese say even today, "a yellow-faced woman," and usually illiterate.

So strong did this tendency become that officialdom grew alarmed at the popularity of such stories among the common people and they were denounced as revolutionary and dangerous because it was thought they attacked the foundation of Chinese civilization, the family system. A reactionary tendency was not lacking, such as is to be seen in *Hui Chen Chi,* one of the earlier forms of a famous later work, the story of the young scholar who loved the beautiful Ying Ying and who renounced her, saying prudently as he went away, "All extraordinary women are dangerous. They destroy themselves and others. They have ruined even emperors. I am not an emperor and I had better give her up"—which he did, to the admiration of all wise men. And to him the modest Ying Ying replies, "If you possess me and leave me it is your right. I do not reproach you." But five hundred years later the sentimentality of the Chinese popular heart comes forth and sets the thwarted romance right again. In this last version of the story the author makes Chang and Ying Ying husband and wife and says in closing, "This is in the hope that all the lovers of the world may be united in happy marriage." And as time goes in China, five hundred years is not long to wait for a happy ending.

This story, by the way, is one of China's most famous. It was repeated in the Sung dynasty in a poetic form by Chao Teh Liang, under the title *The Reluctant Butterfly,* and again in the Yuan dynasty by Tung Chai Yuen as a drama to be sung, entitled *Suh Hsi Hsiang.* In the Ming dynasty, with two versions intervening, it appears as *Li Reh Hua's Nan Hsi Hsiang Chi,* written in the southern metrical form called "ts'e," and so to the last and most famous *Hsi Hsiang Chi.* Even children in China know the name of Chang Sen.

If I seem to emphasize the romances of the T'ang period, it is because romance between man and woman is the chief gift of T'ang to the novel, and not because there were no other stories. There were many novels of a humorous and satirical nature and one curious type of story which concerned itself with cockfighting, an important pastime of that age, and particularly in favor at court. One of the best of these tales is *Tung Chen Lao Fu Chuan,* by Ch'en Hung, which tells how Chia Chang, a famous cockfighter, became so famous that he was loved by emperor and people alike.

But time and the stream pass on. The novel form really begins to be clear in the Sung dynasty, and in the Yuan dynasty it flowers into that height which was never again surpassed and only equaled, indeed, by the single novel *Hung Lou Meng,* or *Dream of the Red Chamber,* in the Ts'ing dynasty. It is as though for centuries the novel had been developing unnoticed and from deep roots among the people, and spreading into trunk and branch and twig and leaf to burst into this flowering in the Yuan dynasty, when the young Mongols brought into the old country they had conquered their vigorous, hungry, untutored minds, and demanded to be fed. Such minds could not be fed with the husks of the old classical literature, and they turned therefore the more eagerly to the drama and the novel, and in this new life, in the sunshine of imperial favor, though still not with literary favor, there came two of China's three great novels, *Shui Hu Chuan* and *San Kuo—Hung Lou Meng* being the third.

I wish I could convey to you what these three novels mean and have meant to the Chinese people. But I can think of nothing comparable to them in Western literature. We have not in the history of our novel so clear a moment to which we can point and say, "There the novel is at its height." These three are the vindication of that literature of the common people, the Chinese novel.

They stand as completed monuments of that popular literature, if not of letters. They, too, were ignored by men of letters and banned by censors and damned in succeeding dynasties as dangerous, revolutionary, decadent. But they lived on because people read them and told them as stories and sang them as songs and ballads and acted them as dramas, until at last grudgingly even the scholars were compelled to notice them and to begin to say they were not novels but allegories and if they were allegories perhaps then they could be looked upon as literature after all, though the people paid no heed to such theories and never read the long treatises which scholars wrote to prove them. They rejoiced in the novels they had made as novels and for no purpose except for joy in story, and in story through which they could express themselves.

And indeed the people had made them. *Shui Hu Chuan*, though the modern versions carry the name of Shih Nai-an as author, was written by no one man. Out of a handful of tales centering in the Sung dynasty about a band of robbers there grew this great, structured novel. Its beginnings were in history. The original lair which the robbers held still exists in Shantung or did until very recent times. Those times of the thirteenth century of our Western era were, in China, sadly distorted. The dynasty under the emperor Huei Chung was falling into decadence and disorder. The rich grew richer and the poor poorer and when none other came forth to set this right these righteous robbers came forth.

I cannot here tell you fully of the long growth of this novel, nor of its changes at many hands. Shih Nai-an, it is said, found it in rude form in an old bookshop and took it home and rewrote it. After him the story was still told and retold. Five or six versions of it today have importance, one with a hundred chapters entitled *Chung I Shui Hu,* one of a hundred and twenty-seven chapters, and one of a hundred chapters. The original version attributed to Shi Nai-an had a hundred and twenty chapters, but the one most used today has only seventy. This is the version arranged in the Ming dynasty by the famous Ching Shen T'an, who said that it was idle to forbid his son to read the book and therefore presented the lad with a copy revised by himself, knowing that no boy could ever refrain from reading it. There is also a version written under official command, when officials found that nothing could keep the people from reading *Shui Hu*. This official version is entitled *Tung K'ou Chi,* or *Laying Waste the Robbers,* and it tells of the final defeat of the robbers by the state army and their destruction. But the common people of China are nothing if not independent. They have never adopted the official version, and their own form of the novel still stands. It is a struggle they know all too well, the struggle of everyday people against a corrupt officialdom.

I might add that *Shui Hu Chuan* is in partial translation in French under the title *Les Chevaliers Chinois,* and the seventy-chapter version is in complete English translation by myself under the title *All Men Are Brothers.* The original title, *Shui Hu Chuan,* in English is meaningless, denoting merely the watery margins of the famous marshy lake which was the robbers' lair. To Chinese the words invoke instant century-old memory, but not to us.

This novel has survived everything and in this new day in China has taken on an added significance. The Chinese Communists have printed their own edition of it with a preface by a famous Communist and have issued it anew as the first Communist literature in China. The proof of the novel's greatness is in this timelessness. It is as true today as it was dynasties ago. The people of China still march across its pages, priests and courtesans, merchants and scholars, women good and bad, old and young, and even naughty little boys. The only figure lacking is that of the modern scholar trained in the West, holding his Ph.D. diploma in his hand. But be sure that if he had been alive in China when the final hand laid down the brush upon the pages of that book, he too would have been there in all the pathos and humor of his new learning, so often useless and inadequate and laid like a patch too small upon an old robe.

The Chinese say, "The young should not read *Shui Hu* and the old should not read *San Kuo.*" This is because the young might be charmed into being robbers and the old might be led into deeds too vigorous for their years. For if *Shui Hu Chuan* is the great social document of Chinese life, *San Kuo* is the document of wars and statesmanship, and in its turn *Hung Lou Meng* is the document of family life and human life.

The history of the *San Kuo* or *Three Kingdoms* shows the same architectural structure and the same doubtful authorship as *Shui Hu.* The story begins with three friends swearing eternal brotherhood in the Han dynasty and ends ninety-seven years later in the succeeding period of the Six Dynasties. It is a novel rewritten in its final form by a man named Lo Kuan Chung, thought to be a pupil of Shih Nai-an, and one who perhaps even shared with Shih Nai-an in the writing, too, of *Shui Hu Chuan.* But this is a Chinese Bacon-and-Shakespeare controversy which has no end.

Lo Kuan Chung was born in the late Yuan dynasty and lived on into the Ming. He wrote many dramas but he is more famous for his novels, of which *San Kuo* is easily the best. The version of this novel now most commonly used in China is the one revised in the time of K'ang Hsi by Mao Chen Kan, who revised as well as criticized the book. He changed, added and omitted material, as for example when he added the story of Suan Fu Ren, the wife of one of the chief characters. He altered even the style. If *Shui Hu Chuan* has importance today as a novel of the people in their struggle for liberty, *San Kuo* has importance because it gives in such detail the science and art of war, as the Chinese conceive it, so differently, too, from our own. The guerrillas, who are today China's most effective fighting units against Japan, are peasants who know *San Kuo* by heart, if not from their own reading, at least from hours spent in the idleness of winter days or long summer evenings when they sat listening to the storytellers describe how the warriors of the Three Kingdoms fought their battles. It is these ancient tactics of war which the guerrillas trust today. What a warrior must be and how he must attack and retreat, how retreat when the enemy advances, how advance when the enemy retreats—all this had its source in this novel, so well known to every common man and boy of China.

Hung Lou Meng, or *The Dream of the Red Chamber,* the latest and most modern of these three greatest of Chinese novels, was written originally as an autobiographical novel by Ts'ao Hsueh Ching, an official highly in favor during the Manchu regime and indeed considered by the Manchus as one of themselves. There were then eight military groups among the Manchus, and Ts'ao Hsueh Ching belonged to them all. He never finished his novel, and the last forty chapters were added by another man probably named Kao O. The thesis that Ts'ao Hsueh

Ching was telling the story of his own life has been in modern times elaborated by Hu Shih, and in earlier times by Yuan Mei. Be this as it may, the original title of the book was *Shih T'ou Chi*, and it came out of Peking about 1765 of the Western era, and in five or six years, an incredibly short time in China, the book became known by the method that is called in China, "You-lend-me-a-book-and-I-lend-you-a-book."

The story is simple in its theme but complex in implication, in character study and in its portrayal of human emotions. It is almost a pathological study, this story of a great house, once wealthy and high in imperial favor, so that indeed one of its members was an imperial concubine. But the great days are over when the book begins. The family is already declining. Its wealth is being dissipated and the last and only son, Chia Pao Yü, is being corrupted by the decadent influences within his own home, although the fact that he was a youth of exceptional quality at birth is established by the symbolism of a piece of jade found in his mouth. The preface begins, "Heaven was once broken and when it was mended a bit was left unused, and this became the famous jade of Chia Pao Yu." Thus does the interest in the supernatural persist in the Chinese people; it persists even today as a part of Chinese life.

This novel seized hold of the people primarily because it portrayed the problems of their own family system, the absolute power of women in the home, the too great power of the matriarchy, the grandmother, the mother, and even the bondmaids, so often young and beautiful and fatally dependent, who became too frequently the playthings of the sons of the house and ruined them and were ruined by them. Women reigned supreme in the Chinese house, and because they were wholly confined in its walls and often illiterate, they ruled to the hurt of all. They kept men children, and protected them from hardship and effort when they should not have been so protected. Such a one was Chia Pao Yü, and we follow him to his tragic end in *Hung Lou Meng*.

I cannot tell you to what lengths of allegory scholars went to explain away this novel when they found that again even the emperor was reading it and that its influence was so great everywhere among the people. I do not doubt that they were probably reading it themselves in secret. A great many popular jokes in

China have to do with scholars reading novels privately and publicly pretending never to have heard of them. At any rate, scholars wrote treatises to prove that *Hung Lou Meng* was not a novel but a political allegory depicting the decline of China under the foreign rule of the Manchus, the word Red in the title signifying Manchu, and Ling Tai Yü, the young girl who dies, although she was the one destined to marry Pao Yü, signifying China, and Pa Ts'ai, her successful rival, who secures the jade in her place, standing for the foreigner, and so forth. The very name Chia signified, they said, falseness. But this was a far-fetched explanation of what was written as a novel and stands as a novel and as such a powerful delineation, in the characteristic Chinese mixture of realism and romance, of a proud and powerful family in decline. Crowded with men and women of the several generations accustomed to living under one roof in China, it stands alone as an intimate description of that life.

In so emphasizing these three novels, I have merely done what the Chinese themselves do. When you say "novels," the average Chinese replies, *"Shui Hu, San Kuo, Hung Lou Meng";* yet this is not to say that there are not hundreds of other novels, for there are. I must mention *Hsi Yu Chi,* or *Record of Travels in the West,* almost as popular as these three. I might mention *Feng Shen Chuan,* the story of a deified warrior, the author unknown but said to be a writer in the time of Ming. I must mention *Ru Ling Wai Shi,* a satire upon the evils of the Ts'ing dynasty, particularly of the scholars, full of a double-edged though not malicious dialogue, rich with incident, pathetic and humorous. The fun here is made of the scholars who can do nothing practical, who are lost in the world of useful everyday things, who are so bound by convention that nothing original can come from them. The book, though long, has no central character. Each figure is linked to the next by the thread of incident, person and incident passing on together until, as Lu Hsün, the famous modern Chinese writer, has said, "they are like scraps of brilliant silk and satin sewed together."

And there is *Yea Shou Pei Yin,* or *An Old Hermit Talks in the Sun,* written by a famous man disappointed in official preferment, Shia of Kiang-yin; then there is that strangest of books, *Ching Hua Yuan,* a fantasy of women, whose ruler was an empress, whose scholars were all women. It is designed to show that the wisdom of women is equal to that of men, although I must acknowledge that the book ends with a war between men and women in which the men are triumphant and the empress is supplanted by an emperor.

But I can mention only a small fraction of the hundreds of novels which delight the common people of China. And if those people knew of what I was speaking to you today, they would after all say, "tell of the great three, and let us stand or fall by *Shui Hu* and *San Kuo* and *Hung Lou Meng.*" In these three novels are the lives which the Chinese people lead and have long led, here are the songs they sing and the things at which they laugh and the things which they love to do. Into these novels they have put the generations of their being and to refresh that being they return to these novels again and again, and out of them they have made new songs and plays and other novels. Some of them come to be almost as famous as the great originals, as for example, *Ching P'ing Mei,* that classic of romantic physical love, taken from a single incident in *Shui Hu Chuan.*

But the important thing for me today is not the listing of novels. The aspect which I wish to stress is that all this profound and indeed sublime development of the imagination of a great democratic people was never in its own time and country called literature. The very name for a story was "hsiao shuo," denoting something slight and valueless, and even a novel was only a "ts'ang p'ien hsiao shuo," or a longer something which was still slight and useless. No, the people of China forged their own literature apart from letters. And today this is what lives, to be part of what is to come, and all the formal literature, which was called art, is dead. The plots of these novels are often incomplete, the love interest is often not brought to solution, heroines are often not beautiful and heroes often are not brave. Nor has the story always an end; sometimes it merely stops, in the way life does, in the middle of it when death is not expected.

In this tradition of the novel have I been born and reared as a writer. My ambition, therefore, has not been trained toward the beauty of letters or the grace of art. It is, I believe, a sound teaching and as I have said, illuminating for the novels of the West.

For here is the essence of the attitude of Chinese novelists—

perhaps the result of the contempt in which they were held by those who considered themselves the priests of art. I put it thus in my own words, for none of them has done so.

The instinct which creates *the arts* is not the same as that which produces art. The creative instinct is, in its final analysis and in its simplest terms, an enormous extra vitality, a super-energy, born inexplicably in an individual, a vitality great beyond all the needs of his own living—an energy which no single life can consume. This energy consumes itself then in creating more life, in the form of music, painting, writing, or whatever is its most natural medium of expression. Nor can the individual keep himself from this process, because only by its full function is he relieved of the burden of this extra and peculiar energy—an energy at once physical and mental, so that all his senses are more alert and more profound than another man's, and all his brain more sensitive and quickened to that which his senses reveal to him in such abundance that actuality overflows into imagination. It is a process from within. It is the heightened activity of every cell of his being, which sweeps not only himself, but all human life about him, or in him, in his dreams, into the circle of its activity.

From the product of this activity, art is deduced—but not by him. The process which creates is not the process which deduces the shapes of art. The defining of art, therefore, is a secondary and not a primary process. And when one born for the primary process of creation, as the novelist is, concerns himself with the secondary process, his activity becomes meaningless. When he begins to make shapes and styles and techniques and new schools, then he is like a ship stranded upon a reef whose propeller, whirl wildly as it will, cannot drive the ship onward. Not until the ship is in its element again can it regain its course.

And for the novelist the only element is human life as he finds it in himself or outside himself. The sole test of his work is whether or not his energy is producing more of that life. Are his creatures alive? That is the only question. And who can tell him? Who but those living human beings, the people? Those people are not absorbed in what art is or how it is made—are not, indeed, absorbed in anything very lofty, however good it is. No, they are absorbed only in themselves, in their own hungers and despairs and joys and above all, perhaps, in their own dreams. These are the ones who can really judge the work of the novelist, for they judge by that single test of reality. And the standard of the test is not to be made by the device of art, but by the simple comparison of the reality of what they read, to their own reality.

I have been taught, therefore, that though the novelist may see art as cool and perfect shapes, he may only admire them as he admires marble statues standing aloof in a quiet and remote gallery; for his place is not with them. His place is in the street. He is happiest there. The street is noisy and the men and women are not perfect in the technique of their expression as the statues are. They are ugly and imperfect, incomplete even as human beings, and where they come from and where they go cannot be known. But they are people and therefore infinitely to be preferred to those who stand upon the pedestals of art.

And like the Chinese novelist, I have been taught to want to write for these people. If they are reading their magazines by the million, then I want my stories there rather than in magazines read only by a few. For story belongs to the people. They are sounder judges of it than anyone else, for their senses are unspoiled and their emotions are free. No, a novelist must not think of pure literature as his goal. He must not even know this field too well, because people, who are his material, are not there. He is a storyteller in a village tent and by his stories he entices people into his tent. He need not raise his voice when a scholar passes. But he must beat all his drums when a band of poor pilgrims pass on their way up the mountain in search of gods. To them he must cry, "I, too, tell of gods!" And to farmers he must talk of their land, and to old men he must speak of peace, and to old women he must tell of their children and to young men and women he must speak of each other. He must be satisfied if the common people hear him gladly. At least, so I have been taught in China.

I think of this great prize now and where it stands, on display in the Foundation building. It is not so important-looking in comparison with some of her other awards. It is a solid gold medal about two inches in diameter and about one-quarter of an inch thick, and truly does not compare in beauty or size with the William Dean Howells Medal of the American Academy of Arts and

Letters, displayed on the same glass shelf of the fourth-floor showcase. The Nobel Prize medal, however, was accompanied by a handsome leather-bound citation hand-illuminated with beautiful Chinese figures, and that citation with its inscription has become one of her most treasured possessions. When I first discussed the correctness of displaying her awards in the Foundation she objected strongly on the grounds that she did not want to look at them. With persistence I won, but only with the condition that the exact thought she had had at the time the Nobel Prize was awarded be on display also. Because it is so characteristic of her brand of determination I include here the words that appear in the display, a quotation from a letter she wrote to an old friend of hers:

"Publishers and literary agents once told me I could never make a success at writing about Chinese people. I thought of that the day I stood before the King of Sweden to receive the Nobel Prize."

I think the child she missed most during her trip to Sweden was her daughter Janice, who remained at home in school. I have concluded this from another little gem I located among her treasures—a small, handmade, handwritten and illustrated booklet entitled "Seasick Rhymes for Janice, from Mother, illustrated by Daddy." The seasick rhymes show a side of her humor I did not see until I came to know her well. I include them here as an excellent example of her marked tongue-in-cheek wit:

> The ocean looks so very nice,
> But really that's its chiefest vice.
> It's very wicked of a saint
> To go and act as if it ain't.

> I think the Aquitania
> Has a mania.
> And as for the Normandie,
> She acted abnormandly.

> To dress for dinner on the sea
> Seems superfluous to me,
> For when my dinners up and left
> I only felt the more bereft.

Oh say what you like about the sea,
Say it's as blue as blue can be,
Say this, say that, say such-and-such of it,
The fact remains there is too much of it.

The ocean may be only water
But innocents it loves to slaughter,
It loves to watch along a rail
A row of faces sick and pale.

The ocean's only watery salt,
But that is still its chiefest fault.
Salt and water dietetically
Act together too emetically.

Ships and seas and sealing-wax,
Rats and snakes and carpet tacks,
All such things had better be
Omitted from Eternity!
(But especially the sea,
Or so at least it seems to me.)

I wonder if the great Nobel
Is not to blame for all this swell?
To feed the fishes
Is not my wishes.

The only thing 'twixt me and Sweden
Is that the ocean is betweeden.
I think that all the Nobel prizes
Should wait until the ocean dryses.

I thank whatever gods there be
Somewhere a shore stops every sea!

There is one final verse under the heading "Postscript by the Artist" and it also is needed to complete the trip.

Higgledy, piggledy,
Steamers are wiggledy.
Flibberty, gibberty,
Statue of Liberty!

Perhaps the most important single fact the Nobel Prize proved was that she was right to hold steadfastly to her own beliefs in her writing. She has always refused to be forced into the mold of "this" or "that" or the "other" as emphatically in her profession as in her personal life. This is pointed out in an article by her, published in *Opportunity* magazine in 1936, and years later in a lecture by Jason Lindsey in Stockholm. He points to this characteristic of her writing as the reason she will always be among the great in literature. I quote first her article, where she frankly refers to all who can be molded and who can have their thoughts formed for them as "lost souls":

I live in a region of innumerable small streams. They flow quietly and slowly enough by nature, lingering in small pools, cultivating along their banks exquisite mosses and ferns and delicate reeds. The water is so clear that one can see a trout flash through it, or the tinge of rusty red stone in the bottom or a bit of green agate inlaid in a gray rock. But they are deceptive streams. They seem so quiet and there comes a change, a wind, a storm, snow—and they go mad. A madness has them then. They are not content to pursue their amiable and individual courses. They are swollen with borrowed waters, dark with mud and debris. And they rush to join some larger stream, and these in turn rush to pour themselves into the river, and the river swells and roars with all these angry and dissatisfied waters and cannot rest until it vents itself into the sea. And in the vastness of the sea all these waters are lost. They will never return to those original pools and brooks—it cannot be—there is no return. When the clouds drop rain again, the waters must go as chance sends them, upon alien hills and unknown lands.

I watch the torrents, thinking how like men's minds they are. I have watched minds rise like that. Men and women live quietly and with serenity of a sort, if not in happiness. Most people live, I suppose, as it has been said, in a state of quiet desperation. And then a tide rises. I do not know from where it comes—perhaps from an excess of despair, or from an unwillingness to believe that life is not more than it is, or from wild hopes, caught, like a disease, from other souls. But there comes a time when the individual souls of people are given up into the tide of mass soul, and they cease to think and feel as individuals.

The world is in such a tide now. That tide has been rising ever since the Great War, and nation by nation, class by class, race by race, men and women are assembling themselves. They are thinking in terms of these groups. Their own names are not so important to them as it is to call themselves by some race or group name—Fascist, Communist, Jew, Gentile, Negro, Chinese, Aryan, and many another. The mass idea has permeated even art and literature. Pictures are painted these days of factories, of a crowd at work, of a laborer who stands not for himself but for a mob. The old days are gone—and it may be well gone, for all I know, since time must move. Once an artist lingered over a single beloved face. Now his art must stand as a symbol. He may not dwell upon a figure for its own sake.

In modern literature, too, there are those who frankly say that the individual no longer has a place. Each character must stand not for himself, but for that group from which he emerges for the moment. He is only named John Doe. The real character is Liberalism, or Communism, or Fascism, or Labor, or Capital. The struggle, the plot, the entanglement, the denouement, must be among these large names. The clash is not now, they say, between men and women, but between ideas and creeds.

In such a time, in the face of such a tide, I must affirm my belief in the individual. I affirm my trust in the individual human heart. I place my emphasis upon the single human mind. No, more, I say that the lowest mind is the mass mind. When men bind themselves together their minds lose clarity, as the brooks do, as the river does, and they overflow into like destruction. I say the coldest, hardest, most inhuman heart is the mass heart, which has lost all sense of individual need, so that it views life and death with callous equal indifference. The most deadened soul is the mass soul, which has no generosities, no impulse of kindness or understanding, no spiritual denominator. That which is common to all is nearest the beast.

Therefore, if I have anything to say, it is to beg men and women never to give themselves up entirely to any cause or creed or mass of race or belief. What each of us has to give of most worth is that which is most peculiarly individual in us. That peculiar individuality is as well our most delicate means of receiving from others what is most valuable and exquisite in life. To lose it is to lose at once our means of receiving the best from others and giving the best of ourselves. To keep it is to keep ourselves clear and untrammeled by confusions; it is to maintain in ourselves a center of tranquillity in a stormy and disheveled world. John Doe is forever himself also, not only one among millions. His life is of value in so far as he most realizes himself. Long ago someone said, "And what shall it profit a man if he lose his own soul?" It is a question to ask again today.

The following passages are quoted from a course of lectures on the six United States winners of the Nobel Prize for Literature given by the American film director Jason Lindsey at Kursverksamheten of Stockholm University 1964–1966:

> The Nobel Prize in Literature has been awarded fifty-three times to fifty-eight writers. Five of the recipients have been women. Two of these, Selma Lagerlöf (who was the first of her sex and the first Swede—in the first eight years it was given to nine other writers, two each from Germany and France, and one each from Poland, Italy, Norway, England and Spain) and Sigrid Undset, are still read in Scandinavia. Only one, however, is still read by as wide a variety of nationalities as when she was at the peak of her fame. She is the most extensively translated of any American writer. I refer, of course, to Pearl Buck, the only woman in the list of U. S. Winners of the Nobel Prize in Literature.
>
> Ask anyone who is more than just mildly literate to name the authors of *Gösta Berlings Saga, The Woman and the Priest, Kristin Lavransdatter,* and *Desolation* and in reply you'll either get a completely wrong wild guess or an "I haven't the foggiest notion," and even when you supply the information that they are the works of, respectively, Selma Lagerlöf, Grazia Deledda, Sigrid Undset, and Gabriela Mistral, all winners of the Nobel Prize in Literature, very few will have any idea of whom you are speaking. But: ask who wrote *Dragon Seed* and *The Good Earth* and almost anyone will answer immediately: "Pearl Buck." Or: do it the other way around; ask who Pearl Buck is and the reply is sure to be: "The woman who wrote *The Good Earth.*"
>
> Pearl Buck *can* write. She *does* write with unflagging energy and purpose. Her works fulfill to the letter the qualifications for the awarding of the Nobel Prize in Literature according to Alfred Nobel's last will and testament. They are works of the highest possible idealistic tendency.

While it is a patently ridiculous mistake to assume that Pearl Buck has no life outside her books, it is not difficult to understand why so many of her readers labour under this quaint delusion, for it is strangely true that more is known about this great woman's works than about the person herself. Nearly every encyclopedia contains basically the same few perfunctory lines which announce that she was born in Hillsboro, West Virginia, on June 26, 1892, of missionary parents who were on leave at the time from China whence they had hied themselves some years earlier to take the message of Christianity to the Chinese. (The *Encyclopaedia Britannica* now and again drops Pearl Buck from an edition but she pops back up again like a daruma and I find that she is in the latest edition.)

She has written more than fifty books which have made her famous the world over as the single person who has striven more than any other to bring about a closer understanding between the white and coloured races. No occidental writer has, as she, plumbed so to the depths of the Chinese problem. No one knows more than she of oriental smells and filth and spices, of the Orient's primitiveness and its potential, of its wild barbarity and its mannered thousands-of-years-old culture. No one has, as she, so clearly divided China's earth from its heaven. But above all, no one has understood China and the Chinese as well as she has. Her books have enjoyed constant international success. Her work has contributed immeasurably to racial tolerance and to Western understanding of oriental customs and problems. She has made oriental civilization understandable and significant to Western readers through her study of Chinese classics and her thorough knowledge of Chinese character. *The Good Earth* is the most effective portrayal of Chinese peasant life in American fiction.

Now, with those facts out of the way, we can get on to the business of finding out what makes Mrs. Buck tick.

Mrs. Buck said, before she returned to live in America, that: "It is people that have always afforded me my greatest pleasure and interest, and as I live among the Chinese it has been the Chinese people. When I am asked what sort of people they are, I cannot answer. They are not this or that, they are just people. I can no more define them than I can define my own relatives and kinsmen. I am too near to them and I have lived too intimately with them for that."

This was quoted by Dr. Per Hallström of the Swedish Academy in his speech of introduction on the occasion of the 1938 Nobel

awards as an indication that it was thus that Pearl Buck had
found her mission as interpreter to the Occident of the nature and
being of China. It explains, in some measure, Mrs. Buck's con-
tention that she did not turn to her mission as a literary speciality
at all but that it came to her without her seeking.

At the banquet following the presentation of the Nobel Prize
to Pearl Buck, Herr Lindblad, Professor of Astronomy, had the
following to say:

"Mrs. Pearl Buck, you have in your literary works, which are of
the highest artistic quality, advanced the understanding and appreciation in the Western world of a great and important part of
mankind, the people of China. You have taught us by your works
to see the individuals in this great mass of people, you have shown
us the rise and fall of families, and the land as the foundation
upon which families are built. In this you have taught us to see
those qualities of thought and feelings which bind us all together
as human beings on this Earth, and you have given us Westerners
something of China's soul. When by the development of techni-
cal inventions the peoples of the Earth are drawn closer to each
other, the surface of the Earth shrinks. East and West are no
longer separated by almost insuperable voids of distance, and
when on the other hand, partly as a natural effect of this phenom-
enon, the differences of national character and ambitions clash to
form dangerous discontinuities, it is of the greatest importance
that the peoples of the Earth learn to understand each other as
individuals across distances and frontiers. When works of literature succeed in this respect they are certainly in a very direct way
idealistic in the sense in which this word was meant by Alfred
Nobel."

The most important thing in Dr. Hallström's speech (as far as
it concerns this lecture) is that he has recognized that Mrs. Buck's
works are what Alfred Nobel had in mind when he dictated the
terms which were to govern the award. In this, Dr. Hallström is
unique. None of his colleagues has seized the opportunity to so
describe the works of any other Nobel Literature Laureate.

Even the most impromptu of Pearl Buck's statements have the
quality of being chiseled in stone or cast in bronze. "Every era of
renaissance," she has said, "has come out of new freedom for peoples. . . . No one escaped the benefits of the Renaissance of the
Middle Ages." Mrs. Buck is looking toward another renaissance
and her mission in life has been to establish real communication
between peoples, to make them realize that all people are alike in

their simple and basic and deep desires, one of which is a desire for new freedom and out of which will evolve a new renaissance. "Nothing," she says, "must be allowed to keep peoples apart for they need each other, cannot, in fact, live, more to the point, cannot survive, without each other." Everyone, everywhere in the world, is obligated to explore every possible means of learning the ways and habits and beliefs and hopes of every other people in the world. It is the duty of mankind to do this, to discover that after all we all long for the same things: for love and home and children, for work to sustain these human rights, for peace, for freedom in which to live and think and grow.

It is not improbable that Mrs. Buck's compassionate understanding of minority groups stems from the fact that for the first forty years of her life she had belonged to a minority race in the country in which she lived. She had suffered, at first hand, some of the indignities of segregation, some of the experience inevitable to anyone who is in the minority in any country.

Americans have not lived together long enough, Mrs. Buck believes, to become unified as the Chinese are, "their racial differences all intermingled and melted into a common colour, and their habits smoothed into uniformity by centuries of living together."

Americans suffer from a lack of curiosity about other countries and other peoples. It is the complaint against England which one most often hears voiced in continental Europe and it is one of the things which has kept England out of the Common Market. England has no real interest in Europe and refuses to admit that she is a part of it. England is all that interests England; and America (for the most part) is really all that interests America.

When the not too distant day arrives that half the population of the world is Chinese, the United States (along with other countries who have failed to appreciate the importance of China in world affairs) will find itself up against the most singularly unified people on earth. One cannot imagine that the other half of the world will suddenly become as unified. Would it not be better then to understand the Chinese half of the world and to face it not as an enemy but as a friend?

Mrs. Buck is tireless in her efforts to bridge the awful gulf which separates mankind from itself. She writes at length and with great skill and insight of all the many things which engage her attention and demand her participation. She has said when questioned: "Why not? I am a writer." She has the curiosity without which any writer is lost. From the moment she made up her mind to become a writer, she has never been idle. She, herself, has admitted that she is "prolific."

Mrs. Buck is surely the most learned of any of the six persons examined in these lectures. Her erudition extends deep into every form of knowledge. One stands mute before it. One's own knowledge palls in comparison. Mrs. Buck is that rarest of rarities: she is wise. And yet she is not sad, for wisdom frequently gives birth to sadness. Mrs. Buck, instead, has hope. The scope of Mrs. Buck's enlightenment is so broad that I am almost afraid to write about her lest I expose my own ignorance. She is, no question about it, the best informed individual in the world today on what ails the world and what can be done about it. I marvel that she has not long since been bodily thrust into the United States Senate or been made Secretary of State or Secretary General of the United Nations. Clearly she has no such aspirations. I suspect her, however, of secretly wanting to be the United States Ambassador to China, a post for which no one has ever been so eminently qualified; and one of the first things I propose to do after inauguration as President of the United States of America is to appoint Mrs. Buck to this post.

Pearl Buck learned one great truth very early in life: that trouble and suffering can always be relieved if there is the will to do it.

The past is the past for Mrs. Buck in that she never longs to dwell again in it as most of us do. Nostalgia she counts as one of the wasted emotions, like hate and envy and regret and prejudice. Mrs. Buck is of, for, and about the present.

Pearl Buck's early reading of writers in English included Mark Twain (she declares that she reads *Tom Sawyer* once a year so that she can understand her son) as well as Dickens and Thackeray and George Eliot and Walter Scott and their company. What she reads nowadays, I don't know—probably everything under the sun. No writer, however, has had any discernible influence on her style. It is her own.

Mrs. Buck had a very small estimate of her powers as a writer, so that in the autumn of 1938 when she heard that she had just been awarded the Nobel Prize in Literature, she didn't believe it and had to confirm it with a telephone call to Stockholm. Even then, she was of several minds about it, unable to understand why it had been given to her. She remembers exclaiming: "Oh, I wish that it could have been given to Theodore Dreiser instead!"

Mrs. Buck and I do not see eye-to-eye with regard to Dreiser.

Like so many writers of extremely high calibre, she lacks the real ability of assigning her fellow writers to their proper places. She is also, sadly, an admirer of Sinclair Lewis, so much so that after his death she made a pilgrimage to Sauk Centre to see the house in which he was born and in which he spent his unhappy childhood. "I saw him (Sinclair Lewis) only once," says Mrs. Buck, "and it was at a dinner given in New York by the P.E.N. Club upon the occasion of the award of the Nobel Prize in Literature in 1938. I went as the guest of honour, but never was there a guest so faint of heart, and even dispirited, as I that night. . . . He sat next to me. I said very little because I felt reticent before so great a writer, and I listened with appreciation to what he said. He was already sad and disillusioned, and I felt a sort of reckless honesty in his words, his fine homely face turned away from me most of the time so that I had to listen carefully while he talked quickly on. Suddenly my turn came to make a little speech, and I got up, intensely mindful of the criticism from some of the very persons who sat that night before me, and looking back to what I had been taught in my Chinese childhood, I told them somehow, and I cannot remember exactly the words and I did not think them important enough to write down, that I had long ago learned that a mere teller of tales is not to be considered a literary figure, and that my novels were only stories to amuse people and make a heavy hour pass a little more easily, and a few more sentences of that sort. . . . When I sat down again, he turned to me with an animation sparkling with anger. 'You must not minimize yourself,' he declared, and I remember every word because they fell like balm upon my wounded spirit. 'Neither must you minimize your profession,' he went on. 'A novelist has a noble function.' And then, as though he understood all I had been feeling, he went on to speak of that function, and how a writer must not heed what others say. I would weary, he said, of the very name of *The Good Earth,* for people would act as though it were the only book I had ever written, but never mind people, he said, never mind! He had often wished, he said, that he had never written *Main Street,* so sick did he get of hearing people speak of it as 'your book.' 'You must write many novels,' he cried with an energy intense and inspiring. 'And let people say their little say! They have nothing else to say, damn them!' What comfort that was from him, and how warmly I felt toward him ever after!"

Mrs. Buck was severely criticized by important writers and critics at the time it was announced that she had won the Nobel

Prize. The award had come quite out of the blue without any knowledge on her part that she was even being considered. The gist of such criticisms was that no woman, except possibly Willa Cather (who never got the prize), deserved the Nobel Prize, and that of all women, Pearl Buck deserved it the least because she was too young, had written too few books of note, and was scarcely even to be considered an American, since she wrote about the Chinese and had lived in China. She was miserably unhappy to know that her fellow writers were against the choice and all the preparations she had to make for the trip to Stockholm were undertaken in the deepest melancholy.

Mrs. Buck took the blast from her fellow writers very badly. It is fairly safe so say that she has not yet fully recovered from the blow. She has written to me: "It is quite true that there was a great outcry of dissent when I received the Nobel Prize. I remember Henry Canby wrote a devastating editorial against the award —it was published in the *Saturday Review of Literature*. All sorts of dreadful things were said. I agreed with them! No one was more astonished than I to receive the Nobel Prize. I remember the outcry, too, when I received the Pulitzer Prize for *The Good Earth*— [the] Nobel Prize of course was *not* for a specific book. [The] Pulitzer outcry was 'why give the Pulitzer Prize to a woman who lives in China and for a book about Chinese peasants?' "

After Lewis's encouraging words and after the actual presentation of the award itself, Pearl Buck felt, as she has written to me, that: "The Nobel Prize came to me at exactly the right time. The first great wave of success, in a popular sense, was over. People were saying, 'can she continue?' I did not know if I could write as I wanted to write. I was trying to accustom myself to my own country—such a profound change! Suddenly the Nobel Prize came as a challenge and a proof of the confidence of others in *me*. I took heart and have never again lost heart."

The American critics have for years ignored the very existence of Pearl Buck, a fact of which she is, naturally, conscious and for which she thinks she has an explanation: "It is true that the American critics ignore me. They do not know what to do with me. I don't mind. I think they are not quite sure I should be included in the field of American literature and writers. Perhaps they are right. The Asians certainly think I belong to *them,* when I go to their countries. Perhaps they are right, too. But I love best my own country in the world I love."

Mrs. Buck says *she* does not mind that she's ignored by the critics. But *I* do; *I* mind for her. She is still one of the most important voices in literature and certainly the most articulate.

At some time during her four days in Stockholm, Mrs. Buck was guest of honour at a luncheon given by Albert Bonnier, her Swedish publisher, in the course of which she met Selma Lagerlöf, who pleased her greatly by confiding that Mrs. Buck's two biographies of her parents, *The Exile* and *Fighting Angel,* had decided her vote for the Nobel Award for Pearl Buck that year.

Within a very short time, half the world's population will be Chinese. There seems to be nothing anybody can do about this. I predict that the works of Pearl Buck, as one of the nonimmediate results, will become newly popular and respected and will be studied and examined more exhaustively than ever before for the simple reason that no one has ever written so understandingly of the problems that afflict the world today and so compassionately of China and the Chinese and their share in the affairs of the world as has Pearl Buck.

I happen to agree totally with everything Jason Lindsey has said about Pearl Buck, and furthermore I think we would have a lot less trouble in the world today if nations, and in particular our own United States, had heeded just one half of what she has said and written. As we go further into this study of her life, public and private, I shall attempt to point out a few of her more prophetic statements.

The Nobel award marked the end of one entire era of a great life. The Chinese period was over. She was to write of Asia many times in the future, of course, but with a subtle difference: while these later books were cognizant of Asia, she was no longer the participant. They were only partly Asian, as, for example, *God's Men, Come My Beloved, Dragon Seed,* or *The Hidden Flower.* Others, though totally Asian, were primarily reminiscent: *Imperial Woman, Pavilion of Women, Peony. Pavilion of Women,* too, is not so much a study of China and Chinese life as it is the study of a woman. There is much autobiographical material in that book, for it is the search that a brilliant and intelligent woman makes to find her complement in a man.

Now she turned her career and talent to the American scene, which previously she had dealt with in only one novel, *This Proud*

Heart. Anyone who is truly interested in her as a writer must realize the importance of her American books, for they mark her complete transition to her own country. And anyone interested in literature will find in them the new unfolding of a writer's talent. Such interest is found more in her European audience, however, than in her American public, who still hark back to *The Good Earth*. I have been glad that so many thoughtful people say they like her later books more than *The Good Earth*. Personally, I have found many that I like better.

The important fact, in any case, is that all of her books are basically about human beings. "Here" or "there" and "now" or "then" makes no difference whatever. They are human, these people of hers, and that is all that counts. From her books, I myself have learned a wisdom and a new approach to my own life today, and this from books of which most are many years old. When I see her, know her and experience all of the wisdom of her many years of varied life through the pages of her books, I am glad she chose to be a writer; for she has left to the world and future generations a richness we would have missed had she chosen another medium.

The awarding of the most coveted prize in literature, the Nobel Prize, was truly a two-edged sword that cut across her life in all directions. Indeed, it marked another beginning. She could not continue her life as before, no matter how much she might have wanted to do so; for after such recognition one belongs to people, and it becomes a duty to share oneself with people. They had bestowed a great honor upon one who, through writing, had enriched their lives, and she has treated that honor as a sacred trust. To have retired into herself then would have been to cheat them in a way of which she is not capable. So Pearl Buck became an object, finally and completely—a Nobel Prize-winning author first, and a human being second—at least in the eyes of the people. Therein lay a dichotomy that was to characterize the next years of her life.

PART II
Dichotomy

Pilloried 'twixt heaven and hell,
my heart its secrets cannot tell.

Hung high upon a cross of praise,
my heart soul's saintliness betrays.

O Soul!

If rise you must, up from the dead,
leave heart behind in that cold bed.
                                    —P.S.B.

WEBSTER'S *New World Dictionary of the American Language* (College Edition) defines *dichotomy* as follows: "1. Division into two parts. 2. a division. 3. the phase of the moon or of a planet in which half of its apparently flat surface seems to be illuminated. 4. in biology, a dividing or forking into parts: bifurcation. 5. in botany, a system of branching by repeated division into two. 6. in logic, division of a class into two opposed subclasses as real and unreal."

In all of these ways—literally, astronomically, biologically and logically—with the awarding of the Nobel Prize Pearl Buck's life became a dichotomy. The two parts? Her life as she personally would have it be and her life as People insist it must be.

I sit this morning in the still and calm of the office, before the workday begins, and reflect on how, exactly, to paint a word picture of her in such a way as to be sure I bring attention to the faults that *are* there, without in any way detracting from the beauty of the one whom I paint.

Behind me as I sit at my desk is the portrait painted of her two years ago by Freeman Elliot in New York. The painting was bought by Huntington Hartford III and hung in his gallery on Columbus Circle before he presented it to the Foundation and it was moved here. I look into the face that returns my gaze from the canvas and I see the woman reserved for the People. I watch the familiar expression, expecting it to change momentarily as in real life her fleeting expressions mirror her feelings. But it remains still, of course, and one knows that, like her as it is, it is not she, for her face is never still for more than a moment.

Most of the actual painting had to be done from photographs

because she announced firmly in the beginning that she would sit only twice, and, true to her word, she sat only twice. The camera, while a marvelous instrument in itself, is nonetheless limited to what the eye can see, and the resulting photograph is necessarily flat; so the artist worked at a distinct disadvantage. He did a very good job under those circumstances. There is kindness in the expression and that is true to her. The graciousness of the pose is hers. The overall effect is one of complete beauty and that is she—but her soul is not there.

The only other portrait of her for which she sat now hangs over the mantel in the library upstairs. It was painted in New York, in 1934, by a Danish artist, Quistguard, and the artist has caught more of the woman she was at that time. He has portrayed the side of her he saw and there she sits forever, her hands folded neatly in her lap, with an expression familiar to all who know her. It is her look of complete and utter boredom and impatience linked with being forced to do anything she does not wish to do. She did not want to sit for her portrait but was told she must, and her expression says, "Well, hurry up and let's get this over with."

That portrait, too, is true to her, but she is not all there. Again, there is no soul. The artists have captured two sides of the woman, two completely different sides, and both photographic.

There is a third portrait painted from memory by the same Danish artist. It hangs now in the small library of her country home and is almost a duplicate of the one upstairs. I say *almost* a duplicate. It has the same pose, the same folded hands, and she wears the same pale green dress, but the duplication stops with the expression. The woman in the third portrait leads me to believe the artist was a dreamer and painted her as he would have liked to see her. The canvas this time holds an expression of the gay wickedness more common to lower professions than to a literary genius. The artist had a vivid imagination.

We have three portraits, of three women and all different, in the physical form of one human female. Never, I'm sure, has any man known all of her and least of all, perhaps, either of her husbands. Through no fault of her own men have never been able to take her as she is, complete and without change. She cannot be this or that or the other, molded as clay into a predetermined pattern. Clay is soft and pliable and she is not. She is herself, whole and complete unto herself, and so she must remain. She compels herself to excellence with her own will and she never fails to be stingy with time and her everlasting energy! She can patiently wait for her efforts to mature, and then when she has done her part she is impatient to a fault, and delay of any kind drives her nearly frantic. She, in turn, drives everyone around her even more frantic with her constant insistence that whatever it is that she wants to happen, must in fact *happen now*. It is no wonder that success is her life. Ordinary persons cannot compete with her determination in any undertaking she chooses.

There was much furor in literary circles when the Nobel Prize was awarded to her, but the aspect that affected her most deeply was that, through this criticism, she became aware that she was not considered an American at all. This hurt her deeply, for she is fiercely American, and pain of any kind always affects an artist's work. Because of this she turned her efforts to this country that did not accept her and began to speak and write about the America she saw and what she thought of it. Now she had a voice that would be heard, for nearly everyone wanted to know what a Nobel Prize winner thought. Oftentimes it was not what people wanted to hear, but she said it anyway.

She uses people's interest in her books in the same way today. When she has an opinion she wishes to express she will not rest until she finds a way to express it. I am reminded of an article she wrote recently for a popular woman's magazine. She had contracted to write six articles about various places where she had traveled. She wrote them as promised, but the magazine refused to publish one article. It was about a certain city in the South which we had visited together, and she reported a conversation we had had with some young people who are citizens of that city. I heard every word of that original conversation and what she wrote in the article is true, but the magazine would not publish it. The city was too easy to identify, they claimed. If she would alter the article they would read it again and perhaps then would publish it. With characteristic stubbornness she refused to change a single word. She put the article in her files, unpublished but not forgotten. The next nonfiction book she wrote, the article came out of the files and into the book it went. She told the truth, like it or not.

The voice may not be heeded if heard, but that is through no fault of hers, for she uses her gift of speaking as well as writing to say what she thinks on an astounding array of subjects. This determination crept into her novels to a marked degree in 1939. In *The Patriot,* she warns of the coming of Communism into China. She tells in detail exactly how and why Chiang Kai-shek turned to the Communist rebels for help to defeat the Japanese invaders. The book is historically true, as are all of her novels. Another example is *Other Gods,* where she points out the fallacy of hero worship as it is found in America. She had been surprised when she returned to America after *The Good Earth* and found crowds waiting for her everywhere. In her own mind she had simply performed her job, as a surgeon or streetcar conductor performs a job, and she was, and is always, embarrassed by adulation from strangers. She did not expect such blind worship, and in *Other Gods* she wrote out her surprise. Her hero, Bert, is a tin god and his wife, Kit, is another of her autobiographical women. She takes the opportunity through the wife to describe how an intelligent person responds to such adulation as well as how she feels with regard to her debt to the people. To explore her own thoughts on those books I include here her "Treasure Book" entry dated January 7, 1940:

"This week has been stormy because of my new book, *Other Gods.* The judges—some of them—of the Book-of-the-Month Club feel that I have made a resemblance between a well known family and Bert Holm and Kit. I cannot so feel it. As a matter of fact, physically my pair are modeled after my parents. The relationship between Bert and Kit is my own unhappy first marriage. The rest is chance.

"Every book I have ever written has been disputed by someone. What protests because of *The Good Earth*—what furors because of the books about my parents! What anguish over *The Patriot!* These were the worst. The last was the worst of all, perhaps. One can pay no heed when one has work to do."

In those years her novels were serialized in the major magazines as well as published in book form. They were, therefore, read by the masses of population who perhaps would not buy a book but did read magazines by the millions. Her sister objected to her writing for magazines, and although I do not know how much of her opinion she expressed in response to her sister, she makes herself quite clear in the "Treasure Book" on January 9, 1940:

"A letter from my sister says she wishes I would not write for the popular magazines. The fact remains that I should not be satisfied if I did not have stories published in the magazines which the mass of people read. The finest and most beautiful do not come from these people, but still they are the root and stock of life. A person so secluded as a writer must not lose touch with them. I value their letters, often so foolish. I *feel* them. Their minds reach mine, and I try to make my mind reach theirs.

"The real objection to magazines is their editorial cutting which reduces every author to a dead level of style. This does distress me, since I write at my own length. I shall try to keep my stories within limits, so that such cutting at least need not be severe.

"I must work hard today. But I shall take an hour to go sledding with the children."

She has had the advantage of living abroad most of her life and she is able to see not only the fine things in the American social structure, but some of its faults. She cannot forget, for example, her shock at discovering racial prejudice in her own country and she began at once to point out the evils of discrimination. She cannot bear to see a people repressed because of the chance of birth that sets them apart from their neighbors. She feels, however, that the Negro must not only demand equal rights but must be prepared to accept all of the responsibility of these rights. As an example of her frank, open approach to this issue, I include parts of her commencement speech on equality, delivered at Howard University in Washington, D.C., on June 5, 1942, and later published in *What America Means to Me*:

These are not ordinary times, and this is no ordinary graduating class. Today the individual must contribute to the human demands of our times or he misses much. Today you are not only a group of individuals beginning your individual lives in a country which is more or less a democracy. You are a specially privileged group, not even because of education, which you have begun here under such excellent circumstances. Beyond that you are privileged because at this moment in human history you are a group with a special opportunity and a special duty to the times which none but you can perform, and this because of what you have been born, as well as because of what you have received. . . .

Let us review your situation at this moment. You are Americans. You are Americans of old families and not of recent immigration. This means that for some generations your families have lived in a country which has believed in democracy and freedom of the individual even if it has not practiced human equality. You belong somewhere near the top of your group or you would not be here today, at a commencement in a good university. You have been accustomed to some financial security, and certainly to some intellectual background or you would not have considered it worthwhile to spend the time and the effort and the money on a university education. Obviously, you are well above the average of all Americans.

And yet I know that I would not be saying anything worth saying if I did not speak of what I know also to be true—that in the heart of every one of you, whether you talk about it or not, there is doubt, not about yourselves, but about your place in society. It is only inevitable that many, if not all of you, are asking how much you can actually accomplish, even with your unusual equipment, and how relentlessly the barriers of race prejudice in your country will hold you back.

I know that some of you, carefully living in a world within a world, can perhaps manage fairly well, in a limited way, to make a life. There is a way in which you can live which avoids the area of race prejudice almost entirely, and which within the circumscribed area of a small nation, subject to a larger one, can give you reasonable security. Those of you who tend naturally to retreat into security will probably choose that world. Who can blame you if you do? There has been nothing to encourage you to break down the walls which race prejudice puts about you, and it has been individual wisdom, perhaps, to live within the walls rather than to waste one's self and spend one's energies in trying to break down what has been until now a relentless barrier.

Yet the hard practical question remains, what are we going to do with race prejudice? If we yield to it and build a world within a world, it simply encourages an evil. Moreover, this deepens the nation's division. Yet if you try to force your way into the white man's world, he resists with the full strength of his prejudice. Moreover, again, although clamoring at the white man's gate has a nuisance value, yet it is degrading to have to keep clamoring for that which is your right. It has an effect upon the colored race that is not good. The continued practical state of inferiority, however unjust and undeserved, does affect very much the colored individual and indeed the whole group. Similarly the false assumption of superiority because of race affects just as unfortunately the white man and his group. Race prejudice affects, in short, the whole life of the nation. A lot of people are wasting a lot of time and thought and energy and emotion on something which is sheer nonsense. But there it is. What are we going to do about it?

What are you going to do about it? You can do one of two things —you can accept the situation as it is, you can consider that it will be safest for you to stay inside your own nation, the Negro nation of a white America that will gradually cease to develop in its growth toward a true democracy because of its own division. Or you can determine that you are going to help America to be that true democracy of which we dream.

The equality of opportunity, therefore, which you have not been given in your country, has become more than an individual handicap, more than a group misfortune. It has become a national danger of the sharpest sort, a rock upon which our whole nation may founder. It is now necessary that all of us who believe with all our hearts in democracy work together to bring about human equality in the world of which our nation is only a part.

There are nations in the world, and great peoples, who may be our friends or our enemies in years to come depending upon whether or not we can believe in and practice human equality. I speak of the peoples of Russia and China and India. These three peoples, combined, make most of the world's population. Combined, they hold the future of the world among them. Two of them, China and Russia, are already resolved on the equality of races, and India wants her freedom. They have suffered, two of them, India and China, severely—India disastrously—from the effects of race prejudice. In a world where these nations will have power, and that is already today, they will not tolerate discrimination between peoples. It is essential that these nations be our friends, yet how can they be if within our own people we are divided by prejudice, one group against another?

You see how important you have become. You are no longer a minority group in one nation. You have become the touchstone of democracy in our own country, in the world.

If I have a criticism to make of the colored people of our country it is that they have been selfish in their interest in equality. They have thought too often of equality only for themselves in this one country—and by doing so they have limited their struggle and robbed it of size and force and meaning for the whole human race. You are not simply a group of people in one country—you are part of the great war of the peoples for freedom. They are not only colored peoples against white—there are many white people on your side, and white people in many parts of the world who are subject, too, to tyrants. You must understand the meaning of the war, and you must wage it on its true scale. By linking your particular battle for your own place in your own country to the whole war for freedom and human equality in the world, you will enlarge your forces and strengthen your cause, and help to win the war for democracy.

And you must remember that if we are really to achieve human equality in the world the war must not degenerate into a war of the races or a war of East against West. Such a struggle between prejudices will win nothing. Your enemies are not of one race or nation, your enemies are all those who do not believe in human equality, who judge a man by his skin and not by what he is as an individual. Your allies are those who believe in and practice human equality and who judge an individual solely by what he is and what he does. As simply as that, you may know your enemies from your allies. You too must not yield to race prejudice. It is as wrong for you to hate the white man because he is white as it is for him to hate you because you are not white. Keep yourselves free from jealousy and revenge that you may do your great work in the world in this time.

And what is your work? It is to be a bridge between your country and those other countries of which I have just spoken. The white man perhaps cannot understand India as India now needs to be understood, nor will he help China as China ought now to be helped. But you can understand India, because you know what India has had to suffer, and you know what China needs now and at the peace table.

Come out of that little world of your own and take your place in America as interpreters of the colored peoples of the world. Be ready to speak for Africa at the peace table, and to speak for Korea. Make yourselves the part of America to whom these peoples turn for understanding. Today you belong in the world, and your demands in our country are part of the world demand for freedom and for human equality.

I have recently heard several of her speeches on the same subject, and they show that the convictions she expressed in 1942 have only been confirmed and renewed with the passing of the years.

It is interesting to note that her speeches, even as early as the one just quoted, have the quality of world scope, even though her delivery is soft, almost intimate. There is none of the "soapbox" quality one often encounters when a speaker is making a point about which he feels very strongly. Her technique is not so easily seen in written text as it is heard in free delivery, where she tucks in often amusing personal experiences. Her audiences find themselves caught up in a web of fact that leads them inevitably to agree at least with her logic, if not always her point. She produces the overall effect of a velvet sledgehammer.

We have recently completed another in the series of speaking tours that has, to date, led us to 238 cities, and I have watched her speaking technique act on audiences all over America—from junior high school groups to senior citizens in retirement communities. Her effect is equally as stunning on all groups, regardless of their backgrounds. I have been told by supposedly knowledgeable persons that her audience consists of those who were adult in the 1930's and who still remember the impact of *The Good Earth,* and that her audience is growing smaller each year. No statement could be less true. The persons who spoke thus have not had the experience of seeing even the most distinguished audiences react to her as schoolgirls do to a current movie idol or singing star. The crowds are always larger than expected by those who arrange her appearances, and while most frequently there is a standing ovation when she is introduced, you can be assured that the audience will rise when she has finished speaking. I have often told her that it is the ending ovation that impresses me. The first one obviously is to pay tribute to what she has done, but the second one pays tribute to what she had to say. And it is the same, regardless of the audience numbers, for I have seen it in groups ranging from six hundred to twelve thousand. A tastefully dressed matron rushed up at the reception recently with this remark, which I quote because it is typical. I was standing next to Pearl Buck in the receiving line as the lady took her hand and said:

"Miss Buck, my mother introduced me to your books when I was in high school, and now my daughter is studying about you in school. The three of us take turns reading each new book as it comes out. You are just about the only interest we have in common. Thank you for enriching our lives."

Could a remark like that allow one to believe in a slowly dying group of fans? Indeed, the opposite is true. Difficult though it is for people to realize, the magic of Pearl Buck is still growing. After the initial impact of *The Good Earth* wore off, there was left a hard core of admirers all over the world that has increased rather than diminished. She is, by the way, America's most translated author.

Her interests have always had the same world scope that they have today, and while the racial problem involved her on the home front during the late 1940's, on the international scene World War II was still affecting her strongly, and her concern over it expressed itself throughout her writing as well as in her speeches. Her feelings on the subject of war in general are best expressed in her "Treasure Book." The first entry on the subject is dated January 20, 1940:

"Last night I sat late reading the [New York] *Times* and became so disturbed by the dreadful possibilities now plain in the European war that I dreamed all night of a war in my own household among the servants, all of whom were quite amiable to me but so bitter toward each other that my own life was embroiled —a sort of symbolism of larger things. My feeling about war boils down to a very small but strong essence. I am not a pacifist, for I perceive that the inequalities of mind and understanding with which people are born make it necessary to apply force to certain persons since they can understand nothing else, but these are individuals and not nations. Force applied to nations is war and war never works. Of that I have become convinced through experience of wars all my life. What they produce is something of a quantity and a quality infinitely worse than would have come about had the people resolutely resolved not to fight, come what would. My objection to war is on entirely practical grounds: war is romantic and utopian and never accomplishes its ends or else accomplishes them with such loss as to be madly extravagant as, for example, our own Civil War. If people would only realize that war does not work there might be a possibility of excluding it as a practical means of accomplishing ends.

"There is, of course, the question of traditional honor. We have so long taught ourselves, generation after generation, to believe in the idea of its being honorable to go to war that we have the difficulty of building new traditions, and yet I believe it must be done."

She never criticizes without offering a solution, and usually in a simple, direct way that cannot be denied merit. It would be interesting indeed if we would try to solve world problems in the way she outlines in the following unpublished article, apparently written during the early 1940's:

A PEOPLES' MANIFESTO

We, who are the plain peoples of the earth, being weary and hard-pressed by the many wars which have been forced upon us, do now declare that the time has come when we ought no longer to be compelled into these struggles whose causes are not made clear to us and whose purposes fail. No war heretofore has bettered our condition, nor increased our happiness, nor made our children safe. On the contrary, as science has perfected the weapons of warmakers, each war has fallen more cruelly upon us. We are not yet at the mercy of bombs and of poison gas but we foresee that should these wars continue we shall suffer still further from the perfected weapons devised by scientists who devote their time today to machines yet more instant in death than those we have. The hour has come when even disease germs and like evils may soon be included in the weapons of war. Unless some clear plan is made, which, put into action, can entirely prevent war anywhere in the world, there is no hope left for us or for our children.

Therefore, we do solemnly declare that the peoples of all countries shall choose representatives and that together these representatives of all peoples shall devise a form of world government which will prevent any nation henceforward the opportunity to begin a war, for any cause whatsoever. For we who are the peoples are determined that never shall war again devastate our countries and waste our families, and we will make this determination plain to our governments, not in any lack of love toward our own countries, but rather for the welfare of all, that in a mutual agreement all may find security and prosperity.

We the peoples desire through our chosen representatives to set up a world government which shall be a real government to which all peoples shall subscribe by the necessity of their being and not by the caprice of any one generation. In this government all peoples shall be members, so long as they exist, by the very fact of their existence, and none shall have the right to secede or to withdraw, because by their very existence they are members of the whole, and should any seek to secede or withdraw, that people is to be held in the world government nevertheless, as though it had not seceded or withdrawn, and for the mutual protection of all, the world government of all peoples must insist and demand of that one people that it shall fufill its obligation.

For this world government which we desire to create cannot be built upon the whims of individual rulers or upon national governments. Rather must its foundation be in a body of laws, shaped and agreed upon and declared valid by the chosen representatives of the peoples of the world, and through these representatives the peoples must bind themselves to this body of law and swear that they will uphold this body of law against any who would break it and thereby disobey the supreme will of the peoples of the earth.

The laws of our world government shall be few and written plain. They shall not contradict the laws of nations except where such laws work harm to other peoples. Mutuality shall be the test of the laws of our world government, and especially must all such laws bear upon those conditions and places and individuals which might prove sources for war. For we know that wars do not come up in a day. The seeds of war are planted early and the harvest is reaped late, and between planting and harvest there is a time when they might be destroyed were they discerned. But we who are the people are busy in the work of our living and neither time nor wisdom is given to us to foresee the evil growth until one day we wake and the harvest is there again, ripe before our frightened eyes, and it is the harvest of death for us and for our children.

Therefore we declare that it shall be the particular duty of our world government to be ever watchful and to discern early the beginnings of war in any of our separate countries. When the beginning is discerned, our world government shall execute through the power of the peoples' law the right to go into that country and to remove the cause of possible war, by just arbitration if there is dispute, by amelioration if there is suffering, and by arrest and removal if the cause be recalcitrant individuals. For we well know that it is never the people of any nation who bring about a war, but the recalcitrant individual, fattening himself upon evil conditions until, grown powerful, he can by his undeserved power force war upon us.

It shall be the duty of the peoples' representatives in the world government, therefore, to arrest and punish according to its laws any such unruly individual in any country whom they deem dangerous to the peace of the world.

And that our world government shall have the necessary power to enforce its own laws, it shall maintain a police force, large enough in numbers to effect the arrest of individuals but never large enough to constitute a threat against the nations. Should an exigency arise whereby additional forces are necessary, then reserves shall be found in the national police forces of individual nations, who would be subject to call for international duty, and these working together would be greater than the force of any single nation.

We who are the common peoples of all countries know very well that wars arise first from discontents among us and discontents arise from hunger and disease and ignorance, all of which are against our will to suffer, and yet which we must suffer unless there be aid to prevent and cure the evils which harass us. Therefore that the very seedbeds of war may be destroyed, it is our will that our world government shall have as its constant duty the examination into the conditions of our several countries in order that those who have particular need may be aided by all others through our world government, so that as quickly as possible the present grave inequalities may be removed from among us, for it is out of such inequalities that wars arise.

This aid shall not be charity, for charity carries with it the hatefulness of inequalities even through its gifts. Rather let our world government determine what is needed by the individual people, and make such loans for reconstruction and education as may be necessary anywhere to better the lives of the people of that country, other peoples subscribing to the loan in proper ways, but the loan itself to be put by our world government, in order that no single government or individual concern shall again have the economic power over people, but that all peoples may support each other in times of crisis and disaster, by mutual aid through our common world government. Such as have sums of money to loan will put these sums at the disposal of the world government on proper security, and such as have need of this surplus of others can draw upon the surplus at proper rates of interest and return, and so a permanent world fund be maintained for the good profit of all and the exploitation of none.

But it is not sufficient that recalcitrant individuals be controlled, and that food and health be made secure to all peoples. It is necessary, too, that the minds of peoples be nurtured in common ideals of humanity and cooperation. All civilizations which have endured have been based upon these ideals, and it is only when the ideals have not been followed but have been contradicted by opposite and evil notions that dissension and war have followed.

It is our will, therefore, that with due consideration for the national lore and customs of each country there shall nevertheless be required of all peoples a minimum and basic common teaching among all schools and the establishment of new schools where they are required. This teaching in all schools of all countries shall be the same, in order that the children of all peoples may grow into common feeling toward one another, so that no more can an evil notion be taught to the young of one people which will cause them to rise up against the young of another in false conceptions of superiority or ruthlessness.

Nor can this common education, to be agreed upon by our world government, be considered tyrannical in any sense, for it shall be agreed upon mutually by all, and it shall have as its end not the impressment of the will of any individual nor the arbitrary shaping of his mind, but rather the development of the individual in all countries into persons considerate of the welfare of all.

Thus we declare ourselves, who are the peoples of the world. Out of our present suffering we demand an immediate beginning of our world government, lest while we wage this war to the final victory, we find peace come upon us when we are at work with war and unready, and lest once again the present comradeship of our nations dissolve into separate and selfish existences.

Now, in the midst of the agony of this present war, let us make peace sure and make it eternal.

A newsman recently posed this interesting question at a press conference:

"Pearl Buck undoubtedly knows more about China and the Chinese people, more about Asia and Asian people, cultures and governments than any other American and possibly more than any other person alive. Why is it that we do not ask at least her opinion of or her advice on our current Asian policies?"

I have received letters from all over the world asking that same question, and I must confess that I cannot answer. The only possible reason I can manage is that our supposedly sophisticated establishment seldom if ever asks a woman's opinion of, or advice on, anything—and should we get it anyway, we seldom if ever pay any heed.

And while she was thinking and writing great thoughts about world subjects, as a woman her heart has always emptied itself of personal sorrow and loneliness in her novels.

The search for companionship that she has made throughout all of the years of her adult life has had a profound effect on almost all of her novels, beginning with *This Proud Heart*. Each book that she has written since then has enabled her to express herself on a situation or feeling or event out of her own life. She has told me that when one creates a novel there must be one character with whom the author can identify completely, otherwise the book will not ring true. Therefore, in all of her novels there is the highly intelligent, deeply sensitive person she herself is, sometimes a man, sometimes a woman, but always there. I have a dream of some day writing a book about Pearl Buck's pivotal characters in which I draw parallels among them. There must be at least fifty, from *East Wind : West Wind* through *The New Year,* who, when examined together, would tell quite completely the story of her innermost life. For example, *The Time Is Noon* was written in the years from 1936 through 1939, although it was not published until 1967. What she tried to express through Joan in that book is her own belief that, whatever blow life deals, and no matter how devastating that blow may be, there is comfort to be found in the natural beauty of small things and one should claim these comforts as birthright, for in so doing one can eventually find happiness within, in spite of great loneliness. She expressed herself freely in that book, and wrote out the unhappy portions of both of her marriages in the story of Joan's own venture. For one heroine to undergo so many emotional blows as Joan has caused some critics to label her a soap-opera character, but nevertheless she served the purpose for Pearl Buck. The relationship between Joan and her husband is taken from the author's first marriage; the relationship with the children and the loneliness from her second. Roger, of course, is her second husband, and as Joan, she exercised the fiction writer's prerogative and decided firmly against marriage, as she felt perhaps she should have in her own life. Instead of her second marriage becoming the complete sharing of self with self, as she had hoped it would, she withdrew from it in spirit, at least. She was the strong one, and as such she must pay the price. In all ways, she must still rely only on herself.

As Joan in *The Time Is Noon,* she also tells how she turned to the children for comfort. She heaped her affection upon these children and they became her life. Perhaps this is why the book was not published during her husband's lifetime, though it is among her best novels. Perhaps he saw this and knew that others would know it as well. All of this becomes especially apparent when one reads in the "Treasure Book":

"I would like to go away somewhere—I don't know where or why. Yet I suppose when night came I would long for home again. The children would pull me back. Without these children how would I live? And yet it rejoices me to see their independence of me—I don't want them to be dependent on me. I enjoy sewing on buttons and seeing that they are properly dressed and well fed and that they are growing as they should—I love to warm my hands at their fire—but I am always conscious that some day, suddenly, I shall not be here, and then the fire must go on burning just the same.

"It is better not to put down on paper the things one feels when one is sad. . . . Keep on growing, my darlings, as long as you live, and I'll be happy, though I am dead.

"I long very much these days for some wisdom of spirit in someone—a selfless, unseeking wisdom, but I do not know where it is to be found—doubtless nowhere. One longs to be approached —or better not approached but just *met*—by a comprehension which is not thinking of itself with any needs, and which indeed needs nothing for itself. That would be a rest of the soul, indeed. Everyone wants something for himself—and shows the want as much in denying it. Well—do I not want something in wanting the rest? Well—I mean I wish to be able to live freely and frankly, sure of comprehension, sure of not wounding. I am perhaps not easily enough wounded. Why should anyone want to wound, I always think, and dismiss it as of no importance if I am wounded. But then that makes me insensitive, perhaps, to others' sensitivity. . . ."

I do not mean to imply that she has not enjoyed her life, save the natural sorrows and the unavoidable ones, such as her eldest daughter's retardation. But she could have so richly enjoyed some of the things she has not had and above all the companionship denied her. When she has found a person with whom such a relationship might be possible, for one reason or another it was impossible to develop the relationship further. Perhaps, for the sake of her art, it is good that this is true. On the other hand, for the woman herself, I know that it is not good, for within her heart there lies a deep unfulfilled need. The lack of fulfillment has not always been due to others; on the contrary, when one is driven by a creative genius to perform a work one must do entirely alone, such as writing, it is all but impossible to share the innermost self with anyone. If one does, then there remains little time in which to create, and a choice must be made. It is unjust that this is true, or perhaps supremely just, but whichever it is, she made her choice, and she has borne with it well all these years. As a "treasure" she has also said, "There is no companionship which does not demand more than it gives."

She has told me that her second husband was always steadfast in his loyalty to her and his love of her in all ways possible to him. He had a good mind; he was a creative editor, appreciative of talent, and discovering authors was his great pleasure. The result was that he numbered many famous firsts in his career—for example, the books of Nehru and Lin Yutang, not to mention Pearl Buck. To him a new manuscript from an unknown author was a treasure to be explored and developed, for there was always the possibility of talent. If encouragement is too infrequently found in editors I must in fairness add that talent is also too infrequently found in writers. To him, above all, his job—indeed, his duty—was to find and develop that rare star quality that sets one writer apart from others. It was his vote alone, for example, that caused his firm to publish *East Wind : West Wind*. He frankly said that he did not publish that book on its own merit but because the writer showed promise of better things to come. And he was right, for he did open the gates to a literary genius that has released seventy books so far. He was not always right on a first book and certainly her case is a rare one. But he did not dwell on his failures. Instead he was always looking forward to his next success. To my mind, this is the mark of a great editor.

They were not a perfect match, however, perhaps because he was not philosophically curious, as she is. Whatever the cause, a secret disappointment with the life she had chosen crept into the "Treasure Book." She wrote:

"Every detail of everyday life is precious these days. I used to think this house would see the end of my life. I would like to die quietly and very old here in this room in my own bed with my face toward the hills—but I have forebodings of how I should die. Yet it does not matter as much as it did. My hold on life has lost a good deal in the last two years, nothing matters quite as much as it did. It seems good, sometimes, to think of simply *not being.* Why people want immortal life I cannot imagine. I hope to be mortal."

In 1934, when the decision was made to remain in this country, she still had not decided to obtain a divorce and remarry. She was being ignored by the so-called intellectuals in America, as she is today to some degree, although hers is one of the purest intellects to appear on the American scene. She is, however, completely American and possesses a love of country and a patriotism rarely found. Not to be considered American by our intellectuals, therefore, and by some few politicians and a handful of literary groups, tears at the core of her proud heart. By 1935 she was fully aware of this situation, and in such a state of complete aloneness she remarried and turned to making a home. She wrote nothing for a while, for she had enough money to do the things they wanted to do and she thought that between her husband and herself they could afford the expenses of expanding the house and the family. In 1937, when he wanted to take the second two children for adoption, she hesitated and was cautious, for by now the unspoken but apparent pattern was becoming established that she was to bear the financial responsibility. He persisted in his desires for a large family, however, and she yielded, too proud to speak her surprise that she must be the family's support. She says she cannot write for money, and in a way this is true, but she writes out of a concern for those persons who are dependent on her, as when she began to write for Carol in China and as she writes today for the displaced children of the world. She will be forever grateful, however, that she yielded on the point of the additional children, for she frankly says that they have been such a joy and comfort to her that she does not know how she would have done without them. This is evidenced again and again in the "Treasure Book." There are many who will maintain, as she does, that she would have written anyway. No doubt this is true—but what kind of books and how many we will never know. By the same token, we will never know whether this pressure was good or bad for her career. Even she wonders. And perhaps her husband truly felt that he was doing his share by publishing her books. Who knows? It is not my role to judge but only to relate fact as it relates to her, and the fact is that this was the beginning of the dichotomy that continued for twenty-five years.

Because she is strong, and by far the superior of the other women in his life, she had more to bear and was given ever-growing burdens to carry alone.

At this point she made one of the decisions of wisdom and finality so typical throughout her life. If she must face a life of inner loneliness without the pleasure and happiness to be found in true sharing, if the deepest companionship was to be denied her in her private self—then she would take everything life did offer her and expect no more of any human being. She enjoyed each detail of her home and garden, planting trees and flower beds, and building additions to the house. What began in 1935 as basically a six-room house has mushroomed into an eighteen-room home today. Her builders were careful, at her insistence, to retain the early charm of the farmhouse. They used the same original fieldstone, and the work was done by old masons and carpenters from the neighboring villages who still used the techniques of building they had learned from their fathers and grandfathers. The result is so effective that only the trained eye can detect where the old leaves off and the new begins.

The children grew day by day, and she recorded their birthdays as "treasures" and wrote of the small things from each day that so greatly enriched her life. As examples of the pleasure she derived from her chosen children I include a random sampling from the "Treasure Book." Each entry is quoted in its entirety, for together they give valuable insight into her response to the world as well as to motherhood.

January 10, 1940: My little children are singing as they dress themselves. I can hear the chorus of voices in the nursery outside my door, each possessing its own happy tune. I long to go and be with them and yet if I did—as I know only too well—they would stop the whole dressing process and instantly turn into babies, all wanting to be held and loved at once. I must build up their self-control and independence because life lies ahead and these are their only security. I love each one so individually and completely. They are flesh of my flesh. Parenthood begins, I am sure, after birth. Physical birth is simply a natural act, but love, the wish to care for, to develop a child, begins when the child is put into the mother's arms. I have felt it with each one of my children. A natural physical act is not enough proof, women want to give their children away when they cannot care for them . . . this I could not do!

January 27, 1940: I have been working on a speech on behalf of Chinese refugees. As always, I want to try to bring something essential from China to my own people. As usual I am at first balked by my own feelings toward China, which are at once strong admiration and almost equally strong repulsion. I am sure that the Chinese are the most civilized and nationally wise people on earth. The new Histomap which Sophie Kerr gave me this week has put this into a simple picture form. The map is five feet of all human history, four thousand years of it. Japan is seven inches, we are five, a long thin wavering line running from top to bottom is India. The other nations are a series of bursting balloons, all except China, which runs along at the extreme right, a strong un-wavering band of orange, strong at the dawn of history, strong today. It is the miracle of all human history. If the individual man lived on and on into centuries, defeating the natural law of death, how precious he would be to scientists and to us all! Yet, of all the nations, only China has lived on. India is another na-tion that has chosen to live on, even though subject, but she has lived by a belief in spiritual things. China has lived more strongly and I think because her peculiar philosophy, spiritual as it is, yet takes account of the material needs of the individual—a com-bination which satisfies the whole man. We ought to send our scientists over to China to discover why she is alive. England, Germany, France, Finland, all at this moment are fighting for material life, yet China has never fought either an aggressive or defensive war. She has poured all her energies into living as she is doing today. It is the law of nature in the physical body to keep the body so vital that it can overcome whatever disease at-tacks it . . . I wish my own country could early learn this in-stead of following the old European traditions of chivalry and a death-dealing patriotism. Far better to live for one's country than to die for it, and sometimes much harder!

February 4, 1940: Richard is four years old today. We had a party in the dining room with tall candlesticks, a cake and candles and toys. I love every bit of our life together. Every detail is a festival in my life. R. said, "You are tired—let's go away." And I thought of going away with dismay. I said, "Where shall we go? All I want in the world is here."

Peace after years of danger from war, quiet after noise. My own house, my own possessions, above all, my children—where could I go? I shall see Richard all my life, sitting gravely at the head of the table on the day he was four years old—God bless my little son!

February 20, 1940: A tremendous snowstorm this last week and my eyes are full of pictures of little children tumbling in the snowdrifts. These children of ours are, of course, the most beautiful and intelligent. I well know I am a fatuous mother, but there are others as fatuous and with only unhealthy, unhandsome, dull little spawns of their flesh as all they have. At least I am reasonably fatuous.

Portrait

Richard in Central Park, feeding peanuts to a squirrel. Having no more peanuts, he puts his hands in his pockets, thereby misleading the squirrel who hopped toward him hopefully. Now it was Richard's turn to be misled. He ran, the squirrel threatened. He ran faster and faster while people stopped to laugh at a very small boy being chased by a squirrel. Richard asked afterwards, "What makes the squirrel bigger and bigger when he runs?"

There is such a storm at this moment as I have seldom seen, the rain beating against the glass and dripping through the crevices.

Jean is so lovely a child. She has just come running in with her cheeks rosy, her eyes very blue, her brown curls fresh. She is a creature born to comfort the hearts of others.

March 18: Richard and John started school today. They were cheerful and eager until they found they were to be left there. John wept, but Richard dissolved completely. When his pride and self-control break, he is in bits, and I am trembling, too, with the sight of it. There is nothing left when he breaks but scraps of wild emotion. The assembling of these into a human being again seems impossible, but he achieves it—no one else can for him.

March 21: The children are all in bed with colds. They all clamor at once, "Mommie, Mommie," and are infinitely less tractable with me than with anyone else. With me they relapse into babies. Actually they are fairly responsible little beings.

Jean is beautiful. I keep trying to imprint her little likeness deep into my memory—chubby still, blue eyes, soft brown hair over her shoulders and curling a little, bangs on her forehead, exquisite hands and feet. But she is the one who gets quickly out of bed when the door is shut and she is supposed to be still for sleep. She gets up and instead of being the demure little thing she appears, she conducts an active, energetic, private life.

At this moment I am sitting in the red nursery. John is in bed, Richard more or less in, Jean is stringing buttons in bed, Edgar playing with blocks. They are ready to burst with energy and bed is prison.

I cut pear branches this morning and put them in the big jar in the library window. The library looked beautiful this morning in the sunlight—quiet and full of the sort of promise that books give when they are waiting in their shelves.

All the children are down and half-down with this virulent cold. Five noses easily seem fifty-five when they are all running at once.

Greatly depressed today, not, however, by a multiplicity of active noses, but by the fact that this morning's paper tells of a judge who confirms the objection of the persons who have accused Bertrand Russell as being unfit to teach in the city college in New York. I care not for Russell or the college, but I care everything for the freedom to speak and I am ashamed of the judge—a fat-faced policeman—but more than anything I was ashamed of a woman, a mother, one of those fools who in the complacency of having given birth to two children, considers that she has the

right to decide upon all matters on heaven and on earth. The
sentimentality which has surrounded motherhood in this country
has produced this folly. This particular fool "accuses" Russell, the
fat-faced crude judge sits up all night to read the philosophical
and authoritative books which have taken a brilliant man a lifetime to write, and decides the man is immoral. This performance
is equal to the Scopes trial on evolution, only in this case *we* have
been made the monkeys.

April 16: Yesterday was Jean's third birthday. The friction
over birthday presents has on each occasion of a birthday been
so acute that we have made up our minds, now that this year's
cycle of parties is over, to have a different plan next year. Instead of having many presents for one child, everybody will
have one present. The birthday child will not be given a party,
he will give a party. Now that these birthdays are over, I take
stock of my children thus:

1) Janice—she is at present a tall overgrown girl who is extremely handsome when she is clean, neat and in a fresh dress
physically, and is content spiritually. Everything depends on
the expression on her face, which can look secretive and mean
or gay and beautiful. She has a fine figure, beautiful hair and
dark eyes. What she will be no one can tell for she has not made
up her mind and she will be what she wants to be.

2) Richard is fun. He is vivacious, quick, temperamental,
deeply affectionate, but inclined to be possessive. He is sensitive
and intensely beauty-loving. He is an exquisite little being and
I fear for him in this world.

3) John is a lovely handsome boy. I can already see the man he
will be—exuberant, exceedingly able, much loved by his fel-
lows, quick to pity—his weakness, a dislike for anything he
thinks of as work.

4) Edgar is a wonder child—handsome, extremely brilliant,
able for anything—but quick to whine and to quarrel.

5) Jean is very pretty—my Jeannie, full of charm and smart-
ness.

Since I wrote these words the European war has been blazing.
France is gone. It is a strange and frightening thing to see a people, a nation, lost in an hour. Somehow one has always the idea

that a nation is long in dying. But France seems to have died before our eyes. Actually, of course, the death began in the last world war. The strongest and best were then gone. She has been weakening through all these years and victory only made her weaker. So death was not as sudden as one thinks.

Now England waits—we all wait. Whatever I am doing I have that feeling of terrible waiting for England to be struck. I believe in her, and if she dies, she may kill her victor with her. She will not die as easily as France.

All of these awful weeks have set me thinking again about war. I feel as I have since I could think with any maturity—that war is savage, stupid, evil and needless. But a police force is essential, internationally. Until we can devise it, we shall be dragged into war as inevitably as any family would if there were no police in the community. It is as simple as that.

This is a beautiful day. Carol is at home—I like to have her here but all sense of flesh, of my flesh, is gone. I feel toward her as tenderly as ever, but I am no longer torn. I am, I suppose, what may be called "resigned" at last. Agony has become static—it is true but I will not disturb it or allow it to move in me.

This morning I mowed the grass for two hours—hard, good work. The sky and land are beautiful. The children picked cherries for a pie which I must make, Mrs. Loris being on holiday and Esther feeling her piecrust to be unreliable. Children cannot be disappointed—not at least in a cherry pie.

The tennis court is finished. I hate games. It is tiresome to run after a ball to see that I lodge it in a particular spot on the other side of a net when I could be reading, walking, wading, cutting flowers in the woods, playing with the children, working at beloved, enjoyable work, anything, anything else! The truth is my mind does not want rest—it wants more activity. The truth is I love so much everything in ordinary life, that I have no desire to escape it. The truth is games bore me to death and wouldn't be an escape anyway. Why should I chase a ball? I am not a child or a young cat or dog. I shall do it as little as possible.

Edgar said when I trimmed the holly tree, "Do we call it holly because it is for holidays like Christmas?" This at three, oh my son! John said, "I feeled badly yesterday." Edgar said, "John, you mustn't say feeled. Field is where the wheat grows."

Elsie told Richard to put on his own pajamas now when he is a big boy and not ask me to help him. He whispered to me, "But I am very little!"

These three boys hold my heart between them—I am entranced with them and a foolish mother, made foolish by adoration and pride in my sons. I won't play tennis with them, though!

The world, my own small private world, is more beautiful this summer than I have ever known it. Trees are growing—the willows are green fountains. To see the children run over the lawns in their bright garments satisfies my last desire of beauty.

John, now four and a half, seeing his baby picture on the motion picture screen, said most wistfully, "I want to be a little boy again."

Jean has gained almost twice as much as anyone this year. On last being weighed she remarked with satisfaction, "I don't have to be weighed any more now—I weigh enough."

Richard is beautifully tender with all animals. He catches a barn cat with infinite cunning and pets and fondles it as long as it will stay. He must always pat the pony's nose when he passes. I spend much time thinking about the sort of world these children are to live in and wondering if this childhood is what they should have.

Fascism seems inevitable. Can Fascism be combined with freedom of press and opinion? We discuss it and wonder. R. says so long as we have freedom of press and opinion, form of government does not matter, but is it inconsistent basically? Not in an ideal society of ideally educated persons who could dedicate power to a chosen dictator and control or renounce him by freedom of opinion publicly expressed! But democracy also would be successful in such a society. It comes back at last to the same old thing—that individuals must be superior if any government is to work—the age-old problem of all humanity!

The roses are wonderful—but one rose is the finest I have seen —beautiful—its bud long lasting, it does not drop its petals, but turns more gold as it grows old. But how thorny! And this is perhaps appropriate.

These are the best days of my life and I keep them so. If these days are not good then there are no others for me.

I hear Edgar outdoors beneath my window asking in puzzlement, "Is this tomorrow?"

I have not found in the "Treasure Book" a single expression of real resentment or a single negative complaint. She simply states a case as it is, good or bad, and then goes on with her life. The nearest I have ever found to a complaint is the occasional statement of fact that borders on bitterness, such as the entries from July 30 and August 5, 1940.

July 30: It is less necessary to be anxious about the weak than the strong in our world. The strong take care of the weak in one hundred ways, they are fed, they are clothed and provided with either no effort on their part or at most only so much as they are able to make. But who takes care of the strong? No one. It is considered that they must be able to care for themselves and they manage it in one way or another because they must, because they know they have only themselves upon whom to depend. If they were given a tenth of the aid, sympathy, compassion, which are given as a matter of course to the weak, the helpless, the ineffectual, they might be more gentle, more compassionate, too, and the world be better for it. For my part I pity the strong.

I am anxious concerning the brilliant, the quick, the able. It is more important that they grow to their full height without bitterness than it is for some dullard or sloth to be fed or clothed. For the human race strides forward upon the feet of the strong, it is the strong who bear the world's burden—those who plan and carry out, not those who stand idle for a lifetime.

For one brief period in my life I had the impulse to confide and share, but being strong I was met with impatience and so I returned to myself.

This has been a beautiful day. I rose early and weeded my garden. I worked all morning surrounded by the voices of children. I sat at the head of my table with two rows of faces on each side of me as we ate luncheon together. The children's appetites were good and we talked of pleasant things. They were quick to see and to hear, the best of company. I worked while they slept, then rested quietly in my room and read. Now we'll go swimming together. Work, beauty, companionship, a good day.

August 5: The ineffectual person is not the one who does not, cannot, accomplish large things—it is the one who does not do well what he is perfectly capable of doing. The dilly-dally, the one who tries to escape the fair share of the day's toil, the incurable sophomore, whose heaven is play, who reads, when he reads, nothing but light stuff that is play for the mind, he is the cheat, who will not pay for his life, though he knows every one must be paid for somehow, by someone. He comforts himself by thinking that he has no ambition to be great. He cannot be great, but he can, nevertheless, be effectual in his place.

This is one of those curiously lonely days, nothing is unusual, nothing different from what I have known and accepted for a long time but there it is. These days come, I am convinced, to prepare us for the long loneliness of death, a premonition of the body and a preparation of the soul.

I am not at all prepared to relinquish the idea of immortality of some sort or another, a continuity somewhere in time or space by one means or another, but perhaps a completely lonely one. In that it is unimportant, except that if there is to be continuance one must be fortified for it, as for the inadequacy of love.

I grow amazed at immaturity where one expects maturity and I feel sometimes too old in wisdom as though life had taught me too much and made me wiser than I wish to be. I will not press wisdom on my children, it is not well to be too wise—wisdom cuts one off from everyone, even the wise, for then one is afraid of so much wisdom, lest, perhaps, it is true that life is less valuable than one wishes it—than it must be if it is to be lived. To enjoy a little work, to enjoy play—this is the best, even though I cannot any more.

I wonder sometimes about friends. Are they somewhere and I have not found them? Not a lover or any passionate being, but some with whom I can talk! I see no one, not knowing whom to see. And yet I love people and would like very much to see a few, especially those of my own age, persons who would not ask me for anything except casual friendship, honest liking, some good talk. I am very much shut away, exactly why and how, is not worth trying to discover.

Having known her for five years and more, I look at the fullness of her life on one hand—and the complete void on the other; full of work, family, admiration and the adulation of fans all over the world, and empty of real companionship and understanding from any source. Moreover, I wonder if such relationship is truly possible for her. I think not. I think that when one explores and develops one's creative being to the extent that she has done, then life itself becomes salt to an open wound. One's heart becomes torn flesh into which one pours all the "natural shocks that flesh is heir to" in order that the characters one is creating may live forever.

Her joy in her children expresses itself in other entries in the "Treasure Book."

I said to Jean, "When are you going to name your new baby doll?" She said, "She is so little we do not know her yet."

The children are so beautiful. We have sent the nurse away and I look after them now. They all go to school so I can. They are rich-hearted children, loving! They are rewarding. They are now my life. I thank heaven for them. They reward me far more than I can deserve. I love to think over each one of them and ponder their looks and their differences. I think about their hands, their feet—I would know them by their hands or feet—I think about the way they laugh and their little voices—they are so right in my life. I want to be as right in theirs.

I said to John, "Do not be naughty while I am away." He said, "What if I can't help it?"

Edgar said, "I have been playing in the snow so long I have a headache in my hand."

Jean said, "What means God? Is it like a boy?"

Last night John talked thus, just after I had tucked him in bed: "Who was Daddy's mommy?"
"Don't you know? Why, Grandmother," I said.
"Is she old?"
"Yes, quite old."
"Will she die?"
"Not yet."
"When?"
"Perhaps when she is very old."
"Will you get old?"
"Yes, some day."
"Then will you die too?"
"Yes."
"But you aren't old yet, are you, Mommy? You will stay with us quite a while?"
"I will always stay with you," I said.
But I could not get death out of his mind. I could see him pondering it and trying to make sense from it. I went to bed thinking about it myself. In spite of the fact that R. does not believe in the possibility of life after death, I have a strange assurance of it. I believe, not with my mind but with some instinct, that there

is life after death. I realize that this may be simply a curious memory of childhood teaching and also my wish to live, but there it is. If I had to say on which side I am I would say, "I am on the side of immortality."

August 3, 1941: How long since I have written here? The children are more beautiful this summer than ever. Now suddenly they have left off their swimming jackets and are diving and swimming by themselves. They are brown and well, and in the water, especially when they are naked, they are inexpressibly beautiful. Jean's hair flows out behind her as dark as seaweed. Every day is a joy with them—yet they are naughty enough to keep me at ease as to their intelligence. I can only try to teach them a few things. To tell the truth . . . because lies are inconvenient and clutter up a life. Order . . . because order is efficiency and time-saving and especially because order is beautiful. Order preserves design. The whole design of a room can be lost or spoiled by disorder. Besides, an intelligent person is always truth-telling and orderly. He gets to his goal more quickly thus. I think I do not try to teach them anything else—well, perhaps kindness to those around them, human and beast.

Yesterday I overheard, while I was in the playroom, Edgar going heavily upstairs. Jean giggled on the second floor and remarked in a pleasant, conversational voice, "We thought it was God coming upstairs but it was only Geggie!"

Esther has left this house this summer, working only in town for us. A curious mood came over her, actually over her younger husband, and I no longer wanted to be at all responsible for her not being with him, so she is gone, and Gretta has come with us. We are only beginning to know her, but I liked her from the first moment I saw her. It is strange to have this fragment of troubled Europe in our quiet and happy household. Her husband is in Russia, she does not know where. Her brother is in a concentration camp. Her old parents she will not, I fear, see again in this life. They are seventy-six and seventy-eight and how can they be brought out? I know that we must keep these tragedies deep and silent, for otherwise life cannot go on as it should for home and little children, and yet I am conscious of pain, death everywhere in the world, the heavier for being senseless.

But I have reached a conclusion somehow about war which, if it makes me any more impatient of it, yet makes me withdraw from it even further. It is that many people enjoy war—especially most men—and this being the case, we will have war so long as these persons are allowed to indulge themselves, just as bearhunting went on, as bullfighting goes on, as any barbaric pastime goes on, so long as it is tolerated. My close reading of newspapers and of popular magazines convinces me that many enjoy war as they enjoy prizefighting, for the sport, the gamble, the danger. This being the case, what hope for peace unless the intelligent ones take hold of the world?

This is part of the game that Gretta's husband has lost in Russia, that she is far from home, that she is so lonely, a young woman, yet no one near who should be near her. She is only one of millions. And am I bringing up these boys of mine to be strong and healthy and sound in order that they take part in the filthy game?

This is a good summer. I have reached a period in my life when I am content with what I have, and what I have not I can do without. I enjoy more deeply than I have mere life—outdoors, the children, the rain that is at this instant pouring down from the summer sky. My work I enjoy more than ever—I have it at my fingertips. Perhaps more than anything my utter content is because I have ceased to care what people are not and only care what they are. To find what they are is enough. What they lack can be supplied in other ways I know. Does this take a certain passion out of life? Perhaps it does, but if so, let it go, too.

It seems to me old age is the best of life. Well, at forty-nine I am not old yet but I am looking at old age. Why the best? Because life itself is the great good—not love, not ambition—though I have never been ambitious—not achievement, not possessions—only life! Sleep at night . . . getting up to the world . . . eating . . . work . . . reading . . . play . . . good enough! But until old age it is not good enough. All I ask of life is to go on exactly as it is. I am living here in this house, working and weeding the garden and looking over the land that lies around me—good enough. I need nothing else except what I have here.

We have a small black dog, our first, named Muffin—he is exactly what a dog should be for children.

October 4, 1941: The children have started school again, all five of them. Janice seems to enjoy her classes for this year. At least she does not hate them. The small four we have divided, the older boys going to Buckingham Friends' School, the small ones continuing at Montessori. Great school rivalry is the result.

Jean: "We have a baby at our school."
John: "That's nothing, we have a turtle."
(And so on up to millions of houses and more cows than there are in the world.) Jean was at last vexed to despair and lay on her back, legs and panties obvious:
Jean: "That's the way the baby did at our school."
Me: "You are too big for it. You're not a baby. You will be five next birthday."
Jean: "When is my birthday?"
Me: "Next April."
Jean: "What, April *again!*"
And so on. Richard is the most independent and the most industrious. He will keep at a job until it is finished. John avoids all work, but works on his play projects with great intensity. Both want to *own* and to be separate. Richard has his things in his own room, bathes and dresses there. Edgar is brilliant, desultory, book-loving, intense. He is an honorable child—the soul of honor. Jean is willful, temperamental, charming, lazy. I believe she will have a sweet singing voice. All in all, they are the joy of my life. I will not let my life be engrossed entirely in them and I struggle to keep my own freedom. It is not only that they are my children or that they are enchanting in themselves. It is that they are growth, life, personality, development, change, youth, individuality, a little sample of the world.

This morning I am in the library alone, at my rare leisure. I have worked too hard recently and without great satisfaction. That is, I do not much care for *Dragon Seed*. Peasant life I am

tired of, war is dull, but still I wrote one more book about these
two things out of a sort of duty to China and what the Chinese
are now enduring. Then I had to write the serial—too fast, though
it is better to write serials fast, I think. Now another serial lies
ahead. Then I hope to do something I really enjoy. Meanwhile,
for a fortnight I am writing nothing except a few small things
long promised. Statements, and so forth, on the world situation.

I wonder if we understand or even acknowledge that impulse
toward excess which is in the blood of every human being. I am
sure it is there and that it is responsible for the madness of war
and the return to war time after time. It is not economic necessity. People will manage better economically without war and do
manage in spite of it. No, it is some feeling of longing to break
out, to have all laws fail for a time, to have bad behavior excus-
able, a smashing, devastating, selfish, bloody impulse.

I have not this whole summer found a really good book to read
and yet I enjoy any book that has reality. Yes, I have read one good
book—*The Fortunes of Richard Mahoney,* a great book, and one
I should have liked to have written.

Autumn comes again. Gertrude Lane [editor of the *Woman's
Home Companion*] died two weeks ago after a long illness. I shall
miss her this winter, not because we were close but because she
was a strong, successful, altruistic, rather simple woman. I like
looking up to people. Now some of the ones I admire the most are
growing old—Ida Tarbell, writing so bravely that she is struggling
against senility, Dorothy Canfield, very fragile and old—the sweet
old shell of herself as once I knew her. I look around for strong
young women. The other day a young woman complained that
now the young "are given no causes for their devotion." It seemed
to me she epitomized her generation. I could not forbear crying
out, "Oh, *take* your own cause!" She looked at me as though I had
gone mad, then said in a frightened sort of way, "I think I see
what you mean."

Every war situation is a local situation, a personal situation.
The next war may be—if the direction of men's minds do not

change, it will be—based on race prejudice. This is a world situation and yet it is in every locality, in every person's life. It must be dealt with there. Bound by this conviction, I have resolved this year to put groups of Negro leaders into touch with the publicists, the persons who have somehow the ear and eye of the public. I have written to eight leading men of this sort and one woman—the women as usual very scarce—and shall see what comes of it.

We sent Janice to Nova Scotia this summer. She had a good summer in that she made friends with the Nova Scotians of her group.

The other side of the dichotomy is her public services. She has worked hard for persons less fortunate than she is, but most of all I think she has worked to overcome stupidity and ignorance wherever she finds them. In her work for the mentally retarded, for example, she spends more time and energy with parents than with the children, for it is necessary first for the parents to overcome their own ignorance and accept the fact of retardation before anything much can be done for the child. Her success is apparent to me from the countless letters of appreciation she receives from parents' groups throughout the world. Also there are the numerous awards and citations on display at the Foundation, among which is a lovely hand-painted Japanese doll from the Association of Parents of the Mentally Retarded in Japan.

Another area of great importance was her work for China War Relief during World War II. The most satisfying personal reward she received from this was her relationship with Eleanor Roosevelt. The success of the program is a well-known fact, but when I ask her to tell me about it she speaks only of Eleanor Roosevelt, and I include therefore a sampling of her thoughts about this remarkable woman:

Whenever I think of Eleanor Roosevelt I think of the first time I saw her. It was in the year when I was getting my master's degree at Cornell. I was on a committee to meet her and stay with her throughout a day when she was booked to give a lecture at the Home Economics Department. I am not in the least interested in home economics. It is my theory that any woman who can read can learn to cook if she wants to do so. Besides, there is so much machinery that it is better for a woman to be a machinist than a housekeeper these days. I was interested in her, however, for I had not known many American women. Therefore I was among those who met her in Ithaca at the railroad station one morning at seven o'clock. I can remember exactly how she looked. It was her energy that struck me most in that day as she came off the train, wearing—and I can remember so well—a long ankle-length purple satin dress, a brown tweed coat and men's bright tan oxford shoes and nondescript hat. She carried a stuffed attaché case and got off the train filled with good humor and quite without shyness. I won't say she had no shyness but it was a disarming kind of shyness. She was full of self-confidence and was anxious to please. She learned in later years to dress well and to be extremely graceful and charming without losing any of her energy. There was a certain childlike quality in her, as there is in all really great people. She wore the long purple satin dress the whole day and explained it by saying that when she got off the train she knew she wouldn't have a minute all day to change, so she decided to get dressed early for the reception to be held at six o'clock that evening. She wore the oxfords because they were comfortable for we had to do much walking. She pursued her way at once into a crowded day as she went over the Home Economics Department. She made a good speech and I remember we were given a luncheon that day which had been invented by the Home Economics Department. It seemed to be mostly raw cabbage. They were very proud of it because it cost only seven cents a person. My private opinion of it was that even seven cents was too expensive for it. It was an uneatable meal so far as I was concerned. Mrs. Roosevelt ate it with great gusto, however, and congratulated the head of the department on having achieved this meal. Of course those were the days before she became famous in her own right. I remember her gay, high-pitched voice commenting on everything.

In the middle of the afternoon I went home and changed into a more formal dress than my everyday suit. Of course I showed up for the reception and was in the receiving line. I stood next to her and she listened as I handed the people on to her one by one. She shook each hand vigorously. She was the soul of good humor and not a whit tired. By that time her coat was gone but as I recollect the oxfords were still there as being more comfortable to stand in. Yes, that was in 1925. Then we proceeded to dinner and when we saw her off on the train I was completely exhausted. As you know, I am usually inexhaustible but I remember being tired that night. She? Not at all! She was in the finest of spirits as she went off on the train in her evening clothes. As I said, in later years she grew far more graceful. She had beautiful hands and arms even when she became quite old. In fact, she grew better looking the older she was. At the time I first met her she had difficulty with her prominent teeth. Later a merciful automobile accident broke those teeth and a dentist improved on nature so that even her teeth looked better when she was older. Of course I met her at various occasions but the next time I remember working with her was on China Relief, in which I hope I gave some help. We used to meet and Mrs. Roosevelt was as brisk as ever. She didn't age, and by that time she had learned how to dress and her voice had modulated—it had been rather high-pitched, a little tiring to listen to for a long time, but her voice changed so that it was really quite a beautiful voice as she grew older. She was very efficient! She was always on time, never late. She always had something useful to say. We went through some difficult times in those days.

None of us knew very much about fund-raising, so we engaged the best fund-raiser we could get. He was a man who had been extremely successful in raising enormous funds for Harvard, but for United China Relief there was no alumni association upon which to count. Before we could turn around we had lost seventy-five thousand dollars. Mrs. Roosevelt said briskly that we had better begin all over again. That is exactly what we did. Harry Luce, who had started the China Relief Fund, kindly paid the deficit and we started all over again and were quite successful.

I met Mrs. Roosevelt at committee meetings in other areas, too. I remember meeting her again, later, at the New York apartment of her mother-in-law, Sara Delano Roosevelt, a redoubtable, still very beautiful woman with whom I went to have tea. I remember that Sara Roosevelt wore an old black silk dress and lovely diamonds and didn't care at all how she looked.

We talked about China. All that she knew of China was that in the days of her ancestors her family had made a fortune in business in Hong Kong.

My next recollection of Mrs. Roosevelt was at a huge meeting at Howard University at which she and I both spoke. More than once she and I both spoke from the same platform. She was deeply interested in civil rights and I was a trustee of Howard University. I remember feeling very proud because the audience gave me a standing ovation just as they had Mrs. Roosevelt when she came in. We always enjoyed these encounters. Neither of us had time for anything like real social life and we used to chit-chat. She was always vital and interesting. And I remember a very pleasant evening I spent with her in the White House when her husband was President. Madame Chiang Kai-shek was then visiting the United States. I had had some difficulty in evading Madame Chiang because I did not wish to speak from the same platform with her. I had lived in Nanking during the years when Chiang Kai-shek was the ruler there and I had all sorts of information that I ought not to have had about her and her family. We were friendly. It wasn't exactly disastrous information, perhaps not more than could be expected from the vicissitudes of China in those days, but I didn't want to appear publicly with her nor seem to endorse anyone or anything. I am a nonpolitical person, you know.

Madame Chiang was imperious and beautiful and expensive, as usual, and when we met anywhere we were friendly enough but we let it go at that. Well, she had just finished her visit to the White House on the night that I was dining there. We had a very intimate and small party and we fell to discussing Madame Chiang Kai-shek. I remember Mrs. Roosevelt said with her delightful and charming smile that it had been very interesting to have Madame Chiang Kai-shek at the White House. I remember thinking as she spoke that she always smiled all over her face and especially with her eyes. She had beautiful eyes, a bright, clear blue.

She told us, laughing gently, while Madame Chiang Kai-shek was staying in the White House that she had to go to a dinner elsewhere. There were no guests planned for dinner at the White House and so it fell about that the President and Madame Chiang would be dining together. She told the President that he would have the pleasure of dining alone with Madame Chiang Kai-shek, to which he said with great decision, "Indeed I shan't! I am going to bed early!"

Then Mrs. Roosevelt added in her inimitable dry fashion, "I don't think that Franklin likes women who think they are as good as he is." This, of course, brought us down in roars of laughter. She knew her husband, too!

Well, we had fun that evening, and then I didn't meet her for quite a long time. She was abroad a good many years. She went to Israel a few times and her life was fulfilling itself in many ways. I always read what she wrote because she really was an original. I remember meeting with her later on a few boards to which we both belonged. I truly admired her, for as she became older she managed her time well. She would come into a committee meeting precisely on the hour. We all knew it was time to begin when Mrs. Roosevelt arrived because it was at the exact moment that the time had been set. She would be very attentive up to the point that she would answer present when her name was called. Then as she grew older she had acquired the very useful habit of drifting off into a quiet, unobtrusive nap. It was the only way perhaps that she could continue her prodigious efforts and maintain her energy. One could hardly notice that she was asleep except that her eyes were closed, for the same interested expression was on her face. She was apparently listening with her eyes closed but after observing this a number of times I came to the conclusion that she really was asleep. Well, anyway, when discussion was over and the committee chairman's voice was the only one speaking she knew it was time to join us again. So she joined us by opening her eyes and still with the same sweet placid expression on her face and she would give in a few sentences a reasoned conclusion, expressing concisely her own ideas on the particular subject that had been discussed. We always received the agenda in advance, of course, and before she ever came to the committee meeting she had thought through what she had to say on the particular subject and she said it! She paid no attention to what anybody else had said, for she was sleeping, but with renewed energy, the little nap having done her a world of good, she said what she had come to say! After she spoke, whether or not it was time for the meeting to be over, she got up and in her graceful fashion gave her excuses for having to leave and then she went on to her next appointment. She was so absolutely honest! You might call her naïve but it was not naïveté. It was ultimate sophistication.

I think we Americans, being so young and unsophisticated, have a completely wrong idea of what true sophistication is. According to Asian definition, which I myself believe to be correct, a sophisticated person is one who has experienced everything, knows everything and has reduced everything to its essence. Sophistication is the final simplicity. And of course that was Mrs. Roosevelt. I remember her very fondly. Although we were never intimate friends, we were often co-workers in various areas and I always enjoyed being in her vicinity. I think she was one of the most useful people that ever lived. I don't think anybody has yet grasped the full importance of her life in human terms, the hundreds and thousands of people whom she helped through what she did in practical ways.

Financial pressure began to be great in the early 1940's and Pearl Buck turned deep into her talent to produce. Yet, she would have written the same books with the same speed, "for the real pressure," she insists now, "was not financial but always from within myself. I have had no financial needs now for decades, and yet I keep writing more and more books, with many others I still want to write. The pressure? It comes, I suppose, from my endless and growing curiosity about life and people, and I cannot keep my discoveries to myself. I put them into books and thus share them."

Her greatest difficulty has been that no public can take books as fast as she writes them. I have heard her publishers argue, "You cannot come out with two major novels in one year, for if you do, the second will kill the sales of the first and neither will ever develop to its maximum earning ability."

Perhaps the publishers are right. It certainly sounds logical enough. Anyway, the publisher always wins, for authors cannot print, bind and market their own books and still find time to write. The author has no choice but to accept the publisher's philosophy.

It was general opinion that any book about China with the

Pearl Buck name would sell because everyone expected her to write *The Good Earth* again and would buy anything she wrote just to see if she had done it. At the beginning of 1940 she had published eleven books and during the next ten years she published twenty-six additional volumes as Pearl Buck. Of those, eight were major novels—*God's Men, Kinfolk, Peony, Pavilion of Women, Portrait of a Marriage, Other Gods, Dragon Seed* and *The Promise*—and were all published by the John Day Company. There were also the two she does not like, *China Sky* and *China Flight,* both of which were made into motion pictures, as was *Dragon Seed* during that same period. These total ten novels by the same author in ten years, with three motion pictures, eight nonfiction works (*The Child Who Never Grew, American Argument, How It Happens, Talk About Russia, Tell the People, What America Means to Me, American Unity and Asia* and *Of Men and Women*) and two collections of fiction (*Far and Near* and *Today and Forever*). In addition to these, she wrote seven children's books. There were also countless newspaper and magazine articles and stories.

As a matter of fact, it was simply too much material to sell during one ten-year period, and yet she had more that she wanted to write. This was the commercial reason behind the decision to begin publishing under an additional name, a pseudonym.

As for her own reasons, she has told me that she was simply tired of being classed or typed as a "writer of Chinese stories." She felt that it was not the subject or the name that made a book sell but the artistry of the author in weaving his characters. She was anxious to prove her point, at least to herself. Thus John Sedges was born. A male pseudonym was created because she has always felt that in the United States a man has the advantage over a woman as a writer. "Sedges" she chose because she had never heard the word used as a name, and "John" because it could be anyone's name.

The rest is history. *The Townsman* was an instant success and a best seller everywhere. It was frankly advertised that John Sedges was the pen name of a well-known author but the content of the book was so unlike anything Pearl Buck had written that not many guessed his identity. At least one man did, however, and that was Francis Hackett, then the critic for the New York

Times. He wrote, "This novel is written in the finest English tradition from George Eliot to Pearl Buck." She knew that he had guessed. "John Sedges" has served his purpose and no longer lives, but any of her real fans would recognize that *The Townsman* is indeed a typical Pearl Buck book. All of her novels fall into one of two basic categories. The first consists of books about a particular person, who could be of any race, creed or color, in a situation in which anyone could find himself. This explains why her writing is called "universal." Some of these are *The Mother, Pavilion of Women, Letter From Peking, Peony, The Time Is Noon* and *The New Year.*

The second group consists of historical, panoramic novels spanning continents or great periods of history, such as *The Good Earth, Sons, Imperial Woman* or *The Living Reed.* Each of the five John Sedges books falls easily into one of these groups. *Voices in the House* fits the former, and *The Townsman* the more exalted company of the latter. *The Townsman* has been called *The Good Earth* of the United States and there is true similarity between Wang Lung and Jonathan, for Jonathan is a man of the land although he is not a farmer. He refused to move on West with his family and friends to California in search of gold and he is not the familiar rough and tough shoot-'em-up Westerner. He stays behind in Kansas and builds a town and becomes the epitome of the kind of man who really built the American West. A critic for the Kansas City *Star* said, "This book must have been written by one who has spent a lifetime in Kansas."

Her whole attitude toward her writing during those difficult years of adjustment is quite clearly summed up in the "Treasure Book" entry of October 28, 1942:

"The chrysanthemums are beautiful—in fact, all the land is beautiful. I am only too overburdened to have time necessary for living in it. I seem to have a genius for acquiring dependents —not children! I would like to just rest for two weeks, say—that is, talk to no one and no one talk to me, except the children, and not write a word—just get up in the morning and not write. It seems to me years since I have had a day to myself. Well, an end to complaining. But I am somewhat tired and feel myself not quite so resistant. At fifty, one takes thought. But my springs are still sound. My joy in sky and land and children, in good books

and fine and simple music is as strong as ever. I feel a certain relief now that I have consciously given up the cultivation of relationships. I let be. The children are very strong and beautiful."

Her own feelings on the subject of being a prolific writer are
summed up in her answer to a newspaper reporter who asked,
"Miss Buck, why do you write so many books?"

"Why not?" she answered simply. "I'm a writer."

The John Sedges "disguise" was retained until the early 1950's,
when her European publishers began to put Pearl Buck in paren-
theses after it. Then it was of no use to her, for she had proved to
herself and others that she could write on subjects having nothing
to do with China. Of the five John Sedges novels there are three
she likes: *The Townsman, Voices in the House,* and *The Long
Love.* The other two are equally good, in my opinion, but she
has developed a dislike for them, as she did for the earlier *The
Young Revolutionist,* though for different reasons. When I ex-
amine a book that she dislikes I find that the basic character is a
person she would not particularly like. I also know that she writes
only out of her own experience. I have therefore drawn the conclusion that in these books she writes out certain incidents that
have made her unhappy, and rereading them or thinking about
the characters is an unpleasant experience for her; thus she dislikes the book.

Everything this woman has accomplished in her life has been
her answer to the world on a subject that concerns her. She acts
or writes out of her indignation. An example of this is *The Good
Earth,* which she wrote because the Chinese intellectuals, whom
she knew so well, ignored the Chinese peasants, whom she also
knew. She wanted her book to be a voice for these peasants. In
The Mother she told how it feels for a woman to desire a man. In
Sons she pointed out the futility of small wars. In *A House Divided* she wrote: "Look out, for these young people are rising up.
They can be dangerous." Each book was her answer to a situation
in which she had become involved and to make herself heard with
force she wrote thought-provoking novels that have been read
around the world. She firmly insists that she writes for no purpose other than to entertain and that if she succeeds in this, then
she is completely satisfied. In her own mind this is true, perhaps;
nevertheless, her books are written with such fire and depth that

while being entertained her reader is learning a lesson as surely as if he had sought only the lesson. It is a lesson in freedom, faith and understanding.

She became interested in more than her own home, family, and career as soon as she was firmly settled into this country. She and her husband then established the East and West Association, a forerunner of the present People-to-People program. She became an active member of the board of directors of the Vineland Training School, where her daughter resides, and later was the chairman of the Governor's Committee for the Mentally Retarded in Pennsylvania. In 1947 she, together with friends, established an adoption agency, Welcome House, Inc., dedicated to finding homes for the so-called hard-to-place child of mixed Asian-American parentage.

During Christmas week in 1947, what she has come to call the world children came to her attention. The first child was a beautiful baby boy—that combination of East and West that results in a new people—and little wonder that she is attracted to them, caught as she herself is between two great cultures. This boy was born of an American missionary's daughter who fell in love with a young East Indian man. The mother's family was a notable one. Her grandfather had founded one of America's largest theological seminaries and her father had gone to India as a missionary before she was born. At the biological age when girls and boys become interested in each other she fell in love with her father's handsome assistant, a young Indian. It was natural for her to do so and natural for him to respond, but both her American family and his Indian family violently opposed their romance and forbade the marriage. True to nature, they culminated their love without the benefit of legal vows. The American family left India and the child was born shortly after they arrived in America. He was turned over at once to an agency to be placed for adoption, for the missionary family would not accept this child. This is where Pearl Buck became involved. The agency called her and said they could not place the baby because they could not match parents to such a racial mixture. To which she replied, "How can one preach the fatherhood of God and the brotherhood of man and not expect this child and accept him as a human being? Send him to me."

Quite by chance at about the same time a second baby boy arrived, the child of a Chinese surgeon and an American nurse. I have heard her tell the story: "I knew my husband and I were too old to take infants so I called adoption agencies and told them of these two beautiful children. Everywhere I was faced with the same answer. They would not place these children because they could not match parents. I was indignant so I started my own damned agency!" Her blue eyes flashed as she spoke.

This led to the birth of Welcome House, Inc. Her first move was to call together a group of her neighbors. She discussed her idea with them and told them she was planning to bring these children into the neighborhood and she wanted to be sure they would be welcomed.

"I remember the very day," she told me. "My neighbors sat in my living room. They were solid Pennsylvania Dutch men and women and they listened carefully. I could tell nothing from their faces, but when I had finished the owner of our village store spoke for them all.

" 'We will be proudt to have these children,' he said.

"So upon this foundation I built Welcome House with the help of many friends. Oscar Hammerstein, friend and neighbor, was president of our board until his death, and one of his daughters adopted two half Japanese babies."

The rest is history for that area of Bucks County, Pennsylvania. One has only to visit Doylestown to find these beautiful young people in strong evidence everywhere.

Soon, however, she was devoting too much time to these activities, although I must not give the impression that her writing did not benefit as well, for out of these experiences many books were to come. Her novel *Come My Beloved* is the story of the romance that led to that first baby boy, although in the book she exercises an author's right to fictionalize and does not allow the child to be born. *The Hidden Flower* is another such novel and so is *The New Year*. *To Whom a Child Is Born* is a collection (not yet published in book form as this is written) of short works of fiction all derived from her experiences with like situations. I have often heard her say that she never seeks material, but I must add that she never comes out of any situation without material for some work of fiction.

Welcome House has not been without a liberal share of problems, but she has stood steadfast in her belief that it was a needed
agency, an opinion confirmed by research conducted by the State
of Pennsylvania before the agency was given its license. The result of her work is that Welcome House is now known and respected all over the world.

The relationship with home and family has always been important to her, but she has maintained other active relationships
as well. She developed interest in activities other than those required to make a home or write her books. As her husband grew
ill and it became apparent she would soon have to continue her
life without the benefit of his companionship, other avenues of
activity began to open and, perhaps subconsciously, she became
more receptive to them than she had been previously. She began
to expand her life personally and professionally in the late 1940's
with the purchase of her Vermont property. What was to have
been a retreat has developed into a profitable business sideline
of real estate development and sales. I asked her to explain how
it happened. She replied with some laughter.

I sometimes wonder myself how I did acquire all that land in
Vermont. But, like most things, it began as an event, or rather an
incident, because it wasn't at the time important enough to be
an event. It somehow built itself through the years. Richard Walsh
published one year a charming small book about maple sugaring
in Vermont. We didn't know the authors, or we thought we
didn't, but when they turned up at the John Day offices they
proved to be Mr. and Mrs. Scott Nearing, and I remembered
when I saw Scott Nearing that I had met him when I was in college decades ago. He had come there as a lecturer. He was then a
young man—much older than I but relatively young. I think he
spoke on economics—anyway I remembered it was rather boring
and consequently I didn't remember what he had said. But I
remembered the name, and he and his wife had written this quite
nice little book about sugaring. I am always eager to know everything about American life and of course I had read about maple
sugaring but I hadn't the faintest idea of what it was, really. In
fact, I didn't even know very much about cold climates and snow.
It sounded fascinating that one could make sugar during the snow

season by gathering sap from the trees. I expressed my interest and Mrs. Nearing hospitably said, "Come and visit us and see for yourself." Well, we went—that is to say it was not just we who went, but Richard Walsh and I and our four children, who were then twelve and thirteen. We stayed in the very interesting stone house which Scott and Mrs. Nearing had built themselves, with a little local help, by that particular method which I have described to you of facing a wooden frame with stones and then pouring cement back of them so that the result looks like a stone house but is really a cement house. Their design of the house was quite good, too, a sort of chalet. It was in late March and there was a heavy snow in the Green Mountains when we arrived. We climbed the hill with difficulty in our car, and deposited ourselves for two days in their house. I'm not sure that they expected such a long visit but we stayed. What nobody had told us, and what our hosts had not thought to tell us, was that they were strict vegetarians and for two days we had nothing to eat but vegetables and fruit, a great shock to Richard Walsh, who was not much on vegetables, and to the children, who were devoted to hamburgers! We staggered through those days, food-wise. I remember for breakfast we had sunflower seeds and a sort of raspberry drink and boiled millet without seasoning. Now I am used to millet from North China but always with something else with it. It was a little difficult to take straight cold millet.

What we had come to see, however, was the sugaring, and we did see it and the children helped with that. And what I fell in love with was not the labor of sugaring, because I didn't care that much for sugar or sugaring, but the snow was so beautiful in those woods and upon the mountains. The mountains reminded me of the mountain place where we used to go every summer when I was a child. The rocks were the same, the ferns were the same. Of course there were no ferns at that time of year but I was enchanted with the place and I made up my mind that I wanted to own a piece of land there. Besides, it occurred to me that it would be a wonderful place to send our boys the next summer and have them learn how to build these stone cement houses. They could build a house with the help of a good master builder and then I wouldn't have the fear that they would be hanging around the village streets in Pennsylvania. I found a piece of land for sale, very cheap—two dollars an acre or something like that —and I bought a hundred acres or so. Thereafter for several summers the boys went up every summer. I rented a little empty schoolhouse from a neighbor which had a stove in it, and we put in cots and they went up there for two weeks at a time. They would come home for a week in order to get cleaned up because I doubt they really did much washing while they were up there, and to get their laundry done and so on. Then they went back for two more weeks and so the summer passed and finally there was a house of sorts to show for it.

I don't think that the boys thought highly of this experiment —in fact, at times they were extremely bored with it. We did engage the general guardianship of a friend who lived there in the mountains, a man who had been a college mate of my husband's. He always had one meal a day with the boys at night. They did all their own cooking and of course there was no electricity— only an old wood range. They lived in a very primitive fashion indeed. A brook ran by the schoolhouse in which they could bathe and keep relatively clean.

The whole experiment had therapeutic value. The boys were able to work out all their desires to fight and quarrel, which three lively boys of the same age seem to have to do, so that when they came home they were friends and understood each other much better than before. Since, as you know, I suffer from an allergy of ragweed pollen and I found I didn't have this difficulty in the Green Mountains, we improved the house, but before we improved the house I ought to add that one other reason for the building of this house was that I wanted the children to know what it was like to live without electricity and without telephone or any of the modern conveniences, as most people in the world still must do. We used oil lamps and candles, we cooked on two big fireplaces at either end of the big house and we bathed in the kind of bathrooms that are to be found in India where there is a drain in the middle of the cement floor and one soaps one's self thoroughly and pours a bucket of water over that self. I wanted them to realize that one can be clean and civilized without any of the modern conveniences. Of course as time went on and especially after Richard Walsh became ill and couldn't walk the mile up through the woods to the house we had to change all

this. By then the lesson was learned, however . . . We modern-
ized the house, and then gradually on the same principle as the
woman in Texas who owned thousands of acres—of course I
didn't own thousands of acres as she did—but I always kept buying the piece of land that was next to me when it was for sale. Yes,
I didn't want anything else but just the land that was next to me,
and so before I knew it I had quite an accumulation of land.

Then as the children grew older and had their own friends I
decided to build a house just for Richard Walsh and myself, and
I built Mountain Haunt, which, as you know, has but three rooms
—my room, which is also a big room, big enough for a work area,
Richard Walsh's room, which is now the guest room, and a huge
living room, which has all the space necessary for dining and a
piano and everything else we use every day. Mountain Haunt
looks out on the beautiful view of rolling mountains topped by
Mount Stratton. We had three happy summers there, by the way,
before Richard Walsh died.

Of those years I don't think it's necessary to speak here because
there are excerpts you might take from *A Bridge for Passing* that
will cover this painful period.

The making of motion pictures is another activity that held
her interest and, for that matter, still does to some degree. As
with other business ventures, her motion picture experiences centered around the talent of one man. I have discussed it with her
numbers of times, but the story is best told in her own words.

Here I will speak of how we met Tad Danielewski. In the days
while Richard Walsh was still able to make decisions I had become acquainted with Tad Danielewski. Our acquaintance began
in a television show, *Omnibus*. When *My Several Worlds* was
published the *Omnibus* people asked me to devote part of one of
their programs on Sunday afternoon to this book, and they assigned to me as director a young Polish-American—that is, he
had been born in Poland and had come here after the war. As a
director he was sensitive, rather silent, very perceptive. He was
married and his wife was expecting their first child when they
came down to visit me in Pennsylvania. I don't remember him
especially at that time except that he was very solicitous that the

program be done in the way that I liked. He was imaginative and understanding and as I went through rehearsals with him later I found that he had planned a beautiful program.

On the final day the business manager came bustling in. To our consternation he changed a number of things and since we were just about to go on the air it was very difficult to carry on. I remember Tad Danielewski's terrifying disappointment. He was crushed that the program was not to be as he had planned, and I sympathized with the director and not with this character who had come in so unfortunately. After the performance was over I felt sorry for Tad and knowing how despondent he was I looked for him. He was standing with his face to the wall in a corner of the studio and saying nothing. I could see he was furiously angry but it was no use to say anything.

Shortly thereafter he left the network and went to a competing network. Then one day unexpectedly he turned up and asked me if I would like to put my book *The Big Wave* on television and, if so, would I write the script. I said, "Yes, I would like to do that." I did write the script and it was put on and was a very successful program. I remember the big headline across the top of the New York *Times* theater section saying ANOTHER MASTERPIECE. Well, of course it was not a masterpiece but it was pleasant to have it called that. Unfortunately Danielewski didn't direct it. The whole program, the whole package, as it was called, was sold to a production firm. But it was done in color, although with an all-American cast. I was only moderately pleased with this Western effort, for I have never been satisfied with Americans impersonating Chinese, even the best of them. Of course Luise Rainer was marvelous in *The Good Earth* but then she has Tartar blood and was very Oriental in her appearance and in her ways. Well, anyhow the critics liked *The Big Wave*. It was another disappointment for Tad Danielewski that he did not do the directing of it, so he came back again and asked me if I would write a script of my story "The Enemy," which was a prize-winning story, and I said I would. So I did and he produced it very well. Two Japanese acted in that play, however. Shirley Yamaguchi, who is a popular and a good Japanese actress—although her grandmother, I believe, was French—stayed over in this country for two months in order to be able to take the leading television part, and she did a beautiful job.

The result of all this cooperation was that one day Tad Danielewski came up to Vermont and asked me if I would consider going into an independent production company with him. I have always been interested in the theater, as you know, and in writing television scripts, though I had never done so before, and I thought it was rather fun. Then, too, I think I foresaw that I was going to have more time on my hands in the future. I mean I realized my life would soon be more empty than it had been, for by now there was no hope for Richard's recovery. In those days, however, he was still able to think and so I said I would not make my decision without his opinion. He was already finding it difficult to follow a line of thought but he concentrated all his effort on listening to Tad Danielewski outline his plan. Then he turned to me and said, "I want you to go into this with Tad. I think you'll find it interesting. It will be something new for you and some day you will want such help." I understood that he was foreseeing the future, too. And so I agreed and, this decision being made, we stopped by the window to look at the sunset on Mount Stratton.

"What do you want to name our company?" Tad Danielewski asked. "What do you want to name it?" I asked in return. He looked up at the mountain which towers over the landscape and he said, "Let's call it Stratton Productions." That was the way the name was chosen, and the company has given me considerable pleasure and interest. It took me to India twice; it took me also to Japan. It brought me into the world of theater. It brought a production on Broadway, not successful but interesting. As usual, my Broadway play was ahead of the times. I mean by "as usual" that it seems I am always doing things too soon, so that people do not know what I am talking about. Well, if I had waited ten years for *Desert Incident,* it would have been an entirely different story.

Out of Stratton Productions, too, has come a film we made in India, *The Guide.* We made a beautiful film in Japan, too, again an art film, of *The Big Wave.* That was financed by and belongs to Allied Artists and they never released it in its full form, unfortunately, but the cooperating Japanese firm, Toho, is still holding it, as you know, hoping it will be released one day in its entirety. Tad has directed Jean-Paul Sartre's *No Exit* and recently has done a documentary in Africa for ABC. At this moment he is in Korea negotiating for *Norbu,* which is probably our next production.

I don't take a very active part in Stratton nowadays except as advisor or in keeping a general knowledge of what is going on because, as you know, I am completely absorbed in the Foundation. But I believe in Tad Danielewski's talent and it has been one of the interests which at a time when I needed it gave me a certain—what shall I say?—a diversion, perhaps. Certainly it enlarged my general knowledge of the world of the theater and television and films and had its effect on me. That is enough, don't you think?

The greatest, perhaps the deepest and most nearly perfect relationship of the entire period of the dichotomy, the struggle between woman and creative artist, is the relationship with Ernest Hocking. She discussed him with me not long ago.

About Ernest Hocking? Now that he is dead I can look back on the part of my life which was shared with him as a whole, very important to me. It was a story in itself, begun in 1918 and finished in 1966. That's a long span of years, yet during most of those years I was not conscious of him. The first time I saw him was in Nanking, China. I was living in the same house in which I wrote *The Good Earth,* one that looked out on Purple Mountain. I was teaching in two Chinese universities and my life was very busy. Fundamentally it was an external kind of life because I had come to the knowledge by then that whatever a good marriage was I did not have it. It wasn't a bad one, you understand, but it wasn't what a marriage could and should be in a human life.

That was the year of the Laymen's Mission to China to investigate Christian missions. I believe that Ernest Hocking was very important in that work, perhaps the chief. I had no knowledge then of his importance in his own field, but I remember very well that he and his wife were guests at a meal with us. They did not stay in our house but they were assigned to me for a meal or so. I remember his coming into the house like a strong wind, very vital and tall, extremely handsome, very blue eyes, very unself-conscious, full of confidence and knowing exactly what he wanted, talkative, humorous, a striking personality. His wife, who was the daughter of James Riley, the Irish poet, was just as striking in her way, though not as attractive as he was because she did not have the brains or the looks that he had. He had a philosophical mind which of course attracted me at once. Hers was not philo-sophical so much as practical, yet it had a sort of Irish quality that was delightful. I remember with pleasure the evening they spent at our house. Then they went back to America and I thought no more of them.

Now all that remains of that meeting of importance is what Ernest Hocking told me afterwards. His interest in me as a per-son, he said, began at that first meeting and he was convinced that I wasn't living where I would eventually live or living as I would eventually live or doing what I would eventually do—all this be-fore I ever knew it myself! Of course he wrote to thank me for our evening. I don't remember that I even answered his letter and there was no special reason to do so. But apparently he kept fol-lowing what I was doing throughout the years after that.

The next time I remember him was after the report was pub-lished under the title *Re-thinking Missions*. It was mainly his work, based upon a compilation of opinions of his whole group, of course, and it was a brilliant job. He comprehended missions and missionary work so clearly, praising where praise was due, yet there was constructive and profound criticism, too, with which I agreed. Of course the churches did not like the book and he came in for a good deal of reproach. I was asked to review the book—I forget for what magazine now. At any rate, I gave it a very favorable review which greatly cheered him, apparently, and he wrote me a wonderful letter, and in that way came back into my life. I remember we met occasionally here and there. I didn't realize then that he was keeping a running account of my life and of the meetings that we had. I was busy and interested in many people. I cannot remember but I do not think I had any personal feeling about him one way or the other, except admir-ation for his brain and his fearless independence.

Then I had my own run-in about Christian missions. It was while *The Good Earth* was making its first impact and when I got back to this country—that was in 1931 or 1932—I found that the mission board under which my husband worked had booked me for many speeches. I was quite indignant about this because I had been working as a professor and earning my own living and not wanting anyone to assume that I was taking church money, for I was not myself a missionary. I declined to keep these engagements, but after persuasion said finally that I would meet confidentially with a few of the Christian leaders and give them my opinion of missions—all this for what it was worth. So I prepared myself and gave a great deal of thought to putting down exactly what I felt after all my years as a missionary child and then as the wife of a man in their employ and then from my observation of living in a missionary community, as I did when I was in Nanking, although I hadn't many associations with Americans, my friends being mainly Chinese, even then. The date was set for a luncheon at the Astor Hotel, which I supposed would be a private one in a private room. I went there at the appointed time and to my horror the luncheon was anything but private. It was arranged in the huge ballroom and tickets had been sold to literally hundreds of people. The ballroom was crowded with little tables, an immense crowd was there, and page boys in various parts of the hotel were shouting, "This way to the Pearl Buck Luncheon!"

I thought, Oh, what shall I do because my speech is not for the public! It's for a few chosen leaders of the mission board. I did not know what to do, and yet I didn't know what else to say except what I had prepared very carefully for a few people and certainly not for the public. I sat at an immensely long head table with the chief of the board and other important religious persons. Well, I had to give that speech and I got up and gave it. When I had finished I sat down. Deadly silence fell upon the room. It was appalling to me. I felt as if I were alone in the middle of the Sahara. But I am nothing if not persistent, as you know, so I sat up straight and looked calm—I hope! Then clapping began and I had a very great ovation. Evidently there were many people who agreed with me but I can't say the people at the head table joined in it. I left rather abruptly, knowing I had done something devastating. When I got back to the hotel the telephone was already ringing. I was asked why I had chosen to make an attack in this public way. "It's not an attack," I replied, "because I gave constructive suggestions about situations which I feel could be improved."

Meanwhile, *Harper's* magazine called to ask me if they could publish my speech as an article and they did so. Later my publishers put it out as a special pamphlet, because there was such a request for it, under the title *Is There a Case for Foreign Missions?* I don't regret one word of it. And now it's quite obvious that Christianity did not take a deep hold on China or it would not be in its present situation there.

As you know, I feel that Christian missionaries are basically good. Certainly I never knew of any Christian missionaries who were thieves or rascals. I did know one or two who had illegitimate children—lonely men without their wives—but they were immediately dismissed. Yet, while missionary standards were high for moral conduct, missionaries themselves were not usually people who understood the Chinese or made much effort to understand the people whose souls they wanted to save —this with some notable exceptions, among them my own father and mother. In general, missionaries lacked the education for a country where the culture was as old as that of China.

After all this rumpus that I had created Ernest Hocking wrote me a marvelous letter. I wish I had it now but I didn't keep it. He kept all of my letters. I didn't keep his until later. In this wonderful letter, which encouraged me, he told me I was absolutely right in what I had said and that it would create a new image of what the missionary should be. It was such a wonderful letter, and I remember that we saw each other after that, although not really in any very personal way. When I created the East and West Association he set it up in Boston for me and we met several times on that. He had the most beautifully ordered mind; he was always calm and philosophical and one could get into immediate communication with him. He was very helpful in those days in Boston and the prestige of his name added a great deal to the work that was done there. I have talked about the East and West Association elsewhere, and I need not do so here. I brought it to a close when the Second World War broke out.

Some years passed before I saw Ernest Hocking again. Indeed, it was only after the death of Richard Walsh. Ernest Hocking's

wife had died some ten years before. He had been devoted to her
in her long illness. I remember he told me of it when we were in
communication again. All by himself he drove her to their summer home in New Hampshire. She was then already very ill in
much the same way that Richard Walsh had been, so that our
experiences were the same. But I don't remember that I wrote
to him, although perhaps I did, after she died. I was engrossed
in other interests. My next vivid personal remembrance of him
comes after Richard's death. Among the hundreds of letters I had
to read and reply to at that time the one from Ernest Hocking
remains the most perceptive, the most understanding, the most
encouraging. He sent me also a book, *The Meaning of Immortality,* which he had written after his wife's death. It expresses the
philosopher's attitude toward immortality, a very helpful book.
He was then retired and living in his house in New Hampshire,
alone, except for his housekeeper. In the summers his children
came to live in farmhouses around him. He had about six hundred acres, a big farm, but he was working on a book, he told me.
Then he asked me to come and see him because he was no longer
able to come and see me. I remember very well that August day
when I reached his house and saw him after a period of years. He
was having his afternoon nap when I arrived but his daughter
and son were there with their families. We sat on a beautiful
terrace outside his living room, which looks out on five peaks of
the highest mountains in New Hampshire, a beautiful view.

When he heard I was there he got up and came downstairs. He
was then over eighty but he looked twenty years younger and very
vigorous. His hair was white, of course, but at least he still had
his hair. His clipped moustache was white, too, but his eyes were
as blue as ever, his step as strong. I remember the feeling of recognition that passed between us . . . we had so much in common.
I spent the afternoon that day, but after that he began to write
to me regularly and with his thoughts occasionally he sent me a
poem. I wrote back, and our friendship—well, I can't say it was
renewed because it was like a new friendship. We began really
to know each other and each summer thereafter I always went to
stay with him about a week. We took walks, he liked to row on
the lake with me until the last summer or two, and we talked
about everything. We grew closer with each letter and in a way I

had companionship with him that I have never had with anyone else. Our minds were sympathetic, we explored philosophical thought together. Did we love each other? Yes, we did. And he took a place in my life that nobody else has, although there was a long span of years between us—twenty, to be exact. He always seemed in wonderful health and spirits and had a philosophical gaiety which I greatly enjoyed.

Then he decided one summer that he would come and visit me in my Vermont house, not too far away. I fetched him in the car and he stayed for a delightful weekend at Mountain Haunt alone with me. He enjoyed it, too. We went sight-seeing all over the mountains and I discovered that among his talents as a musician and a painter he was a very talented artist. He was also a geologist and very much interested in rocks. I learned a great deal about the rocks of Vermont that I never dreamed of and we made a search for books about rocks in that state—very difficult to find they were, too!

It was a productive, rich, rewarding kind of friendship for me at that time. I think the hardest part about losing husband or wife is that abruptly one passes from the years where one has been the center of another person's life and that one the center of one's own life. Suddenly one is alone. Until then there has always been a point of reference, so to speak. When the central person dies there is not The One and one is not The One. For Ernest Hocking and me there came to be no doubt that I had become that one for him and in a somewhat different sense he had for me, too. And yet all the time I knew that it must end very soon because of his age. In 1965, I went to visit him as usual. I knew that this was his last summer and my last visit. Thereafter letters must suffice until the end. We never wrote long letters. I hate writing letters and one page covers the essentials that I want to convey. He wrote one-page letters, too, but very often sent me a verse of poetry as well.

I had said nothing to him during that visit which could lead him to believe it was our last, but I felt sure from the changed look in his face that it was. I was not surprised, therefore, when in the early part of the next year I had word by telephone from his daughter-in-law and son that he was declining very rapidly. He had written me a letter using in its conclusion the old Latin phrase, "We who are about to die salute you," and I understood that he, too, knew that his death was near. It was a great question with me whether or not to go to see him again. He said in that last letter, "I live in the faith that we shall meet again." I didn't know whether that meant meet on this earth or meet in the future, beyond this life.

I decided finally that I did not wish to see him in the last days and carry that memory as I had carried the memory of Richard's last year, the terrible decline and the final change so impressed upon my memory that when I think of him now I have to make myself remember what he was when he was himself, not what he was at the end. I wanted to remember Ernest Hocking when he was still himself. I wrote his children a letter which expressed as best I could my appreciation of their father. It is not often that one meets in life another mind so brilliant as his, which at the same time communicated, in understanding and sympathy, with one's own mind. He was a person to whom I could look up with the conviction that he knew more than I did and was able to think beyond my reach, so that every experience with him was inspiring, encouraging and exciting.

One who has known the tortures of devastating loneliness, defying all reason and borne with a physical pain to a point beyond relief—only one who has known such loneliness can understand. Those who have not known it before will not yet understand. One of the young Amerasians with whom I work said to me one evening, "But all people are lonely. No soul can truly understand another. It is not meant to be, so a person who lives close to himself, one who knows himself, is lonely—whether other people are there or not." This came from a boy of eighteen, and it is profound truth. What he does not know yet is the bone, heart, soul and flesh loneliness that filters through everything in life. It is there always in the gay melody or sad, in every breath. It is a conscious loneliness that never lets one forget that when the time has come each day to retire from the outside world into the place enshrined, one must do so alone. She has known loneliness of the type my young friend describes all of her life, but always she had the physical sharing of her life. I do not mean merely in a sexual way, for that is unimportant to the mature person, but in the comfort of knowing that there is a human being who expects nothing except what can be freely given. I do not mean necessarily one who gives, for such giving can in itself exhaust the one who receives. I mean the person with whom there is neither give nor take because there is no necessity for either. When that person is gone from one's life, then, and not before, one knows loneliness. This aloneness crept into all of her creative expression, but the most personal and revealingly written passages begin with the "Treasure Book" entry of November 15, 1955:

I am now very lonely within for my companion and my love has not been himself for a year and a half—not since that dreadful August 17, 1953, when in a moment's time part of him died forever. The brain is damaged and cannot respond. He is sweet and uncomplaining but the old sharing of thought and communication is gone. We sit in the same room and it is so lonely—so much more lonely than it would be if I were physically alone. I am learning how to find solace, not comfort, in music and in the thoughts of others, in books and in nature again. The hi-fi in the library is a means of keeping up my spirit at twilight . . . I went to see Carol last Friday and tried as usual to satisfy that childish heart in its need for love and communication and then came home to find my poor dear waiting in the living room, doing nothing, just waiting for me—so different, so different! But the heart breaks only once. . . . A soft gray November day, the mists over the hills, the trees standing still and ghostly.

Christmas, 1955: When R. saw the Christmas tree all lighted again for the twentieth time he wept silently and I knew that he was thinking that perhaps it would be the last time for him. Later he told me that he did not want to trouble me but that he could not help remembering he would be seventy his next birthday and that therefore this might be his last Christmas. I said I knew what he was thinking, which seemed to astonish him, and I said he would probably live another ten years. For indeed death need not be thought of; it is already a certainty, only the time unknown. Therefore it is a waste of life to contemplate its end. Whereupon R. drank a large whisky and soda with his usual enjoyment!

Christmas was all it should be—all the children here, no longer children but nearly adult. It gave me content to realize that they no longer need me. That is the fulfillment of parenthood. To-morrow is the last day of the year, another day begins. By this time next week the house will be empty, all but, and certainly quiet. I like it both ways and neither all of the time.

May 13, 1958: R. is still with us in the flesh but his mind has gone away. His habits of affection still remain and the echo of love. The essential nature, all else being stripped away now by a series of strokes, is sweet and patient and good. We take care of him and for him as we do for a child. I do not ask why this has happened. I am alone but I have been alone before. Strange and beautiful compensations come my way, nothing complete or even perhaps profound, but enough to make life bearable through hours of no communication.

The more I learn of her the more sure I am that she wrote *A Bridge for Passing* out of the same motivation that she had earlier written the two novels *This Proud Heart* and *The Time Is Noon*. The motivation? To write "the end" on one entire chapter of her life and to declare the setting of the stage for the next chapter. The obvious difference, of course, was that this time the man no longer lived—hence she need not seek the protective shelter of the novel. Instead she could write freely in first person nonfiction with no danger of hurting another, which has always been one of her greatest fears.

From the beginning of *A Bridge for Passing*, one is over-whelmed by her calm acceptance of fact, completely devoid of any of the feminine hysterics familiarly accorded to a husband's death. This could lead the casual observer to assume that she did not feel deeply. The opposite is true. Richard Walsh was very important in her life. The relationship was not as complete as she would have had it but it was nonetheless deep. There was a companionship, there was a mutual sharing of lives, their own and those of their children, and there was love. His death left the void that has always been in her life even deeper and more absolute than it had ever before been.

The calm acceptance of which I spoke is apparent in the dedication to *A Bridge for Passing*:

It is as it is.
>   —Motto of Edward III, 1340 A.D.

What, then, is to be done?
I take refuge in my heart,
where I love him as I wish.
>   —Paul Valéry

She was in Japan when death finally struck Green Hills Farm. Stratton Productions was making the motion picture version of her children's book *The Big Wave,* and it was necessary for her to be there. She would never have left him had he been aware of her going, but all awareness had faded completely away. Moreover, she needed money for his care. The illness, seven years long, the latter years with three trained nurses, had depleted her, and she was the family's sole support.

"Shall I go?" she asked her physician.

"Go," he said. "There may be years ahead. It has been a long pull and you are exhausted. You must have a change for your own sake."

I shall not attempt to justify her trip, for it is necessary to justify only when one is wrong and I believe her to have been right. I quote some of her philosophical reaction from *A Bridge for Passing.*

I do not know whether it is easier to have the end come suddenly or gradually over the years. I think, if I had been given the choice, I would have preferred a sudden end, shock and all. Then memory would not be entangled with the slow and agonizing fading of perception and speech and at last recognition even of those loved and dear. There is, however, one balm. He did not know of his own decline. And as he was reduced to the elemental physical aspects of his life, his essential nature remained, as I have said, what it had always been, an unselfish sweetness.

Slowly, slowly, the change came. When his eyes failed and he could no longer read, we sent for the records of books. I must here express my permanent gratitude to the Library of Books for the Blind. They kept a continuing stream of records coming into the house, free of charge, and his brain was kept alive and stimulated beyond what we had feared. But this too came to an end. The day came when words ceased to have their meaning, and even music faded, and he was content merely to exist. He would have suffered had he known, and I thank a kind intelligence, wherever it is, that he never knew. The body lived on, relieved of any strain of mind or spirit or emotion, and assumed a strange durability of its own.

"This will last a long time," our family doctor said again. "You must go on about your usual work. You must live, you must travel, you must not let yourself be absorbed by this which cannot be helped."

And indeed it was the only way to endure what was happening to us. I tried to live as usual, insofar as I could. . . .

For the first time in my life I was sad when evening came. The others went to their husbands and wives, but I came back alone to my hotel room. The windows looked over the roofs of new Tokyo—as I have said, not beautiful, for there has not been time enough to create beauty. The city was hastily rebuilt after the war, a pity, for after it was thoroughly flattened by bombing it would have been well, if possible, to design a city with wide streets and parkways, a modern city but beautiful in the Japanese fashion. It was not done. The war had been harsh, people were desperate to begin living again, and the government was all but bankrupt. Houses went up helter-skelter. Today it is still almost impossible to find a house by its number or even by its street. One can only entrust oneself to the unknown. . . .

And always at the end of the day, every day, there came the return to no one! After the problems, solved and unsolved, after the coming and going of many people, the doubt and concern, the excitement of discovery, the shared laughter, the growing confidence in the work, each day had the same end. I went back to my hotel rooms, unlocked the door, went in and locked the door again. Flowers were fresh, the rooms cool, letters heaped on the table—letters from no one. The one letter I longed for could never be written because he was gone. I did not open the others. Let them wait until my Japanese secretary came and I was forced to work in order that she could work. Invitations were many, but I had no enjoyment in accepting them. A few I must accept, those which had to do with the sad and anxious parents of retarded children, a few others from old friends for the sake of past kindness. I fell then into the habit of having dinner sent to my rooms and of eating alone, so that I need not be compelled to smile at strangers who might approach me with questions and praise. When night came, life was suddenly meaningless.

Yet I was not impatient with myself. I knew from experience that time is needed for the absorption of sorrow into one's being. Once that adjustment is made, growth begins again and new life. It was too soon. I found it was impossible to sit alone in the hotel rooms. Had he been with me, it would have been the best part of the day. It always was the best part. Much of our life had to be spent in separation during the hours of day, for each of us had a profession, a work. But how eagerly we looked forward to the evening, and to what lengths we went in order to spend it together! We went together wherever we had to go, I yielding to his necessity, he to mine, depending upon the importance we attached to the specific occasion. And in the twenty-five years of our married life we did not spend a night apart, until it became necessary for him to live and work entirely at home. Even then I refused all invitations that kept me away for a night, until he ceased to know whether I was there or not. And when he ceased to know, everything was different, except memory. . . .

It was as though I were floating and far away, in a strange country in which I had no life. I might have been dead myself, so profound was the silence within. I would never weep again. I knew now there was no use in tears, nor any comfort to be sought or found. There was only this one—myself. Silly to cry for myself. . . .

There would be such moments as long as I was alive, moments of beauty, moments of excitement and exhilaration; above all, moments of achievement. In such moments he and I had turned to each other as instinctively as we breathed. That was no more to be . . . It is not true that one never walks alone. There is an eternity where one walks alone and we do not know its end.

During their twenty-five years together the only philosophical point on which they differed was the immortality of the soul—whether there is continuance of human individuality after this span of life, after the death of the physical body. She continues to ponder the question today, but he never pondered. He was

absolutely convinced that there is no continuance. Her stand remains that it is impossible to make a positive statement of fact
where one cannot possibly know fact! In the last two pages of
A Bridge for Passing she explains clearly and exactly her own
position.

But I have a stopping place in New York, that city of wonders
and grief. He and I always kept a place there. He needed it for his
work and for his spirit, and I have continued our tradition. It is
not the same place we shared for so many years. Within the con-
fines of our old apartment I could not escape the torture of memory. Whether I would have stayed I do not know, but the sky-
scrapers of steel and glass had pushed their way up our avenue,
and the building in which we had made a city home was to be
torn down. I found a place farther uptown in a new building,
where there were no memories except the ones I carry hidden
wherever I am.

And here I tell a story that has nothing to do with the picture,
except that it provides a closing scene for myself. When I was
looking for the new apartment a daughter helped me by sorting
out the impossibles and bringing me at last to see the two or three
possibles. It was night, I remember, when I looked at these places.
I was in haste and it did not seem to matter much where I lived.
We entered bare unpainted rooms. I saw a wide window and
through the darkness I discerned dimly a building whose roof
faced my window, a school, my daughter said, and fortunate for
me, for there would be no high building to cut off the view. I did
not care very much about that, either, for when do I have time in
New York to look at a view? Besides, I have plenty of view in my
Pennsylvania home. So I decided upon impulse.

"I'll take it."

The choice was haphazard, I would have said, a chancy thing.
But I am beginning to believe that there is no such thing as pure
chance in this world. For here is the preliminary to this closing
story:

When I was a child and often reluctant to do my duty, my
father used to say to me firmly but gently,

"If you will not do it because it is right, then do it for the greater
glory of God."

For the greater glory of God then, and for my father's sake, though still reluctant, I did do what had to be done, at least as often as possible.

Now to return to the apartment. I did not once see it while it was being decorated. When all was finished I opened the door and went straight to the big window. It was a bright day, I remember, one of New York's best, the air fresh from the sea and the sky blue. And facing me, across the building, under the eaves and along the roof, I saw these words carved in huge stone letters:

AD MAIOREM DEI GLORIAM

They face me now as I write. To the greater glory of God! What does it mean, this voice from the grave, my father's grave? He lies buried on a mountaintop in the very heart of a China lost to me. I am here and alive and thousands of miles away. Are we in communication, he and I, through my father? It is not possible.

How dare I say it is not?

Some day we shall know. What day? That day, perhaps, when saints and scientists unite to make a total search for truth. It is the saints, the believers, who should have the courage to urge the scientists to help them discover whether the spirit continues its life of energy when the mass we call body ceases to be the container. Faith supplies the hypothesis, but only science can provide the computer for verification. The unbeliever will never pursue the search. He is already static, a pillar of salt, forever looking backward.

There are no miracles, of that I am sure. If one walks on water and heals the sick and raises the dead to life again, it is not a matter of magic but a matter of knowing how to do it. There is no supernatural; there is only the supremely natural, the purely scientific. Science and religion, religion and science, put it as I may, they are two sides of the same glass, through which we see darkly until these two, focusing together, reveal the truth.

On the day when the message comes through from over the far horizon where dwells "that great majority," the dead, the proof will reach us, not as a host of angels in the sky but as a wavelength recorded in a laboratory, a wavelength as indisputable and personal as the fingerprint belonging to someone whose body is dust. Then the scientist, recognizing the wavelength, will exclaim, "But

that's someone I know! I took his wavelength before he died."
And he will compare his record with the wavelength just recorded
and will know that at last a device, a machine, is able to receive
a message dreamed of for centuries, the message of the continuing individual existence, which we call the immortality of the
soul.

Or perhaps it will not be a scientist who receives, but a woman,
waiting at a window open to the sky.

She is the kind of woman who must feel the approval of one
man in her life. This necessity has created the dichotomy. Since
they met in 1932 that man had been her husband. To whatever
she found lacking in him she adjusted herself accordingly, but
he was the man. With the start of his declining health in 1953
there was continually less from him and more adjusting for her
to do. The seven-year period was one of her most difficult, for
the truth is that at those times in her life when she has
most needed help she has been completely alone. The illness
and death of her mother in 1921, the ten years of cruel realization
with her retarded daughter, leaving her first husband in 1933,
the divorce in 1935, all of these life-breaking experiences she had
to face alone. Some will remember that her second husband was
already important to her when she left her first, that he was in
Reno when the divorce was granted, and they were married only
half an hour after the final decree. But those who have suffered
divorce will know that the decision must be made alone and that
after the difficult deciding one must live alone with that decision.
Only one heart can know the pain involved, for no other heart
can share it. Yes, to have shared the knowledge, for example, that
even her second marriage did not fulfill her private hopes
would have affected not only her own life and that of her husband, whom she did love and appreciate, but there were children
to consider as well. During his illness no understanding and no
help came from anyone, and again the burden was hers except
that later in this period there was one man who became a comfort to her—the only solace during this heartbreaking time. I
do not know his name, for I have never asked her and never
shall. I tell of him only because he was important to her at this
time of her life. I doubt that they were ever lovers, but the love

was there. The first sign of it appears as a poem inserted into the "Treasure Book" in 1958; it had been written slightly earlier and transferred here. It is tucked among "treasures" about the children and unexplained.

May, 1958: When Susan [her first grandchild] was born I could not feel her as a person but now at seven months I know her well—a strong, deeply emotional person. She will have a fine life but will be often unhappy.

John is married and has developed in this experience of love.

I am pleased with Joe, too—a lovable young man, right for my tempestuous Jean.

Richard is in Germany. I miss him but I know it is good for him to undergo the discipline.

Edgar I feel more at ease about now than for some time. He is growing and is sensitive.

Janice is a good and useful woman. I was enjoying her pretty face only yesterday.

Henriette is so like me when I was her age. I am close to her. [And then the poem.]

> The heart, it seems, can never know its age.
> I would have said that at this stage,
> I'd never love again.
> Yet here it is—the pain.
> The ecstasy, the joy . . .
> Against you I employ
> My whole will to hide
> Truth I have denied.

The "Treasure Book" stops here for four years as far as personal entries are concerned. There are photographs of the children and of Jean's wedding but only one short handwritten comment:

Arthur Compton died in March, 1962. He wrote the card below after reading Command the Morning.

Miss Pearl Buck:
This is a good job. I am naturally pleased that you find in me a

suitable "hero" around whom to build your story. But I had better not comment about what you say about the hero. After all, this is your story! Except for a few minor factual corrections, the only significant change I have suggested is on the last page, where I alter the words quoted from me to make them more in character. All good wishes,

Arthur H. Compton

She met Arthur Compton when she was doing research for the book. She spent time with him at his summer home, and she went to Washington University in St. Louis, where he taught, and spent long hours discussing with him the drama of the atomic bomb which she later expressed through the hero of *Command the Morning*. She liked Compton and she liked his wife. They never became close friends for it was not possible, involved as she was in her work and her life and he equally involved in his. But she enjoyed the experience of knowing him, however short it was.

In May, 1962, she wrote:

"How many years have passed in this inner silence! This morning I write again . . . The house is still my home. Two darling daughters share it . . . Mary Chieko and Johanna. Henriette is in Westtown School, *growing*. Jean and her family live across the road—three lovely children and another to come. Richard and his wife live in the farmhouse—their baby soon to be born. John and his family in Hilltop house—three beautiful little boys. I came to my office early this morning, and must go back to it, for I am in the midst of a Korean novel, but pause, for some reason, to begin this Treasure Book again . . . I saw Edgar play in *Rashomon* last night—a good job. But he is more than actor, *what,* I don't know and neither does he. His wife Linda sat beside me and we talked about him with love and anxiety. Has he—will he ever have the drive, the energy, so necessary to employ his talent? I think so . . . Perhaps because I hope so enormously . . . Janice is with me between jobs, a chance to know her again . . . I don't feel able yet to write from within myself. This is only to open the book once more. I want to write poetry. When I first began to write, it was with poetry. The time has come once more."

Here she has inserted a poem, written on June 4, 1947, which I find very revealing.

MASCARA (For Women Only)

The real purpose of mascara, my dears,
Is to prevent the flowing of your tears.
Impossible, you will agree,
To let him or others see
When it's time for you to part,
What is happening to your heart.
Stains upon your cheeks
Make you look like freaks.
With mascara, though, my dears,
You can now contain your tears
In the sealed chamber of your heart.
This is a woman's private art.

I find that "bitter-sweet" verse revealing because of her own penchant for mascara. I have never seen her when she was not wearing it, delicately.

The next personal entry was written early in 1963.

"January 26, 1963—Green Hills: Tomorrow, after long indecision and pondering, I leave for three months in India. It seems necessary to me, in the curious way that I am guided. I do not know how to write a full novel on modern India. This means living and working with people there. Mere touristing is not enough. So in a way this is a sort of farewell to home, hopefully only for a few months . . . Snow lies on the ground, with the possibility of more snow. Children and grandchildren wrench my heart. But go I must, for reasons unknown to me. Monday I have luncheon with Alan White in London. Tuesday I shall be in Bombay, God willing . . . Let me live long, to finish all the books I must write."

The trip to India was a success insofar as her writing is concerned. The long novel of modern-day India, *Mandala*, is finished, and she has also brought from India the idea for her children's story *The Big Fight*, which has been published. The beautiful film made on that trip by Stratton Productions from R. K. Narayan's novel *The Guide* is not yet a commercial success. It is an art film and as such is a triumph of glorious color that brings the soul of India to the screen. Perhaps it is too soon for such a motion picture. Perhaps in this venture also she is years ahead of her time. Possibly she will never realize her investment from the income of the film, but she has profited.

She stayed only one month on the first trip, returning in March to attend to pressing matters at home. In April she went again to India, returning this time in June, and on a certain day of that month in 1963 wrote in the "Treasure Book":

"On this day, after a telephone call which resolved my heart, I burned in the fireplace of my office a handful of letters, all short, which I had written over the years to one whom I loved. I burned them because they were dreams never to be fulfilled and therefore they recorded nothing. Now in the fireplace there is only a small pile of ash. This is as it must be, and perhaps as it should be. But many hours of my life lie wasted there, and some of my deepest feelings. And the one to whom the letters were written does not know what has been lost."

Perhaps she found comfort in those letters. In writing from her heart, perhaps she found a release for heartbreak and loneliness. She had asked that her letters be returned, knowing perhaps that this relationship could not continue. At any rate, in this tragedy, the illness and death of her husband, unlike the earlier ones of which I wrote, she was not entirely alone. The sword again swept across her life, separating her two beings, but this time she made the slash. The injury was to her inner self and not to her public self, for no one but she, and possibly he, knew of the cut. Even greater loneliness set in, for at this point of major decision there was no one to whom she could turn for comfort. I am sure the decision for her was based on personal integrity—she made the decision, whatever her reasons, that it was not possible for the relationship to develop into an open one. Basically she is not a secretive person, indeed quite the opposite, and to maintain a secret existence would require so much effort and thought on her part that she would be unable to pursue any creative expression. It was and is impossible for Pearl Buck, the author, to conceal anything, and most of all anything involving her deepest emotions. Would she compromise herself and continue this relationship at the expense of her writing career? It was not so much a question of "to be or not to be" as "what to be."

Often she has had to compromise with others in her life but I have never known her to compromise with herself. And this time was no different from all others. It was her decision not to continue whatever was, and so all was ended. She considered the future years and what she would do. There were still major books she wished to write. One was to be a novel of a triangle—a woman and two men, one older and one younger. Does this represent again the same desire to write "The End" on a chapter of her life? If so, I am sure the woman will be as autobiographical as Susan from *This Proud Heart* or as Joan from *The Time Is Noon*. I am sure the relationship with the older man will be based on her own with Ernest Hocking. And the relationship with the younger man? We must wait and see. As her long period of indecision ended with slow but firm decision, so ended the dichotomy.

PART III
Essence

TO AN AMERASIAN CHILD

Child!
Leave me alone.
I have books to write,
Children of my own.
I cannot atone.
Leave me alone!

Child!
Cease haunting space.
Your eyes are too blue,
In your Asian face.
With your Asian grace,
Cease haunting space!

Child!
Make your own fate.
I never decreed,
In love or in hate,
Your birthplace or date.
Make your own fate!

Too late—too late,
My heart now sighs.
I have seen that face,
I have seen those eyes.
—P. S. B.

ON June 27, 1963, the dichotomy ended forever, and I met her on July 5 of that year. Until we met I had no knowledge of Pearl Buck, of her awards, her life, or even her writings. In fact, at that time I had not only never read *The Good Earth,* I had not even seen the film. I tell this simply to show that my first impression of her was entirely fresh. I had no preconceived ideas of what I would or would not find.

I search for remembrance of first impressions and find that I remember her apparent feelings more than her appearance. She was shy; that was it! Our meeting is recorded in detail in a book we wrote together and I shall not repeat it here except to recall that shyness. I know now how Asian her shyness is. It is not the simple bumbling self-consciousness of youth, for there is none of that in her. It is the deliberate withdrawal from all situations that are unpleasant, whatever creates the situation. I was a stranger and strangers are unpleasant. It was necessary for her to employ every ounce of will at her command in order to go through with that meeting. With every stranger it is the same, and I have watched her withdraw and arrange and rearrange her own thoughts and impressions until the new person fits into place and then the shyness is gone. It is her form of self-protection. She will not give of herself until she is sure the relationship will be pleasant and one that she wishes to develop. It is her sense of order about everything in life; American as she is in many ways, in this she is Asian. She considers a situation in her mind and only when she has it organized, and every detail neatly fitted into place, is she comfortable and relaxed. If she cannot arrange the details into order, she discontinues her presence. She simply goes away.

If she cannot physically leave at that moment, then she goes away in her mind. It is a typical Asian reaction, a firm disinclination to face unpleasantness in whatever form it may present itself. If the unpleasantness is inescapable, it must be faced squarely and with courage and swift measures taken to remove it or solve it—whatever is required to restore order.

This attitude permeates to a remarkable degree Asian thought and each detail of living. Each time we go to Japan, for example, a family of Japanese friends arranges a day of pleasure for us. They meet us at the hotel with several automobiles, for we usually travel as a group with other Foundation executives. Then Madam Yamada, the lady of the family, always graciously sends us on our way, having first seen to our every comfort, only to greet us equally as graciously at our destination. This puzzled me for a time until I came to know Japan well enough to realize that there are poor districts and slums, particularly in Tokyo. Our cars are never permitted by our friends to take a route that may force "Miss Pearl Buck" to view anything unsightly on her day of pleasure. Madam Yamada's own car speeds over the most direct route, which goes through these poorer regions, and she arrives on location many minutes before we do. This gives her ample time to be sure every detail is ready for our arrival and to compose herself to greet us.

Pearl Buck has the same trait of organizing and putting details into order. It manifests itself even in the arrangement of furniture. I have never seen her wholly at ease as a guest in an American home, and it is a very special occasion indeed for her to accept an invitation to visit. Yet in Asia we are frequently entertained in the homes of friends and she is always completely at ease. After pondering this fact one can easily understand it. In Asian homes the lines are straight and simple and furnishings are arranged in perfect balance. Never will one find a chair on an angle or across a corner as is frequently seen in American homes. There are few knickknacks. Everything is carefully and neatly placed to assure balance and beauty. If there is a chair on one side of the room there is one across from it. If there are a table and ashtray at the left, there will also be a table and ashtray on the right, for balance. Pairs are seldom if ever placed together in Asia. When candle holders are not in use one will be placed at one end of a chest and one at the opposite end with something in the middle to balance both. In America the pair may be placed together. For example, there are two silver candelabra on a Chinese chest that stands before the mirrored wall in the Foundation dining room in Philadelphia. For one entire year, each time I entered the room the candelabra had been carefully placed one on each end of the chest with a large fruit bowl in front of a small marble and rosewood screen in the center. Thinking a maid or cleaning woman had arranged it in this fashion, I quickly rearranged it with the pair of candelabra on one end of the chest and the bowl of fruit on the other and the screen in the center. I always moved very quickly before Pearl Buck entered, so that she would not see the disorder. Only after a year did I come into the room and find her rearranging my order to restore her order! The candelabra have remained separate ever since.

Another good example of the permeation of ordered thinking into detail is the problem of the ashtray for any smoker in Asia. I learned fast that when visiting an Asian home I must be sure to sit where a table is decorated with an ashtray, otherwise I would have to use my hand for ashes or move to a chair beside a table with an ashtray. It would never occur to a hostess to put an ashtray on a table where none is intended to be. To do so would throw the room into disorder; and while she wishes you to be comfortable, to her Asian mind no one can enjoy a room which does not balance. If one wishes to smoke, one must have known it before one came in and one should have had enough forethought to sit in a chair near an ashtray. Should one be near an ashtray and happen to move it a couple of inches from where it was placed, the hostess will find a reason, while serving, to move it back, being careful not to call attention to the fact that it was ever moved.

In Pearl Buck's home, in her life, and in her mind I find that same sense of order and balance. When we make one of our rare visits to an American home I watch her struggle to resist the urge to separate that pair or to move a floral arrangement to the center of the table or get up and walk across the room and straighten a chair. Because of this inner struggle she is uncomfortable, and unless she is fond enough of her host to make it worth the struggle, it is more pleasant for all concerned for her to stay home.

In her dealings with people she is equally Asian, particularly if the person is employed by her. An example of this is the cleaning woman in her country house. While taking care of her dressing room the cleaning woman carefully arranged her comb and brush in a diagonal across her dressing table. Each day when Pearl Buck entered her bedroom she straightened them. One would think it simple to speak to the cleaning woman about the comb and brush, but not she. The cleaning woman had been a loyal servant for twenty-five years and she carefully arranged the dressing table as she would have arranged her own. In correcting her one would have run the risk of hurting her. It is a simple detail: the cleaning woman is excellent in other more important areas, and she chooses to rearrange the dressing table herself every day.

Her relationship with her children is also Asian in many ways. One rarely has a chance to observe her with all of her children, but this past year the opportunity came for me. We did not go to Vermont for Christmas as we usually do. We had spent the preceding two and one half months touring Japan and Korea to see how our work was progressing, and after so prolonged an absence office and business duties were too pressing for us to go away. Thus I was able to visit her farm at a holiday time when the family gathered.

On previous Christmases, before we began spending the holidays in Vermont, her many grandchildren had always risen early and opened their gifts at their own houses, then in the afternoon visited Nana, as they call her, and repeated the whole business of opening packages all over again.

"I always feel so sorry for the little ones at Christmas," she told me. "They become so tired that nothing really means anything any more. They just sit and open packages."

I remembered this complaint, and it was I who suggested that this time we have a party on Christmas Eve for all of the children and save our own celebration for the usual time, thereby avoiding the long day for them. She liked the idea, and the time was set for four o'clock in the afternoon before Christmas.

It began to snow steadily in the early morning, and by half past three we had some doubt they would all be able to make it. When the hour arrived, however, everyone was there except for two older children who could not have made it in any case: Edgar, an executive for a leading motion picture company, stationed at that time in Lisbon, and Carol, who lives in a special school. Henriette was home from college. She and the three younger girls bustled about, making last-minute preparations. Only these four still lived at home, for the others had long since gone about their own lives.

One by one they and the other children and the grandchildren all came in on Christmas Eve and deposited packages under the tree, and the huge old house filled up. They gathered about the fire, and I used the opportunity to observe them—Janice, Jean, Henriette, Theresa, Chieko, Johanna, Richard, John, and Jean's husband and Richard's wife, and eight grandchildren. I watched "the chosen ones," as she calls them, and remembered how she had gathered them over the years from 1926 through 1963, one from New York, four from Chicago, one from Germany, then one at a time for a total of three from Japan. Two are part Negro and the rest are combinations of who knows what; yet they are a tightly knit family group, held together by this one remarkably un-motherly woman. Her grandchildren greeted her brightly with "Hi, Nana!" and I couldn't suppress a smile as I remembered the letter she wrote to Jean before a first child was born. "I want you to know, my dear, that I shall spoil your children," she wrote. "Discipline is not my business now. That is your problem. I shall only enjoy them."

I glanced at Jean—Jean, the beauty—Jean, the mother. Now it is she who collects children. In addition to her own five, she gathers neighborhood children and takes care of them. One never knows when she will show up with a new one. "I am just minding him," she will say, and she goes on about her busy life. Yet I have never seen her children other than sparkling clean, happy, healthy and well adjusted. They were, on that Christmas Eve, eight, seven, six, four and three years old, three boys and two girls, and she had a long talk with me about the little girl she wishes to adopt from Korea. The tradition goes on. Richard is the family man of the older group, John is the adventurer and Janice is the tall, handsome, successful career woman. They are a part of her, as much as if she had given birth to them herself.

There were many gifts that evening, of course, but perhaps the most thoughtful was the one from Edgar. It was a small album of photographs taken by him or his wife showing their daily lives in Portugal. Beneath each picture was an explanation in the daughter-in-law's precise handwriting. It was as though the young couple had paid a visit home, and looking at them, Pearl Buck kept a running comment: "Doesn't she look nice?", "Don't you think he has put on a little weight?" When she discusses the children with me, I feel she has a kindred spirit especially with Jean and Edgar. I think she understands them more easily because their basic natures are similar to her own. Certainly she could have developed a very close intellectual relationship with Edgar, for example. It would have been easy for her to find the companionship with this son which she has always needed and which she found lacking even in her marriage. Many women have made this mistake and the result is the type of "momism" too frequently seen today. She made a conscious effort to avoid this, and as a result he has become the most independent of all of her children. After graduation from Harvard he worked in the Manufacturers Hanover Trust Company in Manhattan and was soon considered one of their bright young men with an excellent future. After three years he suddenly announced to her that he had originally taken the job to learn everything he could about money and he felt he had learned enough to know he did not wish to continue the rest of his life there, and abruptly he quit.

She deplored his leaving one job before he had found another, to which objection he replied that with a job he had no time to search for the one he wanted. He was always in her mind, however, and a few days thereafter she happened to be looking at a film in a leading motion picture studio, an executive beside her. She noticed several young men bustling about and upon inquiry was told they were trainees.

"I have one for you," she said.

Three weeks later Edgar was on his way to the Paris office of the motion picture company. He stayed there for almost a year, then was transferred to Lisbon for an indefinite time, and so his new career was successfully launched. This reminds me of her, who as a young woman in 1929 borrowed two thousand dollars from an unknown friend in a still strange country to pay for two years' schooling for her retarded daughter, thereby purchasing two years of personal freedom in which to make a success of herself as an author—and who returned to China and climbed the stairs to an attic room and sat down at a typewriter she did not even know how to use properly and in two and a half months gave the world *The Good Earth*. Birth child or not, Edgar has some of her spirit.

On the other hand, Jean shares in another part of her nature. I visit Jean in her home and I look around. The tables are bare of a woman's knickknacks; the furnishings are solid and indestructible and placed so that there is plenty of room for hordes of small children to play.

"She has many nice things," I was told by her mother. "She had lovely wedding gifts, but she keeps them all put away. 'My children will grow up soon enough,' she says, 'and then there will be plenty of time to enjoy fine things. As for now, I don't want to have to say, "Stop, you will break that," or "Put Mother's such and such down." Let them enjoy their childhood! It is so short.' "

Jean knows when to be firm with a child, for she appreciates the value of discipline, and yet she seems to know as well just when to take a crying youngster on her lap for comfort.

I am reminded of her mother, who spent many thousands of dollars to add a large wing onto the already huge farmhouse. Though it has since become a library, it started as a playroom, "where the children could ride their tricycles and the boys could rough and tumble about without disturbing the whole house," she says of it. And I remember, too, another quotation from the "Treasure Book." The year is 1940:

"The landscape outside the window of my room is spotted with raggedly melting snow. Ice in the lake is beginning to crack loudly. Yesterday the children and I had fun sliding down a great fall of ice by the bridge. Edgar bumped his forehead and said he felt like crying, so I said, 'Sit down there by the big ash tree and cry.' He did, bellowing heartily and with great enjoyment, prolonging it as long as he could while we went on sliding. I asked him if he felt better and he said 'I do.' "

And she, too, knows when to be firm. One of her seventeen-year-old daughters recently complained bitterly: "But, Mother, other girls of my age are allowed to go on dates alone and they can stay out until one o'clock in the morning! You don't trust me!"

"It makes not one particle of difference to me what other people do," she answered. "We are *not* other people, and of *course* I don't trust you! I couldn't trust myself when I was your age. Why should I trust you?" And that was the end of the discussion.

In the woman, as in her daughter Jean, there is the same kind of motherhood, and parts of the motherhood are as Asian as Peony or Madam Wu in the sense of timing, of knowing just when to correct and when to comfort, of knowing exactly how far a parent can go with a child, and of maintaining a position. There is no "buddy-buddy" relationship between Pearl Buck and her children, but the deep mutual respect between parent and child one finds in Asia. She respects her children as human beings, as individuals, as world citizens, regardless of their backgrounds or origin.

She loves the world in which she lives more completely than any person I have ever seen and it is impossible to be with her without being conscious of this ever-powerful love. It is best expressed in her feeling for all children, not the maudlin kind of "smother" love too frequently found among older women but instead an all-encompassing appreciation of human life in its purest form, not yet burdened with the details of daily maintenance of life and position. She firmly insists that each child needs and is entitled to the security and understanding necessary for the development of his or her full potential of mature intelligence. Many persons express great and beautiful thoughts and ideals and then begin trying to convince all others that they are right. Not so with her! She cares not for the verbal approval of others. She is grateful and pleased if people approve her ideals and help to bring these ideals into reality, but mere approval without help means nothing to her except an occasional cause for anger.

I was amused recently when during an important press interview a brash young reporter repeatedly suggested that she had established the Pearl S. Buck Foundation for reasons of self-fulfillment. With infinite patience she corrected him each time the suggestion was made.

"Not at all," she said firmly. "I have set up this Foundation because I wish other Americans to have a tool through which they can assume part of the responsibility for these children of our sons."

"But it is because they are Asian and you are representing the Asian point of view to Americans," he insisted.

"That is not true," she replied. "You miss the whole point! I do this as an American because I believe other Americans will feel as I do when they know of the situation these children face. We are Americans and the world expects more of us than of other people."

"But it is a form of self-fulfillment," he insisted.

Her eyes flashed. "Why should I need fulfillment? I have everything!"

The room filled with laughter, and in the rear a photographer snapped his shutter and said, "In spades, Madam, in spades!" The reporter quickly changed the subject and I left the room to recount the incident to a fellow worker. We have long shared the desire to write a comedy based on such incidents and to be called "Pearl Buck . . . Her Evil Ways."

We threaten her with this often and she smiles and shrugs. "All you young people following me around taking notes!"

She is aware that the many endeavors in which she has been involved may confuse the person who does not know her. Some may think she has tried undertakings that are unrelated. This is untrue. She has tried to restore order and provide understanding. She spoke at some length recently to clarify what are her chief interests in life:

My whole life presents a unity. Everything I have done, even my writing, grows out of a fascinated interest in human beings, in the wonders of their minds and hearts, their sensitivities, their needs, and the essential loneliness of their position in the universe. There are times in sleepless nights when I ponder upon this planet to which we cling. I meditate upon how utterly lost we are in space. We bear the total isolation as we must, for however we may hope there is a God we do not hear his voice and we do not see him and, while faith is a valid emotion, it is not confirmed except through hope. This isolation of the human being has given me concern and consideration for all human beings, but particularly for children, not because of a maternal instinct for, as you know, I am not a very maternal woman, but because children are the future. A child is still malleable. Therefore, knowing that it is impossible for one person to achieve in every area and on all fronts, I have deliberately chosen the area of children as providing the most opportunity for human results.

I first began work with retarded children who seemed to me, at that point, the most needy. Then, too, I understand them through my own retarded child. Later, as our two worlds of East and West, Asia and the West, began to meet face to face, through children of mixed race here in our own country, I felt that the children of mixed race were the most needy. And when this expanded into the children overseas, the children of our servicemen, it was still all of a piece. The adoption agency, Welcome House, became the tool, the means, for the first group who were born in this country of mixed Asian-American parentage and the Foundation became the tool for the children overseas, who are children of our servicemen and Asian women. The only variation, if it can be called a variation, from that pattern, was when the Governor of the State of Pennsylvania asked me to head a committee for the handicapped in the Commonwealth of Pennsylvania. As you know, I am not a person to be interested only in one country, and while I love Pennsylvania because my home is there, I don't think in terms of states, either. I think of the world, its units the countries, and in those countries units of states or provinces. I had never thought of working in so small an area as one state. Nevertheless I decided that I would accept the Governor's invitation partly because I saw in my own state how disastrous it was to have the work for the handicapped as fragmentary and disunified as it was. In one large city, for example, there were twenty-seven agencies for the blind alone. People did not know where to go, which to choose. There were many agencies for the deaf, too, all uncoordinated. I thought such lack of coordination a waste of public funds and I began to work out a plan whereby there could be coordination rather than competition among all these agencies. With the aid of a good executive assistant, Gweneth Zarfoss, I organized a structure of help for the handicapped, based on local needs, which proved to be very sound.

I held that chairmanship through the administrations of two

governors. Then the political situation changed and the work
was not continued, although it had been remarkably successful.
What interested me, however, was the permanent validity of the
plan that we worked out in Pennsylvania for coordination of the
efforts of many agencies who were, each in its own way, trying to
cover the field of aid to the handicapped. As you know, I don't
believe in a welfare state. I think it unfortunate that there are
so many people who don't work or say they can't work, so that the
rest of us have to support them through welfare. I believe a community should care for its own, using federal funds only when
absolutely necessary. I suppose this conviction comes from my
observation of the family as a unit in China. There the big family
took care of all of its members, and when members were out of
jobs they were helped to get on their feet and stay on their feet.
In our country there cannot be security in the family but there
ought to be security in the community. The community may be
a whole county or it may be no more than a city, and I worked
out a very careful plan, a very simple technique, for each community to organize its own agency for the handicapped.

Before we could put this plan into action, of course, I had to
know just what was going on already. Therefore we divided Pennsylvania into nine natural areas, in the center of each an important town or city. In such centers, we held hearings from each
area as to what was already being done for the handicapped, and
what the people would like to have done. For the first six months
we did nothing but learn. All we heard pointed to the fact that
what I had believed was true—there was an enormous waste of
time and effort, yet the handicapped people were not being well
serviced.

Then we had, of course, to find a leader in each center or area.
As you know, I am a great believer in the mind, the personality,
that can lead others. In order to find such persons we called upon
the mayor of each community and asked him to assume local
leadership by inviting all the agencies in the area to meet together and discuss how their work could be coordinated. Thus
we organized a mayor's committee in each community and he
was always the chairman. Each local committee was made up of
leading citizens, both lay persons and specialists. For each community we worked out a central plan which did away with com-

petition and overlapping. This meant that in any community, if a person were handicapped, he could go to that center and find out how to get help. If he couldn't get help in that center, he would be directed to where he could. In this way every handicapped person had someone in his community to whom to turn for the solution of his problem.

I think of one city, for example, where for seven or eight years efforts had been made to coordinate the various agencies for the handicapped, but with no leadership there was no coordination. I remember so well, at one of the hearings, a very dismal report made by a social worker. He said that for seven years he had been trying to get the local agencies to cooperate and coordinate but without the slightest success. They did nothing but meet and argue, and therefore he thought there was no hope for unity of effort. But, thanks to the mayor's committee there, we organized a committee which demanded cooperation and had the power to insist upon it. Today the result of that cooperation is a beautiful center, costing a million and a half dollars, which houses all the local agencies for the handicapped. It is a handsome modern building, simple but well equipped, put up by the citizens, in cooperation with federal and state governments. Now any handicapped person in the area can go to the center and be treated, since all the agencies have their functions in that one center. Or if there is not an agency which can treat him, he will be directed and helped to get to the proper agency elsewhere. Now that was done by the citizens under the leadership of the mayor and that was our plan. If we could have continued, if there had not been changes in the political administration, we would have had the whole state of Pennsylvania so organized.

And, mind you, there was no sentimental charity in all this. My purpose was to work out a means whereby a problem could be solved. This has been the principle upon which I have tried to base anything that I have done. The Foundation was set up in the same way. Here was the problem of the half-American children, thousands of them, all over Asia. It was impossible just to administer relief, and also, as you know, I do not believe in relief except in a temporary emergency. I think it is corrupting to continue relief. So when I set up the Foundation, again it was to organize a tool, to create and shape a means whereby the problem could be solved. Then, of course, we had to enlist the aid of people to cooperate and to use that tool. And under your leadership we worked out the general plan of an opportunity center in each country, a place where an Amerasian child or adult can get help, as needed, to solve his individual problem. The principle of coordination as a means for solution has been behind anything I have done.

I have very little patience with charity, with welfare, with begging. I do know that if a house burns down one must give people shelter until they get another house, or if people are starving one can't say one will do something next year to feed them. But to consider charity and welfare as permanent is futile, to my mind. Physically, some people may have to be cared for to a certain extent. But even they, I believe, can be cared for on an organized basis. I don't want the Foundation ever to appeal for relief funds, or I'll have no interest in it. But I do have a profound interest in helping people to organize their lives so that they can live and work and maintain themselves and this is what the Foundation is trying to do for the Amerasian children in Asia. When a person can maintain himself he also helps the community by being a productive person. And if he has fine talents, as many of these Amerasians have, they are a great source for good—or a power for evil.

I consider the experience of helping the handicapped in Pennsylvania through a coordinated service one of the most valuable in my life. I regret in a sense that it couldn't have gone on and yet I'm afraid if I had given it the time needed, I would not have been able to work on the Foundation and of course I think the Foundation is more important for the world's future. Then, too, I am very ill-fitted to cope with political persons who seek to destroy merely for the sake of the party. There is an element in American life, especially in the states, which for reasons of party politics wants to destroy what others have built. Competition can be very destructive and I am not a competitive person, as you know. I believe in coordination and unification under the best possible leadership.

Now the year is 1968. I look backward and then forward to see what is yet to come, for I have learned from her to seek the future in history, and in her lifetime she has made history. I know that the Foundation will be a success because of her magic. I accept that. I also know that all of the efforts of the Foundation will not be enough to solve the problem of this new child—the Amerasian.

This problem, and Pearl Buck's way of approaching it, are typified by the experience of one boy from Korea. He was a shy withdrawn boy of seventeen in his last year of high school when we made our first trip to Korea under the auspices of the Foundation. He longed to go to medical school, we had been told, and we were asked to interview him and to consider the possibility of a scholarship. We were not ready to consider it, for we had not yet clearly formulated our plans as to exactly what we would do in Korea and we wanted to have that well started before we began any student program. Moreover, we knew almost nothing about this boy and did not relish the idea of having to make a decision without all of the facts.

The boy and his mother had been promised that we would see them, however, so reluctantly we agreed to an appointment. Bob sat rather sullenly while his mother talked and our overall impression was not strong except for one fact. The boy had always wanted to study in America, but his mother had been definitely opposed to the idea until about a week earlier when, while cleaning his room, she had found his diary. After she had read it she had come to the Korean office of the Foundation asking if we would please help him go to America.

At our request, she provided us with a translation of the diary to help us to make a decision, and here are excerpts from it:

> *March 31, 1966:* The history of Korean literature class made me unhappy today. When a friend of mine who was absent was called to stand up and to read a line from the textbook, I stood up and tried to read.
>
> As I began to read, a few classmates yelled and told the teacher that it was not me that was called. I sat down in my chair in smiles. Alas! The innocent smiles of mine had to be offset by a sudden tragedy by the unexpected cry of the teacher, "Hey you bastard Yankee, read." The cry made the entire class quiet, I could not focus my sights upon my textbook. I could see only darkness, and all I can remember is that I felt dizzy.
>
> The silence of all classmates made me even more frightened.

Why did I also keep quiet, when I heard the teacher call me names like that? I should have taken one of my books, moved forward with it and . . . then, I would be in the newspaper headlines "TEACHER BEATEN BY STUDENT."

I could not tell Mother what happened today, when it was most unhappy to me in my life.

May 16, 1966: Today I was talking about the theory of fatherland with my classmates at school. As I thought of it over and over, I have unfortunately found that there is no fatherland to me. The country of my father . . . it is too far away to be called my fatherland by me.

Damn fellow! Why should they talk about nationalism, subjectivity and so on? Is it because they have grown up as I have not?

Whenever political issues are on debate, I must always keep silent or be an outsider, because I do not know whether I should be on the Korean side or on the side of the United States of America. Between motherland and fatherland is there no place for me to stand still?

July 25, 1966: Since I began to tutor Mike, my young Amerasian student, I have discovered myself again. I went to his home at six o'clock in the afternoon as usual. He appealed to me today with rolling tears in his swollen eyes. He had cried all day from anger and sorrow, when he was called a Yankee bastard and was teased by one of his classmates at school in the morning. Mike, the poor fellow, he is also an unhappy boy—like me.

Pity to him who is still too young to formulate his own character and personality, to understand who teases him and to resign all of these affairs! As I listened to Mike's appealing, I felt anger, sorrow and pain burning in my own heart, but I managed to control them with the endurance power that I have successfully built up, and I consoled him and soothed his sorrow, which is mine as well. I felt the same hot blood streaming in my blood vessels as Mike did.

I could not ask Mike to get his lessons, although he wiped the tears from his eyes and cheeks. Looking down at him from his side, I felt a common destiny with Mike . . . and perhaps with all other mixed-blood. I felt it my duty to encourage and to lead these numberless unhappy children, to give them the power to overcome their social environments.

I went to bed after prayer to Holy Mother, Mary.

July 26, 1966: I feel sorry about my mother. She has had to live her life full of sorrow, unhappiness and all that tragic vocabulary can describe. She has walked through the wilderness of her life where only bushes of prickles greeted her, and today she had to fail to hide her weariness, heartbreak and tears before me. I did not know how sorry I was until I saw her tears that she had so carefully covered from me for so many years. I did not know . . .

Who should be blamed for this? Why have I had to live in a different situation from other people around me who can smile? Why should I live failing to meet people's laughing at me and thereby causing more sorrow to my mother? Do I look different? And so what? Why should my mother be hurt for that? Perhaps my ideal world is in the star that is too far away from me to be reached.

October 6, 1966: Something made me unhappy again today. During lunch hour I was unexpectedly grabbed by classmates and brought to an empty room of the school by them and was beaten half dead.

Asked to kneel down and bow before them, I firmly refused and was beaten again. This time heavily on the jaw, with their fists, and my teeth were almost broken. Forgetting my pride and self-respect, I was obliged by their force to kneel down before them.

Of course, I am much stronger than they and although they were two in number, I could resist if I wished. Even during their severe attack on me, there were a number of chances that I could have counterattacked them and beat them down. I would have done so if it were not for the grimace on the face of the Dean of Student Affairs floating before my eyes that I had to face in the Discipline Room yesterday. He hated me anyway because of my racial mixture and threatened to discharge me out of school if I used violence. I wanted to continue my high school education.

I felt shivering all over my body. I was frightened by my own thinking of revenge. Deciding to endure and to forget revenge as well as pride and prestige, I stood up and begged their forgiveness. Forgive me? Why? Oh, what a surrender! What a shame! I went to the bathroom, as I was dreadfully bleeding. After washing I ran to the place where my real friends were waiting for me. I had to tell them a lie—I counterattacked them, I said, but had to surrender on account of a threatening jackknife. Had I told them the truth, they, good friends of mine, would think I was a coward. I was even more afraid of losing friends than of being beaten by foes, and this is why I told them a lie.

Nevertheless, my friend was not satisfied. "Why did you surrender? Why didn't you fight to the last whether dead or alive?"

Perhaps I am really a coward. Am I crying now with tears, before going to bed because I am a coward?

It seems clear and certain that man is created good. I must have been born weak-minded. Am I qualified to become a philanthropist?

The beautiful soul of a brilliant and sensitive young man revealed in this fashion would move anyone. We decided to speak with his teachers to see what additional information we could gather. Although our schedule left little time, we did manage to arrange an appointment but it had to wait until the day before we were to leave Korea and we knew that while there would not be time left to do much to help the boy, at least we would know a bit more about him.

"He has a brilliance in his brain," his teacher said to us that afternoon. "We do not begin to understand it but it is there. Only two students from our school will be accepted to medical school. Now we are eighty percent sure he will be one of them —in four months we will be one hundred percent sure if he works hard, but we do not think he will. Something has happened. We do not understand, but his heart is gone. He needs to study in America."

We talked with him, and it was Pearl Buck who said with characteristic finality, as though the task were completed, "Of course we must do something. We must take him to the States."

It was not possible to do so on that trip, and when we next returned we found him resentful of what he considered our raising of false hopes. But we did in fact manage to cut the red tape this time, and he returned home with us. More of his pent-up feelings came out in a later conversation, after he had burst forth with a condemnation of his father:

"I should not have been born. My father made my mother very poor. She graduated from University—she is very clever. She was well known for her beauty and her cleverness. She was pledged to young man of wealthy family but American captain also wants to marry with her. He is from West Point and has very much money. His family in Philadelphia, they have very much money. My mother marry with him in Korea and then after awhile she is with me. Her sister became angry with her one day and tell me all. She say she get rid of me with operation because she not want. He say, 'No! Have our child. We are in love. We will be together always.' She have me and she name me Robert after him. Then when I am two years old he come one day and he bring gifts to my mother and me and he bring much money and he tell her he have wife in States and he will go back. He go away then and we never hear from him. He had no right to leave her with me. She did not want. Why he make me be born and then go away? I wish I had not been born. I should never be born! I do not want to see him. If I ever see his face I am afraid. I will kill him. I hate him for what he did. My mother has suffered much because of me and did he suffer?"

As suddenly as it started the wild storm was gone.

"You are right—I must success. I must think of my mother."

Pearl Buck has been honored hundreds of times for her many accomplishments, but she has said that the most important day in her life, the happiest, and the most satisfying was June 11, 1967. On that date she dedicated the Opportunity Center of the Pearl S. Buck Foundation in Korea. It was a festive occasion. There were hundreds of Amerasian children playing games on the lawn. Many of their mothers had come to pay tribute to the great lady who cared. Korean and American dignitaries discussed the project together, each thinking of ways in which he could help, while waiting for the ceremony to begin. The schoolchildren's orchestra arrived and it was time to proceed with the dedication. All present had expressed concern about the weather, for the festivities had been planned for outdoors and in the morning the skies had been threatening and overcast. Under dark clouds the orchestra played the Korean national anthem followed by "The Star-Spangled Banner." Then we walked solemnly down the path that had been cleared among the crowd. Suddenly, at the exact moment when we mounted the stairs to the speakers' platform, the dark clouds broke and the platform where she stood was flooded with brilliant sunshine. The crowd was awed to silence as she gave her dedication speech. Then she motioned to a rock on the lawn and said, "On this stone will be engraved these words: 'O children of East and West, by your very being you alone

can best understand both East and West. In this peaceful place
may you learn to save a struggling humanity from final war and,
in so doing, cause the world to bless the day that you were born!' "

Again the orchestra played the two national anthems as we
walked back down the path, but the music could barely be heard
over the cheers of the children and their mothers. Yes, it was the
happiest I have ever known her to be—and I was happy for her.

Our pattern of work is clear now. She has dreamed and planned
in her own way, quite differently from the way anyone else might
dream and plan, and has brought her energy to what might have
been useless dreams. She has begun a whirlpool of activity that
catches everything with which it comes in contact and sweeps it
into the ever powerful depths of her determination. The mind
and heart and success and influence of a beautiful woman have
combined to create the clear, well-ordered pattern to follow
to eventual solution of a problem that only she with her vast
knowledge of East and West could see and solve.

It is easy to see that the Opportunity Center came out of her
experience with the Governor's Committee for the Handicapped
in Pennsylvania. We have gathered the solutions to the problems
of the Amerasians, whatever they may be, into one place. We
must open Opportunity Centers in each of the seven countries
where our men are stationed. Then we choose the most brilliant
from among those with whom we work and bring them to the
United States for higher education. All of these students agree
to return, each to his own country, to work. In this way we will be
able to lift the status of the whole. There is much that remains
to be done but we know now how to do it.

The experiences of all of her lifetime have led us in this big
new undertaking. One of the most important aspects of our work
has been to inform the American public of this problem and somehow to overcome the feeling that the situation is remote. She has
drawn upon her knowledge of world events as they have occurred
during her lifetime and she has tied them together and related
them one to another to bring us to our present thinking. She
has used this material in speeches she has delivered on hundreds
of college campuses in the past several years. While she has written most of it before in one or another of her books, I asked her

if she would write it again in the "Treasure Book," this time tying it all together as she does in speaking but had not yet done in writing. Here is what she wrote:

August, 1967
Mountain Haunt

The dangerous contrast in these days of life is almost insupportable. I sit here at my desk and gaze at the mountains; their peace and calm, strengthening always, deny the violence of the day's news. Daily the dead announce their end. How is it that I am here in the West, while the East, so familiar to me through all my life, is in this fearful conflict? Though here is where I belong by birth and ancestry, I see as clearly as I see these mountains the country scenes of Vietnam which R. and I visited so many years ago, the little thatched villages, the simple people, a gentle childlike people, surely the innocent. And most bewildering, most incomprehensible, these Amerasian boys here in my own house this morning, cheerfully getting their breakfasts! What children are these? They happen to be here, but there are thousands of them in the many countries of Asia where American servicemen are fighting young Asian men. Fighting young Asian men while they, the Americans, make love to Asian women, and of such strange contradiction these boys and thousands of others, boys and girls, are born! These are the new people, these are the Amerasians, the people we never dreamed of, for whom no plans are made, who are not welcome, who have no country, no place in the world. Yet here they are, this very morning, in this my house, one playing the piano superbly, one frying eggs in a skillet, one eating mounds of toast and jam, one playing with the dogs and laughing, laughing as gaily as though he had a place under the sun—which he has not. None of them has. And here am I, committed to them utterly, and with me T.F.H. and all the young men and women he has gathered about us to help in the establishment of a place in the sun, upon this earth, for these whom I call "the new people."

I have, of course, to explain to myself how it happens that these new people appear now upon the human scene. There is much more to it than mere meeting of male and female. The process is history. Had there been no great world wars, had human life proceeded in peaceful ways, the natural coming together of the peoples of Asia and the West would have been in some way slower and more amiable than that of war. In the course of time independence would have been arbitrated for the colonies in Asia, independence would have been achieved and with it the knowledge of government as well as the acquiring of its instruments. Then, all people being acquainted in dignity and mutual respect, prejudices would wane, and children be born who in their ancestry would bring together East and West . . . Instead, the peoples have been thrown together too soon, too abruptly, too harshly, by war. Two great world wars have so weakened the West that the European and British powers have not been able to maintain their hold on restless, rebellious Asian colonials. Before the Asians understood or were able to put into practice among their ancient peoples the principles of democracy they were suddenly independent. Alone among the colonies India was left with a structure of democratic government and a trained civil service . . . Even so, the colonial peoples might have been able to establish their independence securely, in time at least, had there not been an evil concatenation of events in history. These events may be narrowed to the two most powerful in their influence, first, the end of the ruling dynasty in China, complicated by Japan's attack which led to the Second World War, and second, the triumph of Communism in Russia.

The history of China is divided into twenty-four dynasties, each dynasty being the length of rule under a reigning family. As each imperial family declined in power, inevitably the people became dissatisfied with national conditions, the country fell into fragmentation, young rebel leaders rose up, each with his personal army of followers. These leaders, so-called warlords, were contenders for the throne and they fought a series of battles in a so-called civil war, until a victor was proclaimed. This victor always became the first emperor of a new dynasty. The process could take a few years or a century. In the case of the last dynasty, the Ts'ing, it took nearly a century, the deadline delayed by the strong personality of Tzu Hsi, the old Empress Dowager, under whose rule I was born and lived until her death in 1909. Yet in the 1860's the Chinese carried out a rebellion against that dynasty, so nearly successful that it might have been entirely so, had it not been for the skillful action of a British mercenary, Gordon. It was during this rebellion that the ancient enmity of the Chinese against Russians was expressed through the Empress Dowager's reply to the Czar when he offered to send his soldiers to help quell the Chinese T'ai-p'ing Rebellion. Haughtily she replied, "We prefer our Chinese rebels to your soldiers on our soil."

Neither Empress nor Czar could have foreseen the arrival of Russian Communist advisors in China, which led to the acceptance in 1921 of the Chinese Communists as a political party!

I grew up in the last years of the dynasty, and my young womanhood was spent under the dominance of one warlord and another, as battles broke out here, there, anywhere, between the contenders for the Throne in Peking. Then in 1911 the Throne itself was destroyed, a catastrophe so great that its effects are still to be measured, a catastrophe so great indeed that it resulted in the establishment of Communism as the ruling power in modern China, and the end of this is not yet in sight.

I wonder what my revered missionary parents would have thought if they had realized that, innocently and ignorantly, the Christian schools established by missionaries, especially the Americans, had much to do with the coming of Communism into China? For centuries the young men who passed the Imperial Examinations in China were given administrative posts in the government. It was a civil service so modern in concept that no other equals it, although England based her civil service upon the Chinese, and we ours upon the British. Briefly, anyone who could pass the comprehensive Imperial Examinations must have had a superior brain. Therefore, traditional China was governed by her best brains. Moreover, the process was basically democratic. Anyone, regardless of high or low birth—alas, not regardless of sex—could go up for the Examinations. A village lad of humblest origin but high intelligence might be educated at the expense of his fellow villagers and sent to the Examinations to bring honor to his village.

The graduates of Christian schools were not prepared for the Imperial Examinations, however. Missionary schools were attended by those who wished to learn English and Western subjects, but the curriculum was Western and graduates were eliminated therefore from the possibility of getting government jobs. Unable to change this situation, the young modern rebels, under the leadership of Sun Yat-sen, seized the moment of dynastic weakness to overthrow the Imperial Throne, with the purpose of establishing a republic, modeled after the United States. It was an impossibility. Americans had a virgin country upon which to build, few people and those with the same passionate dreams of liberty and justice. China had a vast and ancient country accustomed to traditional ways, and an enormous population, eighty-five percent peasant and illiterate . . . Ten years of effort did not avail to establish the republic. Meanwhile chaos ruled, controlled only by the continuing civil service and the traditional family system. I returned from college in the midst of all this and, accustomed to turmoil, took up life as usual. Warlords contended in old-fashioned ways while Sun Yat-sen and his young followers tried to establish an army and failed, tried to get help from Western nations and failed, tried to elect a president and failed.

Meanwhile, Russia in 1917 had overthrown her traditional empire and had established a Soviet form of government. She now offered to help the Chinese revolutionary party. Doubtful yet desperate, for all other governments had refused aid, Sun Yat-sen accepted. Thus, in 1921, Communism came to China. Sun Yat-sen defended himself merely by saying that he did not believe his people would accept Communism. A military academy, Whampoa, was established in Canton; a young officer, Chiang Kai-shek, was put in command after fifteen months' training in Soviet Russia; and the Second Revolution began its march down the valley of the Yangtze River.

I have told of this in my book *My Several Worlds*, and I have no mind to repeat it here. Suffice to say that the same concatenation of events continued to harass the Chinese people. Chiang Kai-shek turned against the Communists because he disliked the growing power of Russians in China, and he established a government under the Nationalist flag. Thereupon he fought the retreating Communists on one hand while he fought the contending warlords on the other. Before he could totally eliminate the one and vanquish the other, Japan took advantage of China's temporary weakness and attacked. The Second World War broke, and with it eventually the arrival of our American men into Asia

. . . At the end of the war, Chiang Kai-shek made every effort to accept surrender of the Japanese on Chinese soil but at each spot, or nearly, a Communist cell had remained after battle, and lacking other authority, Japanese occupying units surrendered to Communists and so the whole country fell under Communist control . . . I wonder, as I tell this much abridged story, if our American servicemen left little half-American children in Chinese towns and villages? I fear they did—and I say *fear*, for with the present hatred against us, doubtless such children have been killed, even as I hear they have been killed sometimes in other Asian countries. But Asian women are mothers, too, and in the seven countries—perhaps eight—where American men fight today, and die—or live—there are many living children with American blood in their veins, living because their Asian mothers were mothers first and hid their children and saved them. I feel a deep kinship with those children for I, too, belong to East and West. I have no Asian blood in my veins but I have Asian memories, and years of Asian living. I am not willing, therefore, to see these new people wasted. They are too valuable, children of the future, those whom we need, those who may save us one day from the final war, because they belong to both East and West.

In Part I of this book I have tried to build a background of the facts, all necessary, which have made the woman I know. In Part II I have tried to add the delicate shading of the human woman. In Part III of this portrait I try to present the woman as I know her.

Her life has been filled with the things of which women dream. She has loved and lost and she has loved and won. She treasures the letters that Ernest Hocking wrote to her through the years, and I choose the following examples to illustrate their relationship.

April 5, 1964

My Love;

SOLILOQUY
(In dialogue)

The world is too much with us—thee and me—
And yet without this world, we'd cease to be.

I'm *there,* with all thy triumph, all thy pain
Of bringing thought to life, with might and main.

I hear thy music of Beethoven's Third;
I sense the beauty of *The Guide,* unheard;
I feel the firming of great India's will,
Through Rajasthan's pugnacity and skill.

Dear tortured world, envenomed and perplexed,
Praying the gods for guidance to the Next,
As if some other world could breed the love
We lose from sight through wishing an "Above,"
While pain and struggle, distance and delay,
Are substance of the joy that comes each day.

I'm with thee, Love, until my latest breath—
(Be near or far my trust with friendly Death;)
With firm and fearless step mete out our span,
There's only one to serve—the soul of man.

Ernest H.

Tuesday evening, January 9, 62

O My Dearest;

It is here. Saying what one hardly believes a photo-portrait can say—the spirit with which you regard that being—seeking, understanding, loving, evoking whatever is real in it. It is a treasure. (It came perfectly packed and mounted.) It makes one see why— in the heavenly aspects of human life—the woman is so essential —more so than the father-god for most of the human race.

A silly suggestion—but I don't mind being silly with you (that's silly, too)—it reminds me of Rembrandt's historic contemplative bust of Homer (which I saw at the Metropolitan the other day)— Aristotle's look of reverence and pity under which glance blind Homer seemed to be opening his eyes—I don't know what it is you are looking at, but it, too, will come alive.

I love you.

Ernest

1963

Tuesday afternoon, bright, cool and quiet. May the seventh. Raymond outside scraping up leaves, lifting up broken branches of snow-smitten azalea bushes, and wondering whether the cattle, now turned out to pasture, before the grass is strong, will get enough to eat—we are short of hay and all the farm questions of Maytime—happy and a sort of lonely spot in my heart and yet glad that she is not in the midst of all this shifting and cleaning and disorderly fussing prior to settled living.

My Pearl;

You are here—here being a grand big place—too big for soul's satisfaction, but not too big to allow a deep joy in your presence just around the corner. In my welcome-home note I said the library is ready, but that was a remark of hope, for we just scrubbed the floors today and gave the temperature a good test. It's usable, and will be usabler as we get windows and screens into operation.

I know what a chore you are having, to bring India to vocal existence in the USA of this moment; Darling, it's an infinite job, and it has to be done by you. And for me, I'm down a bit. Just got a hurry-up job done for Norman Cousins; he has high hopes of what I could do to conclude his symposium, "Warless World," and I tried—in a hurry. Not too sanguine it's any good. This week is rather peppered with petty responsibilities, but thereafter a fair clearing. I hadn't thought to go to the May Academy meeting, though New York invites and I'd like to welcome Sam Morison, and dear Malvina has a bronze portrait she wants me to see.

But I'm really getting a bit inhibited about travel, and what I long for is chiefly just you, when—if ever—you can find a pause in the day's "occupations"—with just us. Not easy.

I love you.
Your Ernest

My love, my Pearl, my deep, unspoken Rest.

Madison 11/10/62

My Pearl, it is Saturday afternoon—tenth of November—rainy, foggy, one feels like a chimney fire and a chat with my dearest. Been with her all the week via ESP (which can be read extrasensory perception or espionage—much alike—but one is where you belong, the other where you don't). Anyhow, I've been listening-in to you and —— and dimly aware of your wrestling with a mountain of work (same as me only worser). Let me butt in, my Love, with two items;

1. *American Tryp*—no, *Triptych* has come: three John Sedges

novels, with a precious inscription about the things that cannot be spoken (and which—since the best things are just that way— we keep on trying to speak) and that brings me to number 2. In the letter before the "business" letter, I was guilty of trying to say some of the unsayable things. I put them into a bunch of ragged lines which was literally untrue and so has to be confessed!

I said that in a certain "instant" there was spun an immortal tie. As if the tie had no history! We know very well that there were years of history leading up to it. I might have said of these two ships, full-freighted, each one to its own port, that they at least "cross paths, hail, and slip swiftly by"—making the tie- spinning more than credible.

But the remarkable thing is, that the new rapport was *indeed instantaneous!* Our earlier years of friendship were rich, and all within the proper distance of *politesse*—*"politesse"* being a per- fect and silent limit (like one of these new textile fabrics, incred- ibly slight, transparent and firm), such that we might have gone on for all our further years, never taking the step into the imme- diate reality of our feeling, and we might never have known what we had lost—intolerable!

Now I realize what Browning was up to; "O, the little more and how much it is; O, the little less and what worlds away!"

So perhaps the falsity—or let me say the fiction—of the "in- stant" is somewhat truer than the long stepwise approach. Per- haps it *requires* fiction to set a firm hold of truth?

No mystery is without its history. But no history knows its own meaning until the Light arrives, as if unbegotten, suddenly it is *there.*

My Love,
Your E.

September 2, 1963

What is September to me?
It's the month when my Love comes home,
And the life-saving spring once more runs free,
Needing none but itself as poem.

O, my Darling, I am so glad that you and I have the same uncon- cern for dates and ages and birthdays. I am resolved to know nothing about them—though the kind world is likely to insist and one can't reject the friendly interest. I was especially moved by the visit of the Madison village folks, so I'll send you the picture-tale.

After all, who remembers being born? One would suppose that a crisis like that—the first breath, the independent heartbeat, would leave a memory trace—but I never heard of it. We all have to be told when and how it happens. . . . Now the summer-jam breaks—like the ice-jam on spring rivers— . . .

> To some, all birthdays are of grave import,
> The more so as their subject nears the grave;
> But wiser heads may add a touch of sport,
> Prepared to show Old Time how to behave;
>
> Apprised so well of Relativity,
> And having in our love eternal treasure,
> We're unconcerned with years' declivity,
> We "take our Time" untouched by solar measure.

                                            I long for you,
                                            I love you.
                                                      Ernest

                                                      April 29, 64

O, My Love, what a joy—just a word from you—and what a mystery; all the world changes—ceases to be routine, puzzlement, disorder, meaningless complexity, and becomes an inviting task—all the more interesting because it is formidable. That's the miracle wrought by a touch of love.

And there is something else—it has just occurred to me. In the world of physics, if A includes B, then B can't include A. In the world of life and love, A always includes B and B always includes A. How preposterous that E.H. should include the infinite P.B.! Yet, he does. And of course all the time, P.B. includes E.H., and keeps him in his proper corner—an episode in the great world. Mutual inclusion—the truth of the spirit.

Spring has now burst upon us; the ice "went out" of the pond on Sunday the 26th—five days late. The roads are passable. Crocuses and daffodils sing their defiance to the vanishing snow piles. . . . And why does Germany choose this time to confer on me the Order of Merit? I dunno: but it's sort of nice.

O my Love, so much to say to you and such a yearning for a 'touch' instead of a 'say.' It will come—. . . .

I BREAK OFF.

I love you.

Your Ernest

December 4, 1964. Friday p.m.
snow snow snow potential water
WELCOME

O my Love—

How wonderful to hear your voice—

I've been spotwise aware of your travels in the interest of your great work, most recently in the Tampa Bay region, with a little chat at Port-o-Call that got into the "Sun" paper, and thus via my sister to me. And what do I find?! Pearl is moving into the field we are all bound to enter sooner or later—philosophy—in the increasing number of unwanted and displaced children especially in Asia. . . . I can verify the changing of standards or at least the groping for *any standards at all*—a part of the cult of "self expression" in all the arts, including the art of living. . . . I'm thinking I may have to revise one of my poems. I have spoken of these children as offspring of "lonely" boys, suggesting a certain sympathy for the state of mind in which these children are engendered. The loneliness is there, but the relation of responsibility cannot be condoned. Responsibility is a thundercloud sort of word, because—taken in full—it is endless. . . . And I am hoping to carry on. When I wrote you about "my sun is sinking" I was talking literally—I grow aware of limits—but I think the demand to keep going helps the event, and so I say

"But it sinks IN FIRE
     Song without end."

Song to you, my beloved. And the one word I didn't write and don't intend to write just yet is the word *Amen,* which always properly follows the words, "without end."

I love you.

Ernest

Sept. 16, '65

O my Dearest, you have done it, you have made Pearl Harbor and all its brood come alive!

Everybody has his own Pearl Harbor; mine was at a tea-party in President Conant's house; there was a telephone call, and I can see his blanched face as he told the guests. Then—since I had been in Japan recently—he asked me if I had expected any such thing; "No, but I knew the military had been getting out of hand. My friend, Yasaki Takagi had taken me to a secret room——"

But now, O thank you; it's a great book!

All my love, always,
Ernest

Wednesday the 5th, Jan. '66

O my very Dear,
Here I am
    motionless when I
want to fly, silent
    when I want to speak,
    but at least
        moriturus saluto
        and loving you,
        as always,
            I love you.
                Ernest

Thursday, January 27, 1966

Beloved;

How is it possible? "She is thinking of me." O my Darling—can it be true? I must believe—"Always with love—" In spite of all the turmoil in the world, "love never faileth." I must send her word at once. Beloved, nothing must prevent the word from reaching you. Your spark of life may be the only surviving message. I love you always.

God keep you living and assured of life.
Your Ernest

Her "Treasure Book" will go on. Each day is hers in trust to use wisely, and she is unendingly careful that it is so used. Yes, a great life goes on—becoming greater.

Her most recent "Treasures"? She expresses them thus in a poem entitled "These Present Joys":

These are my present joys—
Snow in the valley and rising to the hills,
Moonlight on frozen water,
And I, walking in the night as my heart wills.

O shadows of past joys, retire!
Ashes remain where once was fire.

These are my present joys—
To know that I have stilled a child's despairing cry,
Have fed one's hunger, healed another's ill,
Or, holding someone's hand, have strengthened him
to die.

O shadows of past joys, refrain!
Where death is, also is no pain.

In recent years certain American critics and literary polls have steadfastly refused to admit Pearl Buck into their closed circles. They do this seemingly without realizing the stupidity of omitting the name of the only American woman winner of the Nobel Prize for Literature from the so-called leading author lists. This is understandable if one looks at the situation objectively, for she cannot be grouped with any of our best-selling writers today. Take, for example, the "four-letter" writers, those who use four-letter words, ideas, ideals and situations with little or no plot to stimulate the public erotically and by so doing become successful "authors." She does not of course fit with these, although she writes frankly, when artistically necessary, of love and sex. Another group is composed of those who diligently research an event of our times and then report all the details in a gory "you-were-there" fashion. She does not fit in this company either, for she is an artist, not a journalist. Still another group are those who choose a subject in the news, for example race or religion, and then write page after page about it. I suspect they do this because members of that race, creed or religion will all buy a copy and make it a profitable venture. Pearl Buck cannot be put in that category, either. I repeat again that she writes purely for entertainment and nothing more, and the material is taken from the living facts of her own life, as well as from her observations of human nature.

The blood-and-guts process of living each day has been, and is, her greatest point of interest. She does not have to turn to the make-believe of gore or sex or anything else. These elements are in everyone's life and she knows her own. Her stories seem simple in essence, but they are rich with genuine human beings, with genuine emotions and reactions, and they are told in an exquisite style, direct and unembellished. Anyone can identify with her characters and with the experiences they have because she writes about people and for people. The literary establishment may choose to feel there is no significance here and thus ignore the fact that after thirty-seven years and nearly as many major novels her next novel will still be eagerly received as a major literary event in almost every country in the world.

The Good Earth, considered by many as the book that made her career, has been detrimental to it in some ways. People say, "But it is the book that made her famous. Without it she would not have been able to do so much." That is an opinion too frequently heard—and it is usually expressed by those who are ignorant of her and her work. The majority of the 1,811,000 persons in the United States who bought that book in the first twelve months after publication have missed the true greatness of the woman. They assumed a negative answer to the old cliché, "Now what can *she* possibly do for an encore?" and never followed her career or read her subsequent books. Most newspaper articles about her activities begin, "Pearl Buck, Nobel and Pulitzer Prize-winning author of *The Good Earth* . . ." and there those who assume there can be no "encore" cease reading. Be that as it may, she has retained a hard-core group of true fans who follow her career faithfully, and know that she is worthy of much more recognition and esteem than American critics have accorded her.

It is a comfort to her admirers that other nations and peoples know Pearl Buck very well indeed. Dr. Kyung Cho Chung, a member of the Defense Language Institute and distinguished author of *Korea Tomorrow* and *New Korea,* was asked not long ago to write a review of *The Living Reed* for a newspaper. His closing paragraph is typical of how peoples of other countries feel about her:

Although our only woman Nobel Prize winner for literature is excluded from the absurd recently publicized White House Library list, her works are not excluded from book stores, shelves and tables in the homes of countless readers. She is very much alive, and unwearyingly prolific, giving us now her finest novel of her primary literary domain, Eastern Asia. It is hoped that many in the White House will read it (*The Living Reed*) to better understand not only Korea, but also other newly independent Asian countries which present a challenge to the United Nations, as well as the United States.

In foreign countries she has earned her own place and is accorded the respect due one who has achieved so much.

As the story of her life, this book is incomplete, for in a sense her life will never end. She will live on for generations, not only in the books she has written, but in the great works she has begun. Some are works of such magnitude that it is difficult for the mortal mind of the present to grasp the full importance of her life, which she has lived to the fullest, and mostly for others. Future generations will understand. They will know she had to live. For peace, for understanding, for the human race, she had to live. Thousands of Amerasians, for example, will know that, except for her, they would not have lived. Do they now know? I doubt it.

As I sit here in the Opportunity Center in Sosa, the place she has founded for them, and write these words about her, I am distracted by excited voices from outside my window. A group of Amerasian boys are playing ball, laughing and shouting as young boys will. There goes Hae Chuil. He is a handsome young man of twenty-two, with dark red hair and light hazel eyes and the fair complexion that goes with them. He is winning and there are cheers as he scrambles the ball from another boy and makes a point. Can it be that only one week ago he was begging on the streets of Seoul? I know he was, for I found him there. He was born in Pusan, his mother Korean, his father an American top sergeant "with hair on his upper lip," he told us. His father had stayed with his mother until he was eleven and had then gone away. There had been two letters from his father, each promising to return and take them to the States—then there was nothing. Shortly thereafter his mother died and he heard that his father might be in Seoul. He started working his way here from Pusan, but he could not get a job anywhere because his birth has never been registered. When he reached Seoul, he could not find his father and for at least five bitter winters he begged in the streets, sleeping at night in the alleys. When I found him he—of course, in Korean—said, "Each time I see an American on the streets I think he may be my father." He says now, "At last my father's people have come, and have found me. They will help me." Now he can play ball and laugh and make up for some of the years of horror and loneliness that he has known. His birth will be registered and he will learn a trade so that he can earn a living. Does he know yet that except for her foundation his American father's people might never have come? I think he does not realize the fact. He has been told, of course, but he does not know how to read, and I am sure he does not even know who Pearl S. Buck is. But some day when he is old he will know, and his children and grandchildren will know, and these future generations will love her, even as we, who now know, love her.

Among the many, there are also girl children, but with the girls we must start earlier than with the boys and our job is much more complex. It is so easy for a girl to earn money, at least for a while—and what can one expect of a girl whose mother perhaps became a prostitute after her father left and who was raised to look forward to becoming fourteen so she could "work" and help to support her mother? Peggy is a good example. She is sixteen years old now and I felt a shock the last time I saw her. In fact, at first glance I did not know her. It was only after careful study that I recognized her as the pretty girl whose case history had come to my desk in Philadelphia when she was thirteen. She had been living with her mother in one room and her mother had started "entertaining" a new GI. The girl was unusually bright in school but since the new GI came her grades had dropped off sharply. Our counselor found, after tedious investigation, that the mother would not allow the child to have a light on after the GI came each night, so there was no time for study and, worse still, if the GI chose to stay all night there was only one bed and the child must share it with them or not sleep.

At once we convinced the mother to release the girl to a child-care center where she could live and attend school, and for a while we considered the problem solved. The next few months were peaceful so far as Peggy was concerned, then suddenly she began to run away from the child-care center and school. She was severely teased in school because of her honey-blond hair, but in the past she had chosen to excel in her studies to counter the teasing, so we did not feel this was the underlying cause. Our counselor found her with her mother each time and after the fourth such event she questioned the pair in depth and learned that the mother's GI had not married her as he had promised but instead had "shipped out" for the States about a month earlier and there had been no word from him. The mother was very sad and despondent, for she felt he had really loved her, and Peggy kept running away to comfort her mother. The counselor convinced them it was best for Peggy to remain in school and the girl returned to the child-care center, went back to school and all seemed to be developing well until about a month later when the girl and her mother disappeared. We searched for them for a time and were told by neighbors that they had moved to a small village south of Seoul and were living with relatives. We were unable to locate them, or the village or the relatives, so we had to close our file, at least for a time. Two years passed.

One month ago the Korean newspapers carried the story of a woman's body found in the Han River, clad only in a black lace cocktail dress. The woman had been in the water for at least eight days and could not be identified. The next morning a honey-blond girl came to our office. Her hair was drawn straight back from her face and arranged in a smart Western style. She was tall and beautiful and her perfectly made-up face revealed no hint of Asian heredity, but she spoke only Korean except for a few words of GI slang. Her outfit of tight Western-style pants and sweater, with high-heeled knee boots, told us at once that she was a "business" girl. Yes, the girl was our Peggy! She stayed all day in our office, weeping. She had remembered the black lace dress her mother had worn when she last saw her two weeks earlier, and she went to see the body of the woman found in the river. It was the same dress. Bit by bit, between sobs, the story came out. Peggy had run away from school because her mother was ill when the last GI left and had been unable to "earn" a living. A GI bar near the Demilitarized Zone had agreed to employ the mother as a hostess only if she would bring Peggy with her. Her mother refused for a time, but as things became worse Peggy was convinced that there was no other way. Peggy and her mother worked together as "entertainers," and the girl was very popular indeed because of her blond hair, blue eyes and Western features. Then, two weeks ago, the mother left with a GI for Seoul, where they planned to marry and Peggy had heard no more until the black lace dress. She has been in our office every day since then trying to work out the details of some future life. She does not wish to continue as a prostitute, but until today she had not wanted to come to the Opportunity Center because the other young people would know of her past. The wife of our American director worked with her and today she removed the tight pants, wearing instead a simple pleated skirt and low-heeled shoes. She let down her hair and washed her face and our sweet Peggy is back. She is older, of course, and has had terrible experiences, but at least there is a chance for her here. What would she have done without us? The answer is obvious, I think. Now she will study a trade, dressmaking or beauty culture or perhaps she will become a counselor at the Foundation and help other young people like herself. Because of Pearl Buck, she will do something constructive with her life.

I see another boy running across the playground. It is young Choel. He is younger, perhaps thirteen, he does not know for sure. He has never been registered and has never been to school. Long ago he lost track of time. About two years ago his mother married a Korean man who would not have the half-American boy in his house because it branded his wife as a prostitute. His mother, with many tears, took him to the Seoul train station and told him to wait, that she would come back. But she never did.

After the third day of waiting, an older man who had "be-friended" the boy took him on a train to a small town in the northern part of South Korea. He was told that the man had a home there where he would be cared for until his mother returned, and this he believed, for the man had seemed interested in his welfare. When, after some hours, they reached the small town the terror that was to last for two years began. His "friend" sold him to a group of gangsters who held him captive and forced him to beg for them. He and about five other young boys gathered rubbish and scrap paper all day, which the gangsters sold for money. Then each day at five o'clock they were given pails and went from door to door begging food. The six small boys had to beg enough food for thirty adult men before they, the boys, were allowed to eat. If he tried to run away, which he often did, the gang caught him and beat him severely. One day when he did not beg enough to satisfy them one older man held him while a second burned him horribly on the leg with a red-hot piece of wood from the fire.

Now the horror is over. We found him one day last week, and even though he was afraid and cried with his fear of the gang's revenge, we took him into our car and brought him shaking and sick to Sosa. But for the grace of God, the kind heart of Pearl Buck, and the generosity of Americans she has told about these children, we would not have been in Korea to help him. How long would this son of some American have lived? Not long, I am sure. And what now? Will he go to a regular school, beginning at fourteen? I think not. It may be too late for that. But he will learn a useful trade, and make his own livelihood—and become a good Korean citizen *because* of his American heritage, and *because* of Pearl Buck.

These are her present joys.

Has she been successful? So successful in our first country, Korea, it has been ruled that our work shall not be known as that of a "foreign volunteer agency" but that we shall work as Koreans to help our fellow citizens, the Amerasians. Each child shall be permitted to register himself and establish his own family registry, ending this legal "no-man's-land." He becomes a citizen with all the rights of a citizen, which include education, job, marriage, travel, and all such benefits that we take for granted in our own country. Now that this is so in Korea, other countries will follow.

Her name will be the symbol of the American spirit that has mingled with the Asia in which she grew up, creating a brilliant new people, the Amerasians. And it is fitting that this be so, for while in America we have thought of her as representative of Asia, in Asia she is thought of as the staunchest American. She has represented us always as a good people and true, and Asians, for the most part, have believed her. Now she makes this final

move, which only she can make, to prove it. Yes. Future generations will know her and love her, not only for her books but for
the heart out of which they flowed, leaving still more love for her
fellowman. Is this not the true meaning of all life? Is this not pure
worship of whatever creation is?

No one in Asia, at any rate, would think of comparing her to
anyone else, or anyone else to her, for she *is* Pearl Buck. To them
there never has been and never will be another like her. She has
lived, she has written her own life into her many books, and
we can all read and know that someone, somewhere, has been
through our own joys and sorrows. We can take comfort because
she survived in triumph, and so, perhaps, may we. I can think of
no better way to end this record of her life than with her salute to
the world in her poem, "Essence":

> I give you the books I've made,
> Body and soul, bled and flayed.
> Yet the essence they contain
> In one poem is made plain,
> In one poem is made clear:
> On this earth, though far or near,
> Without love there's only fear.

Bibliography of Books
by Pearl S. Buck

This list is divided into four groups: novels, fiction collections, general, and books for children.

An asterisk following a title indicates that the original edition was published by The John Day Company, Inc. If original publication was by another firm, it is so listed.

Years of original publication are given except when not known.

Notation that a title has been published in languages of Africa, of Asia, or of India means that arrangements have been made for editions in one or more of such languages although available records do not show which have in fact appeared. These languages include Ga, Twi, Ewe, Fanti, Hausa, Yoruba, Ibo, Wolof, Fula, Swahili, Amharic, Luganda, Arabic, Armenian, Indonesian, Malayan, Persian, Peshtu (for Africa and Asia other than India); Bengali, Gujarati, Kanarese, Malayalam, Marathi, Oriya, Punjabi, Tamil, Telugu (for India).

NOVELS

American Triptych, 1958.* Published also in Italian.

The Angry Wife, 1945 * (under pseudonym John Sedges). Published also in Danish, English (in Britain), Finnish, French, German, languages of India, Italian, Norwegian, Spanish, Swedish.

A Bridge for Passing, 1962.* Published also in English (in Britain), Danish, Dutch, French, German, Italian, Japanese, Norwegian, Portuguese, Spanish, Swedish.

Bright Procession, 1952 * (under pseudonym John Sedges). Published also in Dutch, English (in Britain), French, German, Spanish.

China Flight, 1946. Triangle Publishing Company. (Published serially in *Collier's,* 1943.)

China Sky, 1942. Triangle Publishing Company. Published also in Italian. (Published serially in *Collier's,* 1941.)

Come My Beloved, 1953.* Published also in Dutch, English (in Britain), Finnish, French, German, Italian, Norwegian, Portuguese, Spanish, Swedish.

Command the Morning, 1959.* Published also in Danish, Dutch, English (in Britain), Finnish, French, German, Italian, Norwegian, Portuguese, Spanish, Swedish.

Death in the Castle, 1965.* Published also in Dutch, English (in Britain), French, German, Greek, Italian, Norwegian, Portuguese, Spanish, Swedish.

Dragon Seed, 1941.* Published also in Danish, Dutch, English (in Britain), Finnish, French, German, Italian, Portuguese, Oriya (India), Swedish. (Published serially in *Asia Magazine,* 1941-42.)

East Wind : West Wind, 1930.* Published also in Bengali, Danish, Dutch, English (in Britain), Finnish, French, German, Hungarian, Indonesian, Lebanese, Portuguese, Spanish. (Published serially in *Collier's,* 1930.)

The Exile, 1936.* Published also in Danish, English (in Britain), Finnish, French, German, Italian, Norwegian, Portuguese, Spanish, Swedish. (Published serially in *Woman's Home Companion,* 1935-36.)

Father Andrea. United States Information Agency, paperback. Published also in Arabic, English with Japanese notes (in Japan only). Also appears in collections *The First Wife and Other Stories** and *Twenty-seven Stories* (Sun Dial Press).

Fighting Angel, 1936.* Published also in English, Danish, Finnish, French, German, Italian, Norwegian, Romanian, Spanish, Swedish.

God's Men, 1951.* Published also in Danish, Dutch, Finnish, French, German, languages of India, Italian, Norwegian, Portuguese, Spanish, Swedish. (Published serially in *Woman's Home Companion,* 1951.)

The Good Earth, 1931.* Published also in African languages, Arabic, Armenian, Bengali, Burmese, languages of Ceylon, Danish, Dutch, English (in Britain), English language special school edition in territory of Dutch language, English with Japanese notes, Finnish, French, German, Hebrew, Italian, Japanese, Malayalam, Indonesian, Norwegian, Persian, Polish, Portuguese, Serbo-Croat, Slovak, Slovene, Spanish, Swedish, Vietnamese.

The Hidden Flower, 1952.* Published also in Danish, Dutch, English (in Britain), English with Japanese notes, Finnish, French, German, languages of India, Italian, Norwegian, Portuguese, Serbo-Croat, Spanish, Swedish. (Published serially in *Woman's Home Companion,* 1952.)

A House Divided, 1935.* Published also in Bengali, Danish, Dutch, English (in Britain), French, German, Hebrew, Italian, Japanese, Norwegian, Spanish, Swedish.

House of Earth, 1935 * (a trilogy: *The Good Earth, Sons, A House Divided*). Published also in Dutch, German.

Imperial Woman, 1956.* Published also in Dutch, English (in Britain), Finnish, French, German, languages of India, Serbo-Croat, Spanish, Swedish.

Kinfolk, 1949.* Published also in Danish, English (in Britain), Finnish, French, German, Hebrew, languages of India, Polish, Portuguese, Spanish. (Published serially in *Ladies Home Journal,* 1945.)

Letter From Peking, 1957.* Published also in African and Asian languages, Danish, Dutch, English (in Britain), English with Japanese notes (in Japan), Finnish, French, German, Hebrew, languages of India, Italian, Japanese, Norwegian, Portuguese, Slovene, Spanish, Swedish.

The Living Reed, 1963.* Published also in Danish, Dutch, French, German, Italian, Japanese, Norwegian, Portuguese, Spanish, Swedish.

The Long Love, 1949 * (under pseudonym John Sedges). Published also in Danish, Dutch, English (in Britain), French, German, languages of India, Norwegian, Portuguese, Spanish, Swedish.

The Mother, 1934.* Published also in African and Asian languages, Slovak, Danish, Dutch, English (in Britain), Finnish, French, German, Hebrew, languages of India, Italian, Latvian, Norwegian, Portuguese, Spanish, Swedish. (Published in *Cosmopolitan,* 1933.)

The New Year, 1968.* Published also in English (in Britain), Finnish, French, Norwegian, Swedish.

Other Gods, 1938.* Published also in Arabic, English (in Britain), English with Japanese notes (in Japan), Finnish, French, German, languages of India, Italian, Norwegian, Spanish. (Published serially in *Good Housekeeping,* 1938-39.)

The Patriot, 1939.* Published also in Danish, Dutch, English (in Britain), Finnish, French, German, languages of India, Italian, Norwegian, Portuguese, Slovak, Spanish, Swedish.

Pavilion of Women, 1946.* Published also in Danish, Dutch, English (in Britain), Finnish, French, German, languages of India, Italian, Norwegian, Portuguese, Spanish, Swedish. (Published serially in *Woman's Home Companion,* 1946.)

Peony, 1948.* Published also in Dutch, English (in Britain, under title *The Bond Maid*), Finnish (under title *The Bond Maid*), French, German, languages of India, Italian, Japanese, Portuguese, Serbo-Croat, Spanish, Swedish. (Published serially and condensed in *Cosmopolitan,* 1948.)

Portrait of a Marriage, 1941.* Published also in Danish, Dutch, English (in Britain), French, German, languages of India, Italian, Japanese, Portuguese, Serbo-Croat, Spanish, Swedish. (Published serially in *Redbook,* 1941, under title "Man's Daily Bread.")

The Promise, 1943.* Published also in English (in Britain), French, German, Italian, Portuguese, Spanish, Swedish. (Published serially in *Asia Magazine,* 1943.)

Sons, 1932.* Published also in Arabic, Danish, Dutch, English (in Britain), Finnish, French, German, Hebrew, Hungarian, Italian, Latvian, Rumanian, Polish, Portuguese, Slovak, Spanish. (Published serially in *Cosmopolitan,* 1932.)

The Spirit and the Flesh, 1936 * (contains *Fighting Angel* and *The Exile*).
Published also in Spanish in collection of Nobel Prize Winners, de luxe
edition in one volume.

Sylvia. In Japanese only. (Published serially in *Redbook,* 1951, under title
"No Time for Love.")

This Proud Heart, 1948.* Published also in Danish, Dutch, English (in Britain), Estonian, Finnish, French, German, Italian, Norwegian, Portuguese,
Spanish, Swedish. (Published serially in *Good Housekeeping,* 1937.)

The Time Is Noon, 1967.* Published also in Danish, Dutch, English (in Britain), Finnish, French, German, Italian, Japanese, Norwegian, Portuguese,
Spanish, Swedish.

The Townsman, 1945 * (under pseudonym John Sedges). Published also in
Arabic, Burmese, Danish, Dutch, English (in Britain), English with Japanese notes (in Japan), French, German, languages of India, Italian, Portuguese, Spanish.

Voices in the House, 1953 * (under pseudonym John Sedges). Published also
in Dutch, English (in Britain), French, German, Norwegian, Portuguese,
Spanish.

The Young Revolutionist, 1932. New York: Friendship Press. Published
also in German.

FICTION (Collections)

Escape at Midnight. Hong Kong: Dragonfly Books, paperback. Published also
in Arabic, languages of India.

Far and Near, 1934 * (stories of China, Japan and America). Published also in
Dutch, English (in Britain), French, Japanese, Spanish.

The First Wife and Other Stories, 1933.* Published also in Dutch, English
(in Britain), English with Japanese notes (in Japan), French, German,
languages of India (Gujerati, Hindi, Kanarese, Malayalam, Marathi,
Oriya, Punjabi, Tamil, Telegu, and Assamese), Italian, Portuguese, Spanish, Swedish.

Fourteen Stories, 1961.* Published also in Burmese, Danish, Dutch, English
(in Britain, under title *With a Delicate Air*), English with Japanese notes
(in Japan), French, languages of India, Portuguese, Spanish, Swedish.

Stories of China, 1964 (combination of *First Wife and Other Stories* and
Today and Forever).

Today and Forever, 1934.* Published also in Dutch, English (in Britain),
German (Continent of Europe), and in Portuguese (Continent of Europe
and Latin America).

NONFICTION

American Argument, 1949 * (with Eslanda Goode Robeson). Published also
in English (in Canada).

American Unity and Asia, 1942.*

Asia and American Democracy, Editorial Planeta (Spanish).

The Child Who Never Grew, 1950. Training School at Vineland, N. J. Published also in Arabic, Danish, Dutch, English (in Britain), French, Finnish, German, Icelandic, Italian, Japanese, Swedish. (Published in *Ladies Home Journal,* 1950.)

Children for Adoption, 1964. New York: Random House. Published also in German, French, Italian, Spanish. (Published in *Ladies Home Journal,* 1964.)

The Chinese Novel, 1939 * (Nobel Prize Lecture). Published also in Dutch, Spanish.

For Spacious Skies, 1966 * (with Theodore F. Harris). Published also in French.

Friend to Friend, 1958 * (a candid exchange between Pearl S. Buck and Carlos P. Romulo). Published also in German.

The Gifts They Bring, 1935 * (with Gweneth T. Zarfoss).

How It Happens, 1947 * (talk about the German people). Published also in French.

Joy of Children, 1964 * (text by Pearl S. Buck with introduction by Roy Sorenson).

The Man Who Changed China, 1953. New York: Random House (story of Sun Yat-sen). Published also in Arabic, English (in Britain), languages of India, Indonesian, Persian, Spanish.

My Several Worlds, 1954.* Published also in Burmese, Danish, Dutch, English (in Britain), English with Japanese notes (in Japan), French, German, languages of India, Portuguese, Spanish, Swedish, Vietnamese.

My Several Worlds (abridged for young readers), 1954.*

Of Men and Women, 1941.* Published also in Swedish.

The People of Japan, 1966. New York: Simon & Schuster.

The Story of Dragon Seed, 1944.* Written for publication of *Dragon Seed* (limited number printed, none sold).

Talk About Russia, 1945 * (with Masha Scott). (Published serially in *Asia and the Americas,* 1945.)

Tell the People, 1945 * (talks with James Yen about the Mass Education Movement).

To My Daughters, With Love, 1968.* Published also in English in Japan, and in Japanese.

Welcome Child, 1964.*

What America Means to Me, 1943.* Published also in German.

TRANSLATIONS

All Men Are Brothers, 1933.* Translated from the Chinese *Shui Hu Chuan.* Published also in English (in Britain), Italian.

BOOKS FOR CHILDREN

The Beech Tree, 1954.* Published also in French, German, Hebrew. (Published in *Woman's Home Companion.*)

The Big Fight, 1954.* Published also in Danish, Italian, Norwegian. (Published in *Boys' Life,* 1964.

The Big Wave, 1947.* Published also in Danish, Dutch, English (in Britain), French, German, Hebrew, Italian, Serbo-Croat, Spanish.

The Chinese Children Next Door, 1942.* Published also in Dutch, English (in Britain), Italian, Spanish.

The Christmas Ghost, 1960.* Published also in English (in Britain), French. (Published in *Family Circle,* 1960.)

The Christmas Miniature, 1957.* Published also in English (in Britain), German, Italian. (Published in *Family Circle,* 1960.)

The Dragon Fish, 1944.* Published also in Danish, Dutch, German, Hebrew, Italian, Norwegian, Spanish, Swedish. (Published in *Jack and Jill,* 1944.)

Johnny Jack and His Beginnings, 1954.* Published also in English (in Britain), German.

Little Fox in the Middle, 1966. New York: Macmillan Company (Collier Books). Published also in English (in Britain).

Matthew, Mark, Luke and John, 1966.* Published also in French. (Published in *Good Housekeeping,* 1966.)

One Bright Day, 1950.* Published also in Danish, Dutch, English (in Britain), French, German, Oriya (India), Italian, Spanish, Swedish. (Published in *Jack and Jill,* 1950.)

Stories for Little Children, 1949.* Published also in Dutch, German, Italian, Slovene (Yugoslavia).

The Water-Buffalo Children, 1943.* Published also in Danish, Dutch, English (in Britain), German, Hebrew, Italian, Norwegian, Serbo-Croat, Spanish. (Published in *Jack and Jill,* 1943.)

Yu Lan : Flying Boy of Japan, 1945.* Published also in Dutch, English (in Britain), German, Hebrew, Italian, Spanish. (Published in *Child Life,* 1945.)

INDEX

Index